CIVIL WAR LOGISTI

CIVIL WAR
LOGISTICS

A STUDY OF MILITARY TRANSPORTATION

~~~ EARL J. HESS ~~~

LOUISIANA STATE UNIVERSITY PRESS

BATON ROUGE

Published with the assistance of the V. Ray Cardozier Fund

Published by Louisiana State University Press
Copyright © 2017 by Earl J. Hess
Manufactured in the United States of America
First printing

DESIGNER: Michelle A. Neustrom
TYPEFACES: Whitman, text; Engravers' Roman BT, display
PRINTER AND BINDER: McNaughton & Gunn, Inc.

MAP 1 is from *Braxton Bragg: the Most Hated Man of the Confederacy* by Earl J. Hess, University of North Carolina Press, p. 17. Copyright © 2016 by Earl J. Hess. Used by permission of the publisher.

MAP 2 is from *The Iron Way: Railroads, the Civil War, and the Making of Modern America* by William G. Thomas, Yale University Press, 2011, before p. 1. Copyright © 2011 by Yale University Press. Used by permission of the publisher.

LIBRARY OF CONGRESS CATALOGING-IN-PUBLICATION DATA

Names: Hess, Earl J., author.
Title: Civil War logistics : a study of military transportation / Earl J. Hess.
Description: Baton Rouge : Louisiana State University Press, [2017] | Includes
    bibliographical references and index.
Identifiers: LCCN 2017009582| ISBN 978-0807-1-6750-2 (cloth : alk. paper) |
    ISBN 978-0-8071-6751-9 (pdf) | ISBN 978-0-8071-6752-6 (epub)
Subjects: LCSH: United States—History—Civil War, 1861–1865—Transportation.
    | United States—History—Civil War, 1861–1865—Logistics. | Transportation,
    Military—United States—History—19th century.
Classification: LCC E491 .H47 2017 | DDC 973.7/8—dc23
LC record available at https://lccn.loc.gov/2017009582

The paper in this book meets the guidelines for permanence and durability
of the Committee on Production Guidelines for Book Longevity
of the Council on Library Resources. ∞

For Pratibha and Julie, with love

CONTENTS

MAPS AND
ILLUSTRATIONS

MAPS

ILLUSTRATIONS

PREFACE

Logistics have constituted a vital element of warfare, indispensable to the operations of all armies, ever since the origin of organized warfare. But the study of logistics has not always been a visible element in our view of armed conflict. In the many waves of military studies produced by historians over the centuries, it all too often is crowded out of the picture by colorful narratives of battles or biographies of generals. Everyone accepts the fact that armies cannot exist unless they are fed, supplied, and moved to meet the enemy, but relatively few historians seem interested in finding out how those necessary goals of military operations actually worked.

One can find many varied definitions of the word logistics, but this study adopts a simple and straightforward way of defining it. I focus on the transportation of men, material, food, and animals in support of military operations in the field. This approach is supported by the Oxford English Dictionary, which defines logistics as "the activity of moving equipment, supplies and people for military operations."[1]

The topic of supply will not be covered, at least not in full. Supply, the process of obtaining a wide variety of food and material from various sources and later issuing it to the troops, is of course vitally important to understanding the course of military operations. Logistics involves the equally vital topic of transporting that material to the troops in the field or in garrison. Historians tend to treat logistics and supply as one subject because they are so intimately linked.[2] But supply is such a large and important topic that, in my view, it requires a separate study of its own. A detailed and well-rounded study of military transportation in the Civil War is about all that can be fitted into one volume.

Civil War officers tended to view logistics in a variety of ways. According to H. L. Scott, author of a thick military dictionary published at the outset of the conflict, the word logistics derived its origin from the Latin *logista*, designating "the administrator or intendant of the Roman armies." That implies a wider purview for logistics than the one adopted for this study. In contrast, Henry Halleck defined logistics as a term that "embraces all the practical details of moving and supplying armies."[3]

Regardless of where we draw the parameters around the subject of logistics, Civil War officers recognized that the process of supply as well as transportation affected their chances of success. Upon taking command of the Department of the Missouri in November 1861, Halleck worked hard for a month before he could report to George McClellan that the "administration and machinery for the supply of the army is rapidly getting into working order. This was a matter of the greatest necessity, and consequently has absorbed most of my attention. An army is soon disorganized unless properly supplied and its wants provided for." The need for effective logistical support increased when Union armies began to invade enemy territory. As James A. Garfield, who served as chief of staff in the Army of the Cumberland, put it before the Tullahoma campaign, "it is useless to advance into the rebel territory unless we are prepared to hold the ground we win in battle. This cannot be done until we make our supplies secure."[4]

Union and Confederate armies relied on four primary means of transportation during the Civil War, although Southern forces were unable to utilize all of them on the same level as their opponents. The river-based system consisted of civilian steamboats plying the rivers of the West. The rail-based system included large and small railroad corporations and represented the only new element in military transportation by the 1860s. The coastal shipping system consisted of privately owned coastal and sea vessels, both sail and steam-powered. These ships were mostly utilized by the Union army rather than by the Confederates.

All three of these systems were national in scope; to put it another way, they were strategic lines of transportation because they stretched across local, state, and regional boundaries to encompass the entire nation. They were primarily used to shift men and material through friendly territory toward the battlefield, although in the later stages of the journey river steamers and railroads often entered the theater of operations and came quite close to or even into the combat zones. Coastal shipping rarely penetrated deeply into the zone of military operations. Because steamers and trains easily slid from friendly territory to contested areas, they became targets of enemy destruction. In contrast, coastal ships rarely were exposed to enemy attacks.

All three systems of national transportation were either wholly (as in river steamers and railroads) or in part (as in coastal shipping) powered by steam. This was a vital factor in their efficiency. Historian Christopher R. Gabel has estimated that steam engines increased the carrying power of transportation systems by "at least a factor of ten." For example, if a six-mule team could haul one and a half tons of freight in a wagon for 333 miles while consuming one ton of fodder, that amounted to "500 ton-miles of transport capacity generated by that ton of mule forage." A train could travel 35 miles on one ton of engine fuel but haul up to 150 tons, amounting to 5,250 ton-miles. Gabel believes river steamers performed at an even higher rate. The prospects for supporting large armies far afield from their bases increased on a gargantuan scale because of steamboats, train engines, and steamer coastal vessels.[5]

The fourth major system of military transportation in the Civil War con-sisted of old-fashioned wagon trains. This system was entirely tactical, or local in nature. Wagons accompanied the field armies as they penetrated enemy terri-tory and therefore operated almost entirely within the theater of operations and were much exposed to enemy attacks. That is why they were heavily guarded at all times. Ironically, enemy attempts to strike at wagon trains rarely suc-ceeded because field commanders were keenly aware of their importance and vulnerability. They usually assigned adequate numbers of troops to guard them.

All four systems of military transportation were vital to operations in the Civil War. All but the railroads had a long heritage in world military history. Commanders in wars dating back to the ancient Greeks and Romans used river-boats, coastal ships, carts, or wagons to move men and material. The only dif-ference between how Civil War quartermasters used these methods compared to their predecessors lay in the employment of steam power and of course in the sheer size of Civil War transportation needs.

This study pays some attention to other means of military transportation. Civil War officers experimented with the large-scale use of pack animals (mules) but never adopted this method in a significant way. Pack mules were common features in the Civil War, but in very small numbers and for limited purposes. The loads they carried were too small compared to the standard army wagon and they demanded specialized knowledge concerning how to load the pack saddles and how to handle the cantankerous mule.

Cattle herds accompanied every Civil War field army, providing what was popularly called "beef on the hoof" for hungry soldiers. This represented a form of military transportation. For that matter, I consider the individual soldier to be a unit in the logistical chain. After his food, ammunition, accouterments, clothing, shoes, and tent were transported by boat, rail, or sailing vessel to the theater of operations, he put this material on his body and marched to meet the enemy. The soldier literally was a transport unit responsible for taking the material its final step within the theater of operations. Therefore, a portion of one chapter in this study offers some insight into foot power as a legitimate aspect of logistics in warfare.

It is important to understand the vulnerability of these transportation systems to enemy attack in order to get a full picture of the logistical history of the Civil War. Therefore, two chapters are devoted to mostly Confederate efforts to disrupt the Federal river- and rail-based systems, the two systems they had the best chances of hitting. Federal efforts to strike at Confederate logistical systems were more limited and largely confined to efforts aimed at threatening supply lines as part of tactical ploys during large campaigns, such as Sherman's drive toward Atlanta. This book cannot hold a discussion of all the many cavalry raids by Union and Confederate troops during the long war, but at least some indication of the pervasive desire to hurt the enemy by hurting his transportation arrangements can be gleaned.

The study will inevitably deal far more with Union transportation systems than with Confederate transport, not by design but by necessity. The Federal logistical system was far larger, far more successful, and far better documented than its counterpart in the South. The Civil War historian is blessed with a deluge of reports and other documents thoroughly explaining how the four systems worked in the Union war effort. In contrast, the Confederates had far less access to the resources of all four systems. They did not make good use of what access they had, nor did they appoint a quartermaster officer to superintend river transportation and produce reports of what was accomplished. The officers appointed to supervise rail transportation did not have authority to actually change practices and did not file reports of their work. There is only slim evidence that the Confederates used coastal shipping, and they were chronically short of wagons in every theater of the war. It is impossible to understand Confederate logistics with anything like the clarity and depth of information that one can achieve for Federal transportation. Given the near absence of quartermaster reports, for example, one can gain more information about Rebel use of river steamers by looking at W. Craig Gaines's *Encyclopedia of Civil War Shipwrecks* than by looking through the *Official Records*. In contrast, Northern quartermasters filed lengthy and detailed reports that fill hundreds of pages in the *Official Records*. There are also several important collections of archival material relating to quartermaster work in the North, and the personal papers of various officers scattered in repositories across the nation provide important insights into their work.

Until about 35 years ago the lack of attention paid to logistics among Civil War historians had been mirrored in studies of other wars as well. Military transportation and its concomitant topic of supply were acknowledged as important but seldom if ever became the subject of a major study. Edward N. Luttwak believes this came about due to "prevailing literary conventions" and "the writer's need to entertain readers or at least to attract their attention." As a result, "whatever is dramatic easily displaces what is merely important."[6]

This situation did not begin to change until the appearance of Martin Van Creveld's *Supplying War: Logistics from Wallenstein to Patton* in 1977. It was the first major study of logistics to appear and caught a good deal of attention. While the points made in the book were subject to legitimate criticism and revision, Van Creveld's major accomplishment was to focus on an important but neglected aspect of global military history and inspire other historians to pay more attention to it. Unfortunately, he ignored military history in the United States and thus offered no insights into the Civil War.[7]

The logistical studies that appeared after 1977 have been remarkable. Most impressive among them are studies of the classical and medieval eras because the paper trail documenting logistics and supply is so scant for those periods of world history. That has not stopped a number of dedicated scholars from producing insightful studies of supply in ancient Greece, republican and imperial Rome, the Crusades, the Hundred Years' War, and the English Civil War. Despite the shortage of material to work with in the written record, historians have been able to utilize what is available in successful efforts to round out our understanding of how armies across the centuries have been fed and supplied while moving across the countryside. Some historians have turned their attention to logistics and supply for large naval forces as well, with interesting results.[8]

It is almost embarrassing that Civil War historians have to date not done similar studies, especially when one considers the mountain of detailed information readily available on the topic of logistics in the pages of the *Official Records*. A handful of historians have pointed to the direction others ought to go. Charles Dana Gibson has noted that the government use of civilian transport has had no show in the historiography. J.F.C. Fuller has noted in print that Grant "was a consummate quartermaster" while Lee "was one of the worst quartermaster-generals in history." Robert M. Browning Jr. authored a detailed history of the North Atlantic Blockading Squadron, which paid a good deal of attention to logistics and supply. Mark Grimsley has noted that logistical difficulties played a large role in the Northern development of a hard war policy. The importance of logistics as a means of Federal victory in the expansive Western Theater became a theme of my recent survey of the Civil War in the West.[9]

The dearth of detailed studies concerning Civil War logistics has led to only a faint awareness of logistics and supply in our field. The Northern war effort displayed in truth an impressive logistical triumph. Even though many nations had used river transport, coastal shipping, and wagon trains for centuries, Northern quartermasters used all three systems on a greater scale than any nation before them, with the possible exception of Napoleonic armies. Northern quartermasters did a better job of knitting together the junction points of these three systems to create truly national networks of transportation never seen on such a scale before in American or world history. Places like New York, Washington, D.C., Cairo, and New Orleans became points where two or three transportation systems came together. Troop movements could easily utilize riverboats, trains, and coastal shipping as needed. The transfer of John Schofield's Twenty-Third Corps from west Tennessee to Fort Fisher, North Carolina, in the early months of 1865 is a prime example. It is perhaps in this joining of major transportation systems that the Northern logistical effort achieved its greatest triumph, a success never really seen before.

There is no doubt that the American Civil War was the world's first true railroad war. The United States had just emerged as the leading nation in the world as far as the number of track miles was concerned when the Confederates fired on Fort Sumter. Given the huge size not only of the armies but of the opposing territories involved, it was inevitable that railroads would play a fundamental role in the war efforts of both sides.

Prussian authorities led the way in working out procedures for using railroads to quickly mobilize and move large armies before the nation actually declared war, but Americans were unaware of these pre-planned war concepts. As a result, Northern quartermasters had to improvise means of dealing with many problems associated with the joining of rails and war. English historian

Edwin A. Pratt, writing in the early days of World War I, was the first historian to draw attention to the American success at using railroads to support a major war effort. He noted that Northern quartermasters had to work with single-track rail companies; not a single corporation in the United States constructed a double track along the entire length of their line, as was common in France and Prussia. This was not such a problem with the normal run of civilian traffic in peacetime, but it presented a potential for slow travel when war greatly increased the pace of transportation. Northern quartermasters had to devise managerial methods of dealing with trains running in opposite directions on a single track to meet those demands, and they did it superbly.[10]

Pratt also was impressed by the U.S. Military Railroad, especially its large and efficient construction corps consisting of civilians hired by the government to maintain and repair tracks that were under government control in captured Southern territory. The Prussians and French tried to duplicate this (with the Germans translating a major report on how Northerners organized and ran such a corps of workers), but neither was able to do it as efficiently as the Americans. Pratt also was impressed by the level of cooperation between private corporations and government authorities in the Northern logistical effort. He also noted the American development of armored cars and hospital cars as innovations in an international context.[11]

"The American Civil War was practically the beginning of things as regards the scientific use of railways for war," Pratt concluded. "Many of the problems connected therewith were either started in the United States or were actually worked out there, precedents being established and examples being set which the rest of the world had simply to follow, adapt or perfect."[12]

Ironically, the world did not do so. It paid only selective attention to the Civil War as a source of information about current developments in military affairs. Even the small attention paid to the railway construction corps by the Prussians between 1866 and 1871 failed to bring results. The Prussians failed to learn from the American war how to efficiently ship large amounts of supplies by rail; their troops suffered in both wars with Austria and France in this way, compelling them to live off the land more than planned. American quartermasters had worked out systems of moving material quickly from one rail point to another, through a process of trial and error, but no one publicized the details of this effort—or for that matter, any other concerning the logistical triumph of the Union army and the government that supported it. Foreign observers tended to pay attention to what they thought was important, and logistical efforts were very low on the list of priorities.[13]

We must not stress the American logistical triumph too much. It was very impressive and it certainly provided a key foundation for Union army success in the Civil War. But it was not entirely sufficient. The national logistical systems did not provide literally every article of food consumed by Yankee troops; much foraging off the countryside occurred for a variety of reasons, one of which was that the logistical systems had real limits. The rail-based system in particular could stretch only so far. William T. Sherman achieved the biggest logistical success of the war when he fed and supplied 100,000 men operating at the end of a single-track rail line stretching 350 miles from Louisville, Kentucky, to his army group advancing toward Atlanta. But once he captured that important city, Sherman realized the tenuous rail link could not support further operations south of Atlanta. Logistical limitation was the primary cause for a significant shift in Union strategy once the Upper South was conquered and the Deep South became the next Federal target. Instead of connected lines of communication, Federal forces now developed large-scale raids to tear up Confederate transportation and industrial assets in central Mississippi, Alabama, and Georgia during the last few months of the war. Only the Mississippi River and the steamboats that used it could provide Federal armies secure supply routes to penetrate the Deep South and stay there rather than merely raiding.[14]

While the extreme development of logistical capability sets the Civil War apart from the mainstream in Western military history, the need to rely on local sources of food in addition to major lines of supply sets the Civil War firmly back within that mainstream. The truth is that no army in history has ever relied completely on supply lines for literally everything it needed to fight or move, with the possible exception of those created within the past 100 years. Students of logistics in the decades following Appomattox recognized this as an advantage rather than a failure. U.S. Army officer Henry G. Sharpe, who had not seen service in the Civil War, wrote in 1896 of the possibilities inherent in having choices to supply the troops. Any field army tied down to only one option was at a severe disadvantage compared to an army that utilized more than one logistical and supply option. It is not surprising that the majority of commanders throughout history have pragmatically relied on several ways to feed, supply, and move their troops as the situation demanded. A commander who had a robust system of strategic supply lines available could supplement it with foraging in what could be considered an ideal combination of options.[15]

To rely mostly or even entirely on living off the land was the worst option for many reasons. For large field forces such as those used in the Civil War, vibrant formal lines of transportation were essential because large numbers of troops would have eaten up the resources in any given area in very little time. Modern war demands sophisticated logistics, and Northern officials crafted the most sophisticated supply arrangements ever seen up to that time. Their Southern counterparts put together a pale imitation of that Northern system, and this is one of the many reasons the Confederacy lost the war.

This study is set firmly within the heritage of traditional military history, but it does have connections with the study of American society during the Civil War era. Army quartermasters relied mostly on transportation owned and operated by civilians to move men and material across the nation. They in effect became participants in the civilian economy, placing the government on a similar level as any company or individual in civilian life who wanted to transport goods or take a trip. Army quartermasters had to adjust themselves to that civilian economy just as the civilian economy had to adjust its practices to military needs. There is no better way to see how the largest institution in American life during the Civil War affected nonmilitary life than to look at the ways in which the transportation business helped the North and South wage war. This study cannot really explore this interesting avenue of research as fully as it deserves, but it can serve as a starting point for it.

There are many other areas connected with logistics and supply that need to be addressed by historians than can be discussed within the pages of this book. While the reader can find considerable amounts of detailed information about the major transportation systems utilized in our terrible war, future research should flow into the supply area—the administrative infrastructure associated with the purchasing and use of a bewildering variety of food, animals and their feed, and equipment of all kinds by Northern and Southern armies. A study of how army commanders managed transportation as well as supplying their armies from the countryside while moving and fighting within the theater of operations is strongly needed. Much more on the peculiar aspects associated with naval logistics, both at sea and along the western rivers, would be welcome. What soldiers and sailors thought about systems of supply and transportation, the impact these systems had on the civilian business economy, how government agents interacted with private businessmen and their companies, and whether the huge governmental-military effort to procure and transport material actually had an effect on spurring Northern economic growth after 1865 are all fruitful lines of inquiry in which scholars will hopefully engage in the near future.

I owe a debt of gratitude to all the staff members of the archival institutions that are listed in the bibliography for helping make their holdings available for this book. Several graduate student researchers helped me gain access to material at various archives I could not visit, and I gladly extend my gratitude toward them.

Most of all, I am eternally grateful to my wife, Pratibha, for sharing her life with me and for her help in so many ways in making my work better than it could be by myself.

CIVIL WAR LOGISTICS

1

THE LOGISTICAL HERITAGE

Civil War quartermasters were little aware that they worked at the end of a long logistical heritage that stretched back to Greek and Roman commanders who wrestled with many of the same problems they encountered while moving men and material. In every age, problems associated with logistics and supply involved rather similar solutions. River-based transport, coastal shipping, and some type of wagon or cart train were features of military history from the classical era into the mid-nineteenth century. For the most part, military commanders and their governments contracted with privately owned transportation facilities to move their military resources in time of war. Governments also to a limited degree purchased and operated transportation for their armies to supplement the private sector's contribution to war making. Until the nineteenth century, the men who drove the carts and wagons typically were civilian employees of the army. From the earliest evidence of organized warfare, commanders have fully understood the difference between national lines of transportation and in-theater means of moving men and material. They have also utilized a combination of methods designed to feed their armies as they entered enemy territory; reliance on established lines of communication has always gone hand-in-hand with taking food from the countryside.[1]

In the classical era, the Greeks purchased food in local areas and transported some food and forage from elsewhere. Roman authorities "routinely used supply lines to ship provisions to [their] armies in the field," according to Jonathan P. Roth. They heavily utilized ocean transport when territorial expansion took Roman forces across the Mediterranean Sea. Troops as well as supplies moved in civilian merchant vessels capable of carrying up to 40 tons. The Romans never solved the pervasive problem of shipping horses by sea without terribly stressing the health of their animals. Riverboats capable of carrying up to nine tons also became part of the Roman logistical system wherever it was possible to acquire them.[2]

The Romans put together the most impressive military transport system the world had ever seen—one that would not be equaled until the early modern era. "While their skill at arranging supply, and using it as a strategic and tactical tool, is not the only reason for Roman military success, it is certainly one of the major factors in it," Roth concluded. Paul Erdkamp has divided Roman logistical arrangements during the period from 264 to 30 B.C. into three phases: transport to magazines, transport from magazines to field armies, and the maintenance of a large army train to accompany the field force. Roman commanders also worked on "supply from the war zone" to supplement their system of "supply from outside the war zone." Erdkamp estimated, however, that a Roman force could not operate more than 100 kilometers (approximately 62 miles) from its forward magazine. Roman quartermasters could fairly easily transport supplies and material by sea and by river, but the task was more difficult over land because of the limited capacity of the carts and wagons available.[3]

The use of coastal shipping for transporting troops and animals was common during the classical era. The Persians gathered a fleet of 1,000 vessels to move as many as 180,000 men in their invasion of Greece during the fifth century B.C. In contrast, the Greek states could manage fleets of no more than about 200 vessels. Athens used 40 transports to move 6,400 troops and 30 horses to Sicily in 415 B.C. The largest Greek movement of troops by ship during the classical era involved 11,500 Spartans transported a relatively short distance to Doris in the 450s B.C.[4]

Some medieval armies were adept at using transport to gain greater mobility. To prepare for campaigns in Scotland, Wales, and Flanders during the late thirteenth and early fourteenth centuries, Edward I of England faced the fact that land transport was twice as costly as river transport and eight times more expensive than moving men and material by sea. His subordinates therefore crafted a policy of relying on movement by water as far as possible to minimize the cost of shipping on land. Edward pursued a plan to acquire wagons by pressing the Catholic Church to provide them from civilians, by purchasing wagons directly from the civilian population, and by having sheriffs press them directly from citizens, who also were hired to drive them. The crown paid wagon owners a fixed rate for the use of their conveyance and of course paid the civilian drivers.[5]

To make possible the many expeditions to France during the Hundred Years' War, English monarchs sent representatives through the port cities to press suitable ships and personnel into service. They paid standard rates and wages. The crown also compensated owners for damages incurred and released the vessels when they were no longer needed. Most ship owners only reluctantly submitted, because working for the government denied them the opportunity to play the market. The most common type of coastal vessel available, the cog, ranged in size from 130 to 300 tons, and at least 1,291 were available during the era. Quartermasters in the medieval period also found it difficult to transport horses by coastal vessels because the ships had no special accommodations to properly care for them. The horses that Richard the Lionheart took along in the 3rd Crusade were held up in slings for a month and needed several additional months to recover after they arrived at Cypress.[6]

Medieval armies maintained some sort of train consisting of wagons, carts, or at least pack animals. They were drawn from privately owned sources. Yuval Noah Harari has estimated that a typical cart of the fourteenth century could carry 500 kilograms (about 1,100 pounds) of material, but some were large enough to haul four tons. A typical medieval cart could travel 20 to 40 kilometers a day. River vessels along the Seine in France were capable of carrying 150 tons of material and could travel 20 to 40 kilometers a day, while ocean vessels in the 1300s could move up to 300 tons as far as 100 kilometers on a good day for traveling. Medieval armies maintained herds of animals for fresh meat as well.[7]

Harari believes that European armies of the fourteenth century met their logistical needs pretty effectively. They could not rely entirely on only one means of transport or supply, but utilized a variety of methods that included long-distance transport by sea and river, maintaining trains of wagons and pack animals, and living off the land wherever possible. Even when merely raiding enemy country, fourteenth-century armies brought along trains; when intending to stop indefinitely in one place, they usually sought to supply the troops by river transport because of the limitations inherent in wagon capacity. To rely on only one mode of transport was to put the field force in a straitjacket; by balancing several different modes, the commander could increase his options. Feeding animals was always more difficult than feeding men because of the greater amount of food horses required.[8]

Oliver Cromwell used coastal shipping to support an invasion of the east coast of Scotland in 1650 during the English Civil War. The invasion force ranged in size from 11,000 to 20,000 troops. Cromwell used 140 vessels of 150 to 200 tons each; he relied heavily on them to supply most of the land army's needs. Wagons hauled the material from ports to the front lines. For fourteen months this coastal shipping system supported the army so well that little plunder or purchasing of food in local areas was necessary. Fully 94 percent of the bread and 93 percent of the cheese as well as boots, clothes, and tents needed by the army was transported by ship. Hay and oats for the animals and 8,500 replacement troops also found their way north by coastal vessels. The Cromwellian conquest of Scotland represents one of the more impressive uses of coastal shipping to facilitate land operations.[9]

Historian John Lynn has argued that the armies of Louis XIV of France tended to rely more heavily on well-developed systems of transporting food and other supplies to networks of magazines as the major way to feed troops, rather than gathering food from the countryside in which they operated. "Foraging for food was too wasteful of resources, unpredictable in results, and dangerous to discipline to become the primary means of supply." Due to the heavy demand for animal fodder, French armies more often gathered forage from the country than transporting it over long distances. French quartermasters requisitioned carts, wagons, and draft animals from the local area and contracted with civilians to drive them and manage the army trains.[10]

The American Revolutionary conflict of 1775 to 1783 imposed an unusually heavy burden on British transoceanic shipping. Fighting a major war 3,000 miles across the Atlantic Ocean, British commanders wanted to procure resources from the local areas they controlled in North America, but they were severely limited in their ability to do so. After the fall of New York, George Washington pursued a strategy of hemming the British into a close pocket around the city, denying them foraging opportunities and increasing British reliance on seaborne transport to feed their soldiers and animals. With more than 92,000 troops in North America and the West Indies, and about 4,000 horses needing some 14,000 tons of hay and 6,000 tons of oats per year, the strain on British logistics was enormous. Supply ships were vulnerable to storms and to American privateers. Even when British troops penetrated the countryside they found it difficult to forage from the civilian population because of sparse settlement patterns.[11]

In general, British soldiers were adequately fed, but their commanders never were able to stockpile enough supplies to ensure sustained operations that could take advantage of temporary successes against the Americans. They sought a reserve of six months in the American depots, but achieved that level only 23 months out of the 79 months that the war lasted. More often than not, they had no more of a reserve than two or three months.[12]

The main problem lay in administration; government officers were unprepared for the scope of the logistical effort and the administrative system could not expand quickly enough to meet the enlarging military commitment or the duration of the conflict. As Arthur Bowler has put it, the Treasury Department was "cast by time and tradition in a passive mold and the task that fell to it required active, even ruthless, executive supervision. This was not merely beyond its competence but also its comprehension." In the end, the British logistical system worked well enough to avert terrible suffering among the troops who were perched at the farther end of this transoceanic supply line. But the result of this limited logistical power was to severely limit the British army's ability to achieve success in North America.[13]

As one example of the limits of British logistical capability during the Revolution, Matthew Spring has noted that sea voyages decimated the horses sent from Britain to North America for use by the army. Even the comparatively short and calm voyage from New York to Philadelphia during the 1777 campaign for the American national capital saw enormous attrition of horse flesh due to inadequate provisions made on sailing vessels for their safe transport. Virtually every army in history was unable to solve the problem of transporting horses by sea, but the British finally dealt effectively with this issue by the middle of the nineteenth century.[14]

David Syrett has taken a different tack in studying the success of British seaborne transport in the Revolutionary War. He argues that it operated at a surprisingly high level of effectiveness despite its many problems. Syrett points out that the scale of logistical demands in the Revolution dwarfed any previous British conflict conducted outside Europe; in fact, not until World War II would the empire be called on to transport men, supplies, and equipment overseas on such a large scale. The Navy Board's transport service arranged for several large troop transfers: 27,000 men to North America in 1776, 8,000 to the West Indies from October 1776 to March 1780, and 29,000 loyalists shipped out of New York in 1783. These were conducted at a rather leisurely pace compared to those seen in the Civil War, but the numbers of people moved are comparable. Sea transport in the late eighteenth century was dangerous, however, both to men and animals. It was not unusual for half of the horses placed on board seagoing vessels to die before they reached their destination, a loss ratio that would have astonished Civil War quartermasters. Bad food and water and cramped conditions on crowded ships gave rise to sickness among troops as well. Syrett has estimated an average death rate of 8 percent for troop transfers on British ships in the Revolutionary War era. That also is a loss rate that would have stunned Civil War officers.[15]

The Navy Board offered a standard rate for the use of civilian ships and instituted a routine inspection of chartered vessels that included a record of their size and value. Royal inspectors did their job well, often rejecting ships that fell below standards and normally not accepting vessels of less than 200 tons. Ship owners were responsible for financing all aspects of the vessel's voyage, including wages and food for the crew, while the government provided for the soldiers on board. As the war progressed and American privateers took more than 3,000 vessels (more than one-third of which were either recaptured or ransomed back), the Navy Board found it more and more difficult to find adequate transports in the open market. It had no authority to seize vessels. Anywhere from 100 to more than 400 transports worked for the British war effort during any given time of the conflict. Most of them operated on the charter system and were in exclusive service to the government for months at a time. Syrett believes the seaborne transportation system was "one of the best-run organizations in the British government." Its achievements "rank among the greatest military and administrative feats of the eighteenth century."[16]

The Americans suffered enormous logistical problems during the Revolution despite the fact that they were fighting on home territory. John Shy believes the primary problem lay in inadequate roads, draft animals, and wagons. American officers could not use coastal shipping or the coastal roads because British military operations largely denied them access to both, and transportation facilities within the interior were woefully inadequate. They failed to take advantage of inland river transportation although boats were available. American officials suffered from shaky finances, and George Washington was loath to impress civilian property. Beset by localism, lack of faith in the Second Continental Congress, inflation, and a host of other problems, the American war effort nearly foundered on logistical issues until the central authority began to assume more responsibility for procuring food in the period after Valley Forge.[17]

The Second Continental Congress created the posts of Quartermaster General and Commissary General of Stores and Purchases on June 16, 1775. Those officials and their subordinates pursued a dual strategy to acquire transport for Continental army units. They hired teams and wagons from civilians to create army trains and at times resorted to impressment. The civilian drivers often were unreliable. As the war progressed, quartermasters began to purchase wagons and carts and to detail soldiers from the ranks to drive them in order to exert more control over their system of trains.[18]

Not surprisingly, logistical concerns played an enormous role in determining the outcome of many campaigns during the American Revolutionary War. The expedition to Quebec conducted by Benedict Arnold, the Saratoga campaign, the George Rogers Clark Expedition into the Northwest, and the final outcome at Yorktown are examples of campaigns dominated by supply and transportation issues. Armies in the Revolution assembled large wagon trains at times. When William Howe evacuated New Brunswick, New Jersey, in June 1777, his train consisted of 1,500 vehicles (1 for every 10 men in the force) and stretched for nine miles along the road system. Henry Clinton's train was on a similar scale when he evacuated Philadelphia the next year, and even Banastre Tarleton's small, mobile force that was so severely defeated at the battle of Cowpens in January 1781 had 35 wagons, or one for every 30 men in the force. The ratio of wagons to troops in these instances was far higher than in the Civil War, denoting a heavy reliance on transportation systems to keep the troops in the field. Most of the smaller campaigns devolved into efforts by the British to forage across the countryside within the border zones between the cities they occupied and American forces, which tried to deny them access to food in those regions. In one way or another, logistics and supply dominated the thinking of commanders on both sides of the conflict.[19]

Napoleon's brilliant campaigns in the early nineteenth century were to a significant degree made possible by a deliberate strategy of living off the countryside as much as possible to lessen his reliance on wagon trains and lines of fixed communications. This was in turn made possible by the fact that the European countryside he operated in was densely populated. Heavier populations meant higher levels of concentrated food and forage. In short, it was possible for Napoleon to live off the land more easily than armies that operated in sparsely populated areas, such as North America. John G. Moore has estimated that the French countryside of the mid-nineteenth century had 140 people per square mile, in contrast to 17 people per square mile in the United States, a huge difference that would spell more logistical difficulties for Civil War armies than for Napoleonic forces.[20]

American quartermasters faced continual supply and transport problems in their wars, which in the early nineteenth century were largely conducted along the fringes of the United States. They hired or pressed wagons and teams for campaigns in the War of 1812. Although steam power was just beginning to be applied to western riverboats by then, there is no evidence they were used to support American campaigns in that conflict. By the 1820s, however, quartermasters regularly used river steamboats and coastal shipping to supply scattered military posts, hiring them by charter or paying an acceptable rate per man to transport personnel. The government owned a handful of boats to service areas where it was difficult to charter or hire civilian boats. All of these methods would be employed by quartermasters North and South during the Civil War. In times of conflict, quartermasters relied even more heavily on river steamers and coastal sailing vessels to support operations in the field. Pack trains and mule-pulled wagon trains also were prominently used in the Second Seminole War.[21]

Coastal and seaborne shipping served as a mainstay of British imperial ambitions, and the British East India Company used them to project power in the early nineteenth century. Company officials negotiated contracts with private ship owners and established guidelines so their military bureaucracy functioned smoothly while embarking the troops and feeding them along the way. The company shipped a division each from the Madras Presidency Army and the Bengal Army to invade Burma in 1824. Shipping one or two regiments along the Indian coast was easy, but the company found it more difficult to maintain adequate supply lines by sea for two divisions from India to Burma across the Bay of Bengal.[22]

The professionalization of American army logistics proceeded apace after the War of 1812, which had vividly demonstrated the need for a modernized transportation system similar to that crafted in the same period by the British authorities in India. Congress finally created a modern Quartermaster's Department, Subsistence Department, and Medical Department in 1818. The army provided officers to man these departments and developed standard operating procedures for fulfilling their duties. Reforms of the era fostered the creation of a stable and increasingly professional officer corps, which had visible benefits in all support bureaus centered in Washington, D.C. Military transportation came of age in America between 1815 and the 1830s.[23]

The Mexican War tested American military transport like no previous conflict because of the need to sustain sizeable armies thousands of miles from home as they penetrated enemy territory. The new system created since the War of 1812 worked superbly. Some 307 wagons supported Zachary Taylor's 3,000 men as they moved to the north bank of the Rio Grande River in February 1846, amounting to about one wagon for every 10 men. Of that number, 190 wagons carried various supplies while 110 hauled baggage and hospital stores. Pulled by 1,000 mules and 600 oxen, this large wagon train adequately fed Taylor's small force.[24]

American logistical arrangements faced a bigger challenge when the army began to invade Mexico. Quartermasters widely used river steamboats to funnel troops and supplies to the main base at New Orleans. Then they chartered or purchased ocean vessels to set up regular trips across the Gulf of Mexico to sustain Winfield Scott's operations along the coast. By war's end the Quartermaster Department had purchased 52 vessels (including 7 steam-propelled river craft and 15 steam-powered seagoing vessels). It chartered many boats and ships. Some of these vessels connected Atlantic ports with Gulf destinations. The *Massachusetts*, a vessel that combined sail and steam power, made the trip from Fort Washington on the Potomac River just south of the nation's capital to Brazos on the Texas coast in 17 days, a travel time commensurate with the better speed typically recorded by coastal vessels during the Civil War. Quartermasters in the Mexican conflict also negotiated charters with ship owners that allowed the government to purchase their craft after the first trip, an arrangement also to be seen in the Civil War. They found light river steamers on the Ohio River and managed to move a dozen of them across the Gulf in calm weather to operate along the Rio Grande in support of Taylor's operations in that valley.[25]

While the Americans made full use of steam power on the rivers and along the coastal shipping lanes, they encountered persistent problems in trying to acquire enough wagons to support the army. Quartermasters placed orders for new wagons with dozens of firms, but the supply seldom matched demand, leading Taylor to use pack mules, to hire Mexican ox carts, and to purchase Mexican horses when the supply of mules dried up. For his campaign against Monterey in September 1846, Taylor relied on one pack mule for every 8 men

in his 6,000-man army. He allowed three pack mules for each company headquarters and four for each regimental headquarters. His 1,900 pack mules
worked alongside only 180 wagons, an unusual proportion of military transport
for a force this size.[26]

Winfield Scott's drive toward Mexico City challenged American logistics
like no previous campaign in the war. Quartermaster General Thomas S. Jesup
personally superintended the preparation at New Orleans and accompanied
the troops to Vera Cruz, foretelling Montgomery Meigs's trip to Chattanooga
after the Federal defeat at Chickamauga. Jesup's quartermasters rounded
up 53 ocean vessels from the Atlantic coast and 163 ships from the Gulf coast
to transport Scott's army of 10,000 men. Scott estimated he would need up to
1,000 wagons and 3,000 pack animals to haul supplies, plus an additional 500
draft animals to move his siege train for the reduction of Vera Cruz. As he penetrated the interior, Scott was compelled to purchase two-thirds of all his draft
animals from the local population rather than rely on transporting them from
New Orleans. He also came to purchase most of the food needed for his army
in the countryside. A string of wagon trains kept his advancing army in at least
tenuous communication with Vera Cruz. One of the larger trains contained
500 wagons and up to 300 pack mules. With guerrillas a constant threat, it was
escorted by 1,300 troops.[27]

With war's end, the last act of the American transport system was to bring
the troops home. From May 30 to July 2, 1848, 65 vessels moved 18,331 men
from Vera Cruz to New Orleans. Of that number, 16 were owned by the government, 18 were chartered at Vera Cruz, and 31 were chartered at New Orleans.
Quartermasters also arranged for the transport home of many civilian employees of the army later that summer.[28]

Sustaining the enlarged American empire after 1848 imposed new challenges on army quartermasters. The nation had acquired half a million additional square miles of territory, and the army, although small, was scattered
widely over the continent. While only 13.7 percent of the Quartermaster
Department's expenditures had been allocated to transportation costs in 1844,
by 1850 that proportion had skyrocketed to 45.9 percent. Personnel traveled by
ocean vessels that were chartered to run from the East Coast to California by
way of Panama. The cost typically ran to $150 per enlisted man and $225 per
officer. It was cheaper to ship supplies all the way around the tip of South
America than to transfer them overland at Panama. For posts scattered around

the interior of the Far West, wagon trains supplied virtually everything needed. Quartermasters usually contracted with private freight companies, paying a negotiated rate for each 100 pounds to be moved in increments of 100 miles, as it proved to be cheaper than using large government wagon trains.[29]

Well before the Mexican War began, railroads had emerged as a potentially important means of military transport. Several European nations experimented with large-scale troop transfers in peacetime to see how rail transport could be employed in war. As early as 1830, German quartermasters used rails to move a regiment of troops 34 miles in two hours, a trip that normally would have taken two days by foot. The Prussians moved over 12,000 men with their carriages and animals to Cracow in 1846 by using two rail lines, and the Russian army shifted 30,000 men from Poland to Moravia the next year by railroad cars. Austrian quartermasters transported 75,000 troops, 8,000 horses, and 1,000 carriages from Vienna to Hungary in 26 days in 1850. The troops probably could have been marched this distance, 150 miles, in the same amount of time, but administrative foul-ups caused many delays in the transfer. The next year, Austrian quartermasters moved 14,500 men, 2,000 horses, 48 guns, and 464 vehicles a distance of 187 miles in only two days, shaving off 13 days from the time needed to move this force by foot. The first recorded targeting of railroads in conflict occurred in 1848 when Venetians damaged a railroad viaduct used by Austrian troops in their effort to suppress revolutionary uprisings.[30]

The Crimean War of 1854–1856 did not give rise to much use of railroads, but ocean transport lay at the heart of its logistical history. The ability of the British and French to move a large army with thousands of animals from western Europe to southwestern Russia was the key to allied victory. British quartermasters had learned how to take care of the horses on the long voyage to Balaklava, their forward base for the siege of Sebastopol. They made sure proper stalls were built in the vessels and insisted they be cleaned every day, and the holds were well ventilated. Grooms fed the horses carefully, rubbed their legs every day, and washed their mouths and noses with vinegar to prevent communicable diseases. Quartermasters found that using gangplanks were the best method of boarding and unloading the animals. If that was not possible, they preferred slings rather than boxes to hoist the animals on and off vessels. Slings also were used to hold the horses up during rough weather while on board. Of 3,000 horses moved from various Mediterranean ports between June and October 1855, only three died along the way. These precautions were known to U.S. Army officers; the standard tactical manual for field artillery, adopted in 1860, established a set of regulations similar to the British methods for transporting horses by sea. However, it is evident that Civil War quartermasters and ship owners often ignored the regulations.[31]

British procedure for the transport of men and animals over long ocean voyages had been honed by imperial needs for decades. With no overseas empire, the Americans never bothered to learn such lessons. The French also were ahead of the Americans in this area. They moved 309,268 men and 41,974 horses and mules to the Crimea without major trouble. Steam power made such logistical feats possible.[32]

But in-theater military transport during the Crimean War was another matter. While British authorities had honed long-distance ocean transport to a fine point of science, they were woefully behind the Americans in terms of providing wagon trains for field armies. Even though Balaklava lay only seven miles from the siege lines at Sebastopol, British troops suffered needlessly because of supply problems. The British still relied on civilian contractors to provide land transport for their armies in the theater of operations. When these contractors failed them, the authorities hastily organized a new system controlled by English military personnel and operated by locally hired natives. It grew into a large force by early 1856, with 24,000 horses, 14,000 native workers, and 9,000 Europeans. The British government made some form of military land transport service a permanent establishment in its army soon after the Crimean War. The French fared better because their land transport already was under the control of the army. Both allies had to purchase most of the food for their troops in the local area, but they found it quite difficult to find adequate wagons and carts in the Crimea, having to ship most of them from elsewhere.[33]

The British were responsible for an innovation at Sebastopol, the first military railroad. They contracted with a civilian firm to construct a railroad from the port facilities at Balaklava toward the siege lines. Locomotives pulled cars for the first two miles, then a stationary engine hauled eight cars at a time up a steep incline. Horses drew them the rest of the way to the waiting troops. The line operated 5 engines and 40 cars; it hauled up to 700 tons daily by the end of the siege. This line anticipated the Federal military railroad constructed to support Grant's operations at Petersburg by nearly 10 years.[34]

The Second War of Italian Unification lasted from 1859 to 1861 and witnessed, according to historian Frederick C. Schneid, the first "conspicuous part in actual warfare, both strategically and tactically," by railroads. It started over the efforts of Piedmont-Sardinia to coordinate military efforts with France in a plan to eject Austrian troops from Lombardy and Venetia. French authorities agreed to commit 130,000 men to help Piedmont and arranged to transport them at the required time. Two French corps planned to use rail transport to the Alps and then march through the passes to another railhead in Piedmont before completing their journey to Lombardy, the expected theater of operations. Three corps (70,000 troops) planned to cross the Mediterranean to avoid the Alps, mostly in French vessels, but some in Piedmontese ships as well. The French already owned 30 steam-powered transports and contracted enough civilian vessels to make up the difference.[35]

When war opened in April 1859, the French wound up shifting many more than 130,000 troops. They eventually moved 604,000 men and 129,000 horses by rail to the border from April 19 to July 15, 1859, achieving a transport rate estimated to be six times faster than marching this distance. While part of the expeditionary force moved through the mountains to Piedmont, the rest boarded vessels for a short voyage to Italy. More than 79,000 men and over 7,000 horses arrived in a total of 122 shiploads, with each vessel carrying between 200 and 1,700 men. Austrian troops had a short distance to travel to the theater of operations and used railways to get there, but persistent administrative foul-ups delayed the transfer. An Austrian corps took 16 days to move only 47 miles, slower than any rate of normal marching by foot. As a result, the French logistical success brought enough allied troops to Lombardy for a short and successful campaign to kick the Austrians out of the area. The railroads in Piedmont were less capable of handling heavy volumes of troops and supplies, causing some difficulty for the allies, but victory in two large battles turned the tide in this short war.[36]

Historians have only recently recognized the logistical significance of the Italian campaign, having previously devoted a good deal of attention to developments in Prussia during the middle decades of the nineteenth century. Representing a small but potent German state in central and eastern Europe, Prussian officials were thinking about using railroads as a means of rapid deployment to handle the country's complicated defense needs, sandwiched as it was between large and dangerous powers east and west. Privately owned railroad companies in Prussia argued that their lines held an important military potential and sought army support for their business success. By the 1830s, fear of a French invasion sparked the beginning of intensive study by the army to see how it could use rail transport for national defense. In 1839, the army began to transport large numbers of troops on a regular basis by rail to work out the details. Prussia shifted men to several western German states to suppress the revolutions of 1848; when war with Austria seemed imminent two years later, Prussian quartermasters made many mistakes in mobilizing manpower by rail. There was immense confusion and lack of coordination between the army and the privately owned rail companies.[37]

The mistakes of 1850 and the huge expansion of the railroad system that followed compelled the Prussian army to take railroad planning more seriously. Large-scale efforts to establish close cooperative ties with the companies so the army could move large numbers of troops efficiently in time of need were worked out. The government itself became more heavily involved in owning or administering up to half of the country's tracks by the 1860s. Field Marshall Helmuth von Moltke, who became chief of staff on the General Staff in 1858, strongly supported the growing link between the army and civilian enterprise. By 1861 the staff produced the first comprehensive plan for the use of German railroads as military transport; the plan extended out of Prussia to include other key German states. One drawback to the German rail system was that it consisted mostly of single-track lines while the French had a tendency to construct two tracks. Single-track systems could easily become snarled when handling heavy volume over a short period of time. The Prussians planned to stop all civilian traffic when necessary to keep their military assets moving in a timely manner. They worked out detailed instructions for loading troops and set a timetable for trains to make maximum use of available tracks. The Prussians also created a Field Railway Detachment in 1861 that was charged with the task of repairing captured enemy railroads, foreshadowing the U.S. Military Railroad system soon to appear in America.[38]

The army and government of Prussia had gone much further than any other country to prepare for intensive railroad use in warfare. In fact, besides Prussia, only France could point to any significant effort to prepare for rail use before war was declared. One would expect that the first true railroad war, a conflict depending fundamentally on rail transport for a major and sustained military effort, would take place on the continent of Europe. But that was not the case. As soon as the firing on Fort Sumter heralded civil war, the first railroad war in history took shape in North America. Privately owned rail lines provided a huge proportion of the logistical needs of both the North and South from 1861 to 1865, along with river steamers and coastal shipping. Neither the American government nor its army worked out any plans to do so before the conflict erupted, but the end result (at least in the North) was an impressive logistical achievement. Rails played an important role in sustaining four years of massive campaigning by an army that numbered more than 1 million men by 1865. The Americans put together an improvised system of rail, boat, and ship transportation for their military needs, but in general that system worked extremely well for the North and at least reasonably well for a time in the South.

There is no evidence that American quartermasters learned anything from the European example. Although a four-man commission was sent to observe the Crimean War, the publication of its reports was so delayed that the Civil War opened before anyone had much of a chance to absorb them. Prussian efforts to organize rail transport in wartime apparently were unknown to U.S. Army quartermasters before the firing on Fort Sumter.

The global logistical heritage demonstrates several important aspects of Civil War logistics. To start, whether they understood it or not, Union and Confederate quartermasters did not work within a vacuum. Most of their work had deep precedents in global history. Utilizing civilian transportation facilities in river travel, coastal shipping, and land-based wagon, cart, and pack trains had been done for centuries and all across the international spectrum. The relatively new development lay in the growing tendency for armies to purchase their own wagons and detail soldiers to drive them, a trend evident in the American Revolution and later in the Crimean War. American quartermasters had limited experience in using ocean transport before 1861, but then they did not really need to do so during the Civil War either.

The premier new mode of transportation in the nineteenth century was the railroad. Even though America had more track mileage than any other nation in the world by 1861, its army officers spent no time considering how to use the iron horse in wartime. But when forced to do so, American quartermasters quickly crafted a strategy to take advantage of this modern means of travel for military purposes. The Civil War became the first major railroad war, even though European contemporaries and latter-day historians tend to ignore that fact. In this area alone, Civil War quartermasters pioneered new forms of military transportation, working out problems that would continue to stymie German quartermasters in the Franco-Prussian War five years after Appomattox. The world tended to ignore the true lessons of the American Civil War just as American quartermasters tended to ignore the world's lessons in logistics.

2

‡‡‡‡‡‡‡‡‡‡‡‡‡

QUARTERMASTERS NORTH AND SOUTH

Quartermasters were vested with the responsibility for procuring and managing military transportation in the Civil War. They were among a select group of officers in several departments who provided fundamental but often overlooked support for Union and Confederate soldiers. These support departments seldom received much attention from the public. When a special committee of the Confederate Congress investigated their activities early in the war, its report tried to illuminate their significance. "The labors of these departments penetrate the entire military establishment, breathe life into the Army, nurture its growth, give it strength and efficiency in the field, maintaining its health and facilitating its movements." A poor quartermaster "may effectually check the progress of an army, and the demands of an [infantry] officer may destroy the most perfect administration" of the transportation system.[1]

Like the rest of the army, quartermasters were faced with a task of far greater proportions than any yet undertaken by Americans. No previous conflict had seen the raising of 3 million men North and South; moreover, the creation of this huge military force proceeded at a rapid pace. Early in the conflict, the Federal government increased the size of its army by 27 times in only four months. In contrast, the American army increased by only three times in four months early in World War I, and by four times in one year just before the opening of World War II. Quartermaster officers faced with supplying and transporting the rapidly increasing number of soldiers often found the task daunting. "My duties have been & are now ten times more arduous & responsible than those of a Major General in command of a Brigade," Stewart Van Vliet complained to Secretary of War Edwin M. Stanton. Most soldiers took their supply arrangements for granted; a few understood how difficult a task organizing it could be.[2]

Quartermasters were charged with a variety of duties, which included procuring a range of equipment and supplies (other than food for the men, weapons, and ammunition) and arranging for the shipment of literally everything the army needed even if they had not been responsible for obtaining it. As Quartermaster General Montgomery Meigs pointed out, a no less important job was to keep accurate financial records and strive to save the government as much money as possible without stinting the troops. The array of items a quartermaster either purchased, moved, cared for, accounted for, or worried over can be staggering to the reader.[3]

In 1861, the Federal government maintained seven military bureaus to support its army in the field. These included offices run by the adjutant general, commissary general, surgeon general, paymaster general, chief engineer, chief of ordnance, and quartermaster general. The heads of these bureaus did not report to the general-in-chief but to the secretary of war. The quartermaster general acted to coordinate the activities of his subordinate officers in his department and in the field. Department officers were those not assigned to a particular unit in the field; they worked in Washington or in a number of key commercial cities across the country. The number of department officers rose steadily as the war progressed. By May 1862 there were 200 such officers, three-fourths of them volunteers and only one-fourth holding commissions in the regular army. By July 1, 1864, a total of 549 volunteer officers and 76 regular officers worked for the Quartermaster Department. One responsibility of these officers was to organize and manage dozens of depots across the country that acquired, stored, and distributed the array of material and animals needed by forces in the region. While the majority of quartermaster officers working directly for the Quartermaster Department were volunteer officers without military training or prior experience, the minority of professional soldiers they worked with dominated the department, its policies, and its administration.[4]

In addition to officers assigned by the department, there were hundreds of quartermasters embedded in units in the field, from regiments up to field armies. Regimental quartermasters received their appointments from the governor of their state, while those serving on brigade, division, corps, and army staffs were appointed by the president. John J. Metzgar enlisted in the 76th Ohio in October 1861 and served as its quartermaster sergeant from the beginning. He was promoted to 2nd lieutenant a year later and led Company C until he suffered a severe wound at the battle of Ringgold, Georgia, in November

1863 that put him out of action for a few months. When recovered, Metzgar was promoted to 1st lieutenant and assigned as regimental quartermaster. All quartermasters serving with units in the field had authority to procure needed material or arrange for transportation. Each one had to take orders from the commander of the unit he served as well as from his supervising quartermaster officer in the unit above his in the order of battle.[5]

The supply and logistics chain of command ended with the Quartermaster General. Thomas S. Jesup had held that position from 1818 until his death in June 1860. Joseph E. Johnston replaced him but resigned on April 22, 1861, to join the Confederate army. Montgomery Meigs took the position by mid-June. Born in 1816 and graduating from West Point 20 years later, Meigs served as an engineer; his most prominent work was the renovation of the U.S. Capitol and the Aqueduct in Washington during the 1850s. Meigs initially had only 37 officers in his department, one-third of them in office since 1838.[6]

Meigs's role in managing the expansion of the Quartermaster Department and supervising officers in the field cannot be overestimated—he and his officers were responsible for Union logistical success in the Civil War. Meigs submitted estimates of expenses needed in the near future for congressional approval and his office handled a mountain of paperwork flowing in from hundreds of quartermasters in the field. That paperwork largely revolved around vouchers and receipts, which had to be examined by clerks before submission to the secretary of war, who passed them on to the Treasury Department for payment.[7]

Meigs was careful to inform Stanton of the increasing volume of paperwork his men processed as the war continued. He estimated that company-level officers filed 40,000 quarterly statements every year and regimental quartermasters produced an additional 12,000 accounts and returns each year. In addition, quartermasters working on brigade through army levels filed an additional 3,600 monthly statements every year. His clerks had to examine each one of these documents and correspond with officers who did not fill them out properly. Meigs saw this task as second only to the procurement of material because of the enormous amount of government money involved.[8]

He had far too few clerks for the job. By November 1862 Meigs complained to Stanton that his people had been able to process only one-fourth of the paperwork covering the previous fiscal year (which ended June 30, 1862). The unsettled accounts from that previous year amounted to about $105 million.

2.1. Montgomery C. Meigs, Quartermaster General of the U.S. Army. A tower of strength and efficiency, Meigs masterminded the most important department in the Federal war effort. (Library of Congress, LC-DIG-cwpbh-04284)

Meigs wanted at least 120 more clerks to have a reasonable chance of getting caught up in the near future. Stanton responded; by 1863 Meigs had 213 clerks, and at war's end 591. Having started with only 13 clerks in June 1861, Meigs managed to increase his clerical staff by 45 times in four years.[9]

These clerks were highly skilled, experienced accountants and they drew large salaries. They were used even by quartermaster officers serving in the field. Philip Sheridan issued general orders regulating the pay allotted clerks who worked for quartermasters in the Middle Military Division during the late summer of 1864. Those working on brigade-level staffs received $75 per month and those on division and corps level staffs earned $100 per month.[10]

Meigs also managed a major reorganization of the Quartermaster Department from a simple administrative office to a multi-dimensional organization. His subordinates had pointed out as early as 1863 that some officers, such as the personnel responsible for clothing, had such a complicated job to perform that they should constitute a separate unit within the department. Meigs worked out a plan to divide the department's functions into nine divisions, and after some trouble Congress approved the reorganization on July 4, 1864. Three of the nine divisions handled transportation; the 3rd Division dealt with Ocean and Lake Transportation, the 4th Division handled Rail and River Transportation (that is, contracting and chartering privately owned trains and river steamers), and the 7th Division supervised Military Trains and Incidental Allowances (primarily the government-controlled U.S. Military Railroad).[11]

The new divisions reflected an important reality of procurement and transportation in the Civil War. As historian Mark R. Wilson put it, the quartermaster system was "a mixed military economy," combining the utilization of private enterprise with government ownership and management. This dual approach to fulfilling army needs was most prominently seen in the procurement of supplies of all kinds, but it was reflected in arrangements for the transport of this material as well. It has been estimated that the Quartermaster Department managed more than $600 million worth of transactions during the course of the Civil War, and $240 million of that expenditure went toward transportation costs.[12]

Quartermaster officers were aware that their work was fundamentally important but often not appreciated by outsiders. Captain James F. Rusling, who served as chief quartermaster of the Third Corps in the Army of the Potomac, noted after the war that the Quartermaster Department was "the most abused and the least understood of any in the army, though the most important by far of all the staff departments." An old saying emerged from the prewar army that "the first duty of a quartermaster is to make himself comfortable; that his second duty is to make himself *more* comfortable; his third duty, to make himself as comfortable as he *can*; and his fourth duty, to make everybody else uncomfortable!"[13]

But both quartermaster and commissary officers often fought against this negative image. "Any nincompoop will make a good enough quartermaster or commissary in time of peace," concluded H. C. Symonds, who served as a commissary officer, "but in war those offices are in every respect the most important to the commanding general, to the troops, to the government, and to the people." A good quartermaster did not have to be trained at West Point or have any prior experience in the U.S. Army, thought Lewis B. Parsons. "A good business man may enter the service on nearly, if not quite, an equality, so far as practical usefulness is concerned, with any regular officer." Parsons himself held a college degree and good experience in the business world. Simon Perkins

Jr. coupled his business experience with family political connections to secure a position in the army and turned out to be a superb quartermaster. Talent enabled Philip Sheridan to handle both quartermaster and commissary duties in Samuel R. Curtis's Department of the Southwest early in the war. Sheridan thought it was a natural combination, given that Curtis relied heavily on foraging across the countryside to feed his little army as it drove into southwestern Missouri and it made sense to have one man in charge of not only gathering the food but getting it to the troops. "A great quartermaster or a great commissary must . . . be a man of brains" asserted James Rusling. "A good quartermaster is expected to be 'sufficient unto himself,' and to make good the deficiencies of everybody else."[14]

Moreover, quartermasters were legally accountable for their work. They had to file a bond worth $10,000 that made them personally liable for mistakes, and government accountants held them strictly to this pledge. As Herman Haupt pointed out, quartermasters often were happy when generals ordered stores burned in order to prevent them from falling into enemy hands. In those cases, their personal liability for the safety of the material was waived. Haupt heard of cases where quartermaster officers actually celebrated at the receipt of such orders and also heard the same applied to stores destroyed when western river steamers sank or were burned.[15]

Held to strict accountability and given enormously important tasks, many volunteer officers who found themselves doing quartermaster duties in the field suddenly realized they had little idea how the government wanted them to operate. Charles Leib found himself in this situation in the mountainous counties of western Virginia early in the war. He had no experience at army work and there was no copy of army regulations anywhere near his post. Leib "felt as does the mariner cast away in an open boat on an unknown ocean, without chart, compass, or rudder." He soon after wrote a book that recounted with zest his many problems and his attempts to catch up with them, eventually finding himself out of a job because he would not cooperate with unscrupulous contractors.[16]

But as the war effort evolved, quartermaster officers were often given detailed instructions to guide their efforts and order grew out of chaos. Rufus Ingalls, chief quartermaster of the Army of the Potomac for most of the war, lectured his subordinates not to refer trivial matters to higher authority but to exercise judgment about which questions they could decide and which needed the approval of a superior. Ingalls emphasized good business sense, as did William S. Rosecrans when he tried to find a "business quartermaster" for the depot at Nashville early in 1863. "Orders and instructions are not the things," he told Meigs. "Power and energy, with system and business capacity, are what is now wanted."[17]

Rosecrans wrote of the ideal quartermaster; in fact, many of them fit his bill perfectly, while others were lacking in the qualities he described. As with infantry officers, being a quartermaster in a small sphere of responsibility was comparatively easy, but holding a job with wider and more complex tasks required a rare combination of talents in a man. Those talents included not only good business sense, but a professional attitude in dealing with hundreds of people in and out of the army. It also was vitally important that the quartermaster be honest, for he was exposed to innumerable shady businessmen from the civilian world eager to offer bribes for lucrative contracts.

It was not until fairly late in the war that Meigs set up examining boards to evaluate the qualifications of quartermaster officers working directly for the department. The process continued well into the postwar months because those officers had to continue handling mountains of material and hundreds of contracts long after Appomattox as the U.S. Army slowly wound up its wartime business. By October 1, 1865, the boards had examined 283 officers; they found 216 of them qualified for their job and 67 unqualified to perform their duties. Of the latter category, 28 were mustered out, 18 resigned, and no action as yet had been taken on the other 21 officers. The boards still had 245 officers to examine. Almost one out of four quartermaster officers in the department were found unfit for their positions; one can take this statistic either way. Given the need to rapidly expand support activities and having to rely mostly on volunteer officers who came directly from civilian life, the department can be excused any censure for the fact that almost a fourth of its appointees should not have been appointed.[18]

Members of these examining boards were given additional tasks as well. Alexander Bliss was also assigned to serve as president of a board to revise the department's regulations and soon after was told to take over Lewis B. Parsons's job of managing the 4th Division, with responsibility for overseeing all river and rail transport in the country. James F. Rusling served on Bliss's board for revising the army regulations and the manual for quartermaster officers before he was put on a board to examine depots south of the Ohio River. He finished a 200-page report (with an additional 200 pages of tables) on the subject in about six weeks.[19]

"A quartermaster who does his duty sees not many leisure moments," concluded Henry H. Howland, quartermaster of the 57th Illinois. The weight of his duties increased whenever the government seemed not to support him. A. S. Baxter, an assistant quartermaster at Cairo, Illinois, complained to Parsons that Washington failed to provide enough funds for him to pay his civilian workers. Many of them had not seen a penny in six months and were demoralized. "I had rather be in the bottom of the Mississippi than work night and day as I do without being sustained by Government," he moaned.[20]

Baxter's experience was comparatively rare. More often the problem lay not with Washington but with the individual quartermaster. Men who were not up to their duties created many problems. In preparing for the Atlanta campaign, William G. LeDuc was frustrated by a quartermaster assigned over him who seemed to think that prewar routine was good enough for wartime work. He kept rigid office hours from 9 A.M. to 5 P.M., blamed soldiers if their clothing and equipment wore out, and tried to keep transportation costs to a bare minimum. "This was absurd in an army in active service," LeDuc rightly concluded. He learned to stash away extra amounts of all material without reporting it so that he could obtain more control over what his command needed.[21]

James Rusling also understood the needs of wartime. He opened his office as assistant to the chief quartermaster of the Department of the Cumberland in Nashville at 8 A.M. and dealt with a constant stream of people until closing it at 8 P.M. every day. James L. Donaldson (the chief quartermaster), Rusling, and seven clerks worked in this office. By December 1863, Donaldson had more than a dozen quartermasters, 12,000 civilian workers, more than 600 miles of railroad to manage, and over 100,000 men to support. His office disbursed over $5 million worth of business every month. "This is the biggest army depot to-day on the face of the earth," Rusling proudly reported, and managing it was a gargantuan task.[22]

The scale of work and the weighty responsibility attending it demanded highly qualified men at these higher levels, and it was not easy to find them. Colonel C. G. Sawtelle, chief quartermaster of the Military Division of the Gulf, still had 192,000 troops to supply as late as December 1865 because of the continued prospect of dealing with French occupation of Mexico. Sawtelle could not find enough qualified assistants to help him, given that the war was

2.2. Quartermaster's Wharf at Alexandria, Virginia, with Steamer *John Brooks* at the Wharf. A huge stack of hay bales (fodder for horses and mules) lies on the left, while on the right is a large accumulation of either cordwood to fuel the steamers or ties for a railroad track. Also, note the large number of sailing vessels and the relatively small number of coastal steamboats, giving some indication of the relative use of both types of craft by Federal quartermasters. (Library of Congress, LC-DIG-ppmsca-34823)

long over. In fact, the trouble had started back in March during Edward R. S. Canby's campaign against Mobile. An examining board was just then dismissing many quartermasters as incompetent and Sawtelle was forced to detail lieutenants from infantry regiments who had little if any knowledge of quartermaster duties. They also were not bonded at the time.[23]

S. B. Holabird, who managed the quartermaster staff of the Gulf Department in 1864, indicated that the problem of finding suitable officers was deeper and more persistent than Sawtelle realized. It was more challenging to be a quartermaster officer than any other type of support personnel because of the array of duties and the requirement of a bond. "There are abundant other staff positions requiring no bonds, no responsibilities, substantially nothing to do," he complained. Trying to recruit experienced men from civil life proved difficult as well. When Captain Goodwin of Boston, who was "a thorough sailor and gentleman" agreed to work for the army at $200 per month, he went to Pass

Cavallo on the Texas coast to manage the difficult task of getting supplies off steamers and onto land, where proper port facilities were lacking. He took one look at the situation and told the local commander "that he had been promised to be made comfortable and that it could not be done here," and promptly returned to Boston.[24]

Fortunately for the Union army, a handful of highly qualified men took on the heavy responsibilities involved in high-level quartermaster posts and fulfilled their charges superbly. In many men's eyes, Robert Allen stood out among them. A native of Ohio and already 50 years old when the war broke out, Allen graduated from West Point and served conspicuously as a division quartermaster in the Mexican War. During his Civil War service Allen was located mostly at St. Louis and Louisville, from which cities he managed all quartermaster activities in the Mississippi Valley. Allen handled $106,694,657.24 worth of business for the government. In addition, he directed other quartermasters in the disbursement of $90,799,435.88 worth of funds. He bought or supervised the purchase of more than 8 million bushels of corn, over 26 million bushels of oats, more than 377,000 tons of hay, 6,638 wagons, over 100,000 horses, and more than 75,000 mules. Moreover, Allen supervised the processing of 250,000 vouchers submitted by various quartermaster officers within his vast area of responsibility.[25]

Allen was promoted from major at the start of the war to brigadier general and brevet major general in both the volunteer service and the regular army by its end. Yet he never saw duty in the field during the Civil War. Sherman tried to change that. Partway through the Atlanta campaign he wanted to bring Allen to the field because he had no chief quartermaster on the staff of his Military Division of the Mississippi. While Meigs approved the request, Stanton refused to allow it, pointing out that Allen had much more to do than merely to supply Sherman's army group. Allen continued as quartermaster until his retirement in 1878, having disbursed an estimated $111 million of taxpayers' money during his entire career without a penny of it having been contested or disallowed by auditors. While James F. Rusling had worked with many quartermasters East and West during the war, he always placed Allen on top. He was "the Great Quartermaster of our Civil War."[26]

William T. Sherman himself would have made a great quartermaster if fate had not dictated a different career for him. No other general was as concerned with logistics and supply and no other expended as much time and energy dealing with those twin requirements for military success. Lewis B. Parsons was mightily impressed by Sherman when he accompanied the general on the Chickasaw Bayou Expedition in December 1862. "General Sherman is a trump, and makes things move. I like his business mode of doing things, his promptness and decision." Captain Duncan K. Major, who conducted a study of supply in the Civil War many decades after the conflict, also was impressed by Sherman, calling him "his own chief quartermaster and chief commissary." In addition to Sherman, Grenville M. Dodge stands out as a general with a keen sense of logistics. In Dodge's case, it mostly centered on a highly developed skill for constructing and maintaining railroads. Educated at a military school in Vermont, Dodge worked as a civil engineer for various railroads in the West before the war. In filing a report on restoring the railroads in western Tennessee during the summer of 1862, his military correspondence reads much more like an engineer's report than that of a brigadier general in the volunteer force.[27]

On the other hand, there were some generals who had no business or logistical sense at all. John C. Fremont made a royal mess out of his administrative affairs while commanding the Department of the Missouri during the late summer and early fall of 1861. Meigs sensed trouble early on when he saw paperwork coming from St. Louis that indicated Fremont's quartermasters were not following established procedure and were paying far too much for needed items. Torn between protecting the government on the one hand and supporting the army on the other, he decided to approve irregular purchases but then warned everyone that it would be up to Fremont to defend them when Congress realized what was happening and began to investigate. When Henry W. Halleck replaced Fremont in November 1861 he discovered the "most outrageous frauds" in that department he had ever seen. The worst problem lay among Fremont's quartermasters, most of whom were ignorant of their duties and often untrustworthy in a moral sense.[28]

Unfortunately, the problem lay deeper than mere lack of honesty. Even good quartermasters often did not take as much care to save material as they should have done. When Rosecrans's Army of the Cumberland left Murfreesboro for the Tullahoma campaign, many regiments simply left what they did not need behind in their winter camps. Regimental commanders and their quartermaster staff abandoned tools, ropes, stoves, and horseshoes. Many tents were left standing as the army marched away. When Captain J. Warren Clark, an assistant quartermaster at the Murfreesboro depot, saw this, he obtained some wagons and tried to collect it. By then local civilians were already beginning to raid the abandoned camps to take what they could. Clark managed to save about $1,000 worth of government property, only a small fraction of what had been abandoned. Waste was "undoubtedly unavoidable in war," Clark concluded, "but a large portion is needless." It stemmed, in his view, from the fact that regimental officers were not personally responsible for material such as this.[29]

Every item supplied by the government, no matter how small or unimportant, had a role to play in logistics. If a tent was needlessly left behind by members of the Army of the Cumberland at Murfreesboro, eventually it would have to be replaced by a logistical system that was increasing in length with every mile those soldiers marched south. With the increasing length of that supply line, the difficulties of finding enough room in the railroad car for the item increased too, especially when the army crossed the mountains. Rugged topography forced railroad cars to lighten their loads, placing a high premium on space in those cars. Quartermasters understood these problems; common soldiers and their officers never gave them a thought.

More troublesome than thoughtless waste was the possibility of fraud and corruption. Quartermaster officers encountered those possibilities nearly every day of their army service. "If you would spoil an honest man, make a quartermaster of him," ran an old army adage. Handling nearly $34 million worth of government business in one fiscal year, as did Robert Allen, was a severe test of a man's moral stamina. Charles Leib was confronted on a daily basis with civilians who offered him bribes to obtain local contracts for army work or to secure the paperwork necessary to compensate them for loss of property at the hands of the army.[30]

Leib also realized that many army officers did not know how to fill out the paperwork necessary to request, receive, and account for army property. Some even tried to bully him into issuing equipment and supplies without any paperwork at all. He had to stand his ground and insist on procedures or else he would have been held personally responsible for the property. Many quartermaster officers got into trouble not through their own fault, but by the failings of clerks who were dishonest or incompetent. When Henry Clubb was relieved of quartermaster duty pending an investigation into his records, he blamed it on his clerks and was heartened when he heard others say, "Damned shame that Clubb was dismissed. He is too honest for a Quartermaster."[31]

There certainly was corruption in the employment of western river steamers early in the war, at least in the eyes of William J. Kountz. A riverboat owner in western Pennsylvania before the war, Kountz agreed to help his friend George B. McClellan sort out the chaotic transportation system in the Department of the Ohio in May 1861. He took charge of steamer support for the Federal invasion of western Virginia and found a clerk who took bribes to influence contracts granted to certain parties. Kountz opposed him, had him fired, and began a larger crusade to crush corruption. Unfortunately, Kountz had little tack; he was brutally frank and made enemies among the honest as well as among the crooks. Meigs refused to put him in charge of all western river transportation, Ulysses S. Grant got tired of his meddling, and in the end Kountz dropped out of the public service as an honest but self-important and frustrated man.[32]

In contrast to Kountz, Captain John Howland was one of the rare examples of a quartermaster officer who was guilty of embezzlement. A volunteer appointee and temporary chief quartermaster of the Fifth Corps, Army of the Potomac, Howland received a check from Rufus Ingalls for nearly $16,500 to pay teamsters in March 1863. Alexander Bliss arrived to assume the duties of corps quartermaster just as Howland was about to leave for Washington, intending to cash the check there. Howland did not listen to Bliss's sound advice to endorse the check for deposit only and instead took the sum in cash when he arrived in the capital. Howland deserted and spent more than $6,000 of his ill-gotten gain before Federal agents caught up with him.[33]

Howland's case was rare; the government stood to lose much more money through fraudulent procedures in securing contracts with businessmen than by the odd embezzler. Congress tried to reduce fraud by passing a law in June 1862 requiring all contracts to be rendered in writing and to be certified before a magistrate. Meigs rightfully protested that this would not necessarily eliminate fraud and would certainly impose a huge delay on the process of doing business. He thought that quick and sure punishment for fraud would be more effective. Stanton issued a general order ameliorating the worst aspects of this law to keep the process of contracting with civilians going with minimal interference. On the other hand, Congress passed a helpful law in the summer of 1862 specifying that all civilian contractors were subject to army regulations and therefore liable to court-martial for fraudulent practices. Two years later this was applied to all clerks and heads of bureaus in the government as well. These laws had teeth; several courts martial were conducted in the last two years of the war to try contractors for fraud.[34]

Dishonest men like Howland aside, the majority of Union army quartermasters were honest, smart, hard-working men. Many of them stood out in the war years. Lewis B. Parsons graduated from Yale University and obtained a law degree from Harvard University before going west to manage railroads. A friend of McClellan, he rose to prominence as the master of river transportation in the West. Parsons garnered effusive praise from everyone from Grant to Lincoln and yearned for promotion commensurate with his huge responsibilities. At times the pressures of his job led him to hate his lot, calling it a "damnably laborious, perplexing, thankless, position." But he never gave up. After the war Grant wrote a glowing letter of appreciation for Parsons. Lewis's brother Charles, a bank cashier before the war, became his chief clerk in the transportation office at St. Louis.[35]

The financial cost of preserving the Union was enormous. The Federal government spent about $1.8 billion during the conflict, two-thirds of it to sustain the land army. This amounted to more money than the government had spent in all years combined before 1861. Meigs's Quartermaster Department distributed more than $1 billion. In contrast, the Subsistence Department and the Ordnance Department spent only $500 million and the Navy Department spent $300 million.[36]

This level of spending was possible only through a mind-set, a will to enlarge the power of the central authority to meet the increasing demands of the nation's biggest war effort. Washington officials developed "a robust administrative bureaucracy" during the war years. Sherman recalled "how completely we were supplied abundantly with steamers, wagons, horses, mules, clothing" during the war. Rufus Ingalls realized that it was not just the government but thousands of private businessmen who contributed to the supply and logistical success of the Union army. Looking back from the perspective of 1876, Meigs wondered at what had been accomplished. "The elasticity and planning and power of adapting itself to varying circumstances of our Quartermaster's organization properly conducted, is certainly unrivalled. Its conduct during the late war, a war more difficult than that of Germany against France, was satisfactory to the people, to the soldiers, and to their commanders."[37]

The interested historian can easily find a mountain of material written by Union quartermaster officers concerning all phases of their important work in the Civil War, including that related to transportation. This material can be read in the pages of the *Official Records* and in unpublished documents in the National Archives. Moreover, there are many collections of papers kept by Union quartermasters and memoirs written by them that were published after the war. Unfortunately, the same is not true of Confederate quartermasters. Even given the fact that the Confederacy had fewer quartermaster officers, there is still a lamentable dearth of official documents and personal accounts written by them. While we have more detailed information about Union logistics than we can easily digest, historians have far too little information about Confederate logistics than is needed for a full, well-rounded picture of it. The only exception is, to a degree, Southern railroad transportation.

The Confederate government created a Quartermaster Department on February 26, 1861. Lieutenant Colonel Abraham C. Myers was Quartermaster General from that time until August 1863. Born in Charleston, South Carolina, of Jewish descent, Myers was a West Point graduate with quartermaster experience in the Mexican War. He fell victim to public views of mismanagement and inefficiency in the department. Brigadier General Alexander R. Lawton replaced Myers. A Georgian, Lawton graduated from West Point and from Harvard as well, but he was a lawyer and planter before the war and had little experience in quartermaster duties. In addition to the department head, the Confederate government assigned individuals to handle special tasks, such as coordinating rail transport and organizing land transportation (primarily wagons) for the army.[38]

Part of the reason why there is so little material on logistics in the Confederate army is that Rebel officers were terrible record keepers. Joseph Wheeler tried to get his subordinates to maintain good accounts of exactly who handled quartermaster duties in his cavalry corps during the middle part of the war, and only slightly succeeded. He issued a circular on March 4, 1863, requiring regimental and brigade leaders to report the name and rank of their quartermaster and commissary officers and whether they had posted bonds. Wheeler had to request this information repeatedly. He finally warned that any officers not reported would be relieved of their duties by March 15. The next month, Wheeler spelled out clearly in another circular exactly what types of forms had to be submitted each month to the corps quartermaster to ensure timely record keeping so he could know what his command needed on a regular basis. One can search in vain for similar documents in the Union army; Federal quartermasters and officers knew what they were supposed to do without having to be told through circulars and general orders issued by corps or army headquarters.[39]

Confederate transportation history in general tends to be the story of unsolved problems, irreparable difficulties, and frustrated attempts to make a success out of failure. That is not to say that Rebel troops always suffered from logistical limitations, but the difference between Union and Confederate logistics is stunning, and this discrepancy played a huge role in eventual Federal success. In no other area is this as true as in rail-based transportation. Commissary General Lucius B. Northrop fretted, complained, and cried out during the war for improvements in the way the Confederate government handled privately owned railroad companies. A sympathetic Rebel quartermaster who had access to Northrop's letter book noted that he wrote at least 30 long letters to various Confederate officials about this problem during the war; that averages one letter every six weeks. For example, Northrop complained that 1,400 hogsheads of sugar shipped from New Orleans the previous November, destined for troops in the Army of Northern Virginia, still had not arrived as of January 1862. Fifty barrels of pork that started from New Orleans in August 1861 finally reached the army by January 12, 1862.[40]

Many things accounted for the eventual failure of Rebel rail transport, to be more fully discussed in a following chapter, but Northrop realized one of the few problems he could deal with lay in the railroad companies' tendency to give priority to private freight over government business. He pushed for the authority to stop private freight and passenger traffic for short periods of time in order to compel the companies to give priority to army work. Now and then such authority was granted, and it worked for a couple of weeks, until the government relented and the railroads went back to their normal practice of catering to private citizens, who paid their bills on time.[41]

Lack of resources, ranging from funds to iron, impeded Confederate logistics, but at heart its failure lay in an administrative malaise centered in Richmond. Jefferson Davis was never willing to appoint a transportation czar with real power to keep the wheels moving. He was not willing to seize privately owned railroad companies and put capable railroad men in charge of the rolling stock, with full authority to do what was needed to feed his armies. And this failure was not Davis's alone, for the entire Confederate government was loath to exercise the extraordinary power displayed by the Federal government during the Civil War. Historian Richard D. Goff put it well when he concluded that Rebel leaders "fell short of even reasonable standards of supply management. Reacting rather than planning, often arriving at workable policies too late, and making too many mistakes, Davis and those around him bungled supply management and thus contributed in large measure to the defeat of the Confederacy." Goff wrote generally of supply arrangements, but the same could be said largely of military transport as well. By force of circumstances, the Confederate government did implement a few promising elements of an effective supply management system, but it did so in a halting and uncertain way. There was a trend toward centralization of effort that at least was aiming at the high level of effectiveness to be seen in Federal policies, but it never resulted in success. As a result, "Confederate centralization was planless, unco-ordinated, tardy, and impotent."[42]

The Confederate failure in Richmond spelled added difficulties for all Rebel quartermasters, from the chief to those men who served in the field. The Southern transport system eventually deteriorated to the point that it can be said to have largely broken down, and the rank and file suffered far more than their counterparts in blue. This was not so much a failure of Confederate quartermasters as it was a general breakdown of a governmental system that could only be described as weak even on its best days.

3

~~~~~

THE RIVER-BASED SYSTEM

The Mississippi River and its tributaries constituted the central geographic feature of the western states at the time of the Civil War. These waterways defined much of American economics and culture, spawning the development of a new type of river craft in the early nineteenth century that dominated transport and travel in the central portion of the North American continent. The river steamer that carried cotton, grain, and people throughout the Mississippi River basin was uniquely suited for a variety of transportation needs, including that of a military nature, and both governments created a river-based system of logistics with it.

The western rivers provided 16,000 miles of navigable streams to Americans in the 1860s. A steamer trip from the head of navigation on the Ohio River near Brownsville, Pennsylvania, to the head of navigation on the Missouri River at Fort Benton would consume 3,500 miles of travel. The wide Mississippi was more than 2,000 miles long, and the Ohio River was about half that length. The lesser tributaries could be navigated for much shorter distances. The Yazoo River, for example, which flowed into the Mississippi just north of Vicksburg, offered no more than 150 miles of usable watercourse to steamboat captains.[1]

If one flew today in an airplane from Cairo, Illinois, to New Orleans, the trip would cover about 600 air miles. If instead a Federal soldier rode a river steamer from one city to the other, he would have to travel 1,115 miles due to the winding nature of the Mississippi River. The flat delta land that stretches east and west from the Mississippi, from about Cape Girardeau, Missouri, to New Orleans, drains 41 percent of the area of the 48 states. This is a region the size of Austria, Germany, France, Holland, Italy, Spain, Portugal, Norway, and Great Britain combined.[2]

The flat delta land needed protection from the annual spring rising of the Mississippi River, but antebellum governments only partially answered that call. The first levee along the great river appeared in 1727 at New Orleans, but most of the levees in existence at the time of Fort Sumter had been constructed in the middle of the nineteenth century. Some stretches of the river sported continuous levees while many other sectors had nothing. All of the levees were modest in dimension, normally only three feet high. In short, the river contin ued to rise and cover flatlands at the time of the Civil War mostly as it had done long before white men tried to tame it.[3]

Civilization, however, produced a new type of boat with built-in adaptations to the conditions of the western rivers. The first steam-powered boats appeared in the eastern states in the 1790s and on the western rivers by 1811, when the *New Orleans* made the 2,000-mile trip from Pittsburgh to its namesake city in three months of leisurely travel. Six years later a total of 14 boats were regularly steaming along the western rivers. Save for a five-year dip in the mid-1840s and a two-year dip in the early 1850s, the amount of steamboat tonnage on the rivers rose very sharply. It doubled from 1850 to 1860. The overwhelming majority of these steamers were constructed at various places along the Ohio River, and Southerners largely purchased Northern-built craft. These river steamers first exploited the main stem of the river system, the Mississippi-Ohio trunk. Later and in more limited fashion they expanded into the tributaries. Smaller and more maneuverable craft had to be designed to handle the many problems of navigating the tributaries. On average, they were less than half the size of steamers operating on the Mississippi. The innovative designs of the western river steamers attracted the attention of numerous people around the world. Not only the English, French, and Russians, but interested technicians from South America, India, and Mongolia wanted to know how they were constructed.[4]

The number of river craft increased with time. In 1830 the western rivers saw only 187 vessels; thirty years later, on the eve of Fort Sumter, 735 craft provided the engine of economic development and profit on the rivers. These western steamers totaled 162,735 tons in 1860, out of an aggregate of 770,641 tons of carrying capacity among all vessels in the United States. The increase in steamboats was probably faster and greater than that of any other transportation in antebellum America.[5]

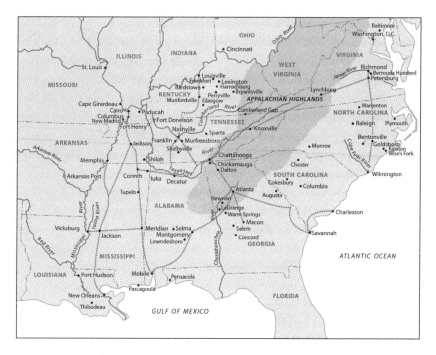

1. Major rivers in the West

As the number of vessels grew, the cost of shipping freight fell sharply. The bill for moving 100 pounds of material from New Orleans to Louisville had been $5 in 1815, but that dropped to only 25 cents by 1860. Downstream rates dropped from $1 per 100 pounds in 1815 to 32 cents by 1860. Freighting on the tributaries was more expensive due to the special conditions on those rivers. During the same period, the average time spent in traveling declined sharply as well. A round-trip between New Orleans and Louisville consumed about 20 days in 1815, but by 1860 the same trip took only 6–7 days.[6]

Steamers typically carried a mixed cargo of freight and added as many passengers as they could to every trip. During the 1850s the average number of passengers per trip between New Orleans and Louisville was 144 upstream and 108 downstream. Two classes of accommodations, cabin and deck, were available. About 40 percent of the passengers paid the significantly higher rates for cabin accommodation. The rest had to make do with what they could find on the deck of the boat.[7]

The passengers suffered along with the crew when the boat experienced any trouble, and lurid reports of fire consuming human lives led governments on both the state and federal levels to investigate. Several western states, including Alabama, Louisiana, Kentucky, Illinois, and Wisconsin, passed safety regulations in the 1820s and 1830s that were largely ineffective. The U.S. government also tried to regulate steamer safety, but its 1838 law was poorly enforced. In 1852, the Federal government finally passed a law that was fairly well enforced. At least it allowed for more detailed information about steamer design, construction, and maintenance than before, even if it failed to eliminate the unique challenges of river travel in the form of boiler explosions and boats breaking up on snags.[8]

Design and construction were indeed the key features of western river steamers. They needed shallow drafts yet significant carrying capacity, and designers worked for decades to perfect the balance between length, breadth, draft, and sturdiness. As Louis Hunter put it, a "long, narrow, flat-bottomed, and straight-sided hull" became the norm. Builders used heavier wood, such as white oak, for the frame of the hull and lighter wood, such as pine, poplar, or cedar, for the rest of the vessel to reduce weight. While the hull was solidly built, the superstructure tended to be flimsy. The entire vessel seemed unusually light, and when a high-pressure engine was added, everyone noticed how the craft vibrated while moving. The overwhelming majority of river steamers were pushed by paddle wheels; only a few small boats used screw propellers. There were both advantages and disadvantages to locating the paddle wheels on the side or the stern of the vessel. Side-wheel boats proved to be more maneuverable in narrow streams and could more readily pull barges behind them, while stern wheel vessels could tie barges to their sides to add to their carrying capacity.[9]

Given the nature of their construction, most western river steamers enjoyed a comparatively short life span. It was by some estimates about 5 years, in contrast to the life expectancy of river steamers in the East (about 20 years) or deep sea whaling vessels (about 40 years). Of 88 western river steamers inspected at Pittsburgh in 1860, the average age was 2.23 years. A survey of inspection reports for a wider variety of cities that year indicated an average age of 8.66 years among 170 vessels. Accidents, lack of proper maintenance, and many other factors came into play to shorten the life of a river steamer.[10]

Boat owners tended to be sharp businessmen out to make short-term profits, and the western river steamer offered many attractive opportunities. The business tended to foster small enterprise. In contrast to railroads, which required huge outlays of capital, riverboats were comparatively inexpensive and several boatyards constructed them. The rivers were a "public highway, free and open to the use of all," in the words of Louis Hunter; a boat owner only had to purchase his craft, staff it with crew members, and he was in business. The vessel cost on average about $100 per measured ton, or about $40,000 for a large craft. In contrast, it would cost about that much to construct just one mile of a well-built railroad line. Even though the rate of depreciation for a river craft was high, one could expect to use it to the full for a few years before it fell apart.[11]

While some larger enterprises existed in the steamer trade (several boats owned by a group of investors), 27.4 percent of boats were owned by individuals in 1860. Partnerships involving two to four men owned about half the boats. Only 6.5 percent of the boats were owned by what could be termed a corporation. The overwhelming majority of owners were Northerners.[12]

Operating costs for the boat owner were largely tied up in wages and board for crew members, insurance, and the 25 percent depreciation per year he had to endure. Wages accounted for nearly one-third of the owner's yearly operating expenses, with fuel being about 26 percent and stores to feed and care for his crew members at about 26 percent as well. On average, each river steamer had a crew of about a dozen men for every hundred tons that the boat could carry. For example, a crew of about 26 men worked a 235-ton craft. Nearly 15,000 people worked on western riverboats in 1851. At the top were the captain, clerk, two pilots, two engineers, and a mate on each craft. The cabin crew (essentially hotel staff) and the deck crew (roustabouts for handling cargo and other duties) rounded out the employees. By 1860, about two-thirds of the deck crew consisted of Irish and German immigrants. Average salaries in the New Orleans–Louisville trade gave captains $1,500 yearly, with clerks drawing $900 per year. Engineers made $100 a month, while members of the cabin crew were paid $25 per month.[13]

The majority of boat owners generated income by roaming the river system seeking cargo and passengers to carry. Called transient or tramp steamers, they had no regular route, no long-term contracts. By 1860, as we have seen, the rates for carrying both freight and people were the lowest in river history, perhaps the lowest of any transportation in the world according to Louis Hunter. It would take only $12 to $15 to travel from New Orleans to St. Louis and $5 from Louisville to St. Louis. The relative income from freight compared to passengers varied widely from boat to boat, but it tended to favor freight as the source of well more than half the steamer's income.[14]

At 500 tons, an ordinary Ohio River steamer could increase its capacity by adding barges and tows. This was done only to a limited degree before the Civil War, probably due to limited engine power and the reduced speed resulting from attaching these vessels to the boat. Increased demands for coal led to the development of large barges capable of hauling 10,000 to 20,000 bushels each. It was not unusual to group five to seven such barges in front of a steamer, forming a mass 160 feet wide and 400 feet long. (The barges were put in front for easier steering.) Still, it is estimated that no more than about 60 boats were doing this trade on the Ohio and Mississippi rivers by 1860. After the Civil War, barge traffic dramatically increased with the addition of bulk transport of grain, timber, and lumber. Barge traffic was developed enough by the time of Fort Sumter, however, to play a role in military transport.[15]

The addition of barges to the steamer presented even more problems of navigation; it greatly increased the mass of floating hardware that had to be handled by the pilot and steersman in unpredictable currents. Generally the pilot always tried, whether he was working with barges or not, to steer the boat in the main channel of the river while going downstream to take advantage of the fastest current. Heading upstream, he had to steer into the shallow water near the banks to minimize the resistance of the strong current.[16]

With time, the bulk of all trade in both freight and passengers came to the steamers, especially on the great central stem of the Mississippi River. The years 1859 and 1860 saw more than $289 million worth of goods transported to New Orleans from dozens of cities spanning the western river system. A total of 1,458 steamboat loads of freight landed at New Orleans in those two years; more than one-third of them originated in Pittsburgh, and slightly less than one third in St. Louis. In fact, those two cities plus Louisville accounted for more than three-fourths of all steamboat departures headed for New Orleans on the eve of the Civil War.[17]

The railroads were beginning to eat away at steamboat dominance of western trade by 1861, although not everyone was thoroughly convinced that the iron horse would win this competition. The construction of major canals in the 1830s had begun to divert some North-South trade along the river system, but the railroads of the 1850s were a more potent threat. Passenger traffic especially was vulnerable, because traveling by rail often was faster than by boat. Some-

3.1. Steamboat Race on the Upper Mississippi. This lithographic print, entitled *Scene on the upper Mississippi* (or *Am Ober-Mississippi*), was published in Berlin by F. Sala and Company sometime in the 1860s. It evokes the excitement, power, and spectacle of steam river transportation in the Civil War era. (Library of Congress, LC-USZ62-94754)

one wishing to go from Cincinnati to St. Louis could look forward to a journey of 339 miles by rail, in contrast to 702 miles by steamboat. While the journey by river would take 50 hours, the passenger could arrive in St. Louis in only 16 hours by rail. The railroad advantage was not yet so clear, however, when it came to transporting freight. While the railroads could move a person from Cincinnati to St. Louis in 16 hours, it needed 30 hours to move a ton of material along the same route. Steamboat travel had seasons that affected hauling capacity and freight rates. In dry times river levels fell dramatically, boats had to carry lighter loads and suffered more delays, and freight rates rose. At these times, the railroad could carry freight more cheaply and assuredly than the riverboats. But in wet seasons, with the river running high, steamboats could outbid railroads in freight haulage.[18]

Given the relatively underpowered steam engines, railroads could assemble only short trains of about a dozen cars. Because of that, river steamers generally had more advantages in bulk hauling than railroads and were largely holding their own against rail competition by 1861. There was only a relative decline in their carrying trade between New Orleans and upstream cities. Steamboats hauled about $2.1 million worth of goods to New Orleans in 1860, compared to $2.8 million worth shipped from the northwestern states to the northeastern states by a combination of rails and canals. But this comparison smacks more of a harbinger of the future than a deadly blow to the steamers in the present. In fact, the riverboat business reached a peak of expansion by 1860 due to the fact that there was still plenty of carrying business available for owners.[19]

"The Mississippi boats were admirably calculated for handling troops, horses, guns, stores, etc.," wrote William T. Sherman after the war. They were "easy of embarkation and disembarkation." Federal officials thought of using them for military purposes as early as May 1861. In developing his famous Anaconda Plan, Winfield Scott envisioned transporting 60,000 troops on 40 steamers to descend the Mississippi River and reopen its navigation to Northern commerce. With hindsight it is easy to see that Scott would have needed at least double that number of craft to move 60,000 men.[20]

Only a month later other government officials provided hard data on the estimated number of river steamers available for use on western streams. Engineer Joseph G. Totten believed that 250 boats, capable of transporting 75,000 men, could be used from the Ohio River trade. Operating out of St. Louis, 150 craft big enough to haul from 45,000 to 120,000 men could be used. Totten also reported that 200 barges capable of hauling a variety of freight were available along the Ohio River and at St. Louis, with another 200 coal barges to be found along the Ohio. He listed all the boat building yards and gave typical water levels at different seasons for the major rivers of the West. Edward D. Mansfield, who helped Totten compile these statistics, warned the engineer to approach boat owners with caution, "for I have no doubt" they would try to get as much money out of the government as possible for their services.[21]

With a modern estimate of 817 riverboats available to the army in 1861, government officials immediately began to use them for military transportation. It was initially done by individual quartermasters for local purposes with no overall guidance or oversight by higher level officials. Reflective of the chaotic nature of the early war effort, engaging privately owned steamers for government service was a circus in the first few months of the Civil War. The government provided a boon to boat owners. The first economic impact of the conflict had been to create a mini-depression in the economy of the river towns, but government business came to save the owners by the end of 1861. In fact, government business led to a boom in new boat construction by 1862 and 1863 as investors sought to cash in on the war while they could. With at least 340 steamers employed in various ways by the midpoint of the conflict, it is clear that the Federal government had a dramatic impact on river transportation business.[22]

The use of riverboats for military transportation was far too extensive and too important to leave it to individual quartermasters alone. The early months of the war were characterized by rampant waste of government funds and widespread gouging by boat owners who took advantage of quartermasters who did not know their business. It took a unique individual named Lewis Baldwin Parsons to bring order, regularity, and balance to the business of dealing with private boat owners. Born in New York and a graduate of Yale University, Parsons also studied law at Harvard University before moving to Illinois and St. Louis. He became the chief executive officer of the Ohio and Mississippi Railroad, headquartered at Cincinnati, before moving back to St. Louis in time to witness the onset of the Civil War. Appointed an assistant volunteer quartermaster with the rank of captain in October 1861, Parsons was assigned to duties in St. Louis with a special charge to oversee steamboat transportation. He brought to this duty a hard-minded business sense and a stern adherence to fairness both for the government and for any honest boat owner he could find.[23]

Parsons soon found that most quartermasters along the western river system were negotiating charters with boat owners wherein the government gained exclusive use of a vessel by paying a fixed sum per diem. The system spawned a range of poor business practices, fraud, and exorbitant rates that wasted much government money. Military officers contributed to the problem by using expensively chartered boats as their personal headquarters or as storage bins instead of constructing sheds on land.[24]

As soon as he took charge in St. Louis in November 1861, Parsons began to switch from the charter system to the contract system. This involved limited arrangements, paying boat owners to haul freight for an agreed-upon rate by the hundred pounds. This was the normal arrangement for civilian business before the war and was far more efficient. Parsons had the full support of his immediate superior, Major Robert Allen, and the military commander of the Department of the Missouri, Major General Henry W. Halleck. Most of the chartered vessels were released and Parsons began to advertise for bids, specifying exactly what and how much material needed to be shipped, comparing the bids, and letting the contracts out. It called for more paperwork than the charter system but was well worth the extra effort. "Order soon arose out of confusion," Parsons reported.[25]

Owners naturally were disappointed at the loss of a system that offered them many advantages for quick profit, but they scrambled to adjust to the new situation. Whether they dealt with government charters or contracts, boat owners tended to negotiate and dissemble to gain every advantage. The easiest ploy was to take advantage of ignorance by the quartermaster officers concerning going rates for boat service. Lieutenant James E. Shields, acting quartermaster at Cape Girardeau, investigated and found that old rivermen considered a charter of $8 per day to be fair for a boat used as a ferry across the Mississippi River, but one owner insisted on a rate of $75 per day. Even the contract system could be abused by greedy boat owners. Flag Officer Andrew H. Foote was so stunned by exorbitant bills for shipping freight on the contract system at Cairo that he refused to pay them, cutting the amount in one case from $300 to only $100. When the owner protested, Foote threatened to take the argument to the Court of Claims at St. Louis. The boatman then caved in, obviously knowing he could not win in court.[26]

Parsons was unable to completely eliminate the charter system because in some cases it made sense. The problem simply lay with dishonest boat owners. Parsons tried during the course of the war to ameliorate problems by cutting the rates allowed and having the government take over running costs because it could do so more cheaply than the owners themselves. For example, the army could round up refugee blacks and use them as deckhands and cooks on the chartered boats.[27]

Parsons spelled out the many instances of gouging by boat owners who took advantage of the charter system. When a quartermaster foolishly agreed to pay the *Platte Valley* $275 a day for 110 days, the bill amounted to $30,284. Parsons refused to pay it and the owner agreed to a huge reduction. He accepted a rate of $75 per day, for a total of $8,140. The owner of the *Bostona* got $200 per day, a rate that would have grossed him $73,000 in one year even though the boat was valued at no more than $22,000. Parsons refused his claim, indicating that a fair rate would have been no more than $80 per day. The story of the *Diligent*, a small vessel of 173 tons, reveals the profits possible for clever businessmen during the war. It was chartered at $90 a day for 18 months, then sold

3.2. The Levee at Cairo, Illinois. Here lay one of those transportation nodes where different logistical systems intertwined. The Illinois Central Railroad ended at Cairo, on the banks of the Ohio River, near its junction with the Mississippi River. It was one of several important nerve centers for the Federal logistical effort in the Western Theater. This photograph shows several wharf boats, used as long-term storage facilities, tied up at the levee along the Ohio. (Library of Congress, LC-DIG-ppmsca-30991)

for $7,000 in November 1862. The new owner spent $1,000 to repair it and chartered the renovated vessel with a different quartermaster for $175 a day. He reportedly made a profit of $14,752 on the deal in only seven months, yet insisted that the government pay for additional repairs, a claim that Parsons refused to honor.[28]

Owners employed many strategies to cut costs and increase profit margins even when agreeing to reasonable charter rates. After concluding a deal with the government, they often released many deck crew members to cut costs by as much as $50 per day, but of course did not pass on the savings to the government. Moreover, fewer deckhands meant a drop in efficiency when it came to moving cargo. Given that the owner was paid a fixed rate anyway, it did not matter to him whether the government's freight arrived on time. The *Des Arc* was chartered as a medical supplies vessel at the exorbitant rate of $250 per day. The owner cut his crew from 40 men down to only five, and Parsons refused to pay the total bill, arguing that the charter rate was twice as high as was fair. The owner quietly approached another quartermaster and convinced him to pay the bill. He received money for six months of light service to the Union that was equivalent to the value of his boat.[29]

Parsons estimated that 75 to 100 steamers were still chartered on the Mississippi River as of June 1863. At least 50 of them were working on the lower river. Many of those chartered boats were used by military officers for flimsy purposes, such as serving as headquarters boats or as dedicated dispatch boats, or for storage of freight. Many of them also had been chartered early in the war and at very high rates. It was not a simple matter to break a charter, for that involved some legal questions and resistance by the owner. Parsons tried to reason with them, putting his foot down when necessary. There is no indication that any owner took him to court over these issues, probably, as we have seen, because they knew they could not justify the inflated charter rates. It also took some time for Parsons to convince high-level army officials to do something about officer misuse of chartered boats. By pointing out that the charter system effectively took vessels out of the market for government contracts, Parsons drove home the point that when the army suddenly needed to transport large numbers of troops for a campaign, his subordinates often found it difficult to round up enough steamers to accomplish the task. Still the army did not issue a general order forbidding officers to use steamboats as quarters until February 1865.[30]

Parsons largely won his struggle against the charter system along the Mississippi River, though some boats continued to operate under that system until war's end. When his authority was extended to the Department of the Cumberland in December 1863, he found again that virtually all government business along the Cumberland and Tennessee rivers operated on the charter system. The same story prevailed; exorbitant rates failed to produce efficient service. Parsons attacked the system vigorously. Boat owners raised a howl of protest, but fortunately Parsons was supported by his superiors. His shift to the contract system produced immediate results. While 123 chartered steamers were employed to supply Major General William S. Rosecrans's Army of the Cumberland in the winter of 1862–1863, Parsons used only 66 steamers on the contract basis to support the combined forces of Major General George H. Thomas, Major General William T. Sherman, and Major General John M. Schofield in east Tennessee during the winter of 1863–1864. A boat owner told Parsons that in switching from charter to contract, most of his colleagues were forced to load their boats with twice as much cargo and run it in only half the time to its destination in order to make a profit.[31]

Captain Frederick S. Winslow provided even more proof that the contract system worked well. He supervised the delivery of 158,016 tons of freight to Nashville from February to May of 1864. Winslow estimated that it would have cost $4,740,493 to do so under the charter system. It actually cost only $1,896,192 to transport it by contracting for payment by 100 pounds of weight.[32]

There is no doubt that for the majority of purposes the contract system was cheaper and more efficient. But Parsons admitted that the charter system still had advantages in certain cases. If the need for transportation was huge and immediate, and if there was a good prospect of that need extending indefinitely into the future, then chartering made sense (but only at fair rates). Parsons wisely created a policy of mixed approaches to the thorny problem of dealing with private boat owners: mostly contract, but open to other methods of utilizing civilian resources for military purposes.[33]

Parsons also purchased steamers on a few occasions to carry mail, for example, or if the need for transport was particularly immediate or indefinite in duration. He kept these purchases to a minimum for the first half of the war, but after July 1863, when the Mississippi River was cleared of Confederate forces, the demand increased. The problem lay in conditions affecting the Department of the Gulf, a Union enclave centered on New Orleans after the city's fall in April 1862. Commanders in that department were starved for river transportation, cut off as they were from the upper Mississippi until the Rebel garrison of Port Hudson surrendered on July 9, 1863. The demand for river steamers in the lower Mississippi was so great that Parsons decided to buy quite a few and send them down to New Orleans to fill a genuine and long-term need in that region.[34]

An alternative to purchase, charter, and contract lay in the right of the government to press civilian boats into military service if the situation demanded it. Parsons did so when there was no time to negotiate charters or contracts. This was only temporary seizure of the boat; owners did not like it, for even though they were guaranteed payment at the end of the seizure, they had no opportunity to negotiate the rate. In fact, Parsons refused to set the rate of compensation at the time he seized the craft, insisting on waiting until the end of the seizure period to settle such things. Precisely because seizure gave the quartermaster all the advantages, Parsons knew he could not employ this method too often or he would alienate the very people he relied on for transportation services.[35]

"There can be no doubt, as a general rule, that it is the policy of the Government to secure its transportation by contract with private parties rather than by attempting to perform it by its own boats and employés," wrote Parsons after the war. Private enterprise "will always perform the same service cheaper than the Government can."[36]

Just how cheaply quartermasters could move men and material depended in large part on the shipping rates agreed upon. Parsons had great faith in making contracts based on what he called "the ordinary mercantile manner by the piece or 100 pounds." Given time, it was most common to advertise the need for conveyance and wait 30 days for the bids to arrive. The advertisement typically specified the starting point and the delivery point, the delivery date, and in general the type and amount of material to be transported. Boat owners typically submitted these bids in laconic fashion, short and to the point, specifying the exact price for hauling freight at lots of 100 pounds, or the price per head for transporting horses and/or men. If time permitted, Parsons also advertised when he needed to charter boats as well. In this case the owner submitted bids for the amount he would accept on a per diem basis. It was not unusual for owners to include a statement such as that written by Joseph Walton: "the United States guaranteeing us against capture & destruction by the public enemy." What he really meant was that the government should agree to compensate him if his boat was damaged, destroyed, or captured by the Rebels, a fully acceptable clause as far as Parsons was concerned.[37]

The contract gained, boat owners typically fulfilled it as quickly as they could in order to clear their boat for another job. Their clerks had to comply with the necessary paperwork required by the government. The side-wheeler *Thomas E. Tutt* was heavily involved in government work throughout the war. At 351 tons, 200 feet long, 35 feet wide, and with a depth of 5 feet, 6 inches, it could be counted as a typical Mississippi River steamer. Built in Cincinnati in 1855, it also was unusually old. In late 1862 the *Thomas E. Tutt* hauled a varied

3.3. The Levee at Vicksburg, Mississippi. In this photograph taken shortly after the fall of the city on July 4, 1863, the busy nature of many levees at river towns in nineteenth-century America is vividly illustrated. De Soto Point can be seen on the other side of the Mississippi River. The bows of these boats are tied up at the levee and their sterns drift downstream with the current. (Library of Congress, LC-DIG-cwpb-01012)

cargo 450 miles from St. Louis to Memphis. The load consisted of 498,428 pounds of quartermaster and commissary stores. This cost the government $2,159.73. The vessel also hauled about 100 horses and mules and a number of officers and enlisted men with a few wagons, but the total cost of transporting everything except the stores amounted to only $152.34. The owner received an additional $220 in demurrage; quartermasters had to hold the boat at St. Louis an extra day to await the arrival of a few intended passengers and offered the extra amount as compensation. With paperwork all in order, exactly spelling out what was hauled, the invoice was stamped approved and paid in the total amount of $2,532.07.[38]

When transporting soldiers, steamer clerks dealt with a different set of papers. The government printed and distributed passes for men to board boats. A typical pass was issued on September 9, 1862, to John Montgomery and three men of the 9th Wisconsin Battery for travel from St. Louis to Fort Leavenworth, Kansas. They were recruits joining their unit in the field. The pass was autho rized by the general commanding the district and signed by Lewis B. Parsons. On the back, Montgomery endorsed it to validate that the four men actually traveled as ordered.[39]

War service offered some unusual dangers that added to the normal challenges of navigating the rivers, and owners were keen on the government covering "ordinary war risks." Quartermasters were willing to allow this, but at times they needed to seek approval from superiors. Grant's Vicksburg campaign involved many boats in the theater of operations and resulted in quite a lot of damage to them. During the Yazoo Pass Expedition of February–March 1863, many boats were taken into narrow, winding rivers in the Mississippi delta, where they were damaged by overhanging tree branches. Montgomery Meigs approved government expenses to repair them or to compensate owners for repairs as long as the damage occurred without fault by the captain and crew and it was greater than the "ordinary wear and tear." Meigs noted that this damage did not occur as the result of enemy action but, considering the circumstances, he felt it was justified for the owners to seek government help. He pointed out, however, that they did not deserve the "full running rate" for the time period when repairs were under way but quartermasters could work out some "reasonable and equitable compensation during this time lost to the owner."[40]

When Grant planned to run steamers loaded with supplies past the Confederate river batteries at Vicksburg in April 1863, he wisely had them appraised by a board before the operation. The *Tigress* was lost to Confederate artillery fire in the run and had been appraised at $22,500. Grant was convinced the boat was actually worth more and he knew the owner, George W. Graham, was exceptionally patriotic. In fact, Graham was still paying interest on the money he borrowed to purchase the boat. Given these circumstances, Grant increased the amount to $26,000 as fair compensation for the *Tigress*. Grant also urged Robert Allen to compensate the owners of two other boats that were sunk and six more that were damaged in this famous series of moves that enabled the

Federals to bypass Vicksburg and cross the Mississippi River to lay siege to the place.[41]

The contract system put into place by Parsons allowed boat owners great flexibility. They could haul government freight and personnel alongside private freight and passengers on each individual trip. When Major General Edward R. S. Canby returned from the mouth of the White River to New Orleans on board the *Mollie Able* in January 1865, one of his staff members noticed that the boat also carried 300 Confederate prisoners going south to be exchanged, "poultry for the New Orleans market," and cattle, cotton, forage, and Union soldiers. Even steamers owned by the government shipped private freight and passengers when possible. During the month of March 1865, government boats in the Department of the Cumberland earned $3,407.89 in profits for the U.S. Treasury.[42]

Parsons could never work out a reliable system of uniform rates for steamers because of the seasonal nature of their trade. At times of low water they had to lighten loads and experienced much delay. Whenever he tried to introduce such a system, the owners invariably complained that the rates were too low. Since the army needed supplies and troop transfers all year round, it could not take advantage of low market rates on a consistent basis.[43]

Nevertheless, the government generally could credit itself with comparatively low rates for moving all manner of things and people during the course of the Civil War. When supporting Grant's Fort Donelson campaign, Parsons moved more than 10,000 men, over 5,000 horses and mules, 56 guns and caissons, thousands of tons of supplies, and 9,000 Confederate prisoners during one week in February 1862. He wound up paying only half a cent per mile for each enlisted man, 1 cent per mile for officers and animals, and $1.25 per mile for each wagon. Hauling the freight cost 7 cents per 100 pounds per 100 miles.[44]

These rates were similar to those specified in contracts let to companies that owned several boats and which agreed to create a regular packet run between different river cities for government use. These rates included $1 per officer, horse, or head of cattle per 100 miles; 40 cents for enlisted men or servants; $1.25 for a wagon, and 5.5 cents per 100 pounds of freight. These rates were reduced if the transport distance increased to more than 200 miles. In these long-term contracts the government agreed to pay the owners at the end of every month, but it also mandated that the boats be safe and manned only by crew members loyal to the United States.[45]

3.4. The Levee at Alexandria, Louisiana. This faded photograph illustrates one aspect of the Federal logistical effort during Nathaniel P. Banks's Red River campaign in March–April 1864. A smaller town than Vicksburg and on a more shallow and narrow river than the Mississippi, Alexandria's levee appears barely large enough to handle this string of riverboats. (Library of Congress, LC-DIG-ppmsca-34025)

Near the end of the war the average price for shipping troops amounted to one-third of a cent per man for each mile traveled. To send one soldier from St. Louis to New Orleans, a distance of 1,250 miles, cost the government only $3.62. Quartermasters could move 20,000 troops from St. Louis to New Orleans for about $85,000. In contrast, average fares for cabin passage between Louisville and New Orleans in the 1850s amounted to $15 and deck passage was $3. In other words, the government was paying for military transportation roughly the lowest fare available to civilians just before the Civil War.[46]

The river-based transportation system evolved into a massive logistical enterprise requiring skillful management on the part of army quartermasters. Those on the lower level of command (regimental, brigade, division, and corps) had fewer demands in this way. But officers on higher levels of responsibility (field armies, districts, and departments) began to feel the pressure of managing far-flung transportation for large commands. The Federals instituted an important managerial innovation by appointing one officer to oversee all river transport along the Mississippi River, and they further sealed the importance of this innovation by choosing one of the best possible candidates. Lewis B. Parsons received enormous support from his superior, Robert Allen, and the army officers who held overall command in the region. Parsons had to work against many competing interests to decrease charters and increase contracts, but eventually he achieved the herculean task of imposing sound business practices on the process of developing an efficient and gargantuan military transport system.

Part of that task included a great deal of personal oversight. By October 1862, Parsons required that all claims for steamboat owners' compensation be sent to his office for processing. More important to the management of the river-based system, Parsons had to act as a troubleshooter. There often occurred shortages of available steamers due to the fact that the government used such a high percentage of the boats on the river system. The biggest crunch occurred between January and July of 1863, when Grant's Vicksburg operations demanded a huge number of craft to support his Army of the Tennessee just north of the Confederate fortress city. Everything had to be hauled from Memphis and St. Louis hundreds of miles away. Parsons also had to deal with many army officers who looked upon the steamers as their own, detaining them unduly at delivery points or using them for unimportant purposes. He worked closely with high-level commanders to deal with problems like these and to assure them he could round up enough boats to meet their needs at short notice.[47]

One example must suffice to illustrate the difficulties encountered by the managers of the river-based system. Parsons's brother, Charles, worked under him at St. Louis. In early October 1863, requests for river transport flooded into the office. A total of 10,500 horses, mules, and cattle had to be sent to Memphis, Vicksburg, Little Rock, and New Orleans. In addition, 600 wagons, 4,000 tons of commissary and quartermaster stores, as well as some coal were slated to be delivered to far-flung posts along the Mississippi and Missouri, including Fort Leavenworth in Kansas. Sherman was taking several divisions of troops from Vicksburg to Memphis and Nathaniel Banks was starting to move westward through Louisiana to Texas. Charles Parsons needed 40 to 50 boats to meet all these needs and to provide the regular runs of supplies to various places, yet he could find no more than five boats unemployed at St. Louis.

This was not the first time that Charles or his brother faced such a crisis; they worked overtime and came up with solutions to the problem, meeting needs more or less in a timely manner.[48]

Some army officers joined in the hunt for alternatives to relying on river steamers. Early in the war Ulysses S. Grant found that wharf boats holding 2,500 tons of freight could be used to store material, allowing steamers to unload quickly if the storage facilities at a given port were overloaded. Grant also believed in using barges to supplement the capacity of river steamers. Barges could transport troops as well as freight. Boat owners themselves resorted to barges and towboats as a way to make up for the steamboat shortage early in 1863 during a critical phase of Grant's operations against Vicksburg. The problem lay in speed of travel; towing barges slowed steamers down considerably, lengthening trips and increasing transportation costs.[49]

With such a high proportion of available steamers employed by the government, the rivers buzzed with traffic. It was not unusual to pass half a dozen boats a day while traveling up or down the Mississippi River. When shifting large numbers of troops in one movement, quartermasters preferred to manage the boats by creating convoys. Their commanders issued orders arranging the dozen or so boats in line and specifying that they should keep within sight of each other as they steamed along. A series of whistles, varied in length and number, constituted a sort of Morse code for the convoy so that any vessel could signal a desire to land, indicate some sort of distress, or report a sighting of the enemy.[50]

River steamers needed fuel on a regular basis, and the prewar system of woodyards scattered along the banks of the Mississippi River provided it. Captains preferred to stop for wood twice a day so as not to carry too much fuel on board, thereby reducing weight on the boat. The privately owned and operated woodyards grew into a large business, but coal began to be used before the war broke out, especially along the Ohio River.[51]

The woodlots operated smoothly during the war. Typically a lookout (usually a black man) kept watch for approaching boats and a white agent of the woodlot owner negotiated the price when it stopped. If well stocked, the wood at the lot was chopped and stacked. It often was still green because the war increased river traffic, with a consequent increase in demand for fuel. If the woodlots were empty and a boat captain was in desperate need of fuel, there was nothing left but to land a party of men with axes to cut their own timber.[52]

The government had a vested interest in making sure this did not happen often, so it rounded up large numbers of refugee slaves from contraband camps near the river system and put them to work for the woodlot owners. In many cases, the government itself established woodlots worked by freedmen who used teams and wagons the government confiscated from nearby plantations. By September 1864, about 1,000 blacks worked in government-owned woodlots and half that number in privately operated lots. The government-owned lots produced more than 60,000 cords of fuel, worth $125,000 to steamers. These lots sold fuel to boats owned by the government at $1.50 less per cord than the going price at privately owned lots, producing a total savings of some $90,000 for the treasury. Most of the money produced by these government-owned lots was used to purchase supplies for the men, women, and children who lived in the contraband camps.[53]

At times quartermasters were willing to provide both fuel and food to privately owned vessels if they needed it on a temporary basis, even though such provision was not part of the charter or contract. In these cases, the owner reimbursed the government when he had a sufficient cash flow. Early in 1863 a quartermaster at Memphis sold commissary stores to the *Thomas E. Tutt* and the owner settled a bill of $593.93 when his contract was finished. Later that year the *Thomas E. Tutt* burned 6 cords of wood, at $3.50 per cord, and owed the government $21 for it in October 1863.[54]

Most steamboat owners and captains kept their political views in abeyance while they made money from the war, but now and then they voiced opinions that seemed to indicate their loyalty was doubtful. The owners of the *Silver Lake* presented a bill for $2,970 that seemed legitimate, but Colonel J. W. McClurg of the 8th Cavalry, Missouri State Militia, heard from others that they were disloyal. The owners were widely thought to be "sympathisers with the rebellion, of a color only *one shade lighter* than those in arms against the Government."[55]

Pilots also could be suspect. These were the most skilled workers on the river, having gone through years of experience in negotiating the many snags and shifting channels in this natural highway that constantly changed from season to season. Concern about their loyalty led Henry W. Halleck to revoke all licenses for pilots and engineers in April 1862. All of them had to reapply for a new license, and loyalty to the U.S. government was an important element in the processing of that application. Given their skilled trade, pilots often tried to gouge the owners when it came to negotiating salaries. Parsons set a maximum salary of $200 per month in 1862, but it was increased to $250 on the western river system north of Memphis and $300 south of that city early in 1864. In contrast, pilots working on seagoing vessels and those that plied the coast received $450 to $750 per month.[56]

We will never know with certainly whether the general fear that most pilots were disloyal was true. Grant felt sure that most were "decidedly disloyal, or at least sympathized with the rebellion." Thus he went out of his way to praise Charles M. Scott for being one of the few, in his mind, who were friends of the Union. Dr. John Vance Lauderdale, a contract surgeon working on the hospital boat *D. A. January,* talked to the pilot, a large, forceful man who weighed 250 pounds. "He has no idea of letting the Mississippi River be cut in two if he can prevent it. He knows this river as well as he knows his fat face and he certainly has a claim to it."[57]

Like any vessel of the era, western river steamers relied on hiring available crew members to man the boat. With two pilots, at least two engineers, captain, clerk, several mates, carpenters, deck crewmen, and cabin and cook people, it was a small but varied lot of workers. The total could come to 25 or 50 men, depending on the size of the vessel. Any number of them could also be disloyal to the government that provided their income. When the *Prairie Rose* received fire while traveling from St. Louis to Fort Leavenworth, a steward and a pantryman refused to help defend the boat. They declared "that they would do nothing against the Confederacy." One of them later claimed to be a veteran of the Rebel army. They were arrested and sent back to St. Louis.[58]

For literally hundreds of thousands of Union soldiers of all ranks, riding on a western river steamer was a memorable experience that most of them had not known before the war. "It was a lively and interesting sight to witness the loading of the steamer," Henry W. Tisdale reported when the 35th Massachusetts embarked on the *Imperial* at Cairo on its way to Vicksburg. "The packing of the men, horses, baggage etc., all seeming to be in a state of inextricable confusion, yet at the last to find all on board in seeming order though closely packed." The 11th New Hampshire and a battery also boarded the boat before setting out at dusk. "We have a large boat, high decks so we have plenty of air and on the whole are comfortably off for room," Tisdale concluded.[59]

The apparent confusion Tisdale mentioned was the primary reason that instructions about how to embark often were issued to unit officers. Quartermasters at St. Louis prepared a generic set of guidelines so that infantry commanders could become acquainted with the special needs associated with steamboat loading. They were urged to inspect the boat before starting the process to make sure it was large enough and in suitable condition. If the officer and the supervising quartermaster disagreed on how many men the boat could hold, the question should be decided by a board quickly appointed to investigate. The quartermaster would provide cooking utensils (at least by the midpoint of the war, when the system's kinks had been worked out), and on the journey the infantry commander was urged to make sure his men kept the boat clean. He also was asked to keep a journal of the trip, but that apparently was seldom done.[60]

One can get an idea of how difficult the task of packing the boat could be when considering that several units typically occupied one craft in order to maximize the utilization of space. The *Jacob Strader*, "a very large boat" in the view of Albert L. Slack, was loaded with the 98th and 121st Ohio, plus 100 wagons, 150 mules, and all the tents, equipment, and baggage of the men. In arranging to shift a number of units from St. Genevieve south to Vicksburg in June 1863, Charles Parsons spelled out which ones should board each vessel. That included dividing the 26th Indiana, 37th Illinois, and 24th Missouri onto the *D. S. Taylor* and the *Hannibal*. The officers had to put no more than 15 companies on each boat, splitting at least one regiment between the two craft. All but 100 men of the 76th Illinois boarded the *Ella* along with all regimental baggage; the 100 who could not fit were placed on the *Pocahontas* along with the 30th Missouri while moving from the mouth of the White River in November 1864. In a more unusual division of units, the 81st Illinois placed three companies on three small boats, while the rest boarded the *Thomas E. Tutt*.[61]

Once on board and moving along the river, soldiers often complained of the crowded, noisy conditions. Charles J. Obriham of the 46th Illinois thought traveling on board a packed boat was "worse than marching." His steamer had more than 2,000 men, 200 horses and mules, wagons, and an artillery battery as it moved swiftly from Memphis to New Orleans in January 1865. "We had hardley room to turn around." The boat hit a snag that punched a small hole in the hull. It took on a couple of feet of water but the pumps kept the vessel afloat and the boat hardly slowed its speed. "No Damage done," Obriham reported, "onley a few men prety badly scared."[62]

Hitting snags or catching on sandbars constituted ordinary experiences. The *Imperial* got stuck twice when Henry Tisdale rode on it. The first time, the men moved to the stern of the boat to raise the front and it was able to back away. The second time two other steamers arrived to help it get off. In addition, the men got soaked every time it rained because there was no room under deck or in the cabin for them. Someone stole Tisdale's shoes and shelter tent on the boat before he learned to tie his belongings to his body while sleeping. When stopping briefly at Memphis, the troops of his regiment and the 11th New Hampshire rushed to buy all the pies that peddlers brought to the boat.[63]

The human cargo was in many ways the most difficult to manage. Colonel Reuben Williams was assigned to lead 1,800 paroled prisoners, captured at Holly Springs in December 1862, from Memphis to Benton Barracks at St. Louis. They boarded nine steamers along with 1,800 other men who needed to go north, plus 100 horses. No one provided armed escorts, which Williams regretted because many of the men had been drinking whiskey just before leaving. He tried to find willing officers on each boat and encouraged them to maintain order as best they could, but Williams admitted that for the first two days of their seven-day journey "Pandemonium reigned. Discipline counted for nothing." The men threatened to throw him overboard when he tried to control them. By the third day the effects of whiskey had worn off and some officers managed to gain authority over their subordinates. Low water caused several boats to ground on sandbars, creating a delay as they were levered off. Then the flotilla was attacked by guerrillas and one man on Williams's boat was wounded.[64]

It took seven days just to reach Cairo; by then rations had run out and the men had grown surly once again. Williams ordered the steamer captains not to tie up at the levee but to anchor at midstream and send small boats for food. He accompanied one of the boats to arrange for resupply, but upon returning three hours later was astonished to find the men drunk again. Some of them had decided to swim to the bank, steal some whiskey barrels, and float them back to the boats. Williams confiscated all he could find and poured it into the Ohio River. He finally unloaded his troublesome cargo at Benton Barracks three days later.[65]

The experience that Williams so vividly described in his memoirs was unusual. Far more commonly troop movements on the river-based system were relatively smooth and easy. Soldiers continued to complain that conditions on board were unhealthy in many ways, especially when the boats were packed and the trip was lengthy. Many soldier travelers commented on the dirt that accumulated when vessels were crowded to capacity and the men had scant opportunity for washing. "We are in a most filthy and sickly condition from being on the boats so long," lamented Cyrus F. Boyd of the 15th Iowa when moving down the Mississippi in January 1863. "No hog-pen can compare." If contagious diseases were inadvertently brought on board, these boats were ripe for their spread. Some of them were "perfect pest-houses," thought David D. Porter, who reported that 30 men on board a transport came down with symptoms of small pox during one voyage.[66]

Maintaining some degree of sanitation was vital to prevent discomfort and disease from decimating manpower. By war's end officers were more alert to this problem, issuing orders for the maintenance of sanitary conditions, which often included letting the men ashore to cook their rations so that the chance of fire as well as the dropping of food material on deck would be lessened. Members of the 19th Iowa found themselves covered with vermin after traveling to the siege of Vicksburg on board the *Henry Choteau*. More than one Union soldier characterized his experience on board a river steamer as being "pened up like a lot of Hogs." On a few occasions the troops disembarked to sleep on land overnight while the boat's crew members cleaned their vessel stem to stern. Responsible infantry commanders detailed troops to help the crew scour the boat on occasion. When Reuben Williams did this during a trip on the *Belle Memphis* the captain and crew were so impressed that they could not thank him enough. "It was the only instance of the kind they had known since the war commenced."[67]

A more immediate threat to life and health lay in accidents. With a high-pressure engine attached to a rather flimsy wooden structure, western steamers were subject to many dangers. Of 576 accidents occurring from 1811–1851, 4.5 percent were caused by collision; 17.0 percent involved fire; 21.0 percent were from an explosion, and 57.5 percent resulted from hitting snags and other obstructions. Explosions alone led to 1,443 deaths on the western rivers from 1816–1848, compared to only 384 deaths due to explosions on watercraft in the rest of the United States. The western rivers were unusually dangerous for travelers. It is estimated that on average 150 people died on the riverboats every year during the entire antebellum period. In addition to deaths, accidents led to the destruction of $5,643,791 in boat property and $12,698,529 in cargo. The vigorous enforcement of the Federal government regulatory law in 1852 failed to stop this trend; steamboat accidents continued to increase after that year.[68]

When the *Sunnyside* caught fire on November 16, 1863, near Island No. 16 on the Mississippi River, up to 40 people perished. A candle started a fire on the *H. D. Bacon* while it off-loaded hemp onto the levee at St. Louis in October 1862. The fire quickly spread to both boats tied up to either side of it. When one of them tried to back away it lodged against two other boats and set both of them on fire as well. In addition to 5 steamers, 600 bales of hemp and 100 bales of cotton were lost, amounting to an estimated $150,000 worth of property.[69]

The steamer *Eclipse* blew up at Johnsonville, Tennessee, in January 1865, killing 10 men and injuring 68 others on board who belonged to the 9th Indiana Battery. The *Pringle* endured one problem after another while trying to reach St. Charles, Arkansas. First a log got tangled in the wheel and damaged it. After several hours repairing the wheel, the *Pringle* grounded on a sandbar. Once off the obstruction it became apparent that the boat had sprung a leak. The pumps were not working and soon more than 10 inches of water filled the hull. Commissary stores were damaged and the *Pringle* only made it to St. Charles because another boat took off 400 troops to lighten its load. All agreed that the pilot was to blame; he was suspected of disloyalty to the United States.[70]

It is also possible that the *Pringle*'s pilot was simply not good at his job. "We have a very poor pilot," reported Irwin Shepard of the man who guided the *Ohio Belle* north from Vicksburg in August 1863. "He has run us on to sand bars 4 times." Once the collision was so hard that the deck wrenched six inches forward of the hull and the engine stopped. To give the pilot his due, the late summer of 1863 witnessed unusually low water levels in the Mississippi. But there were two regiments on board the boat and Shepard was afraid that many of his comrades would perish if the vessel cracked up. The *D. A. January* hit sandbars four times while steaming from St. Louis to Cape Girardeau in January 1862, a distance of 70 miles. It took the boat a total of eight days to reach its destination.[71]

The stories associated with this particular obstacle to transport explain why captains sometimes refused to travel if the rivers were full of trees uprooted by high water. When the *James Watson* hit a snag at midnight of March 1, 1865, 22 of the 80 soldiers on board perished. The boat broke up and survivors clung desperately to chunks of it as everyone continued to float downstream with the current. The passengers on the *Ben Adams* were very lucky; when a snag hit the boat the end of the tree trunk smashed through the side and up through the deck, destroying a good part of the superstructure. It held onto the boat, which continued steaming while dragging the 50-foot tree trunk for hours.[72]

Snags tended to be more numerous at high water, and hitting sandbars tended to be more common at low water. Collisions with other boats could happen at any season but were comparatively less common. Sixty soldiers were killed when the *Courier* ran into the *Des Arc* near Napoleon, Arkansas, in August 1863. Much cargo tended to be lost in such unplanned encounters between boats as well.[73]

Unusual weather conditions also led to accidents. The *Rattler* was anchored at Grand Gulf when a tornado suddenly appeared on the night of December 30, 1864. It drove the boat onto the riverbank, stove in the hull, and partially sank it. Guerrillas later came and burned the part above the water line. A partially rotten rope was blamed for the damage done to the *Mill Boy* by a storm nine miles above Jacksonport, Arkansas, in February 1864. Strong winds caused it to break, setting the boat adrift. No one could find the spare anchor because cargo had covered it up, and the engineer could not get up enough steam to help. The *Mill Boy* hit a snag, which broke open the hull, and the boat sank, destroying 35 tons of commissary supplies and all the forage for horses and mules it carried. No lives were lost.[74]

Severe weather was a concern along the upper Mississippi. Several steamers were caught in ice when a fierce cold front swept across the area in early January 1863. At least 10 steamers were locked in their place when the Mississippi froze solid. Charles Parsons organized rescue efforts from his office in St. Louis, contracting with Captain Spencer Ball to break a passage to the boats with his steamer. He managed to reach several of them before they ran out of food for men and beasts on board. The crews of some steamers threw much of their government cargo overboard in vain efforts to lighten their loads.[75]

Although the wide waters of the Mississippi and its major tributaries were full of obstructions, steamer crews encountered many more on the smaller rivers, especially the upper reaches of those streams. Federal officials gathered as much information on these rivers as they could from experienced pilots and boat captains. The Apalachicola River held tidewater up to the junction of the Flint and Chattahoochee rivers, but farther up from that point steamboat travel was tenuous. Columbus, Georgia, was the head of navigation on the Chattahoochee, with January seeing water levels of 6 feet and summer having only 3 feet of water. Albany, Georgia, was the head of navigation on the Flint, but only from December through March of each year. A total of 16 steamers regularly plied trade along the Apalachicola, Flint, and Chattahoochee rivers just before the Civil War and presumably were available to Confederate quartermasters after Fort Sumter.[76]

Steamboat pilots and their captains sometimes engaged in battles with the elements along these small rivers. When the *Fannie Harris* chartered to bring Thomas W. Sherman's regular battery from Fort Ridgely, Minnesota, to St. Paul in the spring of 1861 it negotiated the winding Minnesota River—the "worst twisted water course in the West," declared George Byron Merrick. "It is a series of curves from start to finish, the river squirming its way through an alluvial prairie." Unfortunately for the 200-foot stern wheel vessel, spring rains had flooded this plain so that the river was well out of its banks. The current in the main channel was so strong the boat was pushed to one side or the other in the curves and lodged against trees. Crew members had to go out in small boats and tie up pulleys to trees on the other side, threading ropes through them so other crew members on board could pull the boat away. This exhausting process forced the *Fannie Harris* to consume four days to make 300 miles. Finally the captain decided to risk his boat by simply crashing through the thin tree line along the flooded bank, breaking down the small trunks by the weight of the boat and steaming effortlessly across the flooded plains that bordered the river. He had to crash back into the channel the same way after many miles. The result was a faster journey and only minor damage to the craft.[77]

Boats chartered by the Confederate government also had to negotiate narrow streams and suffer the consequences. When two steamers transported troops and guns between Tuscaloosa and Mobile early in the war they "scraped the woods." That meant butting trees with the boat. One such tree was taken out by the roots, but a larger tree withstood the battering without injury. Instead, the boat was staggered and lost 20 feet of its guard. "Such incidents were in those days quite common in steamboat travel in low water," concluded the historians of Lumsden's Alabama Battery.[78]

Most military transportation in the river-based system of both sides tended to be centered along the major streams, the Mississippi and its large tributaries. This was partly due to demand and to a wise effort by quartermasters to minimize travel on the unreliable tributaries. For the Federals, St. Louis, Cincinnati, and Louisville were the chief origin points of steamboat transportation. They often sent boats loaded with troops and cargo up large tributaries such as the

Cumberland, Tennessee, White, and Arkansas rivers. Where necessary, they relied solely on railroads.[79]

To the natural hazards of river travel must be added the peculiar dangers associated with military transportation. The *City of Madison* was loading ordnance supplies at Vicksburg in August 1863 when a deckhand carelessly dropped a box of fixed percussion shells. It exploded. There were about 80 men working on deck and on the levee, with another 100 black laborers packing the boxes inside the hull of the vessel. At least 60 men died in the explosion and the boat was torn apart. Mangled bodies were thrown 100 yards from the craft. Another boat tied up nearby also was damaged and people on board were injured.[80]

Lewis Parsons compiled a list of all steamers on the western rivers that were lost in the war. This list included boats not in U.S. government service. The total amounted to 327 steamers from May 1, 1861, through June 2, 1865. The greatest yearly loss occurred in 1864, when 98 vessels were destroyed. The most common cause of loss was hitting snags, with accidental burning being the second. Various kinds of Confederate action took out many vessels. Southerners captured and burned 19 boats, and they deliberately destroyed 39 of their own vessels to prevent them from falling into Union hands. The Confederates also sank 23 of their own craft to serve as river obstructions to Federal boat travel. Rebel agents burned 29 vessels used by the U.S. government, and guerrillas captured or burned an additional 28 Union steamers. Federal forces also captured and burned 24 Confederate vessels and burned 10 of their own boats to prevent them from falling into Confederate hands. Boiler explosions (9), collision (7), and "sundry accidents" (28) accounted for still more casualties among the riverboats. The total loss due to war-related causes amounted to $8,255,000 for the 327 boats. That seems a staggering toll, but Parsons argued it was relatively light considering the frenzied logistical effort launched by the Union army.[81]

If one set aside his worries concerning the safety of steamboat travel, forgot the crowded, unhealthy conditions on board, and ignored the awful shaking of the fragile boat, he could appreciate the many charms involved in this unique mode of transportation. When steamers gathered in convoys they presented impressive sights. A fleet of boats carrying 18 regiments brought reinforcements to William S. Rosecrans's army soon after the battle of Stones River. Many men saw it approach Nashville along the Cumberland River, decks covered with blue-coated infantrymen, the sun glinting off their weapons, and regimental bands playing patriotic tunes. "It was a picture of power and splendor and a revelation alike of the strength and determination of the Federal Government to resume its authority over its rebellious subjects," recalled Henry Aten of the 85th Illinois. When a convoy of 13 steamers moved south past Port Hudson after it had fallen to Union forces in July 1863, each boat was brilliantly lighted in the darkness of a still night. "They presented a beautiful sight as they steamed" past the Union garrison.[82]

The river-based system of steamboats marshaled by the Federal government was by any standard an achievement of epic proportions compared to anything that had taken place in America prior to Fort Sumter. Such a massive logistical system demanded unusually effective management, and a handful of high-level quartermasters in the Union army provided it. The Federals had already instituted an important managerial innovation by assigning Lewis B. Parsons to take control of river transport along the Mississippi River in 1861, the first time that a quartermaster officer was assigned to head such a complicated and huge undertaking. In March 1863, Charles Parsons suggested (and Lewis Parsons strongly recommended it as well the following June) that someone take charge of all river transportation in the western states. All the rivers were connected, and it made sense to have one man superintend everything on the vast natural waterways. Located at a central city, connected by telegraphy, it would be possible for one officer to handle such a load. This prompted Meigs to enlarge Parsons's area of responsibility by extending his authority over the Department of the Cumberland in the fall of 1863. That enlargement put Parsons in charge of most river transportation in the West; his responsibilities increased when Meigs appointed him general supervisor of western river transportation with headquarters at St. Louis in December 1863.[83]

Parsons suggested yet another managerial innovation in October 1863, appointing one man to take charge of all river and rail transportation in the United States. It took some time to do this; Meigs incorporated the idea into a major reorganization of the Quartermaster Department that was approved by Congress in July 1864. Parsons was named head of the Fourth Division of the Quartermaster Department, in charge of all river and rail transportation. This meant he had to move from St. Louis to Washington, D.C., where he took charge of the division on August 26, 1864. His jurisdiction did not include the U.S. Military Railroad, which was lodged in the Seventh Division.[84]

The appointment of Parsons to ever increasing positions of authority over river and rail networks represented an admission that the transportation systems used by the U.S. government were interrelated. They also were interdependent, for they connected at key points such as Cairo, St. Louis, and Louisville so that quartermasters could use both boats and rails to move troops and supplies over hundreds of miles. River and rail transport had their own separate advantages and disadvantages, facilitating the knitting together of the two into an effective whole.[85]

Parsons tended to be very understanding of the railroads. He used polite encouragement when he needed them to give priority to army orders over private freight. But when it came to river steamers, Parsons tended to be tough. Sometimes he browbeat owners into putting aside the hauling of private freight for a couple of weeks in favor of government orders if the military or logistical situation demanded it. In part this was due to Parsons's own experience in the railroad industry and his admiration for the businessmen who ran railroad companies. He often found steamboat owners to be a more unreliable, uncooperative, and dishonest group of businessmen. Moreover, there were far more steamboat owners than railroad managers. Yet it generally was cheaper to ship by water than by rail, especially when moving troops, so Parsons had to deal with the mob of boat owners whether he liked it or not.[86]

While some historians believe that the Civil War represented "a serious blow to river transportation," other scholars convincingly point out that the conflict energized the industry. It is true that steamboat losses were high during the war; in fact, no previous period in the history of steamer transportation came close to matching it. But the government provided literally thousands of contracts and charters, and entrepreneurs were eager to fill the need. Steamboat construction soared during the war years. By 1864 the total tonnage operating on the rivers had reached the prewar level and by 1865 had exceeded it. By the time Appomattox ended the conflict, there were more steamers running the great waterways than ever before. While 817 (195,000 tons) boats plied the rivers in 1861, 1,006 (228,700 tons) were in operation by 1865. A true period of decline set in during the 1880s, which led to the end of steamboating as a major industry by the early twentieth century.[87]

Our understanding of the river-based transportation system in the Civil War is mostly oriented around Federal use of the boats. It is certain that the Confederate government also used river steamers, but on a far lower scale, and it left relatively little behind in the way of documentation. The Confederate government never appointed a single officer to superintend river transportation and therefore we have no quartermaster reports to inform us how Southerners arranged and paid for it. The work was all done by lower-ranking quartermasters. Now and then Southern dispatches mention the names of river steamers in use, and personal accounts by Rebel soldiers sometimes describe riding on boats. Ironically, one of the more valuable sources of information is a comprehensive list of boat wrecks occurring during the Civil War; this list was compiled by W. Craig Gaines and offers a list of the boats under Confederate control that were lost in the conflict. We have no idea how many others were used by Rebel quartermasters and survived the war.[88]

Two companies of the 27th Alabama were transported on a steamer named the *Julius Smith* down the Tennessee River from Florence to Fort Henry in late December 1861. The 20th Alabama divided onto two steamers, the *Dick Keys* and the *Dorrience*, for a trip along the Alabama River in February 1862. When the 31st Alabama left for the war it utilized a combination of rail and river transport across Alabama, Georgia, and into east Tennessee in the spring of 1862. Other regiments, such as the 37th Alabama, also used both modes of transportation.[89]

Albert Theodore Goodloe of the 35th Alabama admitted that his regiment seldom saw the inside of a steamboat. It mostly had short rides along such rivers as the Alabama or across Mobile Bay. Goodloe noted that quartermasters chartered the *St. Charles* to ship the regiment from Montgomery to Selma in April 1863, allowing the enlisted men to use the deck and officers to quarter in cabins. The boat was crowded, but the men enjoyed the novelty of a steamboat ride.[90]

Confederate troops serving along the Mississippi River had many more opportunities to see and ride on boats. At times, Rebel quartermasters could even accumulate enough craft to move an entire division, although this seems to have been rare. John G. Walker's division mounted 14 steamers at Trenton, Louisiana, on May 9, 1863, in response to a Federal expedition into central Louisiana conducted by Nathaniel P. Banks. Walker steamed about 70 miles before turning back upon receiving word that Banks had taken Alexandria. For a time, however, the rare sight of a Confederate flotilla of transports inspired many men who saw it. Upon starting from Trenton, the boats bustled with activity. Flags waved, bands played, "men huzzaing and cheering, with the bank lined with ladies with palpitating hearts and fluttering handkerchiefs," wrote Captain Elijah P. Petty of the 17th Texas.[91]

One wonders at the fact that boat captain J. D. Clarke had to tell Confederate quartermasters that his boat, the *Republic*, was well suited for their needs.

True, the craft seemed an excellent although small boat at 30 feet long, with side-wheel propulsion, and it was big enough to haul 50 men or two tons of freight. The boat was capable of 10 miles per hour downstream or 6 upstream and could tow a flatboat capable of hauling 100 men. Clarke wanted to be of service to the Confederacy. The odd thing about his approach was that he needed to find and tell the quartermasters what he possessed. Federal quartermasters were very proactive in seeking out boat owners and compiling information about their craft. Confederate quartermasters apparently did not take such a wise approach to the problem of finding transportation.[92]

W. Craig Gaines lists a total of 125 Confederate river craft among his compilation of Civil War shipwrecks. There are also many more Confederate coastal vessels in that list, so that the total of Rebel wrecks amounts to 405 craft of all kinds. When the place of construction is noted, it is clear that the overwhelming majority of those vessels (nearly 75 percent) were built in the North. Slightly more than half were constructed from 1857 to 1860. Ironically, the Confederates destroyed more of their own boats than did the enemy. Of 405 wrecks along the inland rivers of the West and along the coast, 174 were caused by the Confederates on purpose while scuttling vessels to obstruct channels to Union incursions or to prevent boats from falling into enemy hands. A total of 157 Confederate wrecks were caused by Federal action and 67 by accidents. Grant's operations against Vicksburg led the Confederates to destroy 12 of their own transports in May 1863 and another 12 the following July to keep them from being used by the invader.[93]

The Confederates had little chance of competing with the Federals on their own terms in the race to utilize steamboats as military transport. There were far fewer boats available in the South after Fort Sumter, and the Union army mounted a vigorous effort to round up as many steamers as possible. Federal quartermasters aggressively sought out, encouraged, and at times argued with steamer owners not only to use their craft but to obtain fair rates. The result was an impressive display of logistical power centered on water transportation. The Federal government itself became the biggest owner of riverboats. By June 30, 1865, it possessed 114 steamboats on the western rivers in addition to 486 barges. Of that number, 91 boats and 352 barges were operating along the lower Mississippi River, where the government also owned 139 coastal craft. No steamer company in the West was nearly this large or important. All these boats were sold, however, by December 1865.[94]

4

++++++++++++++

THE RAIL-BASED SYSTEM

The railroads of America spanned a time period coincident with that of the western river steamers. The first railroad company was chartered in New Jersey in 1815, but the first operating locomotive appeared ten years later. By 1836, the Baltimore and Ohio Railroad was operating 7 engines, more than 1,000 freight cars, and 44 passenger cars with a gross income of over $260,000 per year. Railroad lines began to appear not only from the Baltimore and Washington, D.C., area but from Boston and Charleston as well, all of them stretching west.[1]

By 1840 America was beginning to experience railroad fever. About 200 companies had been chartered and only four out of 26 states had no railroads. The overwhelming majority of the 3,000 miles of track lay east of the Appalachian Highlands, but that was nearly equal to the total miles of canals then operating in the country and contrasted sharply with the 1,800 miles of new track laid in all of Europe during the 1830s. Americans had invested more than $75 million in railroads by then.[2]

Within ten years, by 1850, American railroads increased to 9,000 miles of track. At $310 million, they were about as expensive to build as canals, with an average cost of $34,000 per mile. The increase in railroad companies and consequent increase of mileage was little less than explosive during the decade of the 1850s. While mostly financed by private investors, state governments also offered financial assistance and owned a handful of companies. The Western and Atlantic Railroad, soon to become a key component of military transport in the Civil War, was created and owned by the state of Georgia. The 1850s saw especially heavy growth in the western and southern states. In 1856 Ohio boasted 46 railroad companies, 2,593 miles of finished track, and 2,094 miles under construction.[3]

By 1860, the year before Fort Sumter, America had more railroad mileage than any other nation in the world. Over 30,000 miles had been built, with one-third of it in the New England and Middle Atlantic states, slightly more than one-third in the western states, and slightly less than one-third in the South. There were 400 railroad companies in the country, but most of them were relatively small. Half of the companies operated in New England and the Mid-Atlantic and possessed a bit over 50 miles each. The companies located in the western states were on average twice as big, with more than 100 miles each, and the Southern railroad companies had about 90 miles apiece.[4]

Sheer numbers did not tell the entire story of railroads on the eve of the Civil War. Four major trunk lines had been constructed that linked the western states with the northeastern states, and they were beginning to have an important effect on traditional patterns of trade in the country. Many farmers and middlemen were beginning to ship western products directly east instead of south down the Mississippi River. Chicago was emerging as a major commercial and transportation center, with no less than 11 rail lines linking the city with the rest of the country. Americans had invested a staggering $1.15 trillion in railroads by 1860; the country boasted nearly as many miles of track as the rest of the world combined in that pivotal year in national history.[5]

While the United States was emerging as the world leader in railroad development, it did not have a true national system of rail-based transportation. The 400 companies only loosely cooperated with each other to ship freight and passengers from one line to another. There was no standard gauge in the country. Such a concept existed to some degree because 4 feet, 8½ inches tended to be more common than any other gauge. But Southern railroads tended to set 5 feet as their gauge, and a total of 11 different gauges could be counted in the country by 1860. This meant that freight and passengers had to be off-loaded and re-loaded at places where one company line met another. There were few "union stations" in America—tracks and depots designed literally to meet at these junctions. Passengers and freight had to move a short distance from one company train to another, depending on local businesses to convey material and people between depots. Toledo, Ohio, pointed the way to the future by constructing a union station used by six different railroad companies, but that was rare. Not until the 1880s would railroad consolidation begin to take place, and with it the coming of a standard gauge and the connections between lines that were necessary to create a truly national system of railroad transportation.[6]

While most railroad companies were comparatively small in 1860, a few of them were large concerns. The Erie Railroad possessed 271 engines and 3,500 cars, while the New York Central Railroad used 239 engines and 4,006 cars. The Illinois Central Railroad was still emerging as a major company with 110 locomotives, 2,600 cars, and 3,500 employees. In rolling stock as in railroad mileage, the North far outpaced the South. Three of the largest Northern lines combined with the Baltimore and Ohio Railroad would have possessed as much rolling stock as all the other Southern lines.[7]

In fact, the Baltimore and Ohio Railroad was one of the railroad leaders of the nation even if the other Southern lines paled in comparison. Chartered in 1827, the line serviced the region around Baltimore and Washington, D.C., and stretched westward toward the Ohio River by the 1850s. Three-fourths of its line lay on Virginia soil, and the company constructed auxiliary branches to tap into a wider market. By the time of the Civil War the Baltimore and Ohio Railroad controlled 513 miles of track and used 236 locomotives, 128 passenger cars, and 3,451 freight cars.[8]

Another Southern line that would play a huge role in military transport during the war was the Louisville and Nashville Railroad. It controlled 286 miles of track, upon which only 37 engines, 260 freight cars, and 22 passenger cars operated. In contrast, the Illinois Central Railroad, stretching south from Chicago, had constructed more than 700 miles of track by 1856. It was in fact the world's longest railroad.[9]

With the exception of companies like the Baltimore and Ohio and the Louisville and Nashville, Southern railroads were small and often struggling. The slave states were building track in the 1850s but had a long way to go in order to catch up with the North. Most historians have agreed that many areas of the South were not served by rail traffic when the Civil War began and that a good many of the existing companies had not completed their plans to link with neighboring companies. Moreover, Southern lines depended heavily on the North or foreign countries for the manufacture of rolling stock and other items needed to maintain their equipment. While 19 businesses in the North made railroad engines, only one existed in the South. Northern firms produced 222,577 tons of railroad iron in contrast to Southern production of only 26,252 tons. Capital investment in railroads was on average much higher in the North than in the South. For example, in New York it averaged $52,000 per mile while in Virginia it was only $38,548. Part of this difference may have been due to variations in terrain or higher labor costs, but some of it was related to a Southern tendency to try to keep costs low. North and South comparisons in the railroad business have always indicated Southern backwardness.[10]

But these statistics hid the fact that railroad construction in the slave states proceeded at a rapid pace during the 1850s, even if most of it was playing catch-up with the North. The rate of growth in the industry was 392 percent in the South during the decade, compared to 325 percent in the North. Historian William G. Thomas estimates that access to railroad depots was roughly the same in the South as the North, with an average of 1,800 people per 10,000 of population living near enough to a depot to make use of it. In fact, as Christopher R. Gabel has argued, if the Southern slave states were treated as a separate nation, they would have had the third largest number of railroad miles in the world, next to the Northern states and Great Britain.[11]

We will never know whether Southern railroads would have progressed to a point where they equaled Northern lines if the Civil War had not interrupted their growth spurt in the 1850s. We do know that a preponderance of railroad resources lay in the North by the time Southerners fired on Fort Sumter. The difference was staggering not just in terms of the sheer number of track miles, the number of engines and cars, and the capital available to company managers. It also was seen in the fact that most railroad mechanics were Northerners and the capacity to build needed equipment was lodged mostly in the North as well. As in so many other ways, the slave states were heavily dependent on outsiders for key elements in their economy and would be cut off from those outsiders once the war began.

Americans understood that the railroads created their own culture by the time of the Civil War. "The whole population seems in motion," commented Asa Whitney when taking his first ride on a train in 1844. Indeed, the iron horse introduced a mode of transportation faster than any yet seen. Nineteen-year-old Albert N. Ames of Oswego, New York, wrote a school composition about this idea in the late 1850s. "The Railroads have become so numerous and extensive in the United States that persons can go in nearly all directions through most of the states. They are rapidly increasing throughout the Union and will soon form a vast web over which the shrieking iron horse will spin in all directions carrying passengers and freight wherever they choose to go. This is the quickest mode of traveling now in use."[12]

"The railroad offered a powerful extension of the body—of personal mobility —for anyone who rode in its cars," William Thomas has concluded. It therefore became "one of the first transformative technologies in American history." It must be noted that the western river steamers offered a similarly rapid and far-reaching mode of transportation, but their presence never spawned a similar culture of travel. Steamers could not guarantee regular timetables like the railroads. Or, to put it another way, they did not pretend to guarantee regular time-tables. Railroads printed travel schedules and even published them in blank diary books, which were purchased by Civil War soldiers. "Distances and Times By Railroad from New York to the following places," are the words that grace the first few pages of a diary bought by William Penn Lloyd, a staff officer in the Army of the Potomac. It indicated that a train could travel 1,429 miles from New York to St. Joseph, Missouri, in 64 hours. The travel speeds cited in this table range from 19.5 miles per hour to 22.6 miles per hour. Travelers often took their cue from such travel tables and noted in their diaries exactly how long it took to go from one point to another on the rail system, becoming far more aware of the speed and efficiency of long-distance travel than ever before.[13]

The railroads entered the language of America as well. The word power often was used in association with rail shipping and travel. It was applied to the rolling stock itself. "We have used every available pound of transportation power to bring up supplies," staff officer James A. Garfield wrote during the war. It was common practice to give names to railroad engines just as boat owners did to western river steamers. The names often were those of owners, or family members of owners, or prominent public figures. In addition, there were the charming affectations of "Blue Bird," "Ancient," or "Reindeer."[14]

But railroads also represented a dangerous form of transportation. Accidents were common, more common than in Europe. While 1 out of 188,000 passengers died in American rail accidents during the 1850s, the numbers were only 1 out of 1,703,123 in France and 1 in 6,180,324 in Britain. These are astonishing statistics that indicate how frequently one risked life and limb on American rails.[15]

Setting aside fears and simply concentrating on the rolling stock, a typical freight train in pre–Civil War America consisted of about 17 cars and weighed a total of 225 tons. One car was capable of carrying 5 to 10 tons of freight. Passenger trains were shorter, with 5 to 10 cars. The engine may well have been the

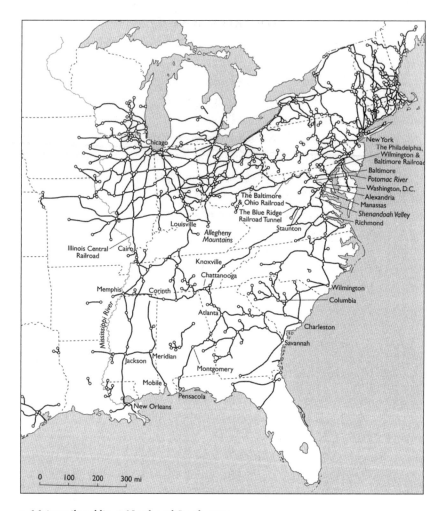

2. Major railroad lines, North and South, 1860

American type, which consisted of four lead wheels and four drivers in what was referred to as a 4-4-0 arrangement. The engine weighed about 20 to 30 tons and for the most part burned wood, although coal was used in limited ways. A ton of coal could move an engine about the same distance as a cord of wood, but it cost less than half the price (6 cents per mile for coal versus 14 cents per mile for wood). One American-type engine cost up to $10,000 to build.[16]

Railroad cars of the Civil War era were mostly designed to haul a variety of freight and thus were simple but usually rugged constructions. With four

4.1. "Genl. J. C. Robinson" at City Point, Virginia. Owned and operated by the U.S. Military Railroad, this engine stands as an example of the success achieved by the government conglomerate that grew to be the largest railroad in the world by 1865. There are two other engines behind the American-type "Genl. J. C. Robinson" as well as large water tanks and, in the distance, a huge wharf. This view offers a compelling vision of the logistical power of the Federal supply base at City Point during the Petersburg campaign of 1864–1865. (Library of Congress, LC-DIG-cwpb-01858)

wheels, freight cars had no springs but could hold 16,000 pounds of material. Weighing about 4,000 pounds, the total weight of a fully loaded freight car amounted to 20,000 pounds, or 10 tons. A train of 15 fully loaded freight cars weighed in at 300,000 pounds, or 150 tons. They were stopped individually by brakemen who worked a braking device, or they were stopped by the engine itself. Companies sometimes used freight cars as storage facilities if they could spare their use for a time. Passenger cars, much fewer in number in all companies, carried 50 to 60 people and had springs for a more comfortable ride. But they were not connected in a way to make walking from one car to another safe or comfortable.[17]

Regardless of what the timetables indicated, train travel, like steamboat travel, was subject to mechanical problems, weather, and a host of other imponderables that could wreck a schedule. It has been estimated that under the best of conditions a light train on a good track could go up to 60 miles per hour. But because trains made many stops along the way, these high speeds did not represent actual travel time. Printed timetables indicated a more realistic travel time based on an average speed of 19.5 to 22.6 miles per hour, but even this often was not met.[18]

The North Carolina Railroad ran a mail train between Goldsboro and Charlotte, a distance of 223 miles. With 23 stops along the way, it took the cars 15 hours to make the one-way journey at an average speed of 15 miles per hour. Many companies placed speed limits on their trains for various reasons, and it has been estimated that the actual speed of freight trains in South Carolina before the war averaged only 12 miles per hour. The highest actual speed one could expect in the prewar South was about 25 miles per hour. During the war itself, speeds often were far less. Federal commissary officer George Williamson Balloch noted that his train from Nashville to Stevenson in October 1863 averaged 9 miles per hour.[19]

Both before and during the war, the condition of tracks was a major factor in the speed and dependability of railroad travel. The technology behind the construction of roadbeds had evolved from fairly simple designs and components. Early on, the strap rail was common, consisting of "a thin iron strap" laid on a wooden stringer. The rail weighed about 18 to 24 pounds per yard. Soon, experiments appeared in the form of U-shaped iron rails that were flanged but still laid on wooden stringers, weighing 60 pounds per yard, to be succeeded by the T-shaped iron rail weighing 35 to 68 pounds per yard. The T rail dispensed with the wooden stringers and was spiked directly onto the wooden ties. Most large companies used the T rail by 1861, but some smaller lines still relied on the old strap rail. Some companies also began to experiment with steel rails, or iron rails that were capped with steel, by 1861. Ties lay on the bare ground with no gravel bed to rest on, and thus had a short life. Experiments with treating them with preservatives were under way by the time of the war.[20]

While it was common for European railroad companies to lay double tracks, allowing free scheduling of trains going in opposite directions along the same roadbed, American companies never adopted this convenient plan because the length of lines common in this country would have significantly increased the already high cost for track construction. To cut costs, American companies also provided only the minimum number of sidings (short pull-offs at critical places). The Virginia and Tennessee Railroad operated 204 miles of track between Lynchburg and Bristol with sidings only at 35 places, and each one was no more than 900 feet long.[21]

Many of the smaller Southern railroads retained cheap, old track methods and material into the war period. The Winchester and Potomac Railroad, which linked that town with the Baltimore and Ohio Railroad in the lower Shenandoah Valley, was branded as "perhaps the worst in the Union." It had strap rails for most of its 32 miles and no sidings. "It has a muddy bed that churns dreadfully in wet weather," reported the operating officer of the Baltimore and Ohio. Any locomotive of more than 12 tons had to slow down to no more than 10 miles per hour to negotiate this hazard. At best, the line could handle the passage of 52 cars per day. The Federal army wanted to increase its capacity to 60 cars per day, but an entire makeover with improved bed, new ties, and T-rails would have been necessary. The Federals decided not to do this and instead tried to get along with what they found. One Union artilleryman recorded that it took six hours to move only 21 miles along this railroad, and even then the engine ran off the strap iron. At other places the men had to get off and walk to lighten the cars.[22]

The Nashville and Chattanooga Railroad was in better shape than the Winchester and Potomac, but its strategic location was such that the Federals invested a great deal of time, labor, and money to completely redo the track. It was 151 miles long and traversed an imposing arm of the Cumberland Plateau. Built cheaply, the track lay on a mud roadbed that barely supported U-rails strapped onto wooden stringers. The stringers quickly decayed and separated, creating many gaps in the track. The line was an essential link in the logistical support of Federal troops in Chattanooga, justifying the reconstruction of the entire length in 1864.[23]

Basic alterations to the roadbed were very expensive. Even something as comparatively simple as changing the gauge of a Southern railroad to suit

4.2. Maintaining Track of the Nashville and Chattanooga Railroad Near Murfreesboro. In 1864, the Federals were compelled to replace the U-rails on wooden stringers used by this Southern railroad with modern T-rails, as shown in this view. Note the untreated wooden ties and the dirt roadway without gravel ballast, unlike modern railroads. (Library of Congress, LC-DIG-cwpb-02135)

Northern standards during the war was a financial burden. Thomas A. Scott estimated that it would cost about $200 per mile of track, but the expense did not end there. The rolling stock of the Southern company also had to have the wheels altered. Scott thought it would cost $38,000 to alter 12 engines and 241 cars.[24]

Roadbeds deteriorated pretty steadily and had to be maintained at substantial cost by companies. The rotting of wooden ties and repairs due to washouts or other natural hazards were common problems. Even grass growing along the roadbed that was not ballasted by gravel could prevent a train from using the track. If grass grew high enough to cover the rails, the engine's drive wheels spun rather than gripped the iron. Such growth was not a problem as long as the track was used regularly, but those lines that saw little traffic sometimes had to have the grass cut before trains could use them.[25]

Trains ran better on level tracks than along uneven ground, but the landscape of America offered many undulations and hills. The issue of grading therefore loomed large in railroad efficiency. There were no large earth-moving machines in pre–Civil War America; only small horse-drawn scrapers and manpower could cut into a hillside or fill in a depression to make a level track. In short, man's ability to command the earth to his bidding was limited. The result was that trains often had to negotiate slopes. The steam locomotive engines of the day provided far less power than twentieth-century diesel engines; a slope that today would not slow a train could in the Civil War era stop it literally on its track.

Many soldiers North and South testified to the delays caused by heavy trains trying to go up modest grades. Adolph Engelmann of the 45th Illinois reported that the heavily loaded train he took from Corinth to Burnsville in Mississippi had to make three attempts to get up "a slight grade." Another train traveling along the Nashville and Chattanooga Railroad stopped partway up a modest grade and could not move farther. The next train coming along slowed down and literally pushed it the rest of the way uphill. An unusually high grade existed where the track ascended the western edge of the Cumberland Plateau, necessitating the placing of a spare engine at this point so that every train could have two locomotives to get up the mountainside. But in level country, such as that along the eastern seaboard, locomotives had no difficulty hauling up to 30 loaded cars rather than the 10 that was typical of the more mountainous areas of the interior.[26]

Wood was the overwhelmingly common fuel for railroad engines. On average, one cord could power a train for about 50 or 60 miles. Companies typically contracted with local people along their line to stockpile usable wood as fuel at designated locations, in a fashion similar to the method adopted by steamboat owners to obtain wood for fuel along the rivers. It was necessary to specify that the wood should be no more than five feet long in order to fit in the burners. Just as with the riverboats, if local conditions during the war led to a decrease in the number of civilians willing to cut wood for railroads used by the Federals,

4.3. Freight Train at Culpeper Courthouse, Virginia. This photograph was exposed by Timothy H. O'Sullivan in August 1862. Grass and weeds grow on the railroad bed in this view, coming close to topping the rails. If that happened, it could lessen the friction needed for the iron wheels to grip the rails, slowing or even stopping a train. One can see an engine and about a dozen cars occupying a siding. (Library of Congress, LC-DIG-cwpb-01078)

Union officers rounded up refugee blacks to perform this labor in order to keep the trains running.[27]

Water was just as necessary for the engines as wood; it was the source of the steam that gave life to the locomotive, and rail lines were dotted with water towers. For many reasons, this system could break down under the stress of war. If a train needed water and there was no tower nearby, it stopped near a creek and passengers formed a line and passed buckets from the stream to the engine before the train could proceed.[28]

Despite the many small problems inherent in the railroad industry, the United States possessed the largest, most robust system of rail transport in the world when the Civil War broke out. Federal quartermasters soon worked out a system of utilizing trains as military transport. One of the earliest issues to deal with related to the rates for moving material and people. Freight rates on pre–Civil War Northern railroads tended to be $1.80 for the first 100 pounds, with lowered rates for each additional 100-pound increment, down to only 70 cents for the 4th 100-pound increment. Passenger rates varied more widely. In 1848 they ranged from 2 cents to 5 cents per mile, depending on the company and the region of the country. Those rates had declined by 1861; one estimate places the passenger rate at 1.8 cents per mile on average.[29]

In the first chaotic months of the war Federal quartermasters tended to offer pretty high rates to railroads for transportation. This problem was worse in the Department of the Missouri when John C. Fremont was in charge at St. Louis. His officers agreed to a flat rate of 2 cents per mile for passengers and the local first class rates for freight. They justified this by citing a circular issued by Secretary of War Simon Cameron suggesting a range of acceptable rates, but this document was never meant to be an order. It merely set a maximum rate allowable. The quartermasters in Missouri made their job easier by accepting the maximum rate as their standard agreement with companies. Montgomery Meigs issued a circular of his own in January 1862 compelling quartermasters to negotiate for better terms and not simply to accept Cameron's previous document as an order.[30]

But something more had to be done, and Cameron's replacement in the War Department, Edwin M. Stanton, did it. A hard-headed administrator, Stanton called a conference of Northern railroad executives in February 1862 and hammered out a schedule of uniform rates for government business. He agreed to a rate of 2 cents per mile for passengers and a freight rate that was 10 percent lower than published local and through rates. It was a smart move. Even though the Federal army would move literally hundreds of thousands of troops by rail, the bulk of government business would be in supplies. By getting a slightly lower rate for freight and a slightly higher rate for passengers, Stanton could save government expenses and give the companies the feeling that he had compromised in the negotiations. It was helpful in the effort to encourage railroad companies to give good service to the army. Moreover, Federal quartermasters had the option of offering a bonus of up to 25 percent if there was an emergency or if it became necessary for companies to set aside their profitable civilian trade for a week or two and concentrate only on government hauling.[31]

For the railroad companies, it also made business sense to compromise with Stanton on rates. There were huge profits to be made from the war. The gross earnings of the Baltimore and Ohio Railroad more than doubled from 1860 to 1864. It is true that companies had more difficulty settling accounts with the government than with private patrons. Railroad agents had to have all their vouchers in order and then find a quartermaster who happened to have enough cash on hand to pay up the account. It often took several months to settle these affairs because of the paperwork and the often uncertain availability of money in quartermasters' offices at any given time. But the increased volume for many companies whose tracks were strategically located for army business certainly made the trouble of settling accounts worth the effort.[32]

The standard freight and passenger rates that Stanton negotiated in early 1862 held firm throughout the war. Despite increased costs for labor and maintenance induced by the war itself, railroad companies did not complain about the standard rate. In fact, the rate continued in effect for government business even after Appomattox. Lewis B. Parsons, who superintended railroad transportation across the country by the summer of 1864, thought the standard rate worked very smoothly. He praised the spirit of cooperation among railroad executives and offered it as a contrast to the often selfish attitude of western riverboat owners.[33]

Parsons did complain about the details involved in arranging for passenger travel by rail. It was typical for the government to purchase tickets for troops before the trip began. As often happened, a handful would not show up and would be left behind, or some would drop off along the journey. The government, in short, lost money by pre-buying tickets. It was possible, with proper documentation, to settle this with the railroad company later, but given the huge volume of paperwork that burdened quartermaster clerks, it could be months before that happened. Parsons suggested as early as October 1863 that a quartermaster in each military department across the country be assigned the task of handling all purchases of railroad tickets and dispose of problems like this more quickly, but this proved to be impractical.[34]

For everyone concerned, freight was more easily handled than passengers, and it constituted the bulk of government business on the railroads. Before the war, from two-thirds to three-fourths of all rail business lay in the hauling of material. For example, even though the Pennsylvania Railroad moved more than 884,000 people in 1857, the receipts it garnered from freight haulage were

4.4. Aquia Creek Landing. This was another node of the Federal transportation system where rail transport met coastal shipping. The landing here supported the Army of the Potomac in the Fredericksburg area during three different periods of the Civil War. Note the large number of sailing vessels, the track and siding, and the wharves. A large supply of wheels for either wagons or artillery carriages is barely visible, as well as piles of coal and lumber, bales of hay, and a wheeled battery forge. (Library of Congress, LC-DIG-ppmsca-35316)

nearly three times greater than receipts from passenger traffic. During the war Northern railroad companies depended heavily on money brought in by their hauling of private freight to strengthen their cash flow while waiting to receive payment for hauling government freight.[35]

In fact, even during the height of the war years Northern railroads derived more income from civilian passenger business than they did from hauling soldiers. The war itself spurred a noticeable increase in civilian travel throughout the Union. "Mr. Gaddis spoke about how odd it was to see such a crowd of citizens around every Steamboat landing & RR depot in his journey home," commented Clement Abner Boughton of the 12th Wisconsin, "now & then a Soldier to be seen among them." Most companies did not keep separate statistics for civilian compared to military passengers, but the Pennsylvania Railroad did tabulate the difference. Only 10 percent of its passenger business consisted of soldiers in 1862, 12 percent in 1863, and 18 percent in 1865. These numbers are typical for the handful of other companies that maintained such statistics. The Pennsylvania Railroad earned $379,393 for transporting 108,524 soldiers in 1862, yet that income represented no more than 14 percent of the company's total revenue from passengers that year. It is astonishing to note that the Pennsylvania Railroad moved 953,397 troops from April 1861 to December 1865, and yet these men represented no more than 18 percent of its total passenger traffic at any given time.[36]

The war increased both passenger and freight hauling for all Northern railroads, but statistics concerning the proportion of military freight compared to civilian freight are lacking. For the Pittsburgh, Fort Wayne, and Chicago Railroad, total earnings from military transport of both freight and men represented less than 10 percent of the company's gross income in 1863. East-bound traffic in grain and livestock was more important in this line's efforts than military traffic. The number of passengers it carried more than doubled during the war years.[37]

But that hugely increased business created problems for all Northern railroad companies. It increased wear and tear on rolling stock and roadbeds alike. Companies could not keep pace by buying more rolling stock or repairing the track. Passenger traffic doubled and freight business increased by a factor of four on the Philadelphia, Wilmington, and Baltimore Railroad, but the company only doubled its number of engines. Its increase in cars didn't even reach that level. The Michigan Central Railroad carried two and a half times more passengers than before the war, but its number of passenger cars only increased from 85 to 100.[38]

Heavier traffic combined with the inability to increase equipment inventories meant that cars and engines alike wore out quickly. Some proportion of this wear and tear was accentuated by the peculiar character of military passengers. Young men in uniform often vandalized cars. Early in the war railroad companies naively provided their best passenger cars for troop transport, but they soon learned their mistake. Good cars "are usually ruined in a single trip," Herman Haupt confessed to Meigs. Companies learned to ship men only in freight cars, sometimes with adjustments to accommodate them. Seats made of boards were at times set up on the bare floor of the car, only to be wrecked by the idle, bored troops during their long journey. Whether seats were provided or not, the tendency was to pack soldiers into freight cars as if they were merchandise. No wonder that many men preferred to ride on top of the car for fresh air.[39]

Vandalism was a problem in the South as well. The president of the Mississippi Central Railroad complained of "malicious destruction by troops *in transit*, without interference of their commanders," while shipping Confederate regiments from Grenada to Canton in January 1863. He pinpointed a key problem: officers often did not or could not superintend their men's conduct, especially when regiments were divided into several cars. The problem grew so serious that Williams S. Rosecrans, commander of the Department of the Missouri, issued a general order regulating behavior when soldiers traveled on both railroads and steamers. They were to obey the instructions of conductors when being assigned cars or seats on the rail lines. Conductors had authority to compel officers to place unruly men under arrest, and officers in turn were required to ride with their troops.[40]

Soldiers in blue and gray overwhelmingly traveled in freight cars, due to both the shortage of passenger cars and their own rough conduct on trains. These freight cars normally had no accommodations for human cargo. Herman Haupt suggested a quick and inexpensive method to provide toilet facilities for troops. He had the idea to cut a hole in one corner and place a square box over it with a hole in the seat. The improvised toilet could be screened by a curtain for some degree of privacy while the human waste would fall on the roadbed. Whether it was done is unclear.[41]

Railroad operations often were hampered by soldiers in ways other than wrecking cars. They had a tendency to walk along the tracks near their encampments if the line was a good route from one point to another, or out of idle curiosity. Passing trains often were compelled to slow down or risk killing them. The problem became so pronounced that Herman Haupt argued it would be impossible to run a railroad if pedestrians had the right-of-way on tracks and "engines must stop and trains stand still until it suits the pleasure of pedestrians to move." Sentinels would need to be posted every 500 feet along the roadbed to prevent strollers from using the track. The only solution was to let men know that they walked along the rail line "at their own risk."[42]

An incident resulting from this problem led to several injuries when a train suddenly came upon a group of soldiers walking on the track. The engineer claimed he was moving at no more than 10 miles per hour and sounded his whistle; still, some soldiers did not get out of the way in time and were hit. The men claimed he was moving much faster, 25 miles per hour, but the crux of the case lay in the fact that soldiers far too often used the roadbed as a walkway and had a habit of waiting until the last minute to get out of the way of a train. Engineers had grown used to it and were somewhat indifferent to the consequences, according to Haupt, who also complained that soldiers often tampered with switches at sidings and other junctions. Haupt also complained about a related problem. One engineer suddenly came upon a lone car on the track used by soldiers to gather wood from the brush near the roadbed. He avoided a collision only by slamming his brakes and reversing the engine. Haupt pressed local infantry commanders to put a stop to such practices.[43]

It is difficult to understand the level of vandalism committed against railroad property by Federal soldiers. They were in fact wrecking the very means by which their food was provided on a daily basis. But vandalism of railroad property had always been a feature of iron horse history, in contrast to the story of river steamers, where one finds no evidence of it. Railroad vandalism before the war tended to be motivated by some hard issue. When the Michigan Central Railroad refused to pay full value for cattle that its trains killed along the track (because the company fenced in its right-of-way), local farmers in Jackson County began to wreck switches and rolling stock in protest.[44]

There certainly were episodes of sabotage by civilians who presumably sympathized with the Confederacy. A man suddenly appeared and threw a switch just in time to cause four cars to derail at Culpeper on the Orange and Alexandria Railroad early in 1864. But such incidents were isolated and infrequent. Ironically, the property of the Orange and Alexandria suffered more from deliberate vandalism by Union soldiers who were assigned to guard it. Fifth Corps troops at Rappahannock Station were in the habit of throwing stones at trains and even at the train crews as they passed by. They knocked out signal lights, almost knocked brakemen off the tops of cars, and tried to interfere with the engine when it was taking on water.[45]

Many guards along the Orange and Alexandria worked hard to steal supplies from passing trains as well. They pilfered food when the train stopped for water or to take on wood. In places where the engine was compelled to slow down to ascend a grade, gangs of soldiers hid in the bushes and managed to snare barrels and packages from open flat cars with a pole and hook, rolling them off the car and collecting the booty after the train had passed. They also broke up some idle cars simply to obtain firewood. The basic problem lay in officers who did not take their responsibilities seriously and failed to oversee the actions of their men. There seemed to be an attitude that the railroad, as public property, was open to use by any Union soldier for his private wants.[46]

George Sykes, commander of the Fifth Corps, issued instructions in an effort to arrest this tendency. "The Orange and Alexandria Railroad is the means of supply for the Army of the Potomac," he lectured his troops. "The supplies passing over it keep that army alive. The safety of the road, its material, and what it transports should be to the troops assigned for its protection a sacred duty." Sykes outlined a plan to compel officers to be more vigilant. Apparently it worked, for complaints about conditions along the track declined.[47]

Idleness, boredom, and hunger were apparent motives for the spate of vandalism and theft that cropped up along the Orange and Alexandria line early in 1864, but one also wonders if troops saw the iron horse ambivalently. It was, after all, dangerous to ride the rails in the Civil War era. Accidents were not uncommon ever since the railroads began operating decades before. More than 100 accidents occurred in 1853, killing 234 people and injuring 496 more. Military passengers were not immune to the dangers. It was not uncommon for a man to slip and fall while the cars were in motion and be run over by the iron wheels. Collisions of one train against another took place in the South with surprising regularity, producing chaos, mangled bodies, and shocked senses among the survivors. Even a simple accident such as an engine running off a track could result in serious injury although moving at slow speeds. One such derailment in November 1862 led to the deaths of 11 men and the injury of 61 others in the 33rd Alabama.[48]

Ironically, the very means of transportation that killed and injured so many also was fitted up with very advanced methods of caring for the sick and wounded. Trains provided the fastest mode of transporting casualties to rear areas. For the most part the injured rode in simple freight cars, and many who experienced it complained about the rough journey. With no springs or bunks, the trip could be absolutely grueling for men suffering from wounds. Soon the railroad companies developed specially designed cars for transporting the injured. Williams S. Rosecrans's Department of the Cumberland is credited with organizing the first regular hospital train service of the war by early 1863.[49]

The spirit of cooperation by railroad companies that resulted in the development of the hospital car was the basis for the rail-based system of military transport. The government and the companies worked out a cooperative arrangement early in the war that held the union of state and corporation together throughout the conflict. But a significant factor in the success of this union lay in the threat of government seizure. Initially Secretary of War Simon Cameron relied entirely on cooperation. He called on key railroad executives for help in sorting out transportation problems in the rail connections linking Washington, D.C., with Baltimore and other cities during those chaotic days following the fall of Fort Sumter. But Major General Benjamin Butler sounded a different approach when he seized the Annapolis and Elk Ridge Railroad and the Washington branch of the Baltimore and Ohio Railroad in the same time period.[50]

Nine months later, on January 31, 1862, Congress approved an act giving the government authority to seize any railroad needed for the efficient prosecution of the war. Two weeks later, Daniel C. McCallum, the superintendent of the Erie Railroad, was recruited to take charge of any lines thus seized and given a commission in the army to lend authority to his position. This aggressive stance by the government probably was a factor in Stanton's ability to negotiate a standard rate for shipping freight and passengers only a few weeks later.[51]

The threat of seizure no doubt helped to shape the spirit of cooperation between rail executives and Federal authorities, but it actually was applied only occasionally to Northern lines. In addition to the Annapolis and Elk Ridge Railroad and a section of the Baltimore and Ohio, seized for a time early in the war, the government also seized a 36-mile stretch of the Western Maryland Railroad for five days in the aftermath of the battle at Gettysburg because the company could not handle the heavy but temporary demands placed on it for removal of the wounded. When the Army of the Potomac moved away in pursuit of Lee, the government gave back all track and rolling stock to company control.[52]

No one in Washington, D.C., was interested in permanent control of any railroad. Driven by compelling circumstances, Federal officers were willing to invoke the congressional act when needed, reverting lines to private owners as soon as possible. "Nothing but a controlling necessity would induce the Department to interfere with the business of any individuals or companies," Stanton assured Cornelius Vanderbilt while explaining why his men had to seize three locomotives being constructed for the transportation tycoon in order to relieve a logistical problem at Chattanooga in the fall of 1863. "This however is a case when the safety and support of an army depends upon the exercise of the authority of the Government and prompt acquiescence by loyal citizens."[53]

4.5. Daniel C. McCallum. Uniformed as a brigadier general, McCallum had been super-intendent of the Erie Railroad before the government asked him to direct the U.S. Military Railroad. His work in that capacity, which lasted from early 1862 until the end of the war, was instrumental in the success of the military railroad. (Library of Congress, LC-DIG-cwpb-05905)

The government overwhelmingly preferred to cooperate with private busi-ness in the North rather than invoke seizure. It was a completely different story in the occupied South. As the Union army penetrated Confederate territory, Southern railroad executives and workers normally fled, leaving much of their rolling stock and track behind. The Union army took over the abandoned re-sources and linked them with Northern lines to form a continuous network across the country and to support further invasion of enemy territory. The government was forced to get into the railroad business in large ways as the war progressed.

Two Southern railroad companies that operated in the border regions managed to avoid seizure. The executives of the Baltimore and Ohio Railroad went above and beyond the call of loyalty to the government to keep their line operating in the face of repeated Confederate attacks. President John W. Garrett spent hundreds of thousands of company dollars to rebuild track and always was eager to serve when a major movement of men or material was at hand. Of course the company did huge business with the government, so Garrett was protecting a major source of income. But the spirit with which he and his subordinates strove to meet any demand of the army went beyond mere financial considerations and demonstrated a soldiering spirit. Under the guidance of William P. Smith, Garrett's chief of operations, the Baltimore and Ohio Railroad may well have been the most efficient rail company in the United States.[54]

James Guthrie's Louisville and Nashville Railroad, serving central Kentucky and Tennessee, managed to avoid government seizure by striving to serve Federal army needs as much as possible. However, Guthrie could not prevent the government from seizing his rolling stock on occasion. From July 1863 to July 1864, Federal authorities took 25 engines and 191 cars for use on other lines, where logistical demands were heavy. In fact, the Federal government controlled nearly half of Guthrie's cars by mid-July. Only because the line took full advantage of the huge government business between Louisville and Nashville, two of the most important logistical hubs in the West, did Guthrie manage to balance these losses with profits. His company did an unusually heavy business in government freight; about half the line's freight hauling was for the Union army. The Louisville and Nashville Railroad netted nearly $2 million in overall revenue during 1864 and more than that the next year.[55]

The Civil War led to an explosion of business for all railroads North and South. Ninety trains rolled into and out of Chicago every day at the height of the conflict. Albany, New York, saw up to 450 freight cars arrive (divided into as many as 18 trains) every day, plus a dozen passenger trains. The heaviest government business was done by those railroads located in the lower Northern states because they lay closer to the theater of operations. The Erie Railroad, located in the upper North, received little government business, but the volume of its traffic soared nevertheless because of the war and the closing of the Mississippi River.[56]

With hugely increased traffic came problems as well as profits. Rolling stock and tracks deteriorated rapidly all across the North as the cost of fuel, labor, and material soared. Accident rates also climbed. It has been estimated that operating costs among some Northern railroads doubled by 1865 compared to three years before. Yet all Northern companies managed to end the conflict with increased profits by making do; the income tended to counterbalance the inflation of operating costs.[57]

Lewis B. Parsons always admired railroad companies and the men who ran them, having had experience with that select community before the war. He lavishly praised their contributions to Union victory in the Civil War. "I think it but just to say that no portion of the community have been more ready to respond to the wants of the Government, more willing to make sacrifices, or labored with a greater earnestness and efficiency in the suppression of the rebellion than have our railroad proprietors and managers." They were "men of superior business capacity." Parsons never made such comments about the owners of western river steamers.[58]

In the South, where large-scale seizure of railroads took place, Federal officers could not rely on company owners or operators to serve their needs. When Daniel McCallum agreed to manage government railroads in February 1862, the only track seized and operated by quartermasters was a seven-mile stretch that linked Washington, D.C., with Alexandria, Virginia, across the Potomac River. The army relaid the line with modern T rails and put tracks on Long Bridge as well to make a secure connection between the capital and the head of the Orange and Alexandria Railroad. The government heavily used this short connection until August 1865.[59]

It did not require a large workforce to renovate or maintain a short line like this, but when the army began to expand its operations in occupied territory such a need arose. In an effort to supply Irvin McDowell's troops at Fredericksburg in the spring of 1862, Stanton asked Herman Haupt to take charge of restoring the Aquia Creek and Fredericksburg Railroad that linked the town with the Potomac River. Haupt had many bridges to rebuild and track to lay using soldiers detailed from the ranks who possessed few skills for the job. Soon he began to hire skilled workers from the North, and his group of laborers grew with the progress of the war. By January 1863, what had by then been designated the U.S. Military Railroad was divided into construction and operating departments. The Construction Corps grew to be a huge concern when

McCallum's organization expanded to include all government-seized railroads in the Western Theater early in 1864. From 300 men in January 1863, the Construction Corps employed 10,000 men by war's end.[60]

McCallum praised Stanton for issuing War Department Special Orders No. 337 on November 10, 1862. It mandated that all army officers cooperate fully with officials of the U.S. Military Railroad, unload its cars promptly, guard its rolling stock with care, and most of all refrain from interfering with its operations in any way. The railroad officers (who also held military rank) had full control of the lines and equipment; any army officer who interfered would be subject to immediate dismissal.[61]

This order was used as a weapon against any officer who tried to impose his own agenda on railroad property or who failed to make sure supplies were unloaded with speed and empty cars sent back for more material. It was "the very foundation of success" of the U.S. Military Railroad, in McCallum's words. "Without it the whole railroad system . . . would have been not only a costly but ludicrous failure. The fact should be understood that the management of railroads is just as much a distinct profession as is that of the army of war." McCallum proudly noted that his personnel succeeded in cases where army commanders tried and failed to have their quartermasters run railroads. The only way they could do so was with absolute control over the details, and this order ensured it.[62]

McCallum put it well when he summarized the objective of the U.S. Military Railroad. It was "designed to be a great construction and transportation machine for carrying out the objects of the commanding generals . . . and it was managed solely with a view to efficacy in that direction." Having extensive experience in managing railroads before the war, McCallum admitted that the economy normally practiced by civilian corporations was impossible in war. Army commanders had imperative demands for timely movement of troops and large amounts of material. "The question to be answered was not 'How much will it cost?' but rather, 'Can it be done at all at any cost?'" The spirit which animated U.S. Military Railroad personnel played a huge role in Union army success; it was to make sure difficult things were done regardless of the problems.[63]

A key to the success of the U.S. Military Railroad lay in the hiring of competent civilians with extensive experience at railroad construction and management, giving them military commissions to lend authority, and then letting them have free rein in their work. These men could have made much more money by continuing to work at their civilian jobs, but they answered Stanton's call out of duty and applied their skills for the Union cause.[64]

Many of these men were inventive, innovative spirits. George Herrick supervised car repairs in the West and devised a wrecking car to clean up train accidents. He developed car repair stations at six locations and put about 20,000 cars back into operation after they were wrecked. E. C. Smeed developed quicker methods of laying track to speed up what often was a lengthy process. Robert E. Lee was deeply impressed by the speed with which his opponent could rebuild bridges. Even though his troops thoroughly wrecked stretches of the Baltimore and Ohio Railroad in late September 1862, he felt it would cause no more than "a few days" delay in the road's operations.[65]

The cost of maintaining track and keeping rolling stock in shape in the U.S. Military Railroad system was enormous. On the Orange and Alexandria Railroad alone, the organization spent on average $90,000 each month on labor costs; $50,000 of that was for maintaining track, buildings, and the roadbed. To acquire more rolling stock the Federals on occasion seized engines and cars from Northern railroad companies or they purchased them on the market. It cost about $750 to make a boxcar and $625 to make a platform car. Government railroads in the Western Theater alone purchased 194 engines and 2,603 cars during the course of the war.[66]

Unlike civilian companies, which could anticipate long-term needs and purchase rolling stock accordingly, the army often issued frenzied demands for increased transportation upon capturing another chunk of Confederate territory. Government railroad officials had to scramble to meet that need. This happened after the Federals captured Corinth and after occupying Chattanooga. It was impossible to meet all of these needs by seizing rolling stock from Northern companies, for they needed what they had, but Lewis B. Parsons thought of a better idea. He suggested the government create a stockpile of 20 spare engines and 300 cars in the East and West to meet sudden emergencies. He estimated it would cost about $1 million but would be well worth the expense. "It seems clear to me that we require arsenals of railroad machinery almost as much as arsenals of arms," he concluded, but there is no evidence this plan was implemented.[67]

Herman Haupt warned McCallum that there was a good deal of inferior iron rails on the market and that government purchasing agents should be very

4.6. Railroad Junction at Hanover, Pennsylvania, August 1863. Two lines served Hanover
Junction, the Hanover Branch Railroad and the Northern Central Railroad. One line, on
the left, has two sidings, but the other line on the right has none. An engine, boxcars,
and passenger cars are visible in this view and the building on the right still stands today,
housing a railroad museum. The tall man wearing a stovepipe hat in front of the building
has been thought to be Abraham Lincoln on his way to Gettysburg on November 18, 1863,
but the original label in the Library of Congress indicates the photograph was exposed the
previous August. (Library of Congress, LC-DIG-ppmsca-35054)

careful of it. This was a matter of no small importance because the U.S. Military
Railroad needed enormous amounts of rails. It purchased 21,783 tons during
the course of the war at prices that ranged from $40 to $130 per ton. In part,
this was why McCallum wanted to put an unfinished Confederate rolling mill
into operation after it was seized at Chattanooga in February 1864. Ulysses S.
Grant approved the project, but completing the mill proved more troublesome
than anticipated. Parts of the plant were not within the fortified line of Chattanooga, so McCallum decided to move the entire operation to a more secure
location. His Construction Corps men did all the work, and by April 1, 1865, the
plant was finished at a cost of nearly $300,000. It made rails for government
use until the following October at a cost a bit lower than the lowest price Mc-

Callum had to pay for rails in the open market. In addition, the Chattanooga rolling mill sold more than 3,000 tons of rails to Southern railroad companies after the war and nearly garnered the cost of reconstructing the plant from that source alone.[68]

The primary role of the U.S. Military Railroad was to serve army needs, but to a degree it allowed civilian traffic on the trains as well. The Orange and Alexandria Railroad charged passengers 5 cents per mile, taking in about $450 each day. The line also collected thousands of dollars to transport the stock of army sutlers, who were civilian contractors selling all manner of goods to soldiers in the field.[69]

The reaction to William T. Sherman's decision to stop all civilian use of railroads that were collecting supplies for his Atlanta campaign was an indication of how much civilians relied on government lines. Everyone from obscure citizens to Abraham Lincoln complained of it, but Sherman argued that it was the only way he could support his operations. Despite this interruption the money collected by government railroads in Sherman's Military Division of the Mississippi during the last year of the war amounted to more than $415,000. Forty-one percent of those receipts came from civilian passenger travel, while 42 percent was derived from shipping private packages. The rest, 17 percent, was generated by civilian bulk freight.[70]

As these statistics indicate, the U.S. Military Railroad expanded into a huge organization as Federal armies continued to invade the expanse of the western Confederacy. McCallum found it necessary to organize the Construction Corps in the Military Division of the Mississippi more thoroughly and in greater detail than in the East because of the enlarged territory it had to cover. Eventually he divided it into seven divisions, with an engineer in charge of each and supervisors in control of each subdivision within the seven divisions. Responsibilities were carefully divided; men responsible for laying track constituted one subdivision, while those who constructed bridges made up another. Each subdivision was further divided into gangs, and the gangs into squads. An array of support personnel, including quartermasters, clerks, timekeepers, surgeons, hospital stewards, and cooks, filled each subdivision as well.[71]

When McCallum began to supervise the western railroads in January 1864, he had to look after only 123 miles of track, 35 locomotives, and 450 cars. By July 1, 1864, his responsibilities increased to 896 miles of track, 165 engines, 1,500 cars, and more than 10,000 employees in the Military Division of the

4.7. Railroad Depot at Atlanta. This photograph by George N. Barnard shows two tracks entering the large depot building, a street crossing six tracks in the foreground, and several piles of loose rails lying about. (Library of Congress, LC-DIG-cwpb-02223)

Mississippi alone. By the end of the war the western railroad crews constructed more than 18 miles of railroad bridges and 433 miles of track. Counting all military railroads in the Western Theater, McCallum's men operated 1,201 miles of track by war's end. The volume of traffic was enormous. The U.S. Military Railroad sent out of Nashville more than 29,000 cars of stores from July 1864 to June 1865, plus 5,673 cars loaded with troops (283,716 men). Almost a quarter of a million tons of supplies left Nashville for various posts by rail during that time period. In contrast, the U.S. Military Railroad operated a total of only 611 miles of track in the East.[72]

The last great service performed for the Union by railroads took place at the end of the war when soldiers wanted to go home. Government railroads and private companies alike cooperated in a massive series of troop movements to demobilize the Union army. Some 6,000 men rode the rails northward from Washington, D.C., every day and another 5,000 were transported west from the capital along the Baltimore and Ohio Railroad. The latter line no longer needed to be guarded against enemy attack, but officers along the route kept guards posted to maintain order among the boisterous veterans. They also closed liquor shops within reach of every station stop. The Baltimore and Ohio Railroad moved 233,300 men plus 27,000 horses west during June and July 1865. Those troops scattered onto other lines as well as onto Ohio River steamers and continued to many other destinations as far away as St. Louis.[73]

The U.S. Military Railroad became the largest railroad conglomerate in the world by 1865. It operated 50 railroad lines, with a total of 2,600 miles of track, 433 locomotives, and 6,605 cars. McCallum reported that he spent a grand total of $42,462,142 during the war but sold rolling stock after the conflict to raise $12,623,965. The net expense to the Federal government for operating the U.S. Military Railroad amounted to just under $30 million.[74]

It must be noted that the Southern railroads operated by the Federal government during the war were returned to their former owners. Most of them were in far better shape than when they had been seized because McCallum's people were compelled to renovate, upgrade, and in some cases literally rebuild entire lines to get adequate service out of them for Union army needs. The Nashville and Chattanooga Railroad was completely modernized from its backward condition when taken. The Western and Atlantic Railroad was also rebuilt quickly after the war so the Federal army could ship thousands of tons of corn to Atlanta in a desperate effort to deal with the near starvation of the population around the city due to war-related destruction.[75]

The transfer of seized Southern railroads to their previous owners was not a smooth or easy process. Many issues had to be worked out, including setting the condition that the owners accept the authority of the Federal government before they got their property back. That meant all employees had to take an oath of allegiance. Federal officials felt comfortable transferring control temporarily to a state board of public works, if one existed in any given state, and trusting the reconstructed state governments to sort out who owned what parts of each company. The Orange and Alexandria Railroad, for example, was partly owned by the state, by loyalists to the Federal government, and by rank secessionists. At least some of the Southern owners seemed eager to haul U.S. government freight if they could regain control of their property quickly enough to take advantage of the opportunity.[76]

Overall, the railroads performed an enormously important service for the Union cause. A total of 75 Northern railroad companies hauled men and material for the army by February 1862, with more to be used as the war progressed. A high proportion of that business was through shipment from one line to another; before the war, local freight and passenger traffic had dominated the business of small railroad companies. Now they had to work out effective systems of linking with other companies, and this helped to set the background for true railroad consolidation after Appomattox.[77]

"The federal government received excellent rail service from the northern railroads," as historian John E. Clark has put it. The companies also benefited enormously from that relationship. They agreed on a reasonable standard rate that helped both sides. The authority to seize roads certainly acted as something of an incentive for companies to do their best in an effort to avoid that unwanted action, but there is plenty of evidence that the majority of railroad executives would have worked hard to meet government needs anyway. Through a misunderstanding, Amasa Stone Jr. of the Cleveland, Painesville, and Ashtabula Railroad in Ohio felt a bit insulted when he thought Stanton snubbed him while trying to recruit his services to round up more rolling stock for the Union army in the fall of 1863. After Stanton explained the misunderstanding, Stone assured the secretary of war that "I allow no personal feelings to prevent my assisting the Government in this its hour of peril when I can."[78]

One of many foundations of railroad success lay in Stanton's wise decision to rely on professional railroad men to manage the roads seized by the army. He also relied heavily on this same class of professionals to organize and superintend the massive transfers of troops the army needed. Stanton recognized that railroad management was a specialized task best left to those who had proven their ability at it in the civilian world.[79]

For their part, the professional railroad men found that working for the army was far different than running their companies in peacetime. Never before had they been forced to devise ways to move so much material and personnel so quickly and so far. It was a real challenge to their professional development. As W. W. Wright told McCallum, his wartime experience had been an adventure and an intellectual challenge. Mostly assigned to managing construction and reconstruction in the West, Wright had met all the challenges; "we have learned how to supply a large army by railroad," he wrote.[80]

"In no other country have railroads been brought to perform so important a part in the operations of war," Meigs accurately reported to Stanton after the conflict. He added that in no other country could so many skilled and dedicated railroad men be found to do it as well.[81]

Probably in no other area of Civil War studies can one see such a stunning contrast between North and South as in the use of railroads. While it is a story of robust logistical power harnessed effectively by the Federal government in the North, the story becomes one of frustrated hopes, inefficient management, and rapid deterioration of track and rolling stock in the Confederacy. Victory literally rode the rails in the North, but it was derailed in the South. In virtually every way imaginable, Southern railroad companies failed the cause, and the men in charge of managing the war effort in Richmond also failed to devise answers to a range of problems that came to immobilize Rebel resources. The Southern rail network could not adequately feed Confederate troops, transport them safely over long distances, or provide offensive mobility for Rebel armies. While Northern railroads prospered during the war, Southern railroads decayed and collapsed. Shortages of repair facilities, funds, and sources of new rolling stock, a lack of a vibrant managerial spirit, and a governmental refusal to seize and operate privately owned railroad companies frustrated Confederate hopes of independence even more than did battlefield defeats.

In January 1862, the very month that the U.S. Congress granted the Federal army authority to seize railroads, a committee of the Confederate Congress recommended that the Richmond government assume similar power. Committee members were worried about the effect on logistical power inherent in the fact that most of the small rail lines in the South were not well connected to each other, impeding through traffic of supplies and troops, and that many companies had too few engines and cars to serve as effective links in a national chain of supply. If the government would seize the principle railroads that linked major transportation hubs, it could set up a truly national system capable of running at least two trains and as many as six along the entire system every day.[82]

The idea of government seizure was not well received in the Confederacy. Given their cultural background of local control, most Rebel leaders were shy about a step that tended toward greater central authority. When Adjutant General Samuel Cooper explained to Braxton Bragg why it was impolitic to seize the Alabama and Mississippi Railroad in order to complete its line for military purposes, he stated that such a move would not only be illegal but enormously expensive. More importantly, it would "irritate the people, and leave open a question between the Government and the company concerning transportation." In short, Cooper saw no end to such a policy until the government seized all rail companies. While Northerners had no difficulty with this "open question," Southerners did, and thus no true government seizure of railroads took place in the Confederacy.[83]

A year later, when Bragg managed to get the Western and Atlantic Railroad to increase supply shipments to his army, Jefferson Davis was happy that it was not necessary to seize the state-owned line. "Any conflict between Confederate and State authority is much to be regretted, and should always be avoided if possible." Davis tried to accommodate railroad companies so as to avoid the need for government seizure. He worked out agreements on standard rates, now and then allowed quartermaster officers to pressure companies into setting aside their lucrative trade in private freight and haul government stores exclusively for a couple of weeks to relieve backlogs, and urged all authorities to bend over backward so as not to antagonize railroad executives. "Efforts have been made to prevent any unnecessary interference with the control of the roads by their respective companies," he assured Virginia governor John Letcher.[84]

That the Confederacy needed more than a laissez-faire attitude toward such a fundamental need as logistical support for its war effort was apparent to some officials in Richmond. Commissary General Lucius B. Northrop early on was convinced that the railroads would fail the country. Given the refusal to seize roads, Northrop advocated that the War Department compel companies to ship only government supplies most of the time, allowing only limited periods for the shipment of private freight. While this was done now and then, it was far too seldom and the periods of sanction were too short to take care of the persistent food shortages suffered by all Confederate troops. Northrop also proposed a plan to help railroad companies maintain their tracks and rolling stock, but it was never implemented.[85]

The Richmond government's policy was merely to appoint a railroad supervisor who had little more power than to negotiate with companies and when necessary arrange for voluntary cooperation in sudden troop transfers across the Confederacy. Three men filled this role. First there was William Sheppard Ashe, former president of the Wilmington and Weldon Railroad, who worked within the Quartermaster Department. He was little more than an inspector with no real authority to compel the companies to do anything. Ashe was replaced in December 1862 by William M. Wadley, president of the unfinished Vicksburg and Shreveport Railroad. Wadley worked for the secretary of war rather than the quartermaster general. Frustrated at his lack of authority, Wadley recommended government seizure as the only solution to the growing railroad problem. Ironically, Congress passed a bill allowing for government seizure in late April 1863, but it also failed to confirm Wadley's appointment, so the disgruntled railroad man left his position in May. Frederick W. Sims, Wadley's assistant, took over his job for the remainder of the war. But because Jefferson Davis refused to implement the seizure law, Sims had no more opportunity to exercise control over the crumbling rail network than his predecessors.[86]

Davis placed most of his hope for rail success on a series of conferences held between his officials and the major railroad companies of the South. These conferences usually devolved into discussion concerning the freight and passenger rates the government was willing to pay private rail lines. Initially, in a meeting held at Montgomery, the authorities offered only about half the regular civilian rates for both freight and people, and the companies agreed to these severely reduced fares out of a sense of patriotism. But they honestly could not hope to continue with such a reduction. At a meeting in Chattanooga held in October 1861, the companies negotiated a raise in rates for freight and passengers moving more than 100 miles—essentially through traffic. While some companies did not honor this agreement, most did, but with time it became unsupportable. At Columbia, South Carolina, in September 1862, new rates were set that cost the government only marginally more money to ship most items.[87]

Wadley called the largest of these railroad conferences to be held at Augusta, Georgia, in December 1862. There he proposed the creation of a truly national system of rail communication with a general car pool to alleviate shortages of rolling stock on some lines, and a comprehensive through schedule effectively linking all lines involved in the major trunk routes across the Confederacy. These proposals would have been a giant stride toward rail efficiency, but the

41 companies represented at Augusta rejected them. Instead, they wanted to talk only about raising the standard rates allowed by the government, which led to an increase in passenger fares.[88]

The frustration Wadley felt at the failure of his grand plan probably contributed to a greater willingness on the part of Congress to act. Secretary of War James L. Seddon called another railroad conference to be held in Richmond in late April 1863, just as Congress was debating the seizure act. Here Wadley laid out for the companies a blizzard of statistics that proved one point: the railroads of the South were approaching a crisis. He estimated a deterioration rate of 25 percent in the rolling stock of all Southern companies with little prospect of finding new engines and cars to replace those wearing out. Wadley also estimated the companies needed more than 49,000 tons of rails every year but that the Confederacy could produce no more than 20,000 tons combined at only two major plants capable of making them. Of course, the railroad companies were fully aware of their own needs and shortages in this way, but Wadley's view was a national perspective and it was oriented on how these companies could support the war effort. Nevertheless, the railroad conference at Richmond merely agreed to the creation of a Railroad Bureau in the Confederate government to coordinate relations between the state and the private sphere.[89]

Nothing really changed. The creation of the Railroad Bureau and the passage of a law allowing for government seizure did not encourage or intimidate the railroad companies. In the next conference, held at Macon, Georgia, in November 1863, again the primary topic of discussion was raising the standard rate, and Sims agreed to do so. The government could not even remove rails from a line that was out of business and use them on a more strategically located line unless it received permission from the company. In the last railroad conference, held at Columbia, South Carolina, in April 1864, again the discussion mainly revolved around the need to raise shipping rates.[90]

There is no doubt that the railroad companies shrewdly understood the power equation in their relationship with the Confederate government. They knew that Davis was so averse to seizure that they could play their hand pretty freely, retaining their share of government business while also deriving as much income from private business as possible. Having started at a very low rate for government work in 1861, the Richmond authorities inadvertently encouraged the companies to focus almost exclusively on raising it in careful increments instead of thinking in terms of larger issues. Stanton's policy of offering a reasonable standard rate from the beginning was far more successful in securing the loyalty of Northern companies.

The Southern railroad companies had a tendency to be lax in their support of army needs. When William J. Hardee temporarily led the Army of Tennessee after the battle of Chattanooga, he complained that the Western and Atlantic Railroad was so unreliable that he seriously worried whether he could feed the troops and animals in his command. Hardee sent one of his generals to talk to company officials face to face, and that visit produced some hopeful results.[91]

If Southern companies found it increasingly difficult to meet government needs as the war progressed, imagine the difficulty encountered when the question of actually expanding the rail network cropped up. As early as January 1862, Congress recommended that many unfinished lines be completed and new tracks laid into agriculturally productive regions of the Confederacy to enhance the ability of commissaries to find food. The latter suggestion proved to be a fantasy; even completing unfinished lines tended to be almost too difficult.[92]

Bragg desperately wanted to complete the 100-mile rail link between Selma, Alabama, and Meridian, Mississippi, as early as June 1862. He worried because there was only one west-east line available to Confederate forces at that time, a roundabout journey south to Mobile and then northeast toward Atlanta. If Mobile fell, there would be no west-east link at all, but completion of this line between Selma and Meridian would provide one. The issue was especially important because Bragg contemplated taking his Army of the Mississippi to Chattanooga. Congress appropriated $150,000 to the Alabama and Mississippi Railroad for the project, but nothing was done and Bragg was ready to seize the company. Higher authorities prevented that and worked out a modus operandi to get the job done. They convinced Samuel Tate, president of the Memphis and Charleston Railroad, to take charge of the project and cooperate with army engineers, who were to supervise the work. Tate's primary role was to work with officials of the Alabama and Mississippi Railroad, which had the legal right to disperse the government money. Tate could use it to hire laborers and purchase material. In this way the government managed to use an incompetently run company, put an effective executive in charge of the project, and complete the link between Selma and Meridian by December 1862, long after Bragg had any use for it.[93]

It took much longer for the government to close another important railroad gap, this one supporting Robert E. Lee's Army of Northern Virginia. A link between the Richmond and Danville Railroad and the system of lines in North Carolina was needed, and a 48-mile track between Danville, Virginia, and Greensboro North Carolina, would provide it. The new line was called the Piedmont Railroad, and Congress appropriated $1 million for the job in February 1862. But Davis hesitated a great deal before spending the money. He wanted to hear all competing views and get the opinion of his engineer officers. When he finally made a decision and work started, the line was not completed until May 20, 1864. "No case better illustrates the weakness of policy, the lack of organization in co-ordinating transportation and the general incapacity of the Confederate government to cope with its railroad problems," concludes George Edgar Turner.[94]

Even after construction, the Piedmont Railroad proved to be less than reliable. Its charter had called for a narrow gauge, which impeded through traffic. All freight and troops had to be unloaded and reloaded at both Danville and Greensboro. By January 1865 circumstances forced quartermasters to rely ever more heavily on this line to supply Lee's troops. Seddon pleaded with North Carolina governor Zebulon Vance to get the legislature to amend the charter so the gauge could be widened to five feet. This expensive project was beyond expectation at this stage of the war and never took place. Instead the government acted; while some historians refer to it as seizure, it was just another example of quartermasters compelling the line to ship only government freight for a while. Rainstorms washed out sections of track at the same time, frustrating quartermasters even more because the line closed for 10 days of repairs.[95]

While railroad companies were obdurate when it came to setting rates and often inefficient when it came to managing their lines, there were many problems they could not overcome. Most railroad mechanics in the South were Northerners, but they fled the Confederacy upon secession. Also, there were few plants in the new nation capable of producing significant numbers of locomotives, cars, and rails. Increased traffic quickly wore out the available rolling stock. Added to expected wear and tear were occasional instances of deliberate vandalism by Confederate soldiers. The president of the Mississippi Central Railroad complained to John C. Pemberton that his officers did not even try to control their men when his company shipped them from Grenada to Canton, Mississippi, in late January 1863, and they wrecked more than one car. Conditions on the rail lines feeding Richmond had become so bad that not even 500 tons a day could be counted on to roll in by March 1865.[96]

Passengers on Southern trains late in the war recalled pitiful sights. In the spring of 1865, Williamson S. Oldham, a senator from Texas, rode on a train through Alabama that consisted of only two platform cars and a decidedly weak locomotive. Five months earlier, Oldham had traveled on a train consisting of two boxcars and one platform car in Louisiana. The box car closest to the engine was carrying 10,000 pounds of powder and many of its boards had been knocked off. Sparks from the locomotive "flew all over around and through the car," and Oldham was lucky they did not set off the powder en route.[97]

J. W. Mallet of the Ordnance Bureau summed up the situation when he wrote that virtually all sidings that were of marginal use had been taken up to provide rails for more important purposes. Smaller lines had been nearly depleted of their rolling stock and rails to supply greater companies. Parts of defunct engines were cannibalized to repair better locomotives and "cars had been mended until they would hardly hold together." Mallet believed that the rail system alone would have forced Confederate armies to surrender within a few months if the war had not ended when it did in the spring of 1865.[98]

Confederate authorities were well aware of this major problem from the beginning of the war. William Ashe warned people of "a most alarming deficiency both in Rails and in Rolling Stock" in December 1861. G. B. Fleece, the superintendent of the Memphis, Clarksville, and Louisville Railroad, faced a huge demand from the Confederate army for transportation into and out of Bowling Green early in January 1862. It amounted to 800,000 pounds of material from Paris, Tennessee, 1 million pounds from Clarksville, and 1.5 million pounds from Nashville, all scheduled to descend on the small town that constituted Albert Sidney Johnston's center of operations. Yet Fleece could muster so little in the way of rolling stock that he could guarantee only one train of about a dozen cars per day between those points. Even if one car could be stuffed with 10 tons of material, one train could carry no more than 240,000 pounds of freight. That amounted to less than one-third of the material needed from Paris; less than one-fourth of the supplies needed from Clarksville; and less than one-sixth of the material needed from Nashville. Fleece also had to deal with a heavy demand for passenger traffic along all three lines.[99]

Fleece despaired of accomplishing more without additional rolling stock taken by the government from other lines. His own company encompassed a total of 225 miles of track, and the normal operating stock for it amounted to 22 engines and 300 cars. By January 1862, however, he had only 10 locomotives,

6 of which were "of limited or ordinary capacity," and 175 cars. In short, within nine months of the onset of war, the Memphis, Clarksville, and Louisville Railroad had witnessed a 55 percent reduction in its locomotive power and a 42 percent reduction in its carrying capacity. "In a word," as Fleece put it, "the entire road is crowded with business to an extent unprecedented in the history of any branch of it."[100]

The East Tennessee and Georgia Railroad, which linked Knoxville with Dalton, experienced increasing pressure to find more rolling stock as the war progressed. President C. Wallace needed at least two more engines and 50 cars by the fall of 1862. He had already purchased several at very high prices and now could find no more. If the government was willing to compel some lines that did little war business to sell their rolling stock, Wallace was willing to pay any price for the hardware.[101]

Many railroad companies lost engines and cars because strategically placed lines needed more rolling stock. The Georgia Railroad, which linked Augusta with Atlanta, started the war with 729 cars but lost half of them by December 1862. The Macon and Western Railroad, which ran from Macon to Atlanta, lost 29 of its 170 cars by that time. With a growing shortage of laborers to cut wood, fuel costs also escalated. The Georgia Central Railroad spent almost twice as much for fuel by 1863 as it had spent three years before.[102]

Brigade commander Daniel H. Reynolds penned an understatement in his diary when he noted that the line linking Vicksburg with Jackson, Mississippi, was "sadly out of repair" in January 1863. Conditions only grew worse as the war dragged out its weary course. When W. W. Wright superintended the restoration of Southern lines in North Carolina to support Sherman's massive sweep through that region in March 1865, he collected all the Southern rolling stock he could find and tried to put it to use. It gave him "a good opportunity to judge of the condition of the rolling-stock in the 'Confederacy.' It was nearly worn out." In listing 16 locomotives, Wright noted that most of them were in need of repair and some were "worthless."[103]

"Everywhere in the Confederacy the railroads grew worse and worse," concluded Philip Daingerfield Stephenson of the 5th Company, Washington Artillery. "Rolling stock and tracks became more and more useless and dangerous." Train speeds slowed nearly to a crawl and accident rates increased. The 80-mile journey between Montgomery, Alabama, and Columbus, Georgia, normally took a morning before the war, but an entire day was consumed in moving from one point to the other by 1865. Many trains could average no more than 10 miles per hour, about half the typical prewar speed. Moreover, freight and passenger rates soared with inflation and heavy demand. Citizens and the government alike were paying more, moving slower, and facing real uncertainty as to whether they or their property would arrive at the destination in one piece.[104]

Making the shortage of rolling stock even worse, some Confederate generals had a tendency to destroy Southern engines and cars in an effort to prevent them from falling into enemy hands. None were more inclined to panic in this way than Joseph E. Johnston, who destroyed 42 engines and 386 cars at Martinsburg, Virginia, in June 1861. He abandoned many locomotives and cars along various lines in north central Mississippi upon evacuating Jackson without a fight in mid-July 1863, most of which had to be destroyed to keep the Yankees from taking them. Even though Johnston had briefly served as Quartermaster General of the U.S. Army just before the war and had demonstrated the utility of using railroads to shift troops quickly to decisive points during the First Manassas campaign, he ultimately failed to appreciate the need to husband rail resources and utilize them effectively. "He destroyed more public property than the enemy he was eternally flying from ever did," sarcastically concluded one of his critics after the war.[105]

Even if they had adequate rolling stock, Southern railroad companies inevitably grew to dislike doing business with the government. This was largely the fault of the government for not offering what John Clark calls "responsible fares." The companies had to compensate for this by doing all the private business possible, to the detriment of military needs. Eventually the government agreed to a passenger rate that was close to what Stanton offered Northern railroad companies, but inflation was far higher in the Confederacy than in the Union, and the ability of the Richmond government to pay its debts plummeted to the point of absurdity. No wonder companies saw the government as a bad risk and preferred private freight and passengers.[106]

The ability of Confederate quartermasters and commissaries to find food and ship it declined sharply over time. Actually, even though the Confederacy was shrinking because of Federal conquest, for the most part it grew enough food to more or less supply its armies, but the ability to transport the food where needed deteriorated alarmingly. Fodder for animals was a particular problem because of its bulk, and all Rebel armies suffered periodic shortages of feed for their horses and mules. "The whole of the middle and southern

Georgia is full of fodder," complained Captain John B. Rowan while his unit was quartered in the northwestern part of the state. "I have seen with my own eyes hundreds and thousands of bales of good fodder actually rotting for want of attention." Making the situation worse, when food was shipped it often was lost due to careless handling or wretched cars. Division commander William W. Loring complained of large losses along the railroad line from Grenada to Canton, Mississippi, in December 1863. Every train hauling corn lost from 50 to 150 bushels along the way. Much of it was loaded onto flat cars exposed to weather, and 6,000 pounds of hard bread were "destroyed" along the route with no explanation as to what happened to it.[107]

Stories of mismanagement, deteriorating equipment, and lack of economic incentive reflect the general trend in the history of Confederate railroads, but one should keep in mind that Southern rail executives could at times rise to the occasion. It was a bit easier to do that earlier in the war rather than later. When the Confederate army evacuated Memphis early in June 1862, much material had to be shifted quickly. From his headquarters Daniel Ruggles coordinated the work of staff officers and railroad executives in accomplishing the task. They found idle engines and cars and encouraged rail managers to work in an emergency mode. President W. Goodman of the Memphis and Charleston Railroad acted in the spirit that animated Northern railroad executives when Stanton called on them for help. "All freights & soldiers can be moved in due time if there is no interference with our trains & we are informed what is necessary," he assured Ruggles.[108]

If the evacuation of Memphis had been reflective of the norm in Confederate railroads, Rebel armies would have been far better supported by the civilian transportation system of the South. But this level of cooperation and efficiency declined steadily with time, and with that decline came many inconveniences for government personnel. For some Confederate troops, riding the rails was a novel and interesting experience. They rarely rode in passenger cars but more often in ordinary boxcars, too crowded for all to lie down at one time. Naturally many of them preferred to ride on the top of the cars to get fresh air and observe the scenery. Even in 1861 the crowded conditions on troop trains produced a good deal of filth in the cars. There always was the danger of accidents that took lives and left survivors mangled for life. Philip Daingerfield Stephenson saw or was involved in at least four railroad accidents during his time in the army, amounting to one every year.[109]

Confederate officers traveling as ordinary passengers on detached assignment or on leave of absence experienced the crowded uncertainties of civilian
passengers on the railroads. G.W.F. Harper of the 58th North Carolina received
a leave for 18 days and spent a good part of it simply traveling to his home
from Dalton, Georgia. He left on December 31, 1863, at 8 P.M. and traveled all
night in a car with wooden benches for seats but without a stove. "A cold and
miserable nights ride," he admitted to his diary. Harper arrived at Atlanta too
late to make his connection to Augusta and waited several hours to board what
proved to be "another slow train but a comfortable car hopelessly behind time
again." Along the way floods prevented the train from proceeding, so all passengers had to walk half a mile to the next station to catch a different train. When
he missed another connection to Charlotte, North Carolina, three days after
starting out, Harper confessed to his diary, "Stock of patience becoming much
depleted, very much depleted." The next day his train to Charlotte was delayed
again by another train that had slipped off the track. On January 5 he had no
opportunity to travel because of a landslide that covered part of the roadbed.
The next day a train took passengers to the slide, where they got off and walked
around the obstruction for six miles. But the train they boarded on the other
side of the landslide stopped for an hour because it ran out of wood. When fuel
was finally found, the train made comparatively good time—60 miles in a little
more than 10 hours. Harper reached Hickory Tavern at 5:45 P.M. on January 6.
Then he walked 19 miles to his home near Lenoir, North Carolina. It had taken
him 6 days (144 hours) to travel 572 miles by rail, at an average travel time of
3.97 miles per hour.[110]

Bradford Nichol, an officer in the Ordnance Department of the Army of
Tennessee, barely survived a harrowing journey from Murfreesboro to Chattanooga during the Stones River campaign. The train carried captured Federal
artillery as well as Rebel ordnance stores. It was a wretched conveyance; every
brake gave out upon descending the steep grade heading toward Stevenson,
Alabama, and the train whizzed along at what Nichol thought was 90 miles
per hour. Worse than this, one of the captured Union guns was still loaded. A
spark from the locomotive touched it off and the piece fired, knocking off the
top of the car just behind it. Somehow the engineer managed to stop the train
and all reached Bridgeport safely. "What an escape!" Nichol commented in his
journal. "Worse than Murfreesboro Battle."[111]

Nichol's experience indicates the worst-case scenario about the conditions of rail travel in the Confederacy; it cannot be taken as typical. But the typical experience was bad enough, especially when compared to the relative efficiency of rail transport in the North. All observers and historians agree that the Confederate government failed to utilize its rail resources effectively and that the Southern railroad companies did not fully cooperate with the Richmond authorities. Neither can be exclusively blamed for the failure.[112]

Richmond probably deserves a greater share of blame for the failure of rail transport in the Confederacy. It had the power to seize lines but refused to do so. Excessive concern for private property and states' rights lay at the heart of this reluctance to exercise power. As historian Robert C. Black has put it, "the nature of southern society" rendered the Confederacy "incapable of either cohesion or the management of large enterprise." But George Edgar Turner has made the compelling point that, even if Davis had allowed true seizure of Southern railroads, it is quite likely Confederate officials would not have operated them any more efficiently than private corporations. "Evidence is abundant that from temperament, disposition and capacity the Confederate government was entirely unfitted for the job." The failure of Southern railroads was at heart a failure by Richmond to meet the many and deep managerial challenges posed by the war.[113]

In the North, Lincoln's government had the spirit, intellect, philosophy, and courage to meet its own numerous challenges in prosecuting a long and bitter war. As Robert C. Black put it, Lincoln controlled "a powerful government that understood its own potentialities and was comparatively unafraid to use them." The war left Northern railroads much stronger and wealthier than before while it shattered the Southern railroad system into pieces. While meeting the huge increase in passenger and freight hauling during the war, Northern railroad companies also laid nearly 4,500 miles of new track during the years 1861–1865. The war experience helped Northern companies learn how to cooperate more effectively with each other because it spurred the creation of a truly national line of transportation for one customer. This helped lay the foundation for railroad consolidation by the 1880s, initiating a golden age in railroad history soon after Appomattox.[114]

5

~~~~~

THE COASTAL SHIPPING SYSTEM

Coastal shipping fulfilled an important role in Union logistics. With control of the sea and an ever tightening naval blockade of Confederate ports, the Federal government pressured the perimeter of Rebel territory by landing troops at key locations along the coast. From these enclaves Union forces threatened Confederate railroads, shut down blockade-running ports, and compelled the enemy to detach troops to occupation duties that could have been used in more important theaters.

Federal troops in these isolated pockets needed supplies, and the only way to fill that need was by utilizing merchant vessels capable of sea coast navigation. The largest and most important enclave surrounded the major commercial city of New Orleans; thus, navigating the long coastal route from New York to the mouth of the Mississippi River constituted most of the coastal shipping work during the war. Forces around New Orleans expanded into the surrounding countryside and eventually moved north up the river to besiege and capture Port Hudson. Troops from the New Orleans area also attempted a drive northwestward through Louisiana, established footholds along the coast of Texas, tried to capture Shreveport in the ill-fated Red River campaign, and mounted a major effort to take Mobile at the end of the war. In addition, largely cut off from its normal source of food in the interior, the civilian population of New Orleans relied on the U.S. Army for much of its subsistence. All of this could not have been possible but for the slim line of ships linking New Orleans with major cities in the Northeast.

Coastal shipping is the least visible of the three Union logistical networks, and as a result its importance has been slighted in the historical literature. For that matter, even maritime historians have paid little attention to what Robert Greenhalgh Albion calls "coastwise shipping." U.S. customs officials did not keep records of coastal trade as they did for international shipping, thus denying maritime historians a ready source of information about the trade.[1]

But enough information exists to patch together a picture of pre–Civil War commercial shipping along the Atlantic and Gulf coasts. The first regular packet making the run between New Orleans and New York began operating in the early 1820s just as the western river steamers began to rise and railroading was still in its infancy. Coastal vessels grew in size and speed with the passage of time, helped by the introduction of steam power. By 1847, 109 steamers navigated the coastal waters, compared to 2,872 sailing vessels. Steam-powered ships could make the run from Charleston, South Carolina, to New York in 55 to 60 hours. They carried not only passengers but freight as well, although steamers working the route from New Orleans to New York carried only light freight, leaving the heavy material to be hauled by sailing vessels. Cotton came to be a major element in the freight carried by packets of both steam and sail as cotton agriculture bloomed in the 1830s.[2]

Coastal shipping occupied a separate niche of the market compared to trans-Atlantic shipping, but comparison between the two trades is instructive. Coastal vessels were smaller than transoceanic ships. The craft linking New York with Liverpool, England, for example, averaged 600 tons, while coastal vessels ranged from 167 tons to 500 tons. By 1833 the number of coastal vessels making regularly scheduled runs was nearly equal to the number of transoceanic packet vessels (36 compared to 38). By 1855, however, the number of ocean packets nearly doubled that of coastal packets. The coastal ships in general were not only smaller than ocean vessels, but cheaper to build and maintain. That is why there were many more single-ship owners and smaller companies in the coastal shipping trade than in the cross-Atlantic business. A good coastal vessel could offer 20 years of service to its owner, much longer than the expected life of the western river steamer.[3]

Passengers could take advantage of regular voyages along the Atlantic and Gulf coasts by the 1850s. It took about 18 days to travel from New Orleans to New York and cost $40 for cabin accommodations, compared to only $25 for steerage. A steamer made the run between Boston and Charleston every 10 days, with cabin rates of $18. The New York to Charleston passenger fare ran $15 for cabin and $7 for steerage. It was possible by the time of the Civil War for a businessman to make regular trips between these far-flung coastal cities with a reasonable expectation that the ship would keep to its schedule.[4]

5.1. Steamer *Fort Jackson* at Hampton Roads, Virginia, December 1864. A typical coastal steamer with two masts for use in case of mechanical breakdown, the *Fort Jackson* had side-wheel propulsion. Hundreds of craft like this supported Federal logistical efforts along the Atlantic and Gulf coasts. (Library of Congress, LC-DIG-cwpb-03830)

This was the coastal shipping trade that Union quartermasters found when the Civil War began. There always was the danger that not only civilian passengers but military personnel would take the availability of coastal travel for granted, but that would have been a mistake. Coastwise navigation often was strained by the unique difficulties associated with sea travel even along the comparatively shallow waters fringing the North American coast. Nearly every voyage from New York, Washington, D.C., or Fortress Monroe to New Orleans was buffeted by sudden storms or gales, especially near the Outer Banks of North Carolina. Ships often grounded on shoals near Florida. The long journey also strained overworked engines, causing breakdowns at the most inconvenient times. Conditions on these vessels, most of which were never designed to haul hundreds of men or horses, often were uncomfortable and even downright unhealthy. It was, after all, an improvised system of military logistics, but the quartermasters, ship owners, captains, and crew members managed to serve the Federal government well considering all the problems associated with the effort.

For obvious reasons, the Confederates were unable to utilize coastal ship-ping to any considerable degree. They had scant need of it, for they were able to use interior rail lines to communicate between one coastal port and another. There is only slim evidence that the Confederates used coastal ships at all; the immediate presence of Union blockading vessels made any significant employ-ment impossible.

But the Federal use of civilian vessels of all kinds was enormous. During the last fiscal year of the war (July 1, 1864, to June 30, 1865), the Quartermaster De-partment used a total of 719 craft. It owned and chartered them, amounting to 224,984 tons. Of that number, 351 were steam-powered coastal trading vessels. Eighty-nine sail vessels complemented the steamers, and 111 tugs operated in various harbors. The department also used 168 barges.[5]

For much of the war these ships had been purchased and chartered by various quartermaster officers with little in the way of central supervision from above. But with the reorganization of the Quartermaster Department in July 1864, Meigs saw the utility of appointing a reliable officer to manage coastal shipping, as he had done for river and rail transport. Colonel George D. Wise took control of the 3rd Division of the Department, which included inland lakes, in December 1864. He soon found that quartermaster needs on the Great Lakes (the principle inland waterways under his jurisdiction) were minuscule in comparison to coastal shipping. In fact, Wise reported using only one small steamer on the Great Lakes. It made regular runs between the mainland and the large Confederate prison camp located on Johnson's Island in Lake Erie.[6]

The process of chartering coastal ships produced problems similar to those seen in the chartering of river steamers. In May 1861, Secretary of War Simon Cameron appointed John Tucker, a former railroad president, as "general agent of transportation for the War Department." Tucker had no experience in work-ing with coastal vessels and came to rely on brokers rather than advertising to secure them for army needs. As a result, there was enormous over-charging by owners and brokers. Bad ships found their way into government service at exorbitant rates.[7]

Only after Tucker quit his job in January 1863 was Meigs able to gain con-trol over the process of procuring coastal shipping. He established a scale of prices for various types of vessels and instituted an examination to see if false information concerning the size and condition of the vessels was submitted in the chartering process. Meigs also used navy officers to inspect and appraise vessels and required all accounts to be sent to his office in Washington for examination. He further insisted on a clause inserted into every charter giving the government an option to purchase the vessel "provided that should prove advantageous." Meigs created an effective system of coastal shipping and gave it to Wise in December 1864. The latter officer merely had to keep it working as established during the last few months of the conflict.[8]

Because of Meigs's insistence on the purchase option, the government became the owner of many vessels by the end of the war. "All charters were made allowing the department to take possession of the vessel by paying 33 per cent. profit on the valuation, and the running expenses and repairs, and be credited with the amount paid for charter," reported Wise. Naval officers were assigned the task of fixing the valuation. The "higher the rate of charter," Wise noted, "the sooner the vessel would pay for itself." Apparently ship owners were happy with this arrangement; they tended to view their vessels as economic investments, and these terms allowed them a profit on each ship.[9]

The department had a wider variety of vessels to choose from in the coastal trade than on the western rivers. It preferred to move troops by steamers if at all possible, given their faster rate of travel, and to haul bulky material such as hay and coal by sailing vessels. Barges of all types were widely used as well. They included open hull craft, others with flat decks, and others with housings over the decks. Canal boats were brought into requisition. Barges of all kinds served as temporary docks or warehoused material for indefinite periods of time.[10]

Just as there were many periods when the army demanded large numbers of steamers on the western rivers, quartermasters responded to urgent calls for coastal vessels to perform particular tasks. When McClellan shifted the Army of the Potomac from northern Virginia to the Yorktown Peninsula, officers quickly gathered dozens of vessels by offering short-term charters at high rates because of the huge demand and the need for quick response. Everyone assumed the term of service would be short, but then McClellan advanced up the Peninsula at a snail's pace, prolonging the need indefinitely. The government was stuck with the high charter rates. This episode was a major incentive for Meigs to insert the purchase option clause in charters later in the war.[11]

Soon after the campaign ended, quartermasters began the process of unloading and discharging as many vessels as possible. A total of 339 ships of all types had been used to supply the Army of the Potomac during the campaign because McClellan had never been able to establish an overland supply line

5.2. White House Landing on the Pamunkey River, Virginia, 1864. There are several canal boats in the foreground, serving as large and stable storage facilities and sleeping quarters for personnel at the landing. Steamers are coming and going into this crowded and busy field port that supported Union military operations for a short while during the Overland campaign. (Library of Congress, LC-DIG-ppmsca-33261)

with Washington, D.C., by railroad; everything had to be shipped by coastal vessels. Of that number, 143 (42.2 percent) were sailing vessels of various sizes and types, 63 (18.5 percent) were paddle wheel steamers, 92 (27.2 percent) were propeller-driven steamers, and 41 (12.1 percent) were barges and canal boats. Officers managed to discharge 122 of those vessels, but only after unloading their cargoes. Nine out of ten of these ships were still loaded with subsistence stores because quartermasters had decided to use them not only as transports but as floating warehouses.[12]

Soon after this was done the army made more demands for coastal shipping in mid-July 1862. Ambrose Burnside's command moved from the coast of North Carolina to reinforce the Army of the Potomac and McClellan shifted his own troops by boat to Washington, D.C. Meigs rounded up all the vessels he could find at Baltimore and Philadelphia, dispatching 200 sailing ships from New York alone. "You now have all the steamboats of the coast which can be procured without breaking up the great ferries and routes by which our new

5.3. The Wharf at Alexandria, Virginia. Andrew J. Russell exposed this view from atop the six-story Pioneer Mill in May 1865. It provides an expansive view of the town, its wharf area, and the broad Potomac River. The foreground also provides a detailed view of the docking facilities, a canal boat (far right), and several sailing vessels and steamers. (Library of Congress, LC-DIG-ppmsca-08240)

levies are to be brought to the seat of war," he told Rufus Ingalls, "excepting the few employed in supplying the Southern posts." In order to do this Meigs had ordered his quartermaster in New York to find transports "capable of ascending the James, the York, and the Potomac Rivers. Schooners, brigs, and ships going out in ballast to load with troops, artillery, wagons, and horses." He wanted them "chartered by the day for not less than ten days and as much longer as the Government needs them." He told his quartermaster in Philadelphia to send "all the roomy schooners he can get" to Fortress Monroe.[13]

Two years later Grant's preparation for the spring offensive of 1864 created another scurry of activity. Meigs told Wise at Baltimore to collect light draft steamers for Fortress Monroe plus 50 schooners and 40 barges to transport the Tenth and Eighteenth Corps to southeast Virginia. Wise tried to find vessels in Baltimore and Philadelphia. "We have a larger number of steamers within reach of Washington," Meigs reported, "which will be made available, and all that are now in service between Philadelphia, New York, and Fort Monroe should be assembled in the Potomac as soon as possible."[14]

Wise quickly secured 17 side-wheel steamers, 11 propeller steamers, and 8 steam tugs to push 50 canal barges. The side-wheelers had capacities that ranged from 350 to 1,500 men apiece, while the propeller-driven steamers could handle from 200 to 400 men each. The canal barges were capable of transporting 150 men apiece but, of course, could not be used except in very shallow water.[15]

Immediate and pressing needs such as those experienced when the Army of the Potomac was on the Peninsula or preparing for the Overland campaign demanded so much shipping that normal logistical needs were strained. Any time army commanders kept vessels beyond their immediate need for them it caused problems elsewhere in the far-flung coastal shipping system. Rufus Ingalls told Meigs that he needed the return of most of the vessels used to transport the Nineteenth Corps from New Orleans to Washington, D.C., in July 1864 to meet the supply needs of Grant's armies at Petersburg and Richmond. In the small Department of the South, which by the summer of 1864 was a backwater of activity, quartermasters had purchased or chartered 28 steamers, but only 6 of them were available for "outside work." That meant that 22 (78.5 percent) of the steamers were tied up in a variety of permanent duties in the department or were undergoing repairs. That was an extremely high rate of dedicated use not justified by the static nature of operations in the department.[16]

Part of the problem lay in misuse of available resources. Meigs was irritated that John G. Foster, commander of the Department of the South, allowed a "powerful and excellent steamer" called the *Ben De Ford* to lie idle for months at a time under government charter with its "fires banked, burning out her boilers and doing nothing." Foster used it as his quarters during that time. It cost $500 per day, or $15,000 per month, plus the price of coal, to maintain him in this fashion. "She is too expensive and valuable for a yacht," Meigs sarcastically told Foster. "A much smaller and less costly steamer ought to serve" the general better. Herman Haupt agreed with Meigs's attitude. When offered a steamer for the comfort of his railroad workers he declined. His men did not need such luxury and Haupt suggested the boat be used to carry wounded soldiers or haul freight.[17]

When Sherman's 60,000 troops neared Savannah at the end of their March to the Sea, Meigs assembled a huge fleet of transports loaded with supplies for them. It "taxed the resources of the department to the utmost extent" reported Wise. In addition to Grant's large concentration of troops at Petersburg and Richmond and the large and small enclaves along the coast from Fortress Monroe to Texas, about 300,000 men depended on coastal shipping for their sustenance. In fact, quartermasters could not provide enough empty ships to transport Sherman's men to Petersburg. They estimated it would take at least two months to do so. Sherman argued that he could march the troops to Grant in six weeks, and he was allowed to try it. Although Sherman was overly optimistic in his estimate, the shortage of coastal shipping played a decisive role in shaping operations and led to the famous Carolinas campaign.[18]

Quartermaster officers often needed specialized craft to perform particular tasks. Ingalls wanted "North River barges" in March 1865, pleading a need for "such vessels very much." When ice choked the Potomac River in December 1862, Meigs tried to find a boat capable of breaking a channel to keep open traffic to Aquia Creek Landing. He found two boats at New York and Philadelphia that might have performed the duty but learned that the Philadelphia ice boat already was in service as a converted gunboat. Dispatch vessels needed to be small and swift. The *Sykes* navigated a regular run between New Orleans, Pensacola, and Ship Island in the fall of 1862. It could travel at 14 miles per hour and left New Orleans every Saturday and Wednesday at 4 P.M.[19]

Coastal vessels of all ages, capacities, and suitability for travel wound up in government service during the Civil War. Members of the 116th New York were surprised to learn that the vessel transporting them to Baton Rouge in February 1863 was an old China trader called the *Chee-ki-ang*. Sudden calms often stranded vessels that depended only on sail. Marianne Edwards accompanied her husband, the captain of a barque, when he made runs along the coast to and from New Orleans. On one such trip in early January 1863 the wind suddenly stopped, and so did the barque. It had to be taken in tow by a steamer to complete the voyage, demonstrating why quartermasters shied away from relying on sailing ships to transport men and animals.[20]

In fact, many steamers were past their prime and unsuited for army use. Captain Anson D. Fessenden of the 53rd Massachusetts gave the propeller ship *Continental* a discerning look after it departed New York for New Orleans in early 1863. It "is long and narrow standing high out of the water," he reported to his parents. "She is the greatest thing to roll I ever saw. At times the railing was under water."[21]

The *James S. Green* was even worse. A 300-ton propeller capable of holding only 200 men, the *Green* "was a frail craft, built for the Delaware & Chesapeake Canal Company, and never designed" for sea according to the historians of the 15th New Hampshire. The *Ella Knight* and *General Meigs* also were hardly capable of transporting troops along the coast. They "were only river craft and not considered very seaworthy," according to the historian of the 1st Connecticut Battery. The *General Meigs* "was an old canal boat" with a narrow and high superstructure that easily caught the wind and rolled dangerously. Both craft hugged the coastline as much as possible while transporting the battery to South Carolina.[22]

Cornelius Vanderbilt controlled one of the largest shipping companies of the day, but members of the 50th Massachusetts discovered that many of his vessels were of poor quality. Three companies boarded the *Jersey Blue* at New York for shipment to New Orleans in December 1862 but found it "a miserable old hulk, not fit for river navigation." It was "so narrow that the weight of one man causes her to list. A small rope running around the entire deck is the only safeguard against falling overboard." Vanderbilt came on board to inspect the craft, pronounced it safe, and the men set off only to hit stormy weather after a few days at sea. The craft put in at Port Royal and unloaded the troops, who boarded a sailing vessel called the *Guerrilla*. It was "a stout craft" that reportedly had been caught trying to smuggle slaves into the country before the war. *Guerrilla* safely transported the three companies to New Orleans.[23]

Five other companies of the 50th Massachusetts also boarded a Vanderbilt ship called the *Niagara* in New York. It was another "miserable and weather-beaten old river craft," and many members of the regiment who were seamen knew of its shoddy reputation. They warned that too many men were crammed on board and the officers protested enough so that Vanderbilt came to investigate. This time he agreed with the troops; one company debarked and found accommodation on a small sailing vessel called the *Jenny Lind*.[24]

Even seaworthy vessels often were not well suited for transporting soldiers. The *Premier* and *Tamerlane* were "both old-fashioned sailing ships built for the Merchant service," according to Colonel William C. Holbrook of the 7th Vermont. They "were ill-adapted and poorly arranged" to haul his regiment to Ship Island in early 1862. As a result, the men had a miserable voyage on these "not over savory" craft.[25]

But when Federals boarded a vessel well suited for troop transport they greatly appreciated it. The *Cambria* moved four companies of the 15th New Hampshire to New Orleans in December 1862. It was "a new iron ship" made in England and equipped with both steam power and sails, captured when trying to run the blockade. The *Illinois* was a large vessel of 4,500 tons capable of taking 1,500 men along the coast, including the 52nd Massachusetts. The *M. Sanford* left New York with 700 men of the 156th New York on board in December 1862. A side-wheel steamer, it was "pretty sea-worthy & rides the waves very well indeed," thought Captain Peter Eltinge. When the Twenty-Third Corps moved from Annapolis, Maryland, to the coast of North Carolina early in 1865, John M. Schofield joined nearly 2,000 of his men on board the *Atlantic*. It was "the crack ship of the Collins Line of New York and Liverpool packets," according to Jacob D. Cox. Meigs also chose one of the best coastal vessels available when he made his way to Savannah early in January 1865. He rode on a propeller steamer of 955 tons named *Nevada*.[26]

George Wise offered good advice to quartermasters concerning the type of ships suitable for transporting men and supplies along the coast. He warned them not to be deceived by craft designed for lake and river travel that had been "boxed up to resemble a sea vessel, but having broad guards only a few feet from the water." A side-wheel steamer had to be specifically designed for sea travel, and quartermasters needed to learn the details and be discerning in selecting proper craft.[27]

Wise was concerned in this recommendation with the safety of the vessel, but the nature of accommodation for both man and animal on these ships also was important. Most of them had not been designed to haul hundreds of troops or dozens of horses and mules. As one soldier who endured two coastal voyages put it, "the comfort of the men who have to do the fighting is of secondary consideration." Thirty years before, the British East India Company had established a formula for transporting troops by ocean or coastal shipping. It allowed 3.9 square feet of space per man, amounting to an area 10 inches wide and 4 feet, 8 inches long. Civil War quartermasters did not work out such statistics, preferring to fit the men to the vessel on an ad hoc basis. Sometimes it worked, and other times they misjudged rather badly.[28]

"It was *awfully* crowded," complained Monroe Joshua Miller of the steamer *Tarascon*, which hauled the 26th Indiana, the 117th Illinois, 230 horses and

mules, and 20 wagons to E.R.S. Canby's Mobile campaign in March 1865. Quartermasters packed the 25th and 26th Connecticut on the *Empire City* for transport to New Orleans in December 1862, one regiment in the hold and the other
on the open deck. The men got little sleep because they were "dove-tailed in"
while lying down. Simeon A. Evans was so irritated at the crowded conditions
endured by the 14th Maine that he told his mother the men were *"packed like
niggers on a slave ship."* Solomon Nelson of the 50th Massachusetts cursed "the
head who designed and contracted for the transport" of his regiment to New
Orleans from New York. He thought the vessel was capable of holding only
100 men, but 300 were shoved on board. Many of the troops had to lie in their
bunks during the entire journey because the deck was too small for everyone
at one time.[29]

When the 25th Connecticut started from New Orleans to return home after
its nine-month term of service in August 1863, the men found conditions aboard
the *Thomas Scott* almost unendurable. It was an "old filthy vessel" filled with
vermin. They put up with it for a week, until debarking at New York. The Connecticut men drank condensed sea water, as did many passengers aboard coastal
shipping during the Civil War. Even though the salt was evaporated and the water filtered, "it was very disagreeable, and sticky enough of itself to make the
men sick," reported a member of the 1st Connecticut Battery. On crowded vessels the potable water had to be rationed, allowing each man one pint per day.[30]

Sleeping arrangements varied from ship to ship. On many vessels it consisted merely of sacking out on the deck. On other craft the owners had in-
stalled bunks. The *James S. Green* sported planks arranged "like shelves in a
pantry" that were large enough for two men to lie side by side. On the *Jenny
Lind*, 50th Massachusetts soldiers lay four in a group on bunks so close together
no one could sit up. They inhaled air that was "reeking with the exhalation" of
500 men. The ship rolled so much that many fell out of their berths, and quite
a few bunks were broken down during the regiment's rough voyage to Louisiana. Even on a good ship such as the *Illinois* accommodations were crowded.
·The owners had arranged three tiers of bunks in the hold, with only 20 inches
of space between each tier. The 1,200 men on board were allowed on deck
only part of the time, and even then restricted to certain portions of the open
space. For nine days the men had to endure these conditions until reaching
Ship Island. When Jesse Macy of the 10th Iowa traveled on board the *Arago*
from Savannah northward early in 1865, he took one look at the overcrowded

conditions in the hold and preferred to sleep wedged between coils of rope on the deck. A severe rain compelled him to head for the hold until his nostrils caught a "whiff of the odors from deep down in the vessel." He turned and went back to his rope coils, letting the rain soak him to the skin.[31]

Soldiers widely complained about a problem no ship owner could address. Seasickness was a "loathsome detestable" illness, wrote Anson D. Fessenden of the 53rd Massachusetts. As Surgeon Simeon A. Evans of the 14th Maine put it, seasickness took away any bit of romance associated with ocean travel. An Iowa man on his way from Louisiana to Virginia in the summer of 1864 estimated that 1,500 of the 2,000 troops on board the *Arago* succumbed to seasickness. Those in the hold were harder hit than those who spent more time on the open deck.[32]

William H. Stevens of the 2nd Rhode Island Cavalry reported that he was not exactly seasick on the *Belle Wood*, but he felt terribly dizzy: "my head was continually swimming, and I could not walk across the cabin or the quarter deck straight for five days." The only men who enjoyed this unique experience were those not affected by it. John Watkins of the 19th Ohio Battery relished the sight of his comrades who struggled with the symptoms. "I could see them begin to get white around the gills," he told his friend, and they walked quietly in an effort to keep the feelings down. Then there "would be a rush for the gunwale and up she would come, some would get over it after that others it would make awful sick."[33]

Far worse than seasickness, a variety of contagious illnesses appeared on board ships during these coastal voyages. It could be measles, small pox, or "ship fever" breaking out among the crew or the military passengers. Ships headed for New Orleans had to pass the Quarantine Station many miles south of the city, where affected vessels were held apart from the rest and not allowed to proceed.[34]

Death in various ways claimed military passengers too. Soldiers who were only in the early stages of illness when they boarded sometimes died before reaching their destination. It was common to bury the body at sea, sewed up in a blanket with weights at the feet. The remains were placed on the end of a plank, which was extended over the water, and then let gently into the deep after the chaplain said a prayer. "It was a sad sight to see him thus cast into the sea," wrote Anson Fessenden of an orderly who died of heart disease on the way to New Orleans.[35]

Accidents also claimed lives. John Thurber of the 116th New York insisted on sleeping in an exposed part of the deck near the railing as the regiment was transported to Virginia in 1864 even though it violated orders. He rolled overboard one night, yelling for help. The ship stopped, but no one could see him and he was lost. A soldier of the 176th New York was more fortunate. He also fell overboard, but crew members threw him a rope and were able to bring him back on board.[36]

What might be termed a typical coastal voyage for soldiers in the Civil War was recorded by Surgeon Benjamin A. Fordyce of the 160th New York. The regiment was on its way aboard a propeller steamer called the *C. C. Leary* from New Orleans to Virginia in late July 1864. The boat was crowded with more than 800 men but made good headway until hitting three days of storms near Charleston, South Carolina. The men became terribly seasick and many could not eat for three days. One man died on the voyage, but he had been ill even before starting. His comrades buried him at sea near the Tortugas.[37]

As the example of the *C. C. Leary* indicates, nearly every voyage had at least a few days of pleasant sailing. When the sea was calm, "smooth as glass," as Captain Jonathan Huntington Johnson of the 15th New Hampshire put it, the troops could lie on deck and read or play cards. They also enjoyed the unique environment of the ocean. Johnson was amazed at the sight of "flying fish." One landed on board the vessel, offering him a close view of the unusual creature. "They are about 6 inches long with two wings,—a very pretty fish," he wrote in his diary.[38]

After his war experience, Wise offered advice about altering coastal ships to better accommodate troops. Owners should install proper water closets, and temporary bathing facilities could "easily be made" he argued. The men needed a few stoves to dry their clothes now and then in case of excessive dampness in the hold. Wise thought it best to take away weapons and baggage from the troops when they boarded and store them for the duration of the trip. Officers needed to inspect their men twice a day to catch any sign of illness as soon as possible. Affected troops had to be segregated immediately from the rest, and most vessels needed to acquire more small boats in case the military passengers were forced to abandon the craft. "While a well-regulated ship is remarkable for health," Wise concluded, "one where proper precautions are not observed soon becomes a floating pest-house."[39]

The government never established regulations such as these for the coastal vessels it chartered, and ship owners did as little as possible to adjust their vessels for troop transport. Conscientious army officers had to make up for this laxness. Jacob Cox issued orders strictly regulating his men's behavior on board the *Atlantic* while traveling from Annapolis to North Carolina early in 1865. Troops were forbidden to handle lights during the night and they were not allowed to smoke in sleeping areas in the hold. Cox wanted the ship's steward to handle all food preparation for the 2,000 men on board. Soldiers were allowed to fill their canteens once per day, marching to the pump in the forward part of the ship. Brigade commanders arranged for regular policing of all areas occupied by the troops, and that included daily inspections and roll calls. They also placed guards at all storerooms and toilet facilities.[40]

A self-regulated unit of men led by conscientious officers could make for a clean and safe voyage, but animals on a ship could not take care of themselves. In fact, horses and mules historically had been difficult cargo when transported by ship. By the time of the Crimean War, the British had worked out effective methods of moving 3,000 horses by sea from various places in the Mediterranean to the theater of operations. They constructed stalls equipped with slings to give the animals some relief from standing on their feet. Attendants cleaned out the stalls and rubbed the horses' legs and cleaned their mouths and noses with vinegar each day. Six gallons of water for every animal was the rule, and proper ventilation was important in the hold. The British learned that it was better to use gangplanks to load and unload the horses. If that was not possible, slings were better than boxes to lift them on and off the vessels.[41]

Unfortunately, the Americans failed to follow the British example in a thorough way. Richard Delafield reported on the British method of transporting animals, but his report was not published until just before the outbreak of the Civil War. Horses often were allowed to stand on their feet in one place for days at a time. When the 1st Connecticut Battery boarded the *Ellwood Walter*, crew members hoisted 160 horses on board, using a crate, as the battery men knocked together some kind of stalls for them. Once on the way to Port Royal, the *Elwood Walter* encountered stormy seas. Most of the battery men became so seasick they could not work, and only twelve of them felt well enough to tend the horses. The animals exhibited signs of distemper and sweated themselves into a lather during the storm. "The horses suffered frightfully," admitted the battery historian, "each morning some were found dead." The Connecticut men cut off the legs of the carcasses and hauled the dead horses out of the hold to be thrown overboard. Thirteen animals died on the relatively short voyage of 11 days.[42]

The callous way horses were accommodated on Union army transports during the Civil War is shocking. Lieutenant Colonel Clark E. Royce of the 6th U.S. Colored Troops took only six horses with his regiment when it boarded the steamer *Salvo* during the First Fort Fisher Expedition in December 1864. During a storm the horses were "all shot and thrown overboard," though Royce failed to explain why that was done. The horses obviously were the private property of officers, making the deliberate killing and disposal of them even more difficult to understand. When the 2nd Rhode Island Cavalry rode to Louisiana aboard the *Belle Wood* in early 1863, so many of its government-owned horses died and were dropped overboard that the sharks had a feast. When the bored cavalrymen tied chunks of meat to the end of strings and dropped the bait into the sea they got no nibbles because the sharks had so heavily feasted on the horse carcasses.[43]

It is true that disease may have accounted for much of this horse carnage aboard coastal vessels, but it is equally true that most animals were not well accommodated even under the best of conditions. When the 19th Ohio Battery traveled from Annapolis to North Carolina on the propeller steamer *El Cid* in 1865, its horses were packed in the hold along the edges of the ship, with the men quartered between them. There was little light and even less air circulating for man or beast. John Watkins had to share the air with 70 horses, and it was horrible: "worse than any stable I was ever in" and "enough to kill well men" he confided to his diary. Watkins survived the experience but argued that it was "the worse hole I was ever in." Another ship, called the *Nereus*, transported Battery D, 1st Ohio Light Artillery, as part of the same Twenty-Third Corps movement that took Watkins to the mouth of the Cape Fear River. After eight days of rough sailing, a total of 36 horses died and were thrown overboard.[44]

At times it was necessary to resort to crude methods for unloading animals from coastal vessels. When Battery F, 1st Rhode Island Light Artillery, landed near Fort Hatteras in January 1862 it was compelled by lack of docking facilities to unload horses "by throwing them overboard and towing them ashore by means of heaving lines, one end around the neck of the horse, the other held in a small boat" that guided them from ship to shore.[45]

For most of the Civil War, New Orleans was the farthest Union enclave on the Confederate coast from the major logistical centers of the Northeast. After a joint naval and army expedition captured the city in April 1862, Federal officers

5.4. "Landing of Horses at Hatteras." Battery F, 1st Rhode Island Light Artillery, unloaded its horses into shallow water because there were no docking facilities on Hatteras Island in 1862. The horses had to be coerced into jumping into the surf and then were led ashore by men in small boats with tethers drawing the animals behind. (Chase, *Battery F*, 27)

scrambled to find river craft in the area that they could use on the inland waterways of south Louisiana. They enjoyed only limited success. Many Southern boat owners hid their craft in the bayous of the region to keep them out of Federal hands. David G. Farragut seized any that were available as "lawful prizes" of war. He refused to give the owners certificates spelling out the exact purpose of the seizure, claiming this could all be sorted out better after the war. Farragut transferred most of these craft to Benjamin F. Butler, who commanded the army units of the expedition and the newly created Department of the Gulf, for his logistical support. There is no readily available record of the number of river craft Farragut was able to secure, but at least nine river steamers were available for Butler to ship 4,000 troops up the Mississippi River to attack Vicksburg by July 1862. When thousands of fresh troops entered the department later that year, however, the number of river craft at the disposal of Union quartermasters proved to be completely inadequate.[46]

The length of the logistical system that linked New York with New Orleans was enormous, stretching for some 2,000 miles along the Atlantic and Gulf coasts. A good vessel such as the sail- and steam-powered *James S. Green* could make at best 10 knots per hour. A letter written by Henry Mitchell Whitney's father on April 12, 1863, reached the 52nd Massachusetts soldier by April 28. "The Department of the Gulf was farthest from the touch and sympathy of the North," recalled David H. Hanaburgh of the 128th New York. Food boxes often arrived with their contents spoiled, and Hanaburgh complained that letters took two weeks to reach their destination.[47]

Despite the distance from major supply bases, Federal authorities not only maintained but strengthened their enclave near New Orleans as the war progressed. When Nathaniel P. Banks replaced Butler, the Federal government sent 10,000 additional troops to reinforce the 15,000 men Butler had brought to the Department of the Gulf a year earlier. Washington officials expected Banks to ascend the Mississippi and take the Rebel stronghold of Port Hudson. Federal quartermasters mounted a major effort to round up coastal steamers for the transportation of these newly raised regiments. They started from various ports and assembled at Fortress Monroe in December 1862. Most regiments split up in order to fit onto the small vessels. The 114th New York placed four companies on the steamer *Thames*, three on the steamer *Atlantic*, and three on the *Arago*. While the latter two ships made it safely to New Orleans, the *Thames* encountered a violent storm off Cape Hatteras that wrecked her engine. It had to be towed to Port Royal, South Carolina, where a board of survey declared the ship unseaworthy. The four companies reembarked on a sailing vessel named the *Voltigeur* on December 17 and reached the mouth of the Mississippi 14 days later.[48]

The storm that wrecked the *Thames* near the Outer Banks of North Carolina also sank the ironclad warship USS *Monitor* and made life difficult for many other ships of the Banks Expedition. Captain Jonathan Johnson of the 15th New Hampshire counted a dozen wrecked vessels near Cape Hatteras on his way through the dangerous area. The rolling of the vessel caused universal sickness among the troops, and it continued off and on while sailing through the Gulf of Mexico. Damage to coastal vessels often was repaired, if possible, by the crew members. Ice covered the riggings of sail vessels during these winter storms, and it was not unheard of that fire should break out in galleys during rough weather. Some vessels of the Banks Expedition grounded on the Florida reefs, necessitating tedious labor to off-load enough men and cargo to lighten the ships and resume the journey. With rough weather and occasional damage to ships, the plan to move Banks's men as a large group was impossible. Ships wound up making their way as best they could and straggled into New Orleans for weeks. The 2nd Rhode Island Cavalry was aboard a sailing vessel called the *Belle Wood*, which was pushed back 100 miles by a strong storm front coming from the west as it neared the mouth of the Mississippi, greatly delaying its arrival.[49]

Most regiments of the Banks Expedition took 20 or more days to journey from Fortress Monroe to New Orleans. Many of the vessels were towed up the Mississippi River because their motive power was not strong enough to stem the current. Upon reaching the city, ship captains found that the unloading facilities were not in good repair. Many of the docks were in fact unsuitable for these vessels, and disembarking became a tedious process of off-loading onto smaller craft. From December 16, 1862, when the van of the Banks Expedition reached New Orleans, the troops streamed in until the tail of the column arrived in February 1863.[50]

Benjamin Butler estimated that it cost the Federal government $300 to transport each man in the Banks Expedition. Such a cost was extremely high compared to inland transportation by rail or river steamer. An additional problem lay in that many of Banks's troops had been allowed to volunteer for only nine months of service. It made little sense to send such regiments so far away at such high cost only to get less than nine months of use out of them in the field.[51]

The Banks Expedition increased manpower in the Department of the Gulf by a large degree, but supporting soldiers was not the only responsibility of the coastal shipping system. When New Orleans fell, Confederate authorities tried to blockade trade between the city and inland areas still under their control. As a result, most of the food sources relied on by the 170,000 residents of New Orleans were cut. Butler had to assume an increasingly prominent role as provider for the city. By the time Banks replaced him, commissary officers reported the Federal government was feeding 20,000 to 25,000 civilians living outside the city with army subsistence. In addition, Banks continued feeding residents of New Orleans throughout most of 1863. By September of that year the government had spent nearly $375,000 on civilian food in only 10 months. "These are unequaled and unheard of charities in any age or country," argued Colonel E. G. Beckwith, "and completely reverse the very general rule of subsisting armies upon the countries in which they operate—for here we actually support the poor of the country we occupy." All of these army rations for civilians, as well as for soldiers, had to be transported by coastal shipping.[52]

Banks's siege of Port Hudson from May to July 1863 strained his logistical network to the breaking point. He was barely able to sustain an army of 30,000 troops 100 miles north of New Orleans for that long. After the fall of both Vicksburg and Port Hudson, however, the Mississippi River was completely open to Northern navigation and Banks called on Ulysses S. Grant for all manner of logistical support. He wanted troops, supplies, and 22 river steamers. Grant found it difficult to comply because he had great need of all these things in his Department of the Tennessee, but he sent what he could. "Accept my thanks for the steamers," Banks wrote. "They will be of great service." Banks also asked for small armed river craft to patrol the shallow waters of bayous and rivers tributary to the Mississippi.[53]

The fact that Banks pleaded so strongly for this material indicates how limited was the effectiveness of coastal shipping to meet his logistical needs. The infusion of 22 river steamers from the upper Mississippi also indicates how few of those craft had been available to him prior to the fall of Port Hudson. These riverboats were uniquely suited to the demands of the western waterways and impressed New England soldiers when they saw them for the first time after the siege of Port Hudson. "These Mississippi River Boats are the most wonderful things going," exuded Henry H. Goodell of the 25th Connecticut. "A mere egg-shell looking as if a lot of empty cigar boxes had been bought up & stuck together, and yet they will stand any amount of banging and hard thumps. They are all engine & pilot house with no room, but some-how they carry enormous loads. They are high pressure and puff away like the blowing of some mighty great giant asleep."[54]

For their part, Grant's men saw a few ocean steamers that made their way up the Mississippi River to Vicksburg soon after the fall of Port Hudson. In fact, it now was possible to transport troops from the Department of the Gulf not along the coast but along the western waterways. Many of Banks's nine-month troops made their way home to New England that way when their term of service expired. The 52nd Massachusetts left Port Hudson aboard the river steamer *Henry Choteau* on July 23, 1863, and reached Cairo in one week. There the regiment boarded railroad cars and speeded through Indianapolis, Cleveland, Buffalo, Syracuse, and Albany to Massachusetts. The 52nd did not have to divide into separate river steamers; although old and slow, the *Henry Choteau* was big enough for the entire regiment.[55]

The 15th New Hampshire, 26th Connecticut, and 26th Maine also had the

5.5. River Steamer *Sallie Robinson* and a Coastal Vessel Transport Confederate Prisoners from Port Hudson, 1863. This image is a superb comparison of these two types of Federal transports in the Civil War. Note the differing style, shape, and design of the two craft as they jointly perform a logistical task along the lower Mississippi River, which was wide and deep enough for most ocean-going vessels as well as river steamers. (*Frank Leslie's Illustrated Newspaper,* August 15, 1863, 336)

luxury of placing all of their men on one river steamer. Even though the 15th lost several hours when a pump broke on the *City of Madison,* the regiment left Port Hudson on July 26 and reached home on August 8 by taking a route similar to that of the 52nd Massachusetts. The New Hampshire unit lost 86 men on the journey who died of illnesses contracted during the siege of Port Hudson.[56]

The river steamer *Omaha* was by no means a pleasure boat. Described as a "rotten old craft . . . overloaded with human freight," it started from Port Hudson with the 50th Massachusetts on board and began to leak within a couple of days. The regiment was transferred to "a large and powerful high-pressure side-wheel steamer" called the *Luther M. Kennett,* yet it still reached Cairo in only eight days. That also accounted for the delay attendant on stopping to bury several men who died on the trip. Conditions on the railroad cars also proved to be cramped and uncomfortable, but the regiment sped forward, reaching Boston 13 days after leaving Port Hudson.[57]

The war experience of these nine-month regiments was remarkable for the exposure it gave them to all three logistical systems employed by the Federal government. They went to war on coastal vessels for 2,000 miles and went home on riverboats for 1,200 miles before transferring to the railroads for another 1,200 miles. All of this, plus the six-week siege of Port Hudson, took place within the space of only nine months.

Riverboats and coastal shipping also transported the Port Hudson prisoners to Confederate-held Mobile. They were sent south to New Orleans with 600 to 800 men on board and transferred to seagoing vessels that flew white flags as they approached the entrance to Mobile Bay. While in New Orleans, many residents brought baskets of food for the Confederates and cheered them when the ships departed.[58]

Coastal vessels continued to work for the government until the end of the war, but now that the Mississippi River was opened Northerners had options. Benjamin H. Grierson visited Washington, D.C., and New York early in 1865 and wanted to return to New Orleans by the coast. But he learned that it would be a wait of several days before "a through or fast ocean steamer" was available, so he decided to travel overland. Grierson left New York by rail on February 17 and reached Cairo five days later even though he stopped at Jacksonville, Illinois, to visit his family. He then hopped on board a river steamer and visited his brother in Memphis while the boat unloaded freight. The craft also made other stops for commercial purposes and was delayed by foggy weather. Still, Grierson reached New Orleans by March 1, having spent 12 days on the way. That would have been considered a short trip compared to traveling along the coast.[59]

Coastal shipping for the army was extended more than 600 miles west of New Orleans when Federal authorities moved the equivalent of a brigade to the Texas coast in October 1863. Napoleon J. T. Dana commanded this force as it established toeholds at three locations near the mouth of the Rio Grande River. The purpose was to inhibit blockade running and counter growing French intervention in Mexico. To support the expedition, quartermasters needed ships that could weather an ocean voyage and yet were light enough to negotiate the shallow waters of the Texas coast. It proved to be very difficult to find them.[60]

River steamers were ideally suited to operate in the shallow waters between barrier islands and the mainland, but they were unsafe while crossing the Gulf of Mexico. Heavier ships with deeper drafts were required to reach the Union enclaves, but they could not cross the many bars inhibiting access to the sounds. That required the use of smaller boats to lighter the freight outside the bar and carry it in. This tedious, time-consuming process greatly delayed the shipping schedule as vessels waited for days until they could be unloaded and returned to New Orleans. Periodic spells of bad weather further slowed the lightering process, and sometimes the lightering vessel itself grounded on the bar. The boilers of boats with high-pressure engines had to be cleaned out every other day because of the salt water used; the tides also were unpredictable, sometimes cresting two or three feet lower than usual on any given day.[61]

Quartermasters in New Orleans tended to put too little cargo on the vessels, perhaps in an effort to enable the ships to cross the bar without lightering. That rarely happened, and the result was a significant decrease in the flow of supplies. "There seems to be no sense or judgment used in shipping rations," complained C. C. Washburn to Banks. "Of articles of prime necessity they send but little, but such as we don't want they send plenty."[62]

Even though the Union presence on the coast of Texas was small, S. B. Holabird, Banks's chief quartermaster, thought it was too difficult to adequately support it and carry on needed logistical functions elsewhere. Holabird had assigned four large steamers to handle the packet runs between New York and New Orleans. They provided "our regular supplies of ordnance and essential and valuable material and stores." But he was compelled to divert two of them to supply Dana's men near the mouth of the Rio Grande. That need evaporated by May 1864 when Federal authorities evacuated the enclaves and sent the troops to more important theaters of operations.[63]

Quartermasters continued to manage large transfers of troops along the coast as the war progressed. Many regiments and batteries from the Federal toeholds along the coast of North Carolina, South Carolina, and Florida gathered in southeast Virginia to constitute the Tenth and Eighteenth Corps of Benjamin Butler's newly formed Army of the James. The shipping process took place in late April and early May 1864, employing "every kind and description of tugboat, sloop, flat, scow, ship and steamer that the mind of man could imagine," recalled the historian of the 1st Connecticut Battery. "Everything that would float seemed to have been impressed into service." The battery left Pawnee Landing, South Carolina, aboard two propeller steamers on April 19 and reached Fortress Monroe three days later after an uneventful voyage. From there quartermasters put the men and horses on a small steamer called the *Convoy* and the guns and caissons on "an old Hudson River barge" named the *L. Durant*. With the barge in tow, the *Convoy* steamed to Bermuda Hundred, where Butler's army was congregating before striking out into the area between Richmond and Petersburg.[64]

Another large troop movement took place in July 1864, when Grant ordered the Nineteenth Corps from New Orleans to Virginia. Regiments located at various posts within the Department of the Gulf first had to be hauled to New Orleans for embarkation on coastal vessels. Not until the ships cleared the mouth of the Mississippi were sealed orders opened and the army officers informed where they were headed. The 116th New York, aboard "a large, new and very staunch craft" called the *Mississippi*, traveled from 249 to 331 miles each day until reaching Fortress Monroe on July 12, totaling 1,400 miles on the five-day trip.[65]

Two expeditions against Confederate Fort Fisher at the mouth of the Cape Fear River required quartermasters to find sturdy vessels capable of braving winter weather off the coast of North Carolina. The first expedition of December 1864 involved moving 6,500 troops from Virginia. One of the transports, the *Admiral Du Pont*, was rammed by a brig that dragged her anchor during a storm and "stove a hole in her port quarter." The *Admiral Du Pont* was forced to put in at Norfolk for repairs and then race to catch up so the 6th U.S. Colored Troops on board could be made available to Butler, who ineptly commanded the expedition. The troops were not even landed before Butler decided to call off the effort and return to Virginia.[66]

The second Fort Fisher Expedition was more formidable and better led by Alfred H. Terry. To support Terry's troops, Cuvier Grover's division of the Nineteenth Corps boarded seven coastal steamers at Baltimore. Grover reported that it took three hours to load each vessel even though some of them had as few as 500 men on board. During the journey to Fortress Monroe the troops were allowed one gallon of water each day. The ships carried enough coal for a fifteen-day voyage.[67]

When Edward R. S. Canby mounted a major expedition to capture Mobile in March and April 1865, he had but a short journey of 150 miles from New Orleans along the coast to the Alabama port city. But with 45,000 troops to transport and supply, Canby was forced to scrape up every viable craft he could find. "I have seized and sent to Mobile all the Mississippi steamers that could make the voyage with any degree of safety," Canby reported, "but have still an insufficient number for as prompt movements as were desired." Monroe Joshua Miller of the 117th Illinois traveled to Mobile on one of these river steamers. Even though the weather was good, the boat still rolled so much as to make the voyage very uncomfortable. The captain hugged every bit of shallow water he could find, always keeping some island in sight until reaching the entrance to Mobile Bay, where he offloaded the troops.[68]

Even those of Canby's men who boarded coastal steamers found the trip unpleasant. The 32nd Iowa packed aboard the *Cromwell* and encountered stormy weather that caused widespread sickness among the men. The troops were lightered from the *Cromwell* by a smaller vessel before being deposited on Dauphine Island at the entrance to Mobile Bay. Job H. Yaggy of the 124th Illinois hated his trip on the coastal steamer *Guiding Star* for the same reason—a rough sea and plenty of sickness. "Thank God, we are on solid bottom again," he wrote upon arrival at Dauphine Island. "I don't wish to take a ship again. A River Transport is a nice thing but an *Ocean Steamer* I don't like."[69]

As these many examples indicate, the Federal government made full use of civilian-owned coastal shipping during the war. There is no doubt that Rebel quartermasters also employed coastal vessels to a limited degree. Larkin Smith, in the Quartermaster General's office in Richmond, listed the names of four steamers, four schooners, and two smaller sailing vessels that were available along the James River in March 1862. These 10 ships had a total capacity for transporting 3,300 men. Smith thought he could increase that capacity by 25 percent if he used barges and other small vessels to transport the troops' baggage. Another steamer was under repair, Smith reported, but would be available in a few days.[70]

Confederate authorities were unable to make full use of coastal shipping for obvious reasons, chief of which was the dominance of the Union navy along the Southern coast. More than 600 warships patrolled that coast by the end of the Civil War and provided safe waters for merchant vessels employed by Union quartermasters to ship men, equipment, food, and ordnance along the coastline of the Confederacy. But, just as with river steamers, the Confederates also destroyed many of their own coastal ships in times of emergency. When Joseph E. Johnston retreated from Yorktown up the Peninsula in May 1862 his subordinates scuttled, burned, or sank 69 vessels to prevent them from falling into Union hands. A total of 280 Confederate coastal ships are listed among the many hundreds of Civil War shipwrecks.[71]

George D. Wise, who became responsible for superintending Union coastal shipping by the end of 1864, reported that an average of 719 steamers, sailing vessels, tugs, and barges, both owned and chartered by the department, worked in coastal waters to support the Federal war effort on any given day during the last fiscal year of the conflict. The cost of this logistical effort amounted on average to $92,414 per day. Slightly more than half of that daily expense was invested in supplying the Army of the Potomac and the Army of the James at Petersburg and Richmond. The cost of chartering vessels ranged widely, from $60 to $550 per day, depending on the size and quality of the vessel. Barges were chartered for more reasonable rates—for example, the 118-ton *General Howard* at $9.24 per day. Quartermasters purchased a number of vessels at costs ranging from $8,500 for the 46-ton screw tug *Reindeer* to $80,000 for the 487-ton side-wheel steamer *Escort*. Only three vessels were lost during that time, all of them due to accidents rather than enemy action.[72]

With the responsibility of feeding Grant's men in Virginia and those of Sherman and Schofield operating in North Carolina, Federal quartermasters employed all the vessels the government owned and they chartered virtually all coastal vessels available along the Atlantic seaboard. Montgomery Meigs proudly reported that "nearly every new steam vessel that had been built in the United States to navigate the ocean" found its way into government service.[73]

When the war ended, the Quartermaster Department moved quickly to reduce this huge fleet of support ships to save government expense. It sold most of the vessels it owned and dropped the chartered ships as soon as convenient. Wise warned Meigs not to expect a profit on the sale of purchased vessels. Most of them were in poor shape because they had always been "under a severe strain" while serving Federal needs. A compilation of all vessels used by the government in the coastal shipping system lists a total of 4,033 craft. That number included 1,966 steamers and 2,003 sail vessels. The overwhelming majority of the sailing craft were schooners. In addition to the expense of purchasing or chartering these craft, the government was responsible for damages incurred as a result of enemy action. Wreckage caused by natural or navigational causes normally did not require government compensation.[74]

Lieutenant Joseph H. Gould, who spent a month on a transport during the First Fort Fisher Expedition, greatly appreciated the services rendered by these civilian craft in support of the war effort. The "perils encountered . . . by those who braved the gales and holy-stoned the decks with freezing fingers, as well as by the thousands of soldiers transported up and down our shores, have not that place in the books, nor in the memory of our people that they deserve," he lamented long after the conflict. He was right.[75]

6

++++++++++++++

WAGON TRAINS

The three major forms of transport used by the armies—riverboats, railroads, and coastal shipping—were not the only elements of Civil War logistics. In every theater of operations some sort of land transportation moved material from the levee, the railroad depot, or the coastal wharf to troops in need of it. Some sort of wheeled vehicle pulled by draft animals and driven by men had been utilized since the classical era to provide logistical support in the theater of operations. Land transportation is therefore an example of logistics on the tactical (or regional) level, as opposed to the strategic or national level of logistics, as represented by river traffic, movement by rail, and shipping by coastal vessels.

Well into the nineteenth century, the British government relied on civilians contracted to work for the army with wagons procured in the theater of operations. Even as late as the Crimean War the British army found this to be a troublesome mode of operating. It had little control over the local civilian drivers. The French army fared much better in this regard because it had established a system of land transportation that the officers could more directly influence. The British hastily put together a better system mixing Europeans with natives and under the administrative control of the army. Near the end of the Crimean campaign the British employed 24,000 horses, 14,000 native drivers, and 9,000 European personnel to support their land force at Sebastopol.[1]

The U.S. Army had worked out a similar system during the American Revolution and continued it to support far-flung military posts on the frontier. The army employed a wagon that had proven its durability. It also hired civilian companies to supply some frontier posts while using government-owned wagons and soldiers to supply other posts.[2]

The army wagon became a staple of military transportation in America. "They were heavy, lumbering affairs at best," commented John D. Billings of

6.1. The Army Wagon. Photographed by Andrew J. Russell, this is a fine specimen of the standard army wagon that carried food, ammunition, medical supplies, and a variety of other necessities for Union and Confederate armies. Sturdy and durable, it had no suspension system and thus provided a particularly rough ride. Note the feed trough on the pole for the six-mule team. (Library of Congress, LC-DIG-ppmsca-08293)

the 10th Massachusetts Battery, "built for hard service, all, apparently, after the same pattern." Although rough to ride in because it had no suspension system of any kind, the wagon was well equipped. It contained a tool box, a feed trough for the mules that pulled it, a wooden bucket for water, an iron bucket for grease, a spare pole, and a canvas covering. Most of the wagons had been manufactured in Philadelphia before the war, but during the conflict many firms in other cities along the Ohio River and the Atlantic coast accepted contracts to make them. The soldiers called these army wagons "Uncle Sam's chariots."[3]

The capacity of the army wagon was as much as 2,674 pounds, or a little more than one ton of material, according to Rufus Ingalls. But the actual load varied widely according to the condition of the roads, the quality of the teams, and many other factors. In preparing for the last stage of the Carolinas campaign, Oliver O. Howard mandated that each Army of the Tennessee wagon should not be loaded with more than 2,000 pounds of material. Twenty-Fifth

Corps wagons had on average only 1,700 pounds of freight apiece at the end of the war, while the Army of the Potomac's cavalry put only 1,500 pounds of grain in each of its 300 wagons during April 1863. One wagon could haul all the hospital tents for one brigade of infantry, with each tent weighing 175 pounds, by early 1864.[4]

When Montgomery Meigs requested suggestions for improving the army wagon, some quartermasters thought it already was as good as could be expected. Others however had a few ideas. L. C. Easton suggested putting side boards around it to increase the height of the box in order to protect the bows and canvas covering when soldiers piled supplies too high. He also suggested fixing the wagon so the entire box could be easily lifted off the frame; that would enable soldiers to haul logs on the frame and axles without damaging the boxes. Richard Batchelder, chief quartermaster of the Army of the Potomac, suggested a brake operable by the driver so the team did not have to bear the entire burden of stopping the wagon. He experimented with a device in the winter of 1863–1864, but it failed to work properly.[5]

The difficulty of developing a brake operable by the driver was largely due to the fact that he did not sit on the wagon but on the left rear mule in the six-animal team. He controlled the mules in the rear of the team formation with short reins, and a longer rein connected him with the lead team of mules. According to John D. Billings, the teamster pulled the long rein to make the lead team go left and executed some "short jerks" to make it go right. An iron bar connected the bits of both lead mules so they were compelled to work together. The most memorable aspect of the teamster's work involved uttering "a sort of gibberish which the mule drivers acquired in the business" and filling the atmosphere with violent curses every time something went wrong. A whip (or black snake, as it was called) completed his equipment.[6]

Teamsters consisted both of soldiers detailed from infantry regiments and civilians hired by the government. The latter oftentimes were difficult to obtain, but they lessened the need to take infantrymen from their units. Thomas Swords complained that he often had to pay as much as $30 per month for civilian teamsters, only to see them quit in two or three months. He felt it was unfair not to pay detailed infantrymen more than their regulation salary of $13 a month for driving teams. Civilians hired as assistant wagon masters received $45 a month, and wagon masters earned $60 a month. All civilian teamsters received one army ration free per day, and sometimes quartermasters had to

6.2. Study of a Mule Team and Driver, September 30, 1863. Edwin Forbes accurately captured the way wagon teams were driven in the Civil War, with the driver seated on the left rear mule rather than on the box of the wagon. He controlled the other mules in the team by means of reins and a whip. Forbes also detailed the harness system used on wagon teams during the Civil War. (Library of Congress, LC-DIG-ppmsca-20592)

pay their transportation costs to get them to the field. These problems were greatly alleviated by hiring refugee blacks to drive teams.[7]

Hired civilian teamsters developed a reputation for unruly behavior. William F. Draper of the 36th Massachusetts recalled that his company boarded the steamer *Express* at Memphis for the trip to Vicksburg in June 1863. Some 200 civilian teamsters were on board as well, and Draper had never seen such rude and undisciplined behavior. The teamsters became angry because they were not allowed to roam anywhere they pleased and invaded the cabin, where company officers were compelled to draw their revolvers to hold them off until guards could arrive to control them.[8]

Land transportation carried the overwhelming majority of all material needed by a field army on campaign. It conveyed three pounds of food for every man and 26 pounds of forage and grain for every horse and mule, every day. A total of 150 wagons were needed to feed the Army of the Potomac

6.3. A Four-Horse Wagon, 1865. This arrangement was not typical of wagons during the Civil War; they typically were pulled by six mules rather than four horses. This image shows the wagon with its end gate in place and canvas covering secured. Note also the vertical pole attached to the rear axle; it is arranged so that the driver (seated on the left rear horse) can apply the brake and take some pressure off the team when stopping with a heavy load. (Library of Congress, LC-DIG-cwpb-01988)

on a daily basis. If commanders contemplated operating for some time away from the railroad or steamers that supplied their troops, the need for wagons increased. One must keep in mind that additional wagons were necessary to carry ordnance supplies, such as infantry and artillery ammunition, plus the personal baggage of officers, medical supplies, and other miscellaneous articles. Sherman believed that, as a rule of thumb, each of his corps in the latter stages of the war required 600 wagons to haul what was needed for a march of 20 days away from sources of supply.[9]

No wonder that Civil War officers used the Latin word *impedimenta* to refer to wagon trains. Not only were they large affairs, but they were extremely vulnerable to enemy action, slow moving, and defenseless. Every army commander had to plan movements with the wagon trains in mind, keeping them close enough to effectively supply the moving infantry, artillery, and cavalry units but not so near the scene of action as to be taken by a quick enemy strike. The larger the train, the slower the army movements; but with a train that was too small, the army could not eat or have adequate ammunition if a large battle suddenly developed.[10]

Alexander Bliss, a quartermaster serving with the Army of the Potomac during the Seven Days battles, experienced the difficulties of moving large wagon trains near the scene of action. Charged with shifting McClellan's trains from Savage's Station toward White Oak Swamp, he exhausted himself and his horse by riding a total of 30 miles to superintend the 7-mile march, taking charge of removing overturned wagons that blocked roads. He forced artillery, cavalry, and cattle herds to ford small streams so the wagons could have exclusive use of the bridges, and he selected fields large enough to park the immense train after reaching his destination so as to keep the roads clear. It took hours to move the wagons this short distance.[11]

The Roman army knew all about these problems. It had developed its train system to a higher level of size and sophistication than any previous military force; indeed, there was no equal to it until the modern era. Using mules and wagons, Roman officers divided their trains into parts that would become roughly familiar to Civil War quartermasters. One part hauled supplies and equipment for a unit, another was designated for the entire field army, a third carried the personal baggage of officers, and a fourth conveyed siege equipment. The Roman army struggled with the need to reduce the size of these trains to balance mobility with supply in the field. They relied on both free and slave servants to drive the teams and loaded soldiers with as much material as they could carry. They also used pack animals to reduce the number of wagons. Roman armies were capable of operating at least 60 miles from their source of supply; at times they could operate up to 200 miles. A typical Roman legion of 5,000 men required 2,000 pack animals and 200 two-horse vehicles in addition to baggage transportation for the officers.[12]

When the Cromwellian government of Britain invaded Scotland during the English Civil War, one wagon was allowed for each regiment. But the troops also carried all they could handle. Carts or wagons were allowed for each regiment to cover its staff needs and medical care.[13]

6.4. First Federal Wagon Train to Enter Petersburg after the Fall of the City. John Reekie exposed this view, presumably on April 3, 1865. The wagons are neatly arranged and the train stretches off as far as one can see into the distance along the street. (Library of Congress, LC-DIG-cwpb-01286)

The U.S. Army gained enormous experience at handling wagon transportation on the frontier. When the 6th U.S. Infantry moved 709 miles from Fort Kearny to Fort Bridger in the summer of 1857, it was on the road for 27 days and marched about 26 miles each day. Captain Winfield S. Hancock managed the regimental train, which was divided into five parts of 25 wagons each. A wagon master was assigned to the whole and one to each of the parts as well. In addition to the six-mule team wagons, the regiment had 2 ambulances, 3 spring wagons, a traveling forge, and 25 extra mules. Hancock proudly reported that the move took place without incident.[14]

In short, the enormous problems presented by the land transportation needs of 3 million Union and Confederate soldiers during the Civil War were solvable because of the American experience. The most persistent problem lay in the size of the wagon trains needed to support the huge armies commanded by Civil War officers who tended to want a lot of wagons for their men early in the war. The 12th Indiana started the conflict with 2 baggage wagons for each company and 3 wagons for the regimental headquarters, for a total of 13 vehicles. The 11th Iowa used 8 wagons for baggage in 1861. Stewart Van Vliet allowed a total of 6 wagons per regiment for the Army of the Potomac, up to and including the Peninsula campaign, in addition to wagon trains to haul ammunition and food for the entire army.[15]

Heavy allowances such as these continued throughout the rest of 1862 as Federal authorities grappled with a surprising problem of material abundance. By the end of the Peninsula campaign the Army of the Potomac possessed 3,100 wagons, 350 ambulances, 5,000 draft horses, and 8,000 mules. Rufus Ingalls, who succeeded Van Vliet as chief quartermaster, thought the allowance of six wagons per regiment necessary. By early August, McClellan instituted new allowances, but they failed to reduce transportation. He mandated six wagons for each regiment, three wagons for each artillery battery, three wagons for each brigade and division headquarters, and four wagons for the corps headquarters. Each officer was allowed no more than a valise or carpetbag, blankets, and a mess kit. The Army of the Potomac saw a sharp increase in its impedimenta, with a total of 3,911 wagons, 907 ambulances, 8,693 draft horses, and 12,483 mules by November 1862. John Pope's Army of Virginia reportedly had an even higher level of land transportation. With 15 wagons per regiment for baggage and a supply train of 40 wagons for each brigade, Montgomery Meigs estimated Pope's command used on average 23 wagons for each regiment. Even so, it hauled no more than ten days' worth of food.[16]

In contrast, Don Carlos Buell estimated that three wagons for each regiment and one wagon for each battery in the Army of the Ohio was a fair ratio. In addition, two wagons were needed to haul the ordnance required by one regiment (at 100 rounds of ammunition for each infantryman). A few more wagons were needed for miscellaneous purposes until the allowance in Buell's army was nearly as large as that of the Army of the Potomac in 1862. Gordon Granger thought this allowance the smallest one could expect; in fact, he thought infantrymen should have 300 rather than 100 cartridges immediately available and postulated that a field army expecting to move 40 miles from its supply depot should take up to 15 days of food in its wagon trains. In his pursuit of Braxton Bragg's Army of the Mississippi north into Kentucky during the late summer of 1862, Buell's army-level wagon train consisted of 1,700 teams moving at about 15 miles per day. It was estimated to be worth more than $2 million.[17]

Bragg's invasion of Kentucky sparked a good deal of frustration and admiration among Union army officers. "When General Buell had to move at a snail's pace with his vast wagon trains, Bragg moved rapidly, living on the country," asserted William T. Sherman. "No military mind could endure this long, and we are forced in self-defense to imitate their example." Gordon Granger also marveled at Bragg's mobility, calling it "almost without a parallel[;] cutting loose from his base of supplies and skedaddling all over the country is something to which history scarcely affords a parallel." Bragg was well aware of what he was doing. "With but one suit of clothes, no tents, Nothing to eat but meat and *bread*, or when we can't get that *roasting ears* from the corn fields along the road, we have made the most extraordinary campaign in military history," he boasted to his wife.[18]

In the end, Bragg was compelled to evacuate the state in October 1862 in part because he did not have a secure line of communications with the South. But he had demonstrated how fast and far an army could move if it severely reduced its land transportation and counted on the endurance of its personnel. The lesson struck many Northern officers. "Napoleon asserted that 500 wagons were enough for 40,000 men," Meigs told Henry Halleck. "We are using at the rate of three times this number. . . . If the army is to move with efficiency, vigorous measures must reduce this luxury of transportation." Halleck reluctantly admitted to Edwin M. Stanton that the Confederate armies had "exhibited much more mobility and activity than our own." Halleck knew it was necessary to reduce the baggage trains but found much resistance. "Once accustomed to a certain amount of transportation, an army is unwilling to do without the luxuries which it supplies in the field."[19]

Meigs attacked this problem with persistence. He explained to Stanton that army trains generally could be divided into three classes: headquarters, regimental, and general. The third class carried the bulk of everything needed by the army, and its size could not easily be reduced. But the first two classes, which carried baggage and supplies for headquarters and small units, were amenable to reduction and typically were larger than truly needed. Meigs also pointed out that the absence of army-wide regulations concerning baggage allowance resulted in field commanders setting their own ratios at anywhere from 6 to 15 wagons per regiment. "The troops generally carry too much useless baggage," he told Stanton. The introduction of the shelter tent, carried on the back of the soldier, reduced the need for wagons to haul the large communal Sibley tents.[20]

Both Halleck and Meigs moved forward to alleviate this problem in the fall of 1862. Halleck issued a general order through the Adjutant General's Office of the War Department mandating that all officers reduce baggage to the minimum. "The mobility of our armies is destroyed by the vast trains which attend them, and which they are required to guard." Meigs proposed a general regulation concerning baggage allowance for the entire U.S. Army based almost completely on McClellan's allowance for the Army of the Potomac. This was issued on October 18, 1862, and set the general allowance at six wagons for each regiment, three wagons for each battery, four wagons for each corps headquarters, and three for each brigade or division headquarters.[21]

Throughout the first half of 1863, Army of the Potomac officers adhered to this standard consistently, except that headquarters mandated fewer than six wagons for regiments that were understrength. While these numbers applied to baggage wagons, Ingalls thought that the general supply train ought to have seven wagons for every 1,000 men for the transport of food, forage, quartermaster's stores, and other material. The ammunition train used four wagons to haul the cartridges for every 1,000 troops. The Army of the Potomac needed a little more than 3,000 wagons, around 350 ambulances, 17,000 horses, and 8,000 mules on a consistent basis to support its operations. Totaling all wagons in the different trains, the army had 30 for every 1,000 men. The Army of the Cumberland and the Army of the Tennessee more or less maintained a similar level of land transport.[22]

The standard allowance set on October 18, 1862, had not really cut land transportation by much, if any; it really operated more as a cap to prevent ambitious officers from increasing the number of their wagons beyond a reasonable limit. But in August 1863, Halleck was greatly dissatisfied with that standard allowance. "We must reduce our transportation or give up all idea of competing with the enemy in the field," he told George G. Meade. "Napoleon very correctly estimated the effective strength of an army by its numbers multiplied by its mobility; that is, 10,000 men who could march 20 miles per day as equal to 20,000 men who could march only 10 miles per day." Halleck therefore issued General Orders No. 274 on August 7, 1863. It set allowances based mostly on those established by Zachary Taylor during the Monterrey campaign in Mexico in 1846. "There is no necessity for the large trains heretofore allowed, and for which there is no parallel in European warfare," Halleck asserted. Corps headquarters were allowed only two wagons, with one wagon for each brigade and division headquarters. Each regiment was allowed one wagon, but several pack animals were permitted to supplement the vehicle's carrying capacity. With General Orders No. 274, Halleck finally engaged the problem of significantly reducing land transportation for the Union army.[23]

Richard Batchelder thought Halleck could go further. He recommended that officers not be given wagons at all but rely entirely on pack animals to haul their personal belongings. He thought that alone would reduce the number of vehicles in an army's train by 20 percent. Moreover, Batchelder thought too much ammunition was carried in an army's ordnance train. He noted that at Chancellorsville the Second Corps of Hooker's army fired the contents of only 9 ammunition wagons out of the 50 loaded wagons available. Even though much more heavily engaged at Gettysburg, the Second Corps fired only 14 wagon loads of small arms ammunition out of 60 available. The Army of the Potomac allowed five loaded wagons of ammunition for every 1,000 men; Batchelder thought it should be reduced to three wagon loads. He also recommended that the amount of hospital stores hauled with the army be cut by half, as that portion of the army's train system constituted 12 percent of the total taken along during campaigns, an excessive amount in Batchelder's view.[24]

Meade instructed his army to adhere to General Orders No. 274, and it did so for the most part. Ironically, Second Corps losses were so heavy at Gettysburg that the corps wound up with far too many wagons for its numbers after the battle and had to turn many of them in to the quartermaster to meet the levels set in this general order. As time went on Meade permitted variations in the allowance, increasing baggage wagons to six per regiment (but with no pack animals to supplement them). Batchelder tried his best to reduce on his own, stripping the ammunition train from five wagons per 1,000 men to only three. Army headquarters was bloated with transportation. About 50 officers worked directly for Meade, but they used a total of 110 wagons, 25 of which carried officers' baggage and official papers, and another 25 hauled food for the headquarters. The army's provost marshal used 47 wagons for purposes not reported, and the rest of the vehicles were employed hauling forage for some 800 animals attached to army headquarters.[25]

Meade prevaricated when he claimed to have given a lot of attention to his army's land transportation and made "every effort . . . to reduce it to the minimum." He actually increased it in some ways and allowed an unnecessarily large number of wagons to serve his own headquarters. By the time the army started on the Overland campaign, its land transportation was about at the same level as the time period before Halleck's General Orders No. 274. When the army settled into static positions at Petersburg, Grant issued more stringent transportation allowances of two wagons per regiment for baggage, three of ammunition for every 1,000 men, seven wagons in the supply train for every 1,000 men, and three for hospital supplies per brigade. Those were still pretty liberal allowances for an army stuck in trenches only a handful of miles from its depot at City Point. When Philip Sheridan prepared his force for highly mobile operations against Jubal Early's command in the lower Shenandoah Valley, he mandated more strict allowances than Grant's. Sheridan permitted only one wagon for each regiment to carry baggage, two wagons for each headquarters from division up to his own, and one wagon for each brigade headquarters. He did allow one smaller spring wagon to accompany each headquarters. Sheridan also ordered each corps commander to reduce his other trains as best he could.[26]

With much longer distances to travel, and thus longer and more vulnerable supply lines, Federal forces in the West were compelled to slash land transportation to the minimum as they penetrated Confederate territory. The ultimate achievement in this regard was accomplished by William T. Sherman in the last year of the conflict. "When we move, we will take no tents or baggage," Sherman told Thomas in preparation for the Atlanta campaign. The men would carry all they could on their persons, the army would use pack animals to an extent, but the number of wagons tagging along behind the troops had to be whittled down to only one for each regiment. Those regimental wagons carried a ton of material, including rations, forage, and baggage. Foraging for subsistence and driving beef on the hoof behind the advancing armies helped in this effort. The result was that Sherman's army group in the Atlanta campaign had fewer wagons but more horses and mules than average for Union armies. Despite this, his men marched with 20 days of bread rations, 10 days of salt meat, 20 days of coffee, 30 days of salt, and 10 days of grain forage for animals. Sherman set an example. "My entire headquarters transportation is one wagon for myself, aides, officers, clerks, and orderlies. I think that is as low down as we can get until we get flat broke."[27]

"Soldiering as we have been doing for the past two years, with such trains and impediments, has been a farce, and nothing but absolute poverty will cure it," Sherman told Meigs. "I will be glad to hear Uncle Sam say 'we cannot afford this and that—you must gather your own grub and wagons, and bivouac and fight, not for pay, but for self-existence.' . . . I assure you I will second any effort you will make looking to economy."[28]

Sherman achieved a level of land transportation for the Atlanta campaign that could have served as a model for all field armies in the Civil War. Operating at the end of a single track of railroad stretching 350 miles to Louisville, his men barely had enough food and his animals barely had enough forage to survive the campaign, but the army group's ability to move was unimpeded. When Sherman broke away from his line of communications after the fall of Atlanta, he was able to maintain roughly the same level of land transportation as during the drive toward the city; he instituted little change in the wagon allowance during the March to the Sea. The Fifteenth Corps took 850 wagons along, each drawn by six-mule teams, plus 150 two-horse wagons and ambulances. Of the 850 army wagons, 225 were filled with ammunition (2,500 pounds apiece), 500 were filled with commissary stores (48 boxes of hard tack in each wagon), and the rest carried medical stores, pioneer tools, camp equipment, and private baggage. The corps transported eight wagons filled with shoes and socks for the troops. Each wagon also carried five days' rations of grain and three sets of horseshoes for the team.[29]

Sherman maintained this level on the Carolinas campaign as well, and his men relied on their own resources to fix wagons as they broke down during the hard marching early in 1865. Traveling forges proved to be unnecessary. In the Fourteenth Corps, small bellows fixed to the end of the wagon box sufficed for all small repairs on the iron fixtures of vehicles and to work on horseshoes. The chief quartermaster of the Fourteenth Corps thought such an arrangement could easily handle the needs of up to 30 teams even under difficult marching conditions. In John W. Geary's division of the Twentieth Corps, only 4 out of 159 wagons and 3 out of 33 ambulances broke down during the Carolinas campaign. His men used parts of these vehicles to repair other vehicles in an effort to keep them moving.[30]

Transportation allowances varied in the West according to the needs imposed by terrain and logistics as well as by the ideas of individual commanders. They ranged from allowances similar to McClellan's in Virginia to much reduced levels similar to Sherman's, although the trend certainly was to lower the allowance over time. Learning his lesson from the bloated transportation that inhibited movement by the Army of Virginia in the summer of 1862, John Pope instructed a subordinate about how to travel light when pursuing Native Americans in the Department of the Northwest a year later. Beef on the hoof should accompany the troops and room should be made in wagons only for sugar, coffee, and hardtack. "Celerity of movement . . . is all-important on such expeditions," Pope concluded, "with much infantry and large wagon-trains, this would be next to impossible."[31]

Confederate transportation allowances generally were lower than Federal standards. Braxton Bragg established slender allowances in preparation for his Kentucky foray in the late summer of 1862. He allowed each man one knapsack and each officer one carpet bag or "small valise." Wagon space was reserved for ammunition and other essential material. Bragg increased the allowance a bit after the Kentucky campaign ended. Overall allowances for the Army of Tennessee went from 35 wagons per 1,000 men in August 1863 to 26 by January 1864. During the Atlanta campaign, the Army of Tennessee managed to cut the number of ammunition wagons by having the men carry a load of rounds on their person. A total of 223 wagons carried 1,772,883 rounds of small arms ammunition, and the men personally carried well more than half the ammunition available, or 1,932,638 rounds.[32]

Robert E. Lee also had to keep wagon allowances to the minimum during most of the war. Daniel H. Hill complained of too few vehicles in the fall of 1862, but Lee pointed out that his division headquarters had six wagons whereas the army-wide standard had been set at only three wagons. Lee reduced this allowance to two wagons by the middle of 1863. In terms of overall averages, Lee was ahead of Bragg in reducing the number over time. While the Army of Northern Virginia was allowed 34 wagons for every 1,000 men in April 1863, the number dropped to 28 per 1,000 men by July 1863. This remained the level into the campaigning season of 1864, but Jubal Early reduced it to one wagon for each division headquarters and one wagon on average for every 500 men in preparation for rapid movement in the Shenandoah Valley.[33]

Transportation allowances set by other Confederate officers were pretty consistent with Lee's and Bragg's standards. John C. Pemberton's command in Mississippi had 27 wagons for every 1,000 men early in 1863. Dabney H. Maury's division of Pemberton's department had a lower ratio of 23 wagons for every 1,000 men. It has to be noted that the low ratio to be seen in most

Confederate commands was often due to the shortage of wagons available to quartermaster officers.[34]

At anywhere from 25 to 35 wagons per 1,000 men, Civil War armies traveled with a comparatively large train. Napoleon more often used 12 wagons to support 1,000 men, but he had the advantage of operating in a European environment that was densely populated and his commissaries could count on finding sufficient food in the theater of war to compensate for limited shipments from his base of supplies. The sparse population of the South compelled Civil War commanders to increase the ratio of wagons and rely more heavily on a fixed line of communications than their Napoleonic predecessor. The U.S. Army continued to allow about 25 to 35 wagons per 1,000 men to support its operations against Native Americans on the frontier after the Civil War, confirming that the Civil War standard was a solid solution to the problem of balancing logistical requirements with issues involving army mobility.[35]

By June 1864, the wagon trains of the Federal army were at their peak size and efficiency. From that point until the end of the war Meigs concentrated on replacing wagons rather than adding new vehicles to the pool. During the last two fiscal years of the war (July 1, 1863, to June 30, 1865), the Quartermaster Department purchased 19,311 wagons, 2,665 ambulances, 1,526 carts, and 188,060 varied sets of harness. It also manufactured 1,443 wagons. Wagons deteriorated at a steady rate due to rough usage. The Second Division, Twenty-Fifth Corps, possessed 73 wagons at the end of the war, but only 40 (54.7 percent) of them "could be called serviceable." That likely was an unusually low ratio of good wagons, but there is no doubt that most of the army vehicles in use by April 1865 had been made and purchased by the government since the outbreak of war. Nevertheless, Meigs noticed when looking at the wagon trains of the Army of the Potomac and of Sherman's army group at the end of the conflict that there were a handful of old wagons that had been in use since 1861; they had survived all the hard service of the war's campaigns.[36]

In contrast, many Confederate teams captured at Appomattox indicated the wretched state of Rebel land transportation. Many mules were so starved that "the bones were very prominent," according to Albert S. Twitchell of the 7th Maine Battery, and many of the harness consisted of "only a collar and hames, with ropes for traces. Some of the collars were merely wisps of straw." Benjamin F. McPherson of the 37th Alabama, detailed as a teamster in the Army of

Tennessee, recalled proudly that his wagon master praised his driving. "My boss often said that I had not given him any trouble at all, never stalled, while others were often breaking tongues out or other parts by carelessness."[37]

An east Tennessee civilian named H. V. Redfield had ample opportunity to observe the characteristics of wagon trains in both armies during the Civil War. He was greatly impressed by the Federal wagons, which were "uniform in size and make, and much stronger and heavier" than their Confederate counterparts. Rebel wagons "had the appearance of having been picked up about the country." Redfield had no doubt which side utilized better land transportation. "There was a strength, uniformity, system, and durability about [Federal trains] that was conspicuous when compared with the rather slip-shod wagon transportation of the Confederates" he concluded.[38]

Regardless of the quality of the train, exactly how far wagon transportation could support advancing troops from their river or rail supply network remained a matter of personal opinion during the war, but army mobility was a question of vital importance. As Joseph E. Johnston sarcastically put it, "we could not expect the enemy to await our arrival and give us battle at the terminus of the rail road." In 1862, Jacob D. Cox, operating in the mountains of western Virginia, thought his lightly loaded wagons could safely haul only 1,000 pounds of material about 12 miles. In the same year William T. Sherman estimated that a hauling distance of 50 miles was too far, while Stewart Van Vliet thought the Army of the Potomac could not rely on a string of wagons that had to go more than 20 miles. Other officers more optimistically thought it could be done as far as 100 miles. Exactly what was to be hauled, the condition of the roads, the threat of guerrilla attack, and the size of the infantry force all played a role in this calculation.[39]

Commanders on the frontier were much bolder in this matter because they were forced to rely almost exclusively on wagons for logistical support. During the fiscal year of July 1, 1862, to June 30, 1863, quartermaster L. C. Easton shipped 662,720 pounds of freight from Fort Leavenworth to Salt Lake City, a distance of 1,837 miles "through a perfect wilderness, where there is no forage or other supplies except grass." He also sent more than 6 million pounds of material to Fort Union, New Mexico, a distance of 735 miles. When John W. Denver proposed an expedition of 5,000 men from Fort Leavenworth to New Mexico in early 1862, he thought 500 wagons and 25 ambulances would give the troops adequate support. That ratio of wagons per 1,000 troops was three times higher than that for armies operating against Confederate forces. It should also be pointed out that Easton's shipments traveled a long distance but were not disturbed by enemy action and they represented regular supply shipments for small garrisons. Feeding and supporting a huge army of hungry soldiers concentrated in one place was an entirely different matter. Officers operating against Rebel armies had a different set of problems and challenges compared to those managing affairs on the frontier.[40]

The travel time of army trains depended on many factors. During Buell's pursuit of Bragg into Kentucky, sections of his train traveled 360 miles in 17 and a half days. A train of 40 wagons and 90 ambulances with William Rosecrans's Army of the Cumberland traveled between Chattanooga and Bridgeport, a round-trip of 60 miles, in six days during late September 1863. With better roads and flatter terrain, Sherman sent a wagon train from Lafayette Station to Memphis and expected it to make the 60-mile round-trip in three and a half days. William G. LeDuc, a quartermaster in the Army of the Potomac, exercised good management of his teams to make a round-trip of 44 miles in 24 hours, including unloading, an average of 1.8 miles per hour. Alexander M. Ayers of the 125th Illinois moved 61 wagons to Kinston, North Carolina, during Sherman's Carolinas campaign, traveling the 20 miles in 28 hours, for a speed of 1.4 miles per hour.[41]

Because Civil War armies were dependent on large numbers of wagons, ambulances, and other vehicles, quartermasters devoted a great deal of time and energy to trying to manage them effectively. Everything from the condition of the harness to the repair of the vehicles, from superintending drivers to working out organizational schemes and coordinating the trains' movements with the rest of the army needed to be developed. As noted earlier, Civil War quartermasters could count on a long history of wagon use mostly oriented toward the army's primary role of managing the frontier environment.

Early in his career, Ulysses S. Grant devoted considerable attention to such mundane matters as harness and mules. While breaking in animals so they could be used as teams, he also complained that the harness supplied his regiment at Jefferson City, Missouri, was so brittle that it broke "with the least strain." Grant was compelled to purchase better harness in the local area to replace it. One of the worst cases of mismanagement in the organization of trains can be seen in John Pope's Army of Virginia, which was gorged with too many wagons and plagued by quartermasters who could not get a handle on them.

"It does not appear that the commander of the Army of Virginia ever knew how many wagons there were," complained Rufus Ingalls, "nor what quartermasters were on duty."[42]

But most commanders and their quartermasters did an effective job of organizing the many wagons they needed. It was important that a quartermaster be placed in overall command of the train with full authority to arrest anyone who did not obey his orders. The marching order was determined by whether the troops were approaching or retiring from the enemy, always placed to be as far as possible from danger but close enough to the infantry to provide ammunition or food as needed. At the end of the day's march the wagons were to be parked in fields so as not to obstruct roads, with fences torn down and ditches filled in to facilitate an early start the next morning. When near the enemy, infantry units of varied sizes guarded the trains.[43]

Delays in long marches were common, but they tired the teams if prolonged indefinitely. William G. LeDuc, chief quartermaster of the Eleventh Corps, advised his subordinates to take advantage of delays to feed and water their mules to keep them "in good heart." They also should close up gaps that developed during the march so as to keep the wagons well in hand.[44]

Often quartermasters had to contend with drivers who were poorly suited to their job or capricious in their judgment. Don C. Buell felt compelled to issue general orders encouraging wagon masters to lock their wheels only when going down truly steep grades. The only way to lock wheels was to stop the wagon and put a chain on the wheels so they could not rotate. Buell thought this was done too often so "that teamsters may in various ways humor their fancies or whims." Eugene A. Carr complained not only of muddy roads and weak mules but of drivers who were "bad" at their job as he dealt with the problems of supplying his cavalry command in Missouri early in 1862.[45]

As a general rule, when trains moved along the same roads with other units of the army, they were to squeeze to the right of the roadway and let the others pass by. William B. Hazen found that habitually moving his Fifteenth Corps division in two columns, trains on the right of the road and troops on the left, shortened his column by half. Early in the Carolinas campaign Hazen noticed that another division, which practiced the normal mode of marching the troops and artillery in front of its wagon trains, had a column five miles long. John A. Logan liked Hazen's idea and mandated it as the normal mode of marching for the Fifteenth Corps. He instructed his division commanders to move their infantry to the side of the trains whenever possible, "studying always to give the road to their wagons."[46]

L. C. Easton thought the best arrangement for Sherman's trains during the March to the Sea was to lead with corps, division, brigade, and regimental baggage wagons in each corps' line of march. These baggage trains were to be followed by the empty wagons used in foraging and then the ammunition train, ambulance train, and all other wagons. The empty wagons fell out of the column during the day to go short distances into the countryside, collecting food and returning to the rear of the entire column. Sherman's quartermasters fully understood the utility of dividing trains into sections of no more than 50 wagons each and assigning wagon masters to each section. Putting the slowest teams in front of each section ensured that gaps in the line (which were inevitable) would develop between sections and not between wagons within each section.[47]

Terrain and weather proved to be the biggest problems faced by Sherman's quartermasters during the Carolinas campaign. When a Twentieth Corps train tried to cross Black Swamp along a narrow causeway on February 4, 1865, it encountered one of the muddiest roadways imaginable. About every third wagon got stuck; the entire line behind it had to stop as men tried to physically lift it out of the muck. The wagons "worked along a few feet at a time," complained Harvey Reid of the 22nd Wisconsin. Night descended along with a chilly fog. The men could not see ten feet ahead, so the train stopped for the night. The drivers found room in the wagons to sleep as infantry details worked to corduroy the roadbed. The wagons managed to get off the causeway by 9 A.M. the next morning.[48]

While some infantrymen might have welcomed assignment to guarding trains as easy duty, many others found it tedious and boring. It was "the worst kind of soldiering," thought William Bluffton Miller of the 75th Indiana. "It makes us late starting and late into camp. Some times we are marching hard and then again we only play along." Those men unlucky enough to be assigned as guards for a small pox train Sherman organized during the Carolinas campaign complained about it because they were afraid of being exposed to the dreaded disease.[49]

Unusual dangers sometimes accompanied the movement of wagon trains in the field. A terrible storm descended on Sherman's columns as he moved toward Jackson, Mississippi, right after the fall of Vicksburg in July 1863.

Ebenezer W. Wells of the 79th New York, who had charge of some Ninth Corps trains, stopped his vehicles to wait it out, but a tree fell onto a wagon, smashed it to pieces, and killed an officer inside. On resuming the march, the first wagon to descend a deep gully was swept away by the sudden rushing of rainwater. The driver managed to save himself, but his team was killed. The chief quartermaster of the Army of the Tennessee also moved his trains through water two to four feet deep for two miles at one point during the Carolinas campaign, and at another point ran them through a burning forest of pine timber that nearly set his canvass-topped wagons on fire.[50]

The greatest danger to wagon trains, however, remained enemy action. When the units they were attached to became engaged in heavy combat, the wagons had to be relatively close to resupply the troops with ammunition, but far enough away to avoid long-range artillery and musketry fire. Because of his long service as chief quartermaster of the Army of the Potomac, Rufus Ingalls developed an effective attitude toward this problem. He positioned the general supply train 25 miles from the fighting at Gettysburg but of course moved ammunition wagons and ambulances close to the troops.[51]

Richard Batchelder served as chief quartermaster of the Second Corps during the Chancellorsville campaign. He left the majority of his 351 wagons at Falmouth before the corps set out up the Rapidan River to flank Lee's position at Fredericksburg. Batchelder moved an additional 70 ammunition wagons, 45 wagons with food, and 30 wagons loaded with medical supplies and forage along with the corps. Batchelder also assigned 35 pack animals to each division for the purpose of hauling ammunition and food from the wagons to the infantry units. Rather than accompany Hooker's main movement up the Rapidan, the Sixth Corps remained at Falmouth to operate across the Rappahannock River and attack the weakened Confederate position at Fredericksburg. Alexander Bliss served as chief quartermaster of the Sixth Corps. He parked his train four miles from the river to keep it safe from artillery fire and kept in close touch with the corps headquarters as the troops captured the heights and moved west, sending forward as much as they needed on a daily basis from his park.[52]

Quartermaster officers on all levels of command in the field managed trains with generally effective methods. In addition, both armies created special high-level administrators to manage the supply of wagons. When the Quartermaster Department was reorganized in July 1864, Meigs relegated this duty to the newly created Fifth Division of his department, which was responsible for supplying everything not specifically falling under the jurisdiction of the other divisions. The Confederates created a central office in Richmond for the inspection of field transportation in the fall of 1862 that performed a somewhat similar service as Meigs's division. This office divided the Confederacy into divisions, with an officer in charge of each. This officer supervised the acquisition of wagons. He also managed the construction and repair of them, and took responsibility for acquiring horses and mules. The office also set guidelines mandating that every regimental quartermaster needed to assign a wagon master and a clerk from the ranks to manage the vehicles assigned the unit. The same was required of brigade and division quartermasters. If wagon masters had to be hired from the civilian population, their maximum pay was set at $50 per month if they managed up to 10 wagons and $75 per month if they took charge of up to 59 wagons. With a much bigger army to serve, Meigs divided much of this work into different divisions. In contrast, the Confederate Transportation Department was far from successful at achieving its goals, but Rebel transportation officers labored under crushing difficulties as the war ground to a conclusion.[53]

Historian Russell Weigley has concluded that "the number of wagons following the Federal armies was probably without precedent."[54] That undoubtedly was true within the context of American military history. Previous campaigns from the colonial era to the Mexican War involved far smaller field armies than either Union or Confederate leaders gathered to fight the Civil War. Within the context of European military history, Federal and Rebel armies were not unusually large, but Europe provided many more opportunities for field armies to live off the land rather than relying on bringing forward large amounts of supplies from the distribution points of logistical networks. But, while the need for large wagon trains was imperative, Civil War officers were able to cope with the demand because they drew on a long heritage of wagon use, mostly due to the expansive frontier environment with its far-flung outposts and crude dirt roads. Civil War quartermasters knew how to handle large trains, and there was a large supply of mules in the civilian economy and hundreds of experienced teamsters. The chief difficulties encountered in the South were the lack of financial power to purchase vehicles and the shortage of wagon-making establishments. In contrast, providing enough vehicles, harness, and mules to the Union army was among the lesser problems faced by Montgomery Meigs.

No matter how important the river and coastal steamers and the railroads were to Civil War logisticians, old-fashioned wagons remained equally important to the armies. They were a vital link in the system of transportation, carrying needed goods over the last gap in the logistical chain. Wagon trains were in fact the tail end of the national logistical systems and the most flexible part of them, cooperating intimately with the moving masses of infantry, cavalry, and artillery who depended as much on the mule team as they did on the iron horse for their daily support.

7

PACK TRAINS, CATTLE HERDS, AND FOOT POWER

A good deal of the military assets associated with every field army was carried by foot power rather than on wheeled vehicles. Pack mules had been a feature of military life since the classical era and they played a large role on the frontier in pre–Civil War America. Beef on the hoof accompanied field armies to provide fresh meat for soldier rations. The men themselves were links in the logistical chain; they carried their weapons, ammunition, and accouterments as well as their food and a few personal belongings wherever they marched. Foot power represented an example of logistics in the theater of operations as opposed to national or strategic lines of communication; it underwrote mobility of armies in the field. Food, equipment, and ammunition needed to keep pace with the most advanced elements of an invading army, and that could not happen without effective roads and methods of crossing streams.

Regulations concerning how the U.S. Army purchased mules had initially been issued in 1818, although quartermasters probably had been using mules prior to that date. The army made large-scale use of mules in the Second Seminole War of 1835–1842 and in the Mexican War of 1846–1848, both as pack animals and to pull army wagons. During the Civil War it was common for every regiment to have one or two mules to haul camp equipment, according to John D. Billings, and sometimes they were used to haul extra ammunition to the firing line. By the latter part of the conflict various headquarters issued orders regulating the number of mules. The Fourth Corps commander, for example, allowed two pack mules for the field officers and staff of each regiment, one for every three line officers, and two to haul the cooking utensils of each regiment.[1]

A basic problem in managing pack mules was how to adjust and load the pack saddle. The idea was to distribute the material over a wide surface to avoid causing sores and undue pressure on the animal's spine. The freight had to be arranged on the saddle so as to keep the center of gravity low, and that meant placing items on each side rather than on top of the mule's back. This demanded a specially designed saddle, and the Mexican aparejo proved to be the best. An experienced and thoughtful packer was also necessary, and the best came from Mexico. He could tie the material to the saddle in a way to leave the mule's backbone free and divide the weight evenly on both sides. If a large number of pack mules were aggregated into a train, all were led by a mule willing to go forward with a bell tied to its neck, and the others tended to follow. On average, one mule could haul about 200 pounds of material.[2]

All these aspects of using mules as pack animals were effectively worked out through the frontier experience of the U.S. Army, especially in the newly acquired territory of the Southwest. But inexperienced Civil War quartermasters had to learn many of these lessons anew after Fort Sumter. Charles Leib was told to create a pack train while supplying troops in the mountainous counties of Virginia early in the war, and the pack saddles sent him were of poor quality. They were "made of bass wood, covered with sheepskin instead of raw hide," and were barely held together with small nails. "The instant they were exposed to damp weather, they almost fell apart. It was next to impossible to fasten the saddles on the mules properly." The mules Leib purchased were rather wild and he had trouble finding someone who knew how to handle them. His first attempt to move supplies by pack train led to the loss of much of his material until superiors sent him several "French Creoles and Mexican Greasers" from the Southwest. They organized a train of 200 mules, found a cowbell, and hung it from a horse's neck to serve as the bell mare.[3]

Even under the best of conditions, pack trains were poor substitutes for wagon trains. A six-mule wagon could carry 25 boxes of small arms ammunition, while a pack mule could haul only 2 boxes. Depending on road conditions, the wagon could convey 2,000 to 4,000 pounds of freight, but the pack animal could haul only 200 pounds. Smaller spring wagons were capable of taking 800 to 1,200 pounds, and even a camel could carry 400 pounds of material. Not surprisingly, army quartermasters found it was more efficient to use the army wagon rather than a pack animal for transport in the field. "We have used 6 Mule Govt wagons almost exclusively in this army," reported quartermaster John J. Metzgar of the 76th Ohio during the Atlanta campaign, "but very few pack animals."[4]

Despite their low carrying capacity, pack mules offered a couple of advantages over wagons. They could better negotiate rugged terrain and tended to be more mobile and less of an impediment than large trains of wagons. Their greater mobility tempted Joseph Hooker to experiment with them during the brief time he commanded the Army of the Potomac. "Don't burden yourself with any transportation not absolutely needed," Daniel Butterfield, Hooker's chief of staff, told the commander of the Third Corps. "Every wagon is one too many in the way where they can be dispensed with." As a result, large numbers of pack mules were issued to the Army of the Potomac in April 1863. The First Corps fielded two mules for every regiment, for example, and they were generally used to carry ammunition. Fifth Corps quartermasters packed 365,000 rounds of small arms ammunition on mules while keeping 2.3 million rounds in their ordnance train.[5]

Alexander Bliss, a quartermaster in the Fifth Corps, thought the pack train worked well in the Chancellorsville campaign. The corps kept its wagon train parked in camp six miles away and relied on mules to carry food as well as ammunition up to the corps' position. One of its wagon masters came up with an idea to tie a rope around every ammunition box so that a loop was handy; packers could hang the box on the pack saddle using that loop for quick loading and unloading. Bliss used 116 of the 320 mules available to the corps to carry ammunition. The rest carried rations and anything else he had to move from the trains to the battle line.[6]

But other quartermasters reported the pack train experiment to be a failure. First Corps officers could not find anyone who knew how to load a mule properly. They kept the animals saddled most of the duration of the campaign, with consequent rubbing of the skin and exhaustion of the mules. First Corps quartermasters were not impressed by the small amounts of ammunition each mule was able to carry and favored the normal method of bringing ammunition wagons as close as possible to the line and then carrying the boxes by hand to the troops. Third Corps quartermasters also noted that they had created their corps pack train by taking two mules from each wagon team. The result was that the train was underpowered and less efficient than normal.[7]

In the Eleventh Corps, William G. LeDuc experienced many problems with the pack train at Chancellorsville. Neither officers nor men had any clue how to handle it. They failed to feed the animals regularly and almost never unsaddled them during the campaign. "The backs of some were scalded and fairly rotten," he reported. Of 59 mules in the First Division, 13 were so injured they had to be condemned. Of 56 mules in the Third Division, one died, one was stolen, one was lost, and one was abandoned during the short campaign.[8]

The results of the pack train experiment at Chancellorsville were so mixed that Hooker decided to give up on the idea of using mules as a major element in the army's transportation. As Rufus Ingalls, his chief quartermaster, put it, they could serve as "auxiliary . . . to wagons, for short distances over rough country, where there are few and bad roads," but not as a main reliance in cases where wagons were feasible. Hooker mandated that at least 200 pack saddles be kept for each corps so that individual mules could be used when needed and trains could also be organized if corps quartermasters thought it was expedient to do so.[9]

The cavalry arm was well suited for pack trains rather than wagons, and Hooker's mounted troops experimented with them during the Chancellorsville campaign. The cavalry "moved, by orders, without wheels, except batteries," reported Butterfield to Meigs. It found plenty of food and forage in the countryside, but C. G. Sawtelle, chief quartermaster of the Cavalry Corps, thought ill of the idea. He could not find enough men who knew how to load the saddles properly. It was "an art which can only be learned by actual and long experience." Moreover, the saddles supplied him were inferior in quality (of "the McClellan pattern"), and saddle blankets were "little better than rotten rags." As a result, two-thirds of Sawtelle's mules were "more or less broken down." Even without these problems, packing supplies for a large force in Virginia was quite different than for a small party on the frontier. Sawtelle told Ingalls that he had to detail one man to take care of every two mules on the march, sometimes one man per mule, thus draining the regiments of able-bodied troops. And for this he could only haul a small amount of material compared to army wagons. In every way, wagon trains were the optimal mode of in-theater transportation, for they maximized quantity of load and minimized the number of men and mules to move it.[10]

Pack mules continued to play a significant role in transportation, but on a small, dispersed scale. They were allowed at all levels of headquarters as a substitute for wagons if the commander chose to use them. The general idea that large pack trains were not efficient continued to guide quartermaster thinking into 1864 and 1865, but General in Chief Ulysses S. Grant continued to allow 200 pack saddles to be transported in each corps train during the Overland campaign. Second Corps officers used mules to carry rations to the troops during the early phases of the Fourth Offensive at Petersburg because rains had worsened the roads for wagons, but frustrated quartermasters declared it "a slow and troublesome method."[11]

Cavalry forces in Virginia continued to supplement their wagon trains with pack mules. When Philip Sheridan led a mounted movement from the Shenandoah Valley toward Grant's concentration at Richmond and Petersburg, tearing up the Virginia Central Railroad and the James River Canal along the way, he moved most of his assets by wagon, although the number was kept to a minimum. In addition, a pack mule was allowed for every squadron and two or three mules accompanied every regimental headquarters for the 350-mile journey.[12]

Far less evidence of pack mule use in the Confederate army exists, unfortunately, but a few documents provide glimpses into the subject. Cavalry commanders in the Army of Tennessee were enjoined to rely on pack mules rather than wagons, allowing one mule for every two men. The idea was to carry everything necessary, including ammunition, to give greater mobility to the mounted arm. Quartermasters were responsible for finding suitable pack saddles.[13]

It is unclear how thoroughly this order was carried out and how well the pack mules worked for the Confederates. One thing is certain: pack animals were more effective when used to support smaller commands as opposed to large units. After the Civil War, back on the sprawling frontier with its isolated posts and small patrols, pack mules were a superb form of in-theater transportation for the army. Twelve mules carried all that a company of 70 men needed for a six-day scout, and there was no fuss or bother with wagons.[14]

Mules played a big role not as pack animals but as draft animals to haul army wagons, which were the mainstay of in-theater transportation during the Civil War. In fact, the mule and the horse teamed up to provide Civil War armies what they needed in animal foot power. Horses were uniquely suited to provide mounts for cavalrymen, to pull artillery pieces, and to carry officers. Mules were uniquely suited to pull wagons under very rough conditions. Six mules had to be teamed to pull the same weight as four horses, it is true, and they were nervous under fire, but they could endure neglect, poor feed, and even abuse more readily than horses. During the Peninsula campaign, the sandy soil of coastal Virginia made for muddy, sticky dirt roads when it rained. "I find that mules are the only animals fit for this rough service," reported Stewart Van Vliet, chief quartermaster of the Army of the Potomac. "Our horse teams suffer severely, and I would recommend that hereafter no more horse teams be provided for our armies, no matter in what part of the country they may be serving, as mules are far more serviceable and economical."[15]

Mules could handle the rough nature of corduroy roads better than horses. Corduroy was made from the trunks of small trees cut to length as a sort of pavement over muddy roads. It could be dangerous to horses because of its uneven nature and the holes between trunks that could catch a hoof. It was a sight to see mules "stepping from log to log with accuracy seldom making a mistake," wrote a member of the 150th New York. If they stepped between logs and got stuck, the hardy mules waited until someone helped to pull their leg free and continued as if nothing had happened.[16]

James S. Wadsworth, commander of the First Division, First Corps, got an idea to experiment with an unusual train following Ambrose Burnside's Mud March early in 1863. He collected the various carts used by refugee blacks who gathered at Union camps and organized them into a train. Then he selected the best steers from the beef herds of the army and assigned an officer who had experience at working with oxen in Wisconsin to train them. Assigning mechanics to fix the carts and fashion suitable yokes, Wadsworth's oxen train was ready for service by the time of the Gettysburg campaign. The oxen moved so slowly that both the horse and mule teams in the Army of the Potomac outpaced them by three miles on the first day of marching. Well before the army reached the Potomac River, frustrated officers dismantled this quixotic experiment and returned the steers to the beef herd.[17]

Mules were far superior to both oxen and horses as draft animals for wagon trains. Quartermaster S. B. Holabird called them among "the most valuable animals in the world for purposes of war." Mules came in differing sizes and temperaments. Those bred in Kentucky and Missouri were heavier, while the mules coming from the Southwest were lighter. The six-mule team for each wagon consisted of three pairs with different jobs. Wheel mules anchored the team and were placed nearest the wagon. Larger, stronger mules made good wheel pairs. The swing pair was placed in the middle; lighter mules were better in this place than bigger animals. Lighter and smarter mules also made good lead pairs at the front of the team.[18]

"A team thus constituted is much more flexible and more easily handled by the teamster," Holabird asserted. The small mules at the lead could get across mud and obstacles and help pull the others across, while heavier mules allowed the driver to restrain the smaller and friskier ones in front. "There was more elasticity in such a team," asserted John D. Billings, "and a good driver could handle them much more gracefully and dexterously than he could the same number of horses."[19]

The driver did not ride on the wagon but on the left-hand wheel mule. He guided the lead pair with what was called a jerk line. Theodore Gardner of the 1st Kansas Battery was detailed to drive a six-mule team and came to appreciate the sturdiness of his animals. Moving in a train at night, it often happened that wagons in front stopped without warning and his team would get jammed up in a bunch. The mules simply waited patiently until the column proceeded; then they had room to untangle by going forward "and away we would go again."[20]

Like everything else in the army, regulations stipulated how many mules were allowed to each unit. It was obvious to William T. Sherman that his division had too many of them while marching toward Memphis in mid-July 1862, and he issued orders for all surplus animals to be turned over to the quartermaster. The number of mules serving the Army of the Potomac remained stable throughout the last year of the war compared to the number of horses. The army's cavalry arm accounted for the overwhelming majority of horses used, and the number fluctuated depending on how hard the cavalry operated. But the supply of mules had to remain relatively constant to pull the wagons needed by the army. While the Army of the Potomac fielded between 23,000 and 25,000 mules during this time period, its supply of horses ranged from 24,000 to 41,000.[21]

The Army of the Potomac had an unusually large cavalry arm; the number of mules serving other Union field armies was higher by comparison. The Army of the Cumberland possessed 19,164 horses in April 1863, but that total came from counting literally all horses (cavalry, artillery, draft, and spare mounts). At the same time it used 23,859 mules. In other words, 55.4 percent of the animals working for William S. Rosecrans's army at the war's midpoint were mules.[22]

Students of the Civil War normally are unaware of how important both horses and mules were to the armies. By 1863 they needed half as many horses and mules as there were men serving in uniform to provide mobility to the armies. Service in the field was arduous to animal flesh, and the civilian supply of horses and mules was not unlimited. It has been estimated that there were about 6 million horses and mules in the North in 1861; initially the Union army started with no more than 15,000 draft and riding animals. Federal quartermasters bought an estimated 1 million mules alone by 1865. It was not possible to breed either horses or mules for the war. With an 11-month gestation period and the fact that they were not ready for the rigors of war until at least four to six years of age, the 6 million animals living in 1861 constituted the only pool quartermasters could draw upon for the duration of the war.[23]

Montgomery Meigs faced the daunting task of providing these animals to the numerous field armies. He sent 18,450 horses and 14,607 mules to the Army of the Cumberland from December 1862 through April 1863. That amounted to almost 7,000 animals every month, at an estimated cost of about $4 million. John Fitch calculated that the average cost amounted to $110 per horse and $105 per mule. In his report covering the last fiscal year of the Civil War, Meigs indicated that the cost of animals sharply rose by that phase of the conflict. He spent from $144 to $185 per horse and $170 to $195 per mule on a total of more than 272,000 animals during that period.[24]

Purchasing animals represented only one phase of government expenses on land transportation. The full ration for a horse was 14 pounds of hay and 12 pounds of grain per day. It was important that it eat both types of feed to maintain a healthy balance. The hay, often called fodder, "provided nutrition and the bulk required by the horse's digestive system," according to historian Ann N. Green. The grain "afforded high-energy food for muscle and energy." Green believes Civil War horses "were probably overfed in camp and underfed while working." By comparison, the daily ration of one soldier amounted to about three pounds. The horse's ration weighed 4.5 times as much as the man's, and part of it, the hay or fodder, was far bulkier to transport. Quartermasters with the Army of the Cumberland stored 24,000 bales of hay at a cost of $25 per ton and 200,000 sacks of grain at a cost of 25 cents per bushel to feed Rosecrans's animals in April 1863. Meigs estimated that the Federal government spent $155,262,732 on fodder and grain alone during the four years of the Civil War. He relied on civilian agents to find and purchase it and paid for shipping costs to army depots.[25]

Apparently mules received the same rations as horses, because reports and regulations do not differentiate between them as far as feeding was concerned. But mules had a different attitude toward food. When hungry they did not hesitate to chew on almost anything that was handy. Since their lives were so tied to wagons, it was not unusual for mules to nibble on various parts of the vehicle they pulled. Favorite parts were the wooden tongues and the end gates. It was not feasible to keep them away from the wagons when in camp, so one quartermaster suggested contractors should place iron strips along the tongues and end gates to prevent the mules from eating them.[26]

Attrition of all kinds ate away at the supply of draft animals, cavalry horses, and artillery mounts at a ferocious rate during the Civil War. Disease exacted a devastating toll. A major outbreak of glanders set in by the winter of 1861–1862 and raged for many months, never entirely going away by war's end. It was a communicable disease that resulted in high fever and the discharge of a thick nasal mucus. Many horses died, but others merely weakened. The survivors carried the disease for years, leading to periodic outbreaks over time. Tens of thousands of horses perished in this way during the war.[27]

Battle also created casualties among animals. More than 500 artillery horses and over 1,000 cavalry horses were killed at the battle of Stones River. An estimated 5,000 animals perished at Gettysburg, representing about "2.5 million tons of horseflesh." When Philip Sheridan served as a quartermaster in Samuel R. Curtis's Army of the Southwest in Missouri early in the conflict, Curtis told him to count on losing 10 percent of his animals every month due to a variety of causes.[28]

Early in the Atlanta campaign, Cyrus Clay Carpenter recorded the loss of 42 mules from his wagon train, which was attached to the Left Wing of the Sixteenth Corps in Sherman's army group. This was from a total of 960 mules in the train. The loss ratio, 4.3 percent, represented only one day's attrition, compared to Curtis's benchmark of 10 percent per month. Extended to a 30-day period, Carpenter's loss rate would have amounted to wiping out all his available mules and more in a month.[29] But Carpenter encountered unusual difficulties in getting his train from winter camps to northwest Georgia in time for the start of the Atlanta campaign; we cannot take his loss ratio as typical.

Twenty-Third Corps troops also encountered similar conditions while moving from east Tennessee to join Sherman early in May 1864. "You have no idea how many horses and mules die along the road," Marshall Mortimer Miller told his wife as Battery F of the 1st Michigan Artillery continued marching toward Georgia. "It is almost impossible to breathe in some places." Up to 4,000 horses and mules had been transported to a corral near Bridgeport, Alabama, the previous winter, where they could recuperate from exhaustion, malnutrition, and disease. Many of them did not survive. Jenkin Lloyd Jones took 38 horses and 3 mules of the 6th Wisconsin Battery to this corral in December 1863 and was appalled by the sight and smell. "Its presence was manifested by the stench from far off from the carrion of the dead. They filled for acres the woods to a number almost incredible, starved to death."[30]

Attrition increased its toll when, pressured by high demand for mules, quartermasters purchased inferior or juvenile animals that could not withstand the rigors of field service. It also was possible for horses and mules to fall while being transported in boxcars that usually were not designed to carry animals. Typically they were simply led into an empty car that had no specially designed stalls and not even feed or water troughs. Cooped up for hours on end, train travel was a trying and dangerous experience for animals.[31]

Specific campaigns were especially hard on horses and mules. The operations around Chattanooga in late 1863 were conducted in rugged mountains, and the ability of railroads to transport large amounts of fodder and food was severely limited. Horses and mules suffered enormously, as we have seen at the corral located near Bridgeport. Meigs estimated that 30,000 draft animals either died or were so emaciated that they had to be taken out of service during the Chattanooga campaign, surely the most devastating operation as far as animals were concerned in the entire war.[32]

Sherman began his March to the Sea with a weak force of draft animals. Prior to setting out, John Bell Hood had broken the rail link between Chattanooga and Atlanta in several places, and the teams left behind in the latter city suffered a great deal from food shortages. At one point they were reduced to only half rations of fodder and no grain at all. Even those animals belonging to troops that set out in pursuit of Hood fared poorly. In the Seventeenth Corps, 150 horses and mules were lost in one day's march. By mid-October, Sherman ordered his trains stripped to the minimum in order to pursue the enemy more effectively.[33]

After Hood escaped into north Alabama, Sherman redirected his troops eastward and prepared for the March to the Sea. His men were compelled to kill or abandon 3,116 horses and 1,603 mules along the way from Atlanta to Savannah, mostly because of their weakened condition due to food shortages the previous two months. But the Federals vigorously scoured the Georgia countryside to find 3,450 horses and 4,930 mules to more than replace those losses. Moreover, they found these Georgia animals to be in far better condition than their own. Sherman's move through the Carolinas early in 1865 produced harsh marching conditions, leading to an even bigger loss of draft animals than in the Georgia campaign and with fewer opportunities to replenish them from farms along the line of movement.[34]

Both Union and Confederate authorities established a system of animal care consisting of camps where sick or run-down horses and mules could recuperate. Meigs reported that 60 percent of the animals sent to the Union system recovered and were returned to service. There are no comparable reports for the success rate of the Confederate system, but the corral at Lynchburg, Virginia, took in 6,875 horses from October 1863 until February 1865, and only 15 percent of them recuperated enough to return to service. The Lynchburg corral had better success with mules; out of 2,885 of them, 56 percent recovered and returned to duty.[35]

At war's end, Meigs sold off surplus draft animals to save taxpayer expense. From May to October 1865, he reduced government stock by nearly 54,000 horses and over 52,000 mules, bringing in well over $6 million. Mules continued to play a large role in U.S. Army operations after the Civil War. They were indispensable as pack animals and for wagon teams on the frontier and in every major war the country conducted overseas for the next century. They saw service in the Filipino War of 1899–1902, and more than 30,000 American mules were transported to France during World War I (three-fourths of them died, principally from inadequate care). Pack mules became indispensable in negotiating the mountainous terrain of Italy during World War II, as well as in the jungled landscape of the China-Burma-India Theater in Asia. They were used in Korea, but the army decided to discontinue its heritage of mule service by "discharging" the last mules from the military in 1956.[36]

Horses and mules play a visible role in our view of the Civil War, but cattle remain obscure. They accompanied every field army, providing beef on the hoof for soldiers. Drovers chose a docile steer to carry their camp equipment and lead the herd as they plotted a course across the countryside, leaving the roads to troops, trains, and artillery. Quartermasters killed some every day using rifle muskets, slaughtered them on the spot, and issued the meat to the troops. In large field armies the cattle herd was divided into brigade, division, and corps herds, with a general reserve for the entire force.[37]

The Army of the Potomac had from 8,000 to 10,000 steers when it began the Overland campaign in May 1864. By July, the general reserve for the army numbered 3,000 head of cattle. Moving the herds across the wide James River during Grant's march from Cold Harbor to Petersburg proved difficult because the few bridges had to be reserved for troops, wagons, and artillery carriages. Besides, allowing the steers to walk across a pontoon bridge in any way they wished courted disaster. They would tend to group and put too much weight on some parts of it, possibly breaking up the string of boats. It would have been necessary to segment the cattle into groups of only five, with men between each group, to make a crossing of pontoons safe, and that would have taken several hours. Instead, drovers found some small boats to escort the herd as it swam across the river.[38]

Of course, it was far easier to drive cattle along roads than across streams, and several beef herds accompanied Sherman's army group during the Atlanta campaign. Captain Edward C. Dale, a commissary officer, took charge of 589 head of beef at Nashville. There simply was no room on the overcrowded railroad cars for them, so he had to move the cattle all the way to Sherman on foot. Sixty soldiers guarded the herd and 30 civilians drove the cattle. Dale made about 14 miles each day after setting out on May 29, 1864. By mid-July he delivered his charge and was back in Nashville ready to take another herd of 1,000 head to Sherman. At the same time, cattle herds were moved to other parts of middle Tennessee to feed garrison troops along Sherman's rail network. Some 800 head moved from Murfreesboro to Tullahoma in five days. Beef generally was considered an important part of a soldier's diet, and the method of delivery avoided unnecessary strain on the heavily taxed railroad system.[39]

Confederate armies also relied on cattle herds when they could, but the supply was uncertain in quantity and often in terms of quality. Thomas B. Wilson, a Rebel cavalryman who served as a courier, recalled a herd of Texas steers issued to the Army of Tennessee just before the onset of the Tennessee campaign. A herd of 3,000 crossed the pontoon bridge over the Tennessee River at Florence by dividing them up into groups of two or three, but when they arrived on the north bank everyone was astonished at their emaciated condition. The beef cut from their carcasses "was so devoid of fat that the boys would amuse themselves by throwing their steaks of it against trees to see it stick to the bark."[40]

Whether in the Union or Confederate army, cattle butchering produced an enormous mess. Rosecrans's army killed 50 to 60 head every day while lying stationary at Murfreesboro during the first six months of 1863, and local residents recalled years later the sight and smell of butchering. Initially an area of about an acre was covered with "the entrails, heads and feet, left lying there." But as time went by the affected area increased to include several acres. When spring brought warm weather, the "smell became very offensive." Civilians worried about the effect of such carrion on the air and water of the locality, but fortunately army officers detailed men to dig pits and scrape the offensive matter into them.[41]

Cattle herds represented an element in the logistical chain of Civil War armies because they took an important part of the soldier ration where it was needed. Marching soldiers themselves were another important element in that chain because they moved weapons, ammunition, and food while invading enemy territory. In effect, they were the leading element in the logistical chain supporting army movements, fed and supplied by the long strings of steamboats, railroad cars, and ocean transports behind them.

"On foot was our normal method of locomotion," recalled Albert Theodore Goodloe of the 35th Alabama. "This involved weariness extreme, and sore feet and corns without limit or stint." Everyone in his war experience came to the point of exhaustion and physical breakdown at one time or another, even though for most of their service they managed to keep up with the regiment. In fact, Goodloe was quite aware that men reacted differently to the rigors of marching. "Some would struggle, while others would maintain their places steadily in the ranks; some would yield to weariness with much readiness, while others would with much determination resist it; some would continue to keep their guns in proper position, while others would carry them with such looseness as to inconvenience or strike those nearest them; some would give attention to their feet and keep them in good condition as long as possible, while others would neglect them from the start and soon have them smarting with sores."[42]

Successful soldiers learned during their first march to lighten the load they carried. The gun, ammunition, accouterments, and food could not be compromised; they were essential. But the personal baggage could be reduced to almost any point and men tended to throw away what they thought they could do without. Spare clothing could be dispensed with until only the essentials were left. According to Thomas Sewell of the 127th Illinois, this amounted to "a pair of socks, an undershirt and a pair of drawers."[43]

Throughout their long war service, Union and Confederate soldiers experienced some particularly strenuous marches that tried even hardened men. For the 36th Illinois it came when the division moved from Batesville, Arkansas, to Cape Girardeau, Missouri, in May 1862. The weather was unusually hot, the roads were particularly dusty, and there were hills and rivers to cross. "Not a third of the troops were able to keep up with the marching column," declared regimental historians after the war. Crossing the deep and swift Current River on a small ferryboat led to the drowning of nearly a dozen men in the 15th Missouri when the craft capsized midstream. Partway through the journey the weather changed and downpours were common for two days, yet the troops continued their heavy pace of 20 to 30 miles per day. New shoes issued at Batesville were of such inferior quality that many of them wore out well before the journey's end, leading to cut and sore feet in the 36th Illinois. After nine days of hard marching, the regiment finally reached Cape Girardeau, with the men in tattered clothes and looking "like a crowd of vagabonds."[44]

A sense of urgency sped the 36th Illinois and its companion regiments along the road to the Mississippi River, but when Sherman planned his famous March to the Sea he could set a more measured pace. Moving 60,000 men in the first leg of a planned trip to Petersburg, Virginia, Sherman mandated a rate of 10 to 15 miles per day. Feeding his troops from the countryside, he had to slow the march to allow for the dispatch of foraging parties and the protection of wagon trains.[45]

No matter the purpose of the march, every soldier wrestled with the problem of making his load as light as possible, and the only way to do that was to get rid of personal belongings. The tendency always was for new troops to be overloaded with items they thought they needed, only to find that a stripped-down mode of marching was far better. Colonel Montfort S. Stokes's 1st North Carolina State Troops was mustered into Confederate service in May 1862 and brought with it the personal baggage accumulated during a year of service in static positions. It was far too much for field service; moreover, the men had not even learned how to pack and secure their personal belongings for marching. As one observer noted, they had "too much baggage and have no care or skill in securing it, thus rendering it a great impediment in moving."[46]

It has to be pointed out, however, that even experienced troops could accumulate unnecessary material while lying in camp for extended periods of time. After several months of comparative idleness at Murfreesboro in early 1863, Rosecrans's troops held company inspections, after which officers ordered them "to pack up all spare 'duds.'" They were allowed to keep one pair of shoes, two pairs of drawers, two shirts, one cap or hat, one coat, one pair of pants, and one blanket.[47]

After the war, Sherman concluded that the average soldier was capable of carrying up to 50 or 60 pounds while on the move. The load included his musket and equipment, 60 rounds of ammunition, a shelter tent, a blanket or overcoat, and extra pairs of pants, socks, and drawers. Rather than a bulky knapsack, Sherman advised that the soldier roll up whatever could be folded into his blanket and wear the roll over his shoulder. The haversack filled with "bread, cooked meat, salt, and coffee" was indispensable. Thus set up, the troops of a corps could carry what would require 500 wagons to transport, thus cutting down on the size of the army's trains.[48]

Sherman's troops learned through hard experience—and at the insistence of their commander—how to travel as light as possible. This was a goal that many Federal officers thought about as well. A French manufacturer named Alexis Godillot had tried to develop equipment for the French army designed to provide all that soldiers needed in a way for them to carry it in the field, thus dispensing with trains entirely. Montgomery Meigs was interested and acquired a copy of Godillot's catalog and purchased sample pieces of equipment and supplies from him early in the war. By January 1862 Meigs began to forward a paper prepared by Godillot concerning his system to Union generals. He thought some of the Frenchman's ideas were impractical, but others were worthy of consideration.[49]

Joseph Hooker was particularly interested in these ideas after he took command of the Army of the Potomac and tried to devise an American approach to reducing personal baggage for the men. He mandated that they carry eight days' worth of rations on their persons during an active campaign. Wagons would carry forage for animals and ammunition for the troops, with pack mules moving the rounds from trains to the firing line. The men set out on the Chancellorsville campaign with loads estimated at 45 pounds. The articles almost duplicated Sherman's postwar list of essential items.[50]

But the troops of the Army of the Potomac did not do well in this experiment during the trying days of late April and early May 1863. Rufus Ingalls concluded they were too heavily loaded because they dropped an unusually large amount of material along their short marches to outflank Lee's army. Ingalls estimated that at least 25 percent of all knapsacks were dropped in the field and thus lost to the soldier and his government. This was an item that Sherman thought should not even be issued to the troops. Ingalls came to the same conclusion after Chancellorsville, advising that as many items as possible be wrapped up in a blanket to be slung over the shoulder. "Our men are generally overloaded, fed, and clad, which detracts from their marching capacity, and induces straggling," Ingalls wrote.[51]

The loss rate of government-issued material was very high among some units in Hooker's army, much higher than the overall 25 percent loss rate for knapsacks. Fully half the knapsacks issued to a brigade of nine-month New Jersey regiments in the First Corps were tossed along the roadside, and two-thirds of the new clothing issued another brigade in the corps was discarded during the relatively short campaign that culminated in the battle at Chancellorsville. Quartermasters in the Second Corps requested enough new knapsacks, haversacks, blankets, and shelter tents to indicate a 25 percent loss ratio for all these items in the campaign. Fifth Corps troops readily got rid of more than 5,381 knapsacks, 1,681 haversacks, 877 canteens, and 3,891 shelter tents.[52]

Troops of the Eleventh and Twelfth Corps began to discard material even before they left their winter camps. The ground was "covered with blankets and overcoats, and the road was lined with abandoned property, which was being collected by the inhabitants of the country," reported quartermaster officer William G. LeDuc. He compiled a lengthy list of material abandoned or lost by the Eleventh Corps during the campaign. It included 16 separate items of personal clothing, equipment, and accessories for the common soldier. More than 6,000 knapsacks, over 4,000 shelter tents, 3,000 pairs of trousers, and 13,000 pairs of stockings were on the list. The Eleventh Corps suffered a devastating defeat in Stonewall Jackson's famous flank march of May 2, 1863, which no doubt contributed greatly to the loss of material. The corps lost more material than any other unit in the Army of the Potomac during that ill-fated campaign.[53]

LeDuc voiced the views of many Federals when he condemned the knapsack issued to Union troops. It was "clumsy, uncomfortable, expensive, and entirely too large," which contributed to the soldier's readiness to throw it away while marching. "So far as my experience goes," wrote Quartermaster J. J. Dana in the Army of the Potomac, "troops, both regular and volunteer, will throw away their knapsacks before any other article of equipment, even on comparatively short marches." While LeDuc advocated the design of a smaller knapsack that would leave the spine free for cooling air to circulate along the back, other officers, such as Sherman and Ingalls, wanted to do away with it entirely. Noting the unusually warm weather during the Chancellorsville campaign, Ingalls understood that the men acted on an impulse "almost irresistible" to "throw off all impediments, under such circumstances."[54]

Quartermasters wrestled with a problem that had varied components. They wanted to give the soldier all he needed to be effective in the field, but not so much that it would impede his mobility or tempt him to throw things away and lead to waste of government resources. They also wanted to reduce the wagon trains accompanying the army by increasing the amount of material each soldier carried. Joseph Hooker supported this effort when he took command of the Army of the Potomac, appointing a board of officers to consider how his men could carry more than three days of rations on campaign and reduce the number of wagons. Board members found that a loaded knapsack typically weighed 15½ pounds with a blanket rolled and strapped to its top. With increased rations it amounted to 19 pounds. Hooker therefore ordered his men to carry eight days' worth of rations when the army set out on the Chancellorsville campaign and he counted it a successful experiment. Meigs was excited by the news when he heard about this order, but Hooker's chief of staff, Daniel Butterfield, warned him that it would be injudicious to pack a soldier with eight days of rations if he was expected to meet the enemy in battle carrying that kind of load.[55]

In short, placing more than three days' rations on each soldier for an active campaign was impractical. Expecting them to carry anything more than absolutely necessary even for a simple march through the countryside was naive. Meigs was stunned by reports that 800 overcoats had been thrown away by one regiment during a march that took place on an unexpectedly warm day, only to be succeeded by several days of cold rain during which the men suffered greatly for the want of those coats. Meigs bemoaned the practice of stripping for battle by placing all knapsacks, blankets, overcoats, and other items on the ground, only to leave them there after the battle or find they had been stolen. The expense to the government of providing replacements amounted to a huge proportion of its total expenditure. The modern concept of strategic consumption, the need to account for supplying an army more than it actually used, has few better examples than the wanton discarding of personal equipment during the Chancellorsville campaign.[56]

"Every soldier feels that it won't pay to carry a mule load of clothing on his back," concluded Joseph Cross of the 11th New Hampshire, "so every hot day that he is on the march he will reduce his load as much as possible & even in many cases throw away every thing he has except what he has on." Cross estimated he saw 5,000 overcoats and 10,000 blankets along the side of a road used by the Ninth Corps one day during the 1864 campaigns in the East.[57]

Confederate soldiers were not so providentially supplied as their counterparts in blue; rather than throwing away needed articles, they tended to scrounge across battlefields looking for spare items of clothing and equipment. On fields such as Stones River and Chickamauga, where Rebel troops held the field for some time, they often found a bountiful harvest of material. Everything from Union overcoats, underwear, and metal canteens to Federal blankets, hats, and shelter tents found their way into Confederate hands. Captured Northerners also became targets of opportunity for many Rebels, who "traded" their worn-out clothing and equipment with that held by captives. "The spoils of war were an important item to them," commented a captured Federal artillerist about his captors.[58]

Soldiers had an ambiguous relationship with the government-issued clothing and equipment they used during the Civil War. In some ways, the Federal government gave its soldiers too much, while the Confederate government gave its men far too little. This contributed to the impression that Rebel armies moved with more celerity in many campaigns of the war; Bragg's Kentucky campaign is an example, as is Lee's raid into Pennsylvania. Union soldiers in particular did not hesitate to callously throw away a great deal of the equipment they received from the government, yet they complained when the little they had left was lost due to the exigencies of war. Troops of the 22nd Iowa lost all their personal belongings and camp equipment at the battle of Cedar Creek, "through no neglect of their own," commented Colonel Harvey Graham. He thought the men should be compensated for their loss by the government, a suggestion that of course was not taken seriously. The Federal government did allow honorably discharged soldiers to keep their knapsack, canteen, and haversack at no charge at the end of the war. It is not known how many of them did so.[59]

If the individual soldier was a unit in the logistical system, carrying war-making material as well as what was needed to feed, clothe, and keep him warm while moving through the countryside, then the nature of roadways in the South comes into play as an adjunct to the logistical system. Steamboats used the rivers, steam engines used artificially constructed railroads, and coastal ships used the shallow coastal waters as their highways. Field commanders

7.1. Bailey's Crossroads, Virginia. The scene of a skirmish on August 28–30, 1861, the junction of Columbia Turnpike and Leesburg Pike is in the foreground. The photographer was standing on the Leesburg Pike looking southeast in the direction of Alexandria five miles away. The roadbed is graded but unpaved. (Library of Congress, LC-DIG-ppmsca-34809)

relied on wagon roads and bridges to move their soldier logistical units forward through enemy country.

Most roads in the Civil War South were comparatively crude affairs, a single lane that was wide enough for one wagon, snaking across the landscape with minimal grading or earth-moving. Most roads also were unpaved, merely dirt lanes vulnerable to the weather. They also were not of uniform quality, and officers paid a good deal of attention to assessing the state of any roads they planned to use in order to gauge what problems they would encounter. Some roads were in good shape, but many others were not. Based on reports, Nathaniel Banks concluded that one road near Culpeper and Sperryville was "very bad, not traveled nor repaired for many years. It is hardly practicable for any force, unless cavalry, and small bodies at that."[60]

A few major roads in Civil War America could be classified as improved road systems, based on several methods of constructing modern highways. The idea of planking a dirt road, using split logs or thick planks, began in Russia and was adopted in Canada by 1834. The first plank road in the United States linking Syracuse with Lake Oneida, New York, appeared in 1846. That state boasted 182 plank road companies by 1850. Stringers were laid on the ground and cross planks nailed to them, with sand, gravel, or sawdust spread in a layer over the wooden pavement.[61]

Such a road needed continual maintenance. Federal troops participating in John Pope's campaign against Island No. 10 encountered planked sections of an old Spanish road, the King's Road that linked Sikeston with New Madrid, in southeast Missouri. The well-graded pike ran through several swampy areas that had to be planked. With nearly 200 army wagons using it, the planking became quite cut up and rough.[62]

A paving method devised by an English surveyor named John Louden M'Adam in the early 1800s proved to be far better than planking. He applied a layer of small stones on the surface of a dirt road without anything such as earth or clay to adhere the stones, relying only on weathering and dust to form a coherent layer. It was cheaper and faster than paving with admixtures and soon became so popular that his name gave rise to the term macadamized to denote this type of road pavement. In the United States this method became the most common mode of making turnpikes, and several major pikes served the needs of Union invaders of the Confederacy. Most Americans viewed this method of improving roads as the most advanced, at times referring to them as gravel roads. They mostly were located in the upper South rather than in the lower South.[63]

Macadamized pikes were far better than dirt roads and planked roads combined for moving army wagons, and many soldiers thought they were better for marching as well. "First rate traveling, all day on a McAdamized Pike," commented William Henry Jackson of the 12th Vermont. But many soldiers noticed that the limestone used in this paving tended to produce a good deal of dust in dry weather. Marching over a macadamized pike near Newport, Kentucky, William Garrigues Bentley of the 104th Ohio called it "the nicest road that I ever saw, though it was very dusty and we all looked like millers as the road is made of limestone and the dust is nearly as white as flour." The pike linking Georgetown with Lexington, Kentucky, produced so much dust that Harvey Reid of the 22nd Wisconsin could hardly see the length of his company moving along it. "The dust of a limestone road is not the most agreeable stuff in the world to have a person's eyes, nose and mouth stuffed full of," he concluded.

Limestone dust from the pike near Murfreesboro, Tennessee, coated the cedar trees lining the roadway when troops marched along during dry weather. When it rained heavily, the dust became a sloppy liquid that covered level places of the roadbed.[64]

Randolph Abbott Shotwell of the 8th Virginia recalled that atmospheric conditions, the limestone of a macadamized pike, and the bare rocks lining the roadside along the Chambersburg Pike near Cashtown, Pennsylvania, produced difficulties for his comrades. "As we approached the Cashtown Gap about noon the vertical rays of the sun seemed like real lances of steel tipped with fire! The broken rock of the McAdamized turnpike and the broad flat flagstones of mountain slate reflected the heat until a perfect steam arose in our faces as we trudged along and the choking dust gathered in throats and eyes causing infinite annoyance."[65]

Shotwell pointed out an important fact. Even though providing a solid surface, paved roads often were hard on marching soldiers. "The glare of the sun on the limestone pike was dreadful," reported a soldier of the 18th U.S. Infantry about his march toward Louisville in 1862. "My tongue was so swollen that I could scarcely articulate, and it was with the greatest difficulty that the men were kept in ranks." The stone pavement hurt the men's feet as well. "We are used to dirt roads," complained Chesley Mosman of the 59th Illinois, "and as the macadam road does not give under foot we are simply 'stove up' by that march. A footsore crowd. It is worse than twenty-five miles of dirt road." A 30-mile march from Murfreesboro to Triune and back in January 1863 took George D. Wagner's brigade over a pike with recently laid stone pavement. The stones were sharp and cut the shoes of his men so badly that he requisitioned 700 new pairs of footwear for his command. Moreover, wagons with iron-rimmed wheels made a loud noise while moving along a macadamized pike. John A. Nourse of the Chicago Board of Trade Battery could not sleep while lying within twenty feet of the Nashville Pike during the Stones River campaign because of the noise produced by wagon trains during the night.[66]

Even the best pike could be wrecked by overuse. Less than two months after the battle of Stones River, the Nashville Pike linking the state capital with Murfreesboro had degenerated into "one dense mass of mud" in the words of an observer. Heavy use by army wagons cut the pavement so badly until it was broken up and the roadside was littered with the carcasses of mules and wrecked wagons. Several Federal soldiers remembered this road as one of the best pikes they had ever seen, but it was destroyed by the logistical demands of Rosecrans's army. Even the stone mile posts were nearly all knocked over by careless teamsters.[67]

The Nashville Pike represented a good example of the best kind of improved, paved roadbed in Civil War America, but there were some roads that had been improved (or graded) but were not paved. One existed near Lawrenceburg, Tennessee, which the local people referred to as a "dirt pike." Grading certainly made dirt roads easier for travelers, whether in a wagon or on foot, but they still were vulnerable to weather and needed time to dry out after a hard rain.[68]

The overwhelming majority of roadbeds used by Union and Confederate soldiers were unimproved and unpaved. They often became impassable in wet weather, while turnpikes continued to offer good traveling. The sandy, level countryside of the coastal plain east of Richmond posed particularly difficult problems for the Army of the Potomac during the Peninsula campaign. Stewart Van Vliet, McClellan's chief quartermaster, reported that even empty army wagons sometime sank to their axles in the soft, quicksand-like mud of the roadbeds. Hundreds of soldiers were detailed to cut small trees and lay the trunks down as improvised plank paving (corduroying), and even then it was a rough, difficult passage that stressed the wagons. Teamsters could haul little more than half a load (1,000 pounds) per wagon.[69]

One of Van Vliet's quartermaster officers, B. S. Alexander, believed the bad roads were a major factor in the failure of McClellan's Peninsula campaign. He thought it would have been feasible to construct a major new road system to support the army, envisioning two military roads—one to handle wagon traffic forward to the front line and one to take empty wagons back to the base of supplies. Alexander thought detailed troops could have constructed this road system at the rate of two miles per day. He took his suggestion a step further by suggesting that a similar road system be constructed to support the next On to Richmond offensive in November 1862. This time it would start from the Rappahannock River and extend some 60 miles to the Confederate capital. He envisioned two roadbeds, each wide enough to handle two-way traffic. The roadbeds would be raised on causeways to negotiate low, swampy areas and be paved with timbers laid longitudinally along the direction of travel, a layer of brush and dirt on top of the timbers. Alternatively, Alexander suggested traditional planking 3 inches thick and 8½ feet long positioned crosswise compared to the direction of travel. He estimated that 4,224 men could construct one mile of roadway every day, including necessary bridges. Once the road was finished for a distance of 40 miles from the base of supplies, Alexander thought army wagons could make the round-trip over this road in only four days.[70]

Alexander laid out a rather fantastic scheme for road building; understandably, it was never taken seriously and reliance continued to be placed primarily on railroads, with the army's wagon trains providing the connecting link between the advanced rail head and the moving infantry force. Those trains continued to rely on preexisting roads, with army pioneers and detailed infantrymen improving the roads as needed. Despite the problems, this was the least troublesome mode of operation in logistical support. But Alexander's vision to a limited degree foreshadowed the interstate highway system of the mid-twentieth century, with its large-scale deployment of men and resources for construction and its multilane travel scheme.

The road problems encountered on the level terrain of Virginia were a far cry from the problems to be found on the roads that crossed the Appalachian Highlands. From the initial incursion into the mountainous counties of Virginia to the Chattanooga campaign, Federal armies had to adapt their wagon-driving techniques to high ridges, dangerous hills, and roaring mountain streams. In western Virginia, Jacob D. Cox thought a smaller, lighter wagon was needed to negotiate these mountain roads, but the standard army wagon remained the only one available.[71]

The road across the Cumberland Plateau that ran alongside the Nashville and Chattanooga Railroad was "the roughest rockiest and crookest road I *ever* saw," complained Surgeon William Harrison Githens of the 78th Illinois. "It was up, up, up—and then down, down—teams stalling—wagons breaking down or upsetting." A bit farther north the 84th Illinois traveled along a partially macadamized pike that linked McMinnville with Dunlap, Tennessee. It ran in a zigzag course up the western side of the Cumberland Plateau, causing weary teams to pull 3 miles to get only 1½ miles up the slope. Extra mules were added to the wagons to accomplish this feat. When descending the western side of the Sequatchie Valley, the teams were in danger of falling off the roadside hundreds of feet down sheer rock walls.[72]

There were many spots along these mountain roads where the roadbed literally was nothing but exposed rock carved out naturally by erosion in a series of uneven steps. Teamsters collected tree branches to position in the angle of each step to create something a bit more even, then whipped their mules to climb as fast as possible and hoped to get the wagon up this obstacle. While traveling from Lexington to Knoxville in December 1863, Jacob Cox found when trying to cross Pine Mountain "only a rough track alternating in mud and rock, that had never been good even in mid-summer." His entourage doubled the teams and still took all day to move five miles. Further on they encountered a stepped section of the road ascending another mountain. The teamsters whipped their mules so fast that the wagons literally bounced up the rock steps. "We zigzagged along as the road sought the easiest places among the rocks," Cox remembered. Such roads were very hard on the mules. Cox counted 150 dead draft animals lying along just 20 miles of the roadway during his eight-day journey. That averaged about one dead mule for every 250 yards of the trip.[73]

The roads linking Nashville with Chattanooga could not support the large numbers of troops vying for possession of the latter in 1863; even the railroad was inadequate at that stage of the war. Edward C. Dale was impressed by the wagon road crossing the Cumberland Plateau near the railroad when he moved cattle herds along it during Sherman's Atlanta campaign of 1864. The road "winds around over a solid mass of rocks, which appear as if they had been showered down from heaven & fell promiscuously, some standing on their ends, some on their edge & in fact in every conceivable shape except the right one. I am certain that nature never intended a road to be made over rocks projecting 2 or 3 ft. above the surface, & its so more or less for 7 or 8 miles." Marching along such roads hurt the men's feet and forced them to adjust somehow. The Anderson Pike, which crossed Walden's Ridge to enter Chattanooga from the north, negotiated two places on its descent with very sharp hairpin turns difficult for teams to make safely. In addition, heavy rains caused a great deal of erosion and created soft spots in the roadbed that resembled quicksand. This awful stretch of the pike required constant corduroying, shoveling, and immense care when driving wagons over its treacherous course.[74]

After the Chattanooga campaign, when western armies operated in the piedmont and coastal plain of Georgia, they encountered mostly unimproved and unpaved roads. Every time it rained these dirt roadways became quagmires cut up by wagon wheels and marching feet. Officers tried to get the trains to vary their routes so that all the wagons of a particular train did not use the same road. Of course, they could not count on local governments to repair the roads, as Jacob Cox noted, but had to rely on army resources for quick and temporary repairs; sometimes that amounted to nothing more than a teamster stopping long enough to throw some fresh dirt over a mud hole before climbing back on his mule and resuming the journey. When the road problem grew worse, army, corps, division, and brigade commanders detailed men to large work parties. Confederate officers often pressed black laborers to repair or construct roads for military use.[75]

Sherman's March to the Sea and his campaign through the Carolinas placed a good deal of strain on the road repair methods used by the army. The problem was not so bad through Georgia, but one road that ascended a steep slope proved difficult for the wagon train of Sherman's lone cavalry division. It was raining and the dirt, which consisted of heavy clay, was slick. Quartermaster G. E. Dunbar told his pioneers to shovel a layer of this clay off the road, mix it with drier dirt from the shoulder, and place a layer of the mixture over the roadbed to provide traction for the teams. Other roads encountered periodic low-lying areas that required attention. Twentieth Corps pioneers worked for a total of 10 days to corduroy roads during Sherman's 30-day March to the Sea. As the Federals approached the coast, they traversed the Georgia coastal plain and encountered swamps. Near Springfield one road wound through a swampy area for five miles, and over 100 wagons became stalled in the mire.[76]

In the Carolinas, Sherman steered a course as near the junction of the coastal plain with the piedmont as possible, but the roads during these winter months of January through March were in terrible shape. "The worst roads I ever saw, mud 2 feet deep," lamented Captain Alexander Miller Ayers to his diary on February 24. His wagon train made only three miles that day. Thousands of men were detailed to construct corduroy out of necessity, with long stretches of rough timbered pavement the result. Rockfish Creek in North Carolina, a wide and sluggish stream, proved a major obstacle to the Twentieth Corps. Every inch of the ten-mile approach to the stream had to be corduroyed. "I have never seen so spongy and treacherous a road as to-day," reported corps commander Alpheus Williams on March 10. "If made of jelly it could not have been less firm."[77]

Without corduroy, Sherman could not have made it through the Carolinas, but fortunately the Federals had deep experience at making improvised wooden pavements. Engineer Peter S. Michie spelled out the typical way to do so after the war: "lay a sufficient number of stout sill-timbers lengthwise, and to place crosswise on these saplings of about 4 to 6 inches in diameter, which were tied down by side rails, secured by anchor pickets." Or rather, it should be noted that Michie described the *ideal* way to make corduroy; actual field conditions often led to less care taken in constructing it. At times it did become necessary to make two layers of wood, but typically soldiers were so pressed that they could only lay one layer without rails or pickets.[78]

Many corduroy projects required large numbers of troops. Thomas J. Wood took charge of improving the road linking Danville with Somerset, Kentucky, in January 1862. He detailed an entire brigade to the task, armed with 1,000 axes, 1,000 picks, 500 shovels, and 500 spades. Headquarters instructed Wood to split small tree trunks and "make a species of puncheon floor" at least 16 feet wide. "You are aware of the difficulties and dangers to animals in passing over a road of this nature unless it is well made," warned James B. Fry, Don Carlos Buell's adjutant general. Wood was given 10 days to complete the road, which likely needed corduroy along its entire length of 50 miles, with the knowledge that "the supply of our troops depends upon its successful and early completion." The troops completed the task, cutting down chestnut trees, splitting them, and laying them on the "almost unfathomable mud."[79]

Struggling to enhance the transportation of supplies into Chattanooga after the battle of Chickamauga, Rosecrans wanted a double wagon road between Bridgeport and Battle Creek to allow wagons to go one way along one route and return along the other. "The corduroy should be of the most permanent kind," he instructed, "three heavy stringers or sleepers, then the cross-pieces or corduroy of logs, not less than 8 or 10 inches in diameter, tied at proper distances by forks." While struggling to bring four divisions from Mississippi to Chattanooga, Sherman's men often had to corduroy stretches of road along the way. They tended to do it right, laying stringers before placing cross pieces up to 10 feet long. Even then wagons often sank in places where the wooden pavement traversed quicksand-like soil, forcing the work details to add a second and even third layer of cross pieces to get them across.[80]

Corduroy was nothing more than a temporary expedient, requiring a great deal of hard, unpleasant labor and producing at best a rough, serviceable roadway for a short while. It was "hard, dirty, disagreeable work for the men," commented Philo Beecher Buckingham of the 20th Connecticut. There was no possibility of finding crosspieces of uniform diameter, and thus men, horses, and mules often stumbled along the road, especially when rain made the pieces slippery. Moving casualties along such a road was sheer torture. "As they jolted over the rough corduroy roads the poor fellows would scream and holler with pain," vividly recalled Captain William Merrell of the 141st New York. One could experiment with different types of material to make the corduroy road-bed. Fence rails were a bit more uniform in size but of limited supply. Sherman thought that pine saplings ten inches thick, split into two halves with the flat side laid down, "make a better road."[81]

The Carolinas campaign witnessed the most extensive corduroy work of the war, and the amount of labor invested in it was astonishing. Hartwell Osborn of the 55th Ohio estimated that the Federals constructed 150 miles of corduroy along the 465-mile journey from Savannah to Goldsborough from January to March 1865. That figure has not been confirmed by other reports, but it is true that the Third Division, Fifteenth Corps, laid down 23½ miles of corduroy and the Third Division, Seventeenth Corps, made nearly 26 miles of it during the campaign. In the short advance of 45 miles from Goldsborough to Raleigh, the Fifteenth Corps constructed 13,196 yards of corduroy and the Seventeenth Corps made 16,918 yards of it.[82]

Reliable shoes were an important support for the soldier if he were to fulfill his role as an element in the logistical network; unfortunately, many of the men could not count on the quality of their footwear. Long marches such as the so-journ through the Carolinas proved that the wear and tear of campaigning ate up even well-made shoes by the thousands, and poorly made footwear wore out even faster. The chief quartermaster of the Fourteenth Corps blasted any idea that sewing was an effective way to keep the parts of a shoe together during a rigorous march. The pieces separated and the shoe fell apart. He had faith only in shoes held together with pegs. Some quartermasters believed that western soldiers were larger than those who grew up in the East and therefore needed shoes slightly bigger than their eastern counterparts.[83]

Climate and terrain often produced conditions that were particularly hard on marching feet and the shoes that attempted to protect them. Winter weather in east Tennessee made dirt roads so stiff with frost that shoes broke apart and thousands of Union and Confederate soldiers essentially walked barefoot across frozen mud, cutting their feet in the process. "There were places where I saw the road marked with bloody tracks from the wounded feet of the soldiers," recalled Jacob D. Cox. Even in warm weather, the rocky roads of mountainous areas had a similar effect on men's feet. Preparing to move into the mountains, William G. LeDuc tried to keep an extra supply of shoes handy because he anticipated that rocky mountain roads would prove hazardous to footwear. "I knew the gravel of the southern mountains had not been ground smooth by the glaciers of the ice period, and the sharp angles would cut the contract-made shoes," he recalled in his memoirs.[84]

Soldiers operating along the flat coastal plain often found that watery conditions affected footwear, too. A Virginian named Catlett Conway waded through several pools of water along a road from Suffolk to Richmond in the early spring of 1863. "The sand stuck to our wet shoes, got inside and ground the skin from our feet so that we were forced to take off our shoes and socks and march barefoot all day." Later the road became hard, but by then Conway's feet had swollen so much it was painful to force his shoes over them.[85]

The Union army had the resources to replace shoes by the thousands, but Confederate quartermasters were severely limited in their ability to help Rebel soldiers. Very often, they resorted to expedients, such as rounding up anyone in the ranks who had experience at shoe-making, acquiring raw leather, and setting them to work cutting and sewing. The result often was little better than a crude moccasin that lasted only a few days in rough weather.[86]

In addition to footwear and the condition of roads, Civil War soldiers depended on bridges to achieve the kind of mobility necessary to move personal equipment forward in the logistical chain. They could not count on uniformly made or entirely safe bridges, for, like roads, the condition of stream crossings depended much on local governments. In fact, the majority of stream crossings had no bridges at all; if there was a viable ford near the course of a road, it was utilized as the cheapest way to take traffic across. Small bridges often were poorly built or poorly maintained, and commanders needed a structure that not only could support marching men, but artillery and wagons as well. Major stream crossings tended to have more reliable bridges, particularly those constructed by railroad companies for their trains.

"The movements of armies are always much embarrassed by forests, marshes, and water-courses," remarked Henry W. Halleck in his book on military science, published well before the war. When Herman Haupt agreed to help Union authorities arrange railroad transportation in Virginia, he became interested in this problem, recognizing that "mobility is essential to success" for any army operating on the strategic offensive.[87]

The U.S. Army had no organized wagon train to carry bridging material before 1846 but had put together two trains of india rubber pontoon boats for the

Mexican War. They were stationed at the U.S. Military Academy at West Point, to be used by the cadets for drill purposes after the conflict. Worn out by 1858, the army contemplated how to replace them before adopting the French model of wooden pontoon boats for a reserve train and the Russian model of a canvas pontoon for the advance bridge train. A trestle called the Birago also was adopted, serving as a modular replacement for a damaged bridge that could be assembled on the site.[88]

When the Civil War broke out, the Union army used all four types of bridges (rubber, wooden, canvas, and Birago) but tended to rely more heavily on two of them. Engineers liked the wooden pontoons for their durability and weight, viewing the canvas as too likely to rot through long exposure in contact with water. The Army of the James maintained a typical pontoon train in the waning months of the conflict. It consisted of 15 canvas boats and 4 Birago trestles that provided up to 380 feet of bridge material. Engineers hauled this material in 22 pontoon wagons, a wagon to carry extra planking, and 8 wagons to carry forage for the teams plus a traveling forge.[89]

Pontoons were vital elements of army mobility in the Civil War. Portable as well as durable, they provided the best temporary bridges of the conflict. Herman Haupt calculated how they could support heavy weight such as artillery pieces and found that the key was distribution of weight. As long as one gun did not rest all its weight on one pontoon for more than a few seconds (assuming that no more than 18 feet separated the center of one pontoon from another), a battery could pass safely over the bridge. Even troops were cautioned to space out a bit and break their cadence so that they did not march in unison while crossing a pontoon bridge. Haupt developed a variation on the canvas boat, using what he called blanket material instead of canvas. He estimated it could be set up as a bridge in only one hour and was capable of moving 10,000 men over a stream every hour.[90]

Pontoons of all kinds were used extensively in every theater of operations. Heavy wooden pontoons took Sherman's men across the Tennessee River to attack the north end of Missionary Ridge during the Chattanooga campaign. They made "one of the prettiest Bridges that I ever Crossed on," thought W. G. Buck of the 17th Iowa. The Twentieth Corps used canvas pontoons to cross the Chattahoochee River during the Atlanta campaign. Sherman made sure each of his four corps had enough pontoons to make 900 feet of bridging material during the March to the Sea.[91]

In the Carolinas, Sherman's army group used rubber, canvas, and wooden pontoons. The rubber pontoons were inflated by air pumps until 14 feet long and 15 inches in diameter, and three of them were attached to form one "pier" of the bridging material. The canvas boats leaked, but soldiers operating small pumps managed to get most of the water out. Teamsters had to be careful in crossing; moving too close to the edge of any pontoon bridge would tip the whole over, as happened one night while wagons crossed the Wateree River. If not enough pontoons were available to span a particularly wide stream, engineers scrounged up any sizeable boat they could find to help. Orlando M. Poe used four "large wooden boats" he found on the Roanoke River to span nearly 200 feet of the stream because he had only 580 feet of pontoon bridging to cover the 740 feet of water. He anchored the boats in the center of the river and constructed trestle work to link them, laying the pontoons from each bank toward the assembled boats.[92]

Despite the numerous crossings provided by pontoon bridges, Civil War soldiers crossed most small streams by fording or by improvising bridgework. Herman Haupt focused a good deal on expedient methods of crossing watercourses so that armies did not have to rely on cumbersome bridge trains. "*Resource* is almost omnipotent," he wrote, "with it, few impossibilities are found; without it, slight impediments become insurmountable difficulties." Haupt thought pontoons could be improvised from wagon boxes, although he did not address the problem of how to make them waterproof. In addition to using locally available boats as bridges, as Poe did in the Carolinas, Halleck advocated fashioning rafts or constructing footbridges of rope.[93]

Soldiers in the field typically did not resort to unusual expedients, such as converting wagons into boats or making rope bridges. They scrounged timber and planks from nearby buildings to rebuild small bridges or felled trees across narrow streams to serve as footpaths.[94]

Sherman encountered a major obstacle when attempting to cross the Little Tennessee River during his march to relieve the siege of Knoxville in December 1863. His men improvised two crossing points. At Morganton, the water was five feet deep and cold, stretching 240 yards across. Over the course of 24 hours, the troops tore down nearby buildings and cut trees to fashion a rickety bridge barely capable of handling wheeled traffic. At Davis' Ford, other Federals used 30 wagons abandoned by the Confederates at nearby Loudon, drove them into the shallow water, and lined them up, connecting them with planks taken from nearby buildings to use as a footbridge from one wagon box to another. This bridge stretched for 1,000 feet across the river. Philip Sheridan's division constructed a similar footbridge made of wagons to cross the French Broad River northeast of Knoxville in January 1864, with the pole of each wagon run under the rear axle of the preceding wagon and the tail boards opened so that troops could walk from one wagon box to another without planking to connect them.[95]

Bridges of all kinds, whether improvised or ready-made for deployment on site, provided an essential element of mobility for Civil War armies in the field. Immediate logistical support was one result. Moving equipment, food, forage, ammunition, artillery, and soldiers were all part of a matrix covered by the subject of army mobility, and Civil War armies were highly mobile because of all elements in the logistical chain.

That logistical chain started deep in the home territory of both belligerents in the Civil War. It extended for hundreds of miles across protected geographic space—along rivers, over specially built railbeds, and through shallow coastal waters—until reaching the theater of war. Here material was loaded onto wagons or more rarely onto the backs of pack mules. Additionally, small items of personal use to soldiers wound up in knapsacks, haversacks, and rolled up in a blanket slung across the shoulder for the final stage of logistical power supporting penetration of hostile territory. In its own way, every article of war that traveled along this logistical chain completed a journey of monumental importance for the prosecution of the Civil War.

8

########

TROOP TRANSFERS

In April 1862, before the railroads had fully proven themselves as reliable arteries of troop movements, Peter V. Daniel Jr. warned Confederate secretary of war George W. Randolph not to expect too much. The president of the Richmond, Fredericksburg, and Potomac Railroad had consulted a friend who knew something of how the French had used railroads in the Second War of Italian Unification three years before. They had the benefit of a double track and Daniel knew that under favorable conditions large-scale troop transfers were feasible. "But to rely on [railroads] as a means of transporting any large body of troops, besides what is needed to supply and maintain them, is certainly a most dangerous delusion and must inevitably result in the most grievous disappointment and fatal consequences."[1]

Daniel tried to say that the Confederate rail system could provide some emergency service in shifting large numbers of troops quickly if the details of the movement fitted its capacities. He did not think it wise to rely on railroads for more than this limited role. Large-scale troop transfers on a continuing basis were beyond a reasonable expectation; small-scale shipments spread out over time were already being made on a fairly reliable basis.

While the Confederate rail-based system labored under severe problems that limited its usefulness in consistent, high-volume transfers of men over thousands of miles, the Northern rail-based system was fully capable of handling this new and demanding role for locomotives and cars. Northern railroad companies and the reconstructed Southern lines that the Union army captured and used became exemplars of logistical power, capable of shifting massive numbers of Federal troops over long distances at nearly a moment's notice without dangerously interrupting the normal flow of traffic in passengers and freight. Union quartermasters created the first impressive example in global history of the potential inherent in a well-developed railroad industry for rapid movement of large military units across the length and breadth of a huge nation. Even the struggling Confederate railroad system managed to pull off a handful of impressive large-scale troop transfers on occasion.

This chapter does not deal with the normal logistical needs of either government at war in the 1860s, but with the unusual necessity of rapidly displacing large numbers of troops from one location to another in order to meet an important military need. By default this chapter deals more with Northern success in moving troops than it does with Southern success because Lincoln's government had a far more capable logistical system at its disposal than did Davis's government. The most prominent troop transfers of the war involved the movement of Longstreet's two divisions from Virginia to the area around Chattanooga in September 1863 and the corresponding transfer of two corps from the Army of the Potomac to Tennessee by the Federals a few weeks later. But many other important troop transfers by both governments took place during the course of the war that are worthy of attention.

Lewis B. Parsons enumerated at least twenty major troop transfers by rail and steamer that took place within the Western Theater of operations. They involved a total of 236,000 men in increments ranging from 2,000 to 40,000 troops for each transfer and covered tens of thousands of miles. He started with the movement of 2,000 men under Nathaniel Lyon up the Missouri River to capture the Missouri state capital in June 1861, and ended with the transfer of John M. Schofield's Twenty-Third Corps from western Tennessee to Annapolis, Maryland, early in 1865. In most of these examples quartermasters transported animals, wagons, and artillery along with the men.[2]

Some large-scale troop transfers took place in the Eastern Theater that Parsons did not list. When George B. McClellan started his Peninsula campaign the Army of the Potomac required a huge fleet to move from the Washington area to Fortress Monroe. Federal quartermasters rounded up a total of 405 vessels of all types, representing a total of 86,278 tons. Of that number, 71 were side-wheel steamers, 57 were propeller-driven steamers, 187 were schooners, brigs, or barks, and 90 were barges. At the start of this movement, the Potomac River "was filled with every variety of transport," D. H. Rucker told Meigs, "from the ocean steamer *Constitution*, with a carrying capacity for 5,000 men, to the smallest tide-water barge." This was the logistical requirement to move 100,000 men with their wagons, artillery, cavalry, animals, and supplies about 150 miles in March 1862.[3]

Four months later, a large troop transfer over a much greater distance *almost* took place. With Union successes in the West and Confederate resistance in the East, Edwin M. Stanton told Henry W. Halleck to send 25,000 men from the area around Corinth, Mississippi, to Virginia. Halleck warned that Don C. Buell would have to give up his slow advance toward Chattanooga, and there was no guarantee that Federal garrisons in west Tennessee could hold their ground with the loss of so many men. When Lincoln intervened and reduced the transfer to 10,000 troops, Halleck still could not guarantee the fulfillment of military goals in his department if he lost such a number. McClellan's defeat in the Seven Days campaign increased the pressure to bring reinforcements to Virginia, but Halleck staunchly opposed draining his manpower. "I must earnestly protest against surrendering what has cost us so much blood and treasure, and which, in a military point of view, is worth three Richmonds." In the end, the Washington authorities relented and no men were transferred, but they did order Halleck himself, Franz Sigel, and John Pope to the East in the futile hope that these western generals could engineer victory.[4]

Ambrose Burnside's Ninth Corps earned the reputation of a well-traveled unit. Having served along the North Carolina coast before joining the Virginia campaigns in late 1862, two divisions were shifted to Kentucky in easy stages early the next year. Starting from Falmouth, just across the Rappahannock River from Fredericksburg, the troops reached their destination in the West in one month. Ten thousand of them were later shifted to support Ulysses S. Grant's siege of Vicksburg in June 1863, having traveled some 2,500 miles from Falmouth according to artillery officer Jacob Roemer. Parsons had hardly more than an hour's notice to move these men from central Kentucky to Vicksburg. He routed them through Ohio, Indiana, and southern Illinois by rail and then boarded them on steamers at Cairo within 48 hours of their departure from camps in Kentucky. Within three days they were at Haynes' Bluff just north of Vicksburg after traveling about a thousand miles in five days.[5]

After the fall of Vicksburg, Burnside needed what was left of those 10,000 men for his planned drive into east Tennessee. Quartermasters shipped them from Haynes' Bluff as rapidly as possible. The 20th Michigan left at 3 A.M. of August 4 and reached the mouth of the Yazoo River at dawn. Running all day and night, the steamer reached Memphis at 5 P.M. on August 6, having made 475 miles in three days and two nights. The boat needed to be cleaned and resupplied with coal and did not leave Memphis until 4:30 P.M. on August 7. Although running slowly, it reached New Madrid at 6 P.M. on August 8, then Island No. 10 an hour later, Columbus at 11 P.M., and Cairo at 5 in the morning of August 8 after making 240 miles in the past 36 hours. The regiment unloaded for two hours, boarded railroad cars at noon, and left Cairo at 3:45 P.M. Running night and day through the countryside, stopping and changing cars, the 20th Michigan hit Cincinnati at 9 A.M. of August 11 to complete one of the most rapid troop movements of the entire war.[6]

The constant shifting of Burnside's two divisions from East to West, and within the Western Theater of operations, was hardly noticed by anyone, but it was as important to the success of Union military operations as any other troop transfer in the war. Grant reinforced Nathaniel Banks with the Thirteenth Corps of his army after the fall of Vicksburg, and that also was viewed as routine, garnering little attention from contemporaries or historians. By this stage of the war, Parsons provided not only the transport for troops but also a commissary boat to accompany the transfer, loaded with meat and butchers, and a hospital boat to tend to the troops' medical needs.[7]

The shipment of the Eleventh and Twelfth Corps from the Army of the Potomac to Virginia following the battle of Chickamauga stands as the most visible and best documented troop transfer of the Northern war effort. On the night of September 22, two days after the devastating defeat of William Rosecrans's Army of the Cumberland, Stanton called an emergency meeting attended by Lincoln, several cabinet officers, and Halleck. Stanton believed that the rail system could deliver 20,000 men from Virginia to Nashville, the van of the moving column arriving within five days, but Lincoln and Halleck doubted it could be done so quickly. Stanton persisted and convinced other members of the meeting that the idea was feasible. Joseph Hooker was brought off the shelf and placed in command of both corps for the movement west.[8]

It was truly a daunting prospect. The plan involved more than 20,000 men, their artillery, baggage, and transportation, and a distance of 1,166 miles. Orders were not issued until September 24, indicating the authorities might have given the plan more thought the day after the meeting. Stanton assigned Daniel McCallum of the U.S. Military Railroad to oversee the loading in Virginia. McCallum telegraphed William P. Smith, an executive of the Baltimore and Ohio

Railroad, for at least 140 cars for the men and 50 for the stock. He planned to load the first men of Oliver O. Howard's Eleventh Corps at Bristow Station the next day, but soon realized the sidings were inadequate and instructed Howard to move to Manassas Junction.[9]

Stanton exercised general supervision of the movement from his office in Washington, D.C. He recruited the help of John W. Garrett, president of the Baltimore and Ohio Railroad, and Samuel M. Felton, president of the Philadelphia, Wilmington, and Baltimore Railroad. Stanton made Thomas A. Scott, vice president of the Pennsylvania Railroad, an assistant quartermaster on Hooker's staff and sent him to Louisville because he knew that city was a choke point in the logistical chain. He also asked Meigs's advice about the carrying capacity of the Louisville and Nashville Railroad. It would be necessary to recruit extra cars from several Northern railroad companies to make this transfer work, so Stanton sent telegrams to several company officials. Stanton also authorized Hooker to take military possession of all rail lines involved in the transfer if that seemed necessary.[10]

Halleck informed Rosecrans that help was on the way and would arrive within seven days. Rosecrans was relieved. He told Halleck that it was not wise to bring the reinforcements all the way to Chattanooga, his fortified refuge following the defeat at Chickamauga, for the rail line leading into the city was inoperative and he could barely feed the men already there. Upon their arrival, Hooker's troops should take up positions at Stevenson and Bridgeport, Alabama, as well as points in middle Tennessee to secure his rail communications. The 30-mile gap between Bridgeport and Chattanooga would have to be bridged by some means to be devised later.[11]

A meeting of the railroad officials involved in the transfer took place on September 24 in Washington. In this conference, it was decided that the Baltimore and Ohio personnel would handle the troop transfer from the District of Columbia to Louisville by way of Bellaire, Ohio, and Indianapolis. Scott would handle everything south of Louisville. Garrett worked his men without relief to assemble 194 cars for troops and 44 for stock, with more promised. How to organize all those cars now became the issue. William P. Smith pointed out that each Baltimore and Ohio engine could pull 40 loaded cars from Washington to the Relay House 30 miles west, but from there the terrain was such that they could only pull 20 to 22. Smith suggested to McCallum that he organize trains of 30 to 32 cars in Virginia to make it easier to divide them into 3 separate trains at the Relay House. J. G. Devereux, manager of transportation for the Orange and Alexandria Railroad, agreed to try, but he pointed out to Smith that his military line also had to supply the Army of the Potomac and he could not afford to take too much time in organizing details such as this.[12]

The first shipments of troops were rolling by September 26. By 11 A.M. that day, 12 trains had passed the Relay House carrying 7,000 of Howard's men. In fact, McCallum loaded these troops much faster than anticipated and Twelfth Corps troops had to wait because there were not enough empty cars immediately available, even though Smith provided them faster than initially planned. "It is impossible to avoid more or less confusion in such an extraordinary movement," Smith assured McCallum, and the delay was short at any rate. McCallum put 36 to 45 men in each car, depending on the capacity, and most of these cars had seats. He started to load Howard's animals on September 27, packing 15 horses in each stock car. The Eleventh Corps' artillery marched to Washington, where it could find better loading facilities, and Devereux promised to provide platform cars for it. McCallum had initially been told Howard would ship only 5,500 men, but the number wound up being 7,500; this necessitated a scramble to find more cars. Stanton took on the task of helping to round up extra cars by telegraphing a number of railroad companies for their cooperation.[13]

Carl Schurz, one of Howard's division commanders, nearly threw a monkey wrench into this smoothly running machine when he ordered the Baltimore and Ohio agent at Grafton to hold the cars carrying his troops for a while. Smith refused to let Schurz order his agent around and the cars ran forward on schedule. Schurz also had to be stopped from commandeering an engine for his personal use. Stanton was very upset when informed of this and issued instructions for Schurz's arrest if he persisted. The division commander tried to explain his motives by pointing out that companies and regiments were broken up on loading, making it difficult for officers to control their men. He heard reports that some of them had climbed on top of cars and fallen to their deaths. Schurz tried to get to the head of his division column; that was why he wanted to commandeer an engine, believing it would not have delayed the shipment appreciably, but Stanton ignored this explanation and the concerns expressed in it.[14]

The first four trains carrying Howard's corps reached the Ohio River by 11 A.M. on September 27. They had moved 2,500 men a total of 412 miles from Washington, D.C., in a little more than 24 hours. As Smith proudly reported, they arrived two hours earlier than anticipated. The bridge spanning the Ohio

River, consisting of barges and scows "strongly connected," was ready for the trains, and adequate numbers of empty cars were waiting at Bellaire for the troops and animals. At Louisville, Scott had arranged to ferry them across the Ohio River because there was no railroad bridge at that city.[15]

For many soldiers, the train ride through the mountains presented grand scenery. "The Road is very crooked, winding like a huge serpent among the mountains, which rise on either side to an immense height," reported George Williamson Balloch, Howard's chief commissary. Several tunnels and iron bridges added interest to the traveling experience. "The road cost an enormous sum of money & is the best built road in the country," Balloch told his wife. Captain William Wheeler of the 13th New York Battery rode atop the cars as his train passed through the splendors of the mountainous terrain, enjoying the "delicious autumn" weather during the day and the "lights and shadows of a perfect moonlight autumn night."[16]

By September 28, W. P. Smith could report much progress. Some 16,000 troops had passed the Relay House heading west, and more than 200 cars, carrying some 8,000 men, had left Bellaire, the first train reaching Columbus, Ohio, by 3 A.M. In the conference of September 24, Smith had advised bypassing Indianapolis because he knew the railroad officials there were not used to rapid shipment of large numbers of troops. His suggestion seemed prescient, for the Eleventh Corps was delayed six hours while transferring from one line to another, marching one mile across the city. Smith had suggested an alternative route by way of Cincinnati to board the men on steamers for the trip to Louisville, but that seemed to involve much delay and trouble. After some investigation it turned out that the two depots involved in Indianapolis were not actually one mile apart, but rather the men had marched one mile from the depot to the Soldiers' Home for food and hot coffee. The two depots actually were close to each other and the transfer would have been quick and easy if not for the fact that food had not been provided on the train and the soldiers were famished.[17]

The transfer of Hooker's command proceeded with astonishing speed and smoothness while on the Baltimore and Ohio Railroad from Virginia to the Ohio River, and then on several smaller rail lines across Ohio and Indiana. But the real problem lay from Louisville south. Thomas Scott highly recommended changing the gauge of a branch line extending from Louisville to Lexington so as to open a secondary rail route from the Ohio River at Cincinnati to Louisville. He also wanted to extend the Louisville and Nashville track all the way to the wharf on the riverbank at Louisville. Stanton approved these suggestions; the former one of course could not be done in time to help Hooker, but the latter could be accomplished quickly.[18]

But the Louisville and Nashville line and the Nashville and Chattanooga line were the real problems. The former railroad still remained in complete control of the company that owned it because President James Guthrie had tried to accommodate Federal government needs so as to avoid military takeover. Guthrie could barely handle the volume of government logistical needs on a regular basis, and the coming of Hooker's men was not by any means business as usual. Stanton initially thought to take over the Louisville and Nashville line because its "equipment and rolling stock are inadequate to the purposes of the Government in the movement both of troops and supplies." He wanted Amasa Stone Jr., president of the Cleveland, Painesville, and Ashtabula Railroad at Cleveland, Ohio, to be general superintendent of all military railroads south of the Ohio River, but Stone reported that he was far too busy with his own business to do so. Stanton then asked his help at least in rounding up spare cars from Northern railroads to aid Hooker's movement, and Stone agreed to try. Immediately after, Stanton turned to John B. Anderson, the former superintendent of the Louisville and Nashville Railroad, and authorized him to find up to 500 cars and 20 engines to be used south of the Ohio River, forgetting Stone altogether. Stanton's assistant, P. H. Watson, also telegraphed Quartermaster Robert Allen to locate any cars of the proper gauge for the Louisville and Nashville line and send them to the city.[19]

The task of the Baltimore and Ohio Railroad was nearly done by the time September 28 drew to an end. W. P. Smith proudly reported to Stanton that "everything has worked with the most desired success, exceeding our promises and anticipations." The line had dispatched 30 trains and a total of about 600 cars loaded with troops, artillery, and animals during the past five days. The actual number of men wound up being 20 percent more than initially reported to the railroad, and the number of horses exceeded the initial estimate by 50 percent, but these surprises did not delay the movement or cause undue problems because Smith was used to such things and was able to assemble enough cars. Stanton was ecstatic. "You have fully justified my most sanguine expectations, and have deserved well of your country," he told Smith.[20]

The flow of men, animals, and equipment slowed only a little when it reached the Ohio River. Because there was no bridge at Louisville, troops on the first train debarked at Jeffersonville, Indiana, and boarded river steamers to move across the Ohio. They arrived in Louisville at 4 A.M. on September 29 and Thomas Scott was ready for them. He provided food for the men and sent the first train on its way by 5:30 A.M. The second train reached at 7 that morning, the third three hours later, and the fourth within 15 minutes of the third. After a de-lay of two hours the fourth train left Louisville, and the fifth train, which carried Carl Schurz and 800 men, departed at 11 P.M. Scott had a busy day, but he ex-pected the lead train to reach Bridgeport, Alabama, by 6 A.M. on September 30.[21]

Scott's estimate was off by three and a half hours, for the first train rolled into Bridgeport at 9:30 on the morning of September 30. Even while he con-tinued to process the remaining trains as they arrived in Louisville, Scott told Rosecrans to unload the cars at Bridgeport as fast as possible because he des-perately needed empty cars to shift Hooker's men and carry on some degree of normal supply at the same time. Scott also told Stanton that the railroads of Kentucky and Tennessee needed 300 freight cars, 15 passenger cars, 50 plat-form cars, and 25 engines to run smoothly. It was up to Anderson, Stone, and Allen to find these if they could.[22]

The sixth, seventh, eighth, ninth, and tenth trainloads of men left Louisville several hours apart from each other, from 1:20 A.M. to 6:30 P.M. on Septem-ber 30. Hooker and his staff spent that night in Louisville. Scott was able to report that the first four trains had reached Bridgeport by 10:30 that night. The next day, October 1, Hooker left at 8 A.M. and Howard arrived for a stay of a few hours in the city, leaving by 4:30 P.M. Scott reported that a total of 15 trains had departed Louisville by the end of the day, carrying 9,470 men. All of the Eleventh Corps and a part of the Twelfth Corps were on Southern soil and on their way to various posts along the line from Nashville to Bridgeport. The Bal-timore and Ohio Railroad had fulfilled its mission by October 1, boarding more than 20,000 troops, 10 batteries of artillery with horses, and filling 100 cars of baggage and sending all this on its way west. Smith reported that, overall, the total of men and material shipped was 35 percent over the initial requisition on the railroad.[23]

Enough spare cars were immediately provided by various railroad compa-nies of the North to handle the shipment of Hooker's men, but, as Scott had reported, the lines in Kentucky and Tennessee required many more cars to handle the everyday demands of the government on them. Anderson ordered 100 new cars from manufacturers in Michigan City, Indiana, and requested a limited number of cars from various railroad companies of the northwestern states, which represented in Scott's words "a light tax upon each" one. Scott was able to obtain 11 engines from other sources and understood that an agent of Rosecrans was in the eastern states purchasing engines as well. He hoped to obtain all needed rolling stock by the end of November.[24]

By the night of October 2, Scott reported shifting a total of 21 trains containing 13,615 men and four batteries from Louisville. Three empty trains had returned to the city from Bridgeport thus far. "Circle is now complete," he announced to Stanton, "and we could keep up the present rate of movement without difficulty." But there *was* a difficulty. Hooker's command had left its wagon trains behind in Virginia. These wagons took up a good deal of space on railroad cars, and it was deemed more important to get the troops and weapons to Tennessee than their trains. But Joseph Wheeler's Confederate cavalry struck at Rosecrans's wagon link between the railroad and Chattanooga, destroying some 350 wagons and making it even more important that Hooker's transportation be shipped from Virginia as soon as possible.[25]

Another round of concentrated effort was needed to do this. Garrett rounded up all the cars he could find for the movement, promising Stanton he would alter some of them so as to accommodate wagons more easily. By October 4, Baltimore and Ohio personnel had loaded 40 wagons and 300 mules, and they planned to load an additional 140 wagons and 650 mules as soon as possible. The first shipment left Washington that day, but the rest took three days to load. D. H. Rucker estimated that the total transportation of the Eleventh and Twelfth Corps included 570 wagons and 150 ambulances (720 vehicles), plus 2,502 mules and 912 horses (3,414 animals). Garrett used 350 railroad cars to load all this, about three-fourths the number needed to transport the troops and their artillery. He had to request cars from McCallum's military railroad and from the Northern Central Railroad. Meanwhile, the process of converting Baltimore and Ohio cars to accommodate wagons and animals proceeded night and day. Garrett told his employees that if the workers exhausted themselves they should get more laborers from other railroad companies to finish the conversions.[26]

The transfer of Hooker's Eleventh and Twelfth Corps to Tennessee justly has been regarded as a remarkable event in the Civil War, demonstrating the power of rail transport in warfare. Participants were proud of their achievement. But it also has to be noted that the transfer was not easy to accomplish. It strained the resources of all railroad companies involved and temporarily interrupted normal supply shipments. The large number of cars and engines needed to move Hooker's men meant that tents and overcoats could not be delivered for weeks in the fall of 1863 as winter neared various military posts throughout Tennessee and Kentucky. Forage could not be shipped to Stevenson, Alabama, for some time. The draining of cars and engines from lines North and South affected a huge logistical area for much longer than the actual traveling time of Hooker's command; it took some time for the cars and engines to be returned to their lines and schedules, and many of them were never returned at all, given the added logistical burden placed on the Louisville and Nashville and Nashville and Chattanooga lines, which now had 20,000 more troops to feed and supply.[27]

On a lesser scale, the trip itself was anything but easy for the men and animals involved. The hasty rush to board trains and enduring hours on the road with only occasional chances for refreshment and relief of body functions stressed the troops. Captain William Wheeler of the 13th New York Battery reported that "both men and animals were more distressed and pulled down by it than by the severest forced march." Horses and mules especially were strained by the trip and needed time to recuperate upon arrival in Tennessee. Moreover, a number of the troops died along the way. Many of them insisted on climbing onto the tops of cars to get more air and see the sights. At least eight men of the Eleventh Corps fell off and died.[28]

While the shipment of Hooker's command has garnered the lion's share of attention from historians, many other significant troop transfers continued to take place with little fanfare. Grant wanted to move two divisions of the Nineteenth Corps from the area around New Orleans to Virginia, and the order prompted quartermasters to begin rounding up ships on July 1, 1864. Colonel C. G. Sawtelle used all government boats in the Department of the Gulf and pressed every private vessel near New Orleans, shipping the troops in installments until he had moved 20,923 men. The last installment left New Orleans on July 20.[29]

Andrew J. Smith's Right Wing of the Sixteenth Corps had participated in the Red River campaign and then in operations taking place in Mississippi during the summer of 1864 before shipping out for Missouri to counter Sterling Price's invasion of that border state during the fall. Eventually, his two divisions were needed at Nashville to help George H. Thomas deal with Hood's Army of

Tennessee. The troops boarded 22 steamers at St. Louis and began leaving on November 21.[30]

Smith issued strict orders governing his men while on board the boats. Any time the craft touched shore, subordinate officers had to post guards and prevent men from leaving the boat. The senior officer on board any craft was in charge of all men on the vessel. The boats ran together as a group governed by a system of whistles that signaled what they should do in any conceivable case. Mimicking Morse code, the number and duration of the whistles indicated where the boats should close up or spread out, whether enemy troops or artillery had been sighted ahead, and where the craft should head for shore to refuel or accomplish any other task. One boat, the *W. L. Ewing*, sank along the way with the loss only of wagons and harness. Smith's command reached Nashville by November 30 after traveling some 500 miles.[31]

Federal quartermasters arranged an unusual shipment of troops on a low visibility mission to support the presidential election of 1864. Troops were detailed from the Tenth and Eighteenth Corps of the Army of the James to form a Provisional Division under Brigadier General Joseph Hawley. They boarded five vessels (at least three of them were large ferry boats) for transport to New York City. Federal officials were worried following the terrible draft and race riot of July 1863 that trouble might attend the election. The division unloaded at New York but remained quietly near the wharves. After several days of calm, Hawley's men reboarded and steamed back to Virginia. Hardly anyone outside those responsible for the movement knew it had taken place.[32]

Another major troop transfer on the order of magnitude of Hooker's took place in the winter months of 1865. John M. Schofield, whose Twenty-Third Corps contributed mightily to the defeat of Hood at Franklin and Nashville, chafed under Thomas's command. Friction between the two added to Thomas's slowness in mounting a follow-up invasion after his victory at Nashville led Schofield to propose shipping his men by a northern route to join Grant's concentration at Petersburg and Richmond. Grant agreed and issued orders for the transfer in mid-January 1865.[33]

By now Lewis B. Parsons had been appointed to head the Fourth Division of the Quartermaster Department, which was responsible for superintending all river and rail transport in the country. While Stanton had masterminded Hooker's transfer, Parsons took sole responsibility for managing Schofield's movement. Stanton's assistant, Charles A. Dana, issued the order to Parsons on

January 11 and suggested it would be best to ship the troops by steamer from Clifton, Tennessee, down the Tennessee River and up the Ohio to Parkersburg, West Virginia. From there they could use the rail system to reach Washington, D.C. If that was not feasible, perhaps they could steam to Cairo and utilize the Northern rail system.[34]

Of course, the details and the final decision about routes lay entirely in Parsons's hands, and he worried about the unreliability of steamboat navigation on the upper Ohio River, especially in winter. Thus Parsons quietly telegraphed several railroad companies in the North and asked them to assemble a number of empty cars so he could within twelve to twenty-four hours' notice get them to Cairo, Cincinnati, or Louisville for Schofield's troops as needed. Given the cold weather, he also arranged for "an abundance of hot coffee" to be gathered for distribution.[35]

Parsons left his office in Washington, D.C., five and a half hours after receiving Dana's order and reached Louisville to find that Schofield had already begun using the steamers readily available to him. He gathered more boats and started up the Tennessee River, meeting the first shipment of five brigades coming downstream. Parsons was surprised to see all of them overloaded, so he accompanied them to Cairo, where he rearranged the troop placement on board to alleviate this potentially dangerous problem. The first shipment left Cairo at 7 A.M. of January 18.[36]

By the time these first five brigades reached Louisville on the evening of January 20, the weather began to turn bitterly cold and reports filtered down the valley that ice was forming on the upper reaches of the Ohio. Parsons consulted with Schofield, Robert Allen, and many experienced steamboat men, who all agreed that it would be too dangerous to carry the men by boat to Parkersburg. Parsons issued orders for the vessels to unload at Cincinnati, but even that proved troublesome. Because the Ohio was falling rapidly, the larger boats could not get over the falls located just south of Louisville. He had to unload them, find smaller boats for the troops, and then proceed through the canal that bypassed the falls. Battery D of the 1st Ohio Light Artillery, for example, had been on board the *Loretta* but divided onto the *Baltimore* and the *Rose Hite* for the trip through the canal and to Louisville. The first boats began to reach Cincinnati on the morning of January 21 as reports confirmed that ice had so choked the river upstream from the city as to close navigation for the next three or four days.[37]

Parsons now had to rely on the accumulation of empty cars he had providentially arranged. In fact, more cars were desperately needed than those already accumulated and Parsons instructed his quartermaster officers to impress them if necessary. He managed to start the first 600 troops out of Cincinnati, followed by 2,500 more, before dense fog began to force the remaining steamers on the Ohio River to stop where they were between Louisville and Cincinnati on the evening of January 21. As the boats dribbled in, Parsons continued to send trainloads of troops by different rail lines out of Cincinnati so as not to overload any one company's resources. He sent 4,000 altogether by midnight of January 22. Meanwhile, the fog lifted and the rest of the boats came into Cincinnati; Parsons sent another 4,000 men out of the city on January 23.[38]

Parsons evidently saw the river as a more convenient logistical link than the rail system. When prospects seemed to indicate a sudden warming trend on January 23 he ordered some boats to continue upstream to Parkersburg. But before the vessels could start, all predictions of warming temperatures were blasted by increased cold. Parsons ordered the boats unloaded as planned and scraped up more empty cars at Cincinnati.[39]

With the temperature plummeting to just 5 degrees, Parsons ordered stoves to be put on board each car and hay or straw to be issued the troops. Reports that the Ohio Central Railroad was having serious trouble coping with the transfer began to filter in. The cold weather added to the problems posed by old, worn-out tracks, causing some trains to derail. With ice flows cruising down the Ohio at Bellaire, Parsons found "heavy iron bound Ferry Boats" to transfer the men over the river. Only these craft, he thought, could deal with the ice.[40]

Parsons was very lucky. The boats carrying Schofield's troops barely managed to get into Cincinnati before the coldest weather and heaviest ice on the Ohio descended on the city and points below. By January 27, Robert Allen reported that at Louisville it was "intensely cold. The river is full of ice and frozen besides the Ohio is gorged with ice thirty miles below the falls." The city was cut off from river navigation both above and below. The few steamers located below the ice blockade were needed for normal supply shipments. The Mississippi River also was closed by ice from Cairo to St. Louis.[41]

By January 29, Parsons had crossed many trainloads of troops over the Ohio River and given them to the capable hands of the Baltimore and Ohio Railroad. The next day, officials of the Ohio Central Railroad managed to complete their shipment of Schofield's men, having dealt with the many problems posed by their substandard facilities. By this time Parsons reported that the "incessant labor of all connected with the movement by night and day" had worn everyone out.[42]

Parsons traveled along the Baltimore and Ohio route on January 30 and found everything "passing well over the Road." Army commanders closed liquor shops in towns along the way to avoid tempting Schofield's men, offering them plenty of hot coffee instead. Many of John W. Garrett's railroad operatives suffered from the severe cold, enduring "frozen hands and feet," and Garrett had difficulty finding skilled men to replace them. Still the trains rolled from the mountains onto the coastal plain and into Washington, D.C., without undue delay.[43]

Parsons reached Washington on the night of February 1, having been gone three weeks to manage this difficult and complicated troop transfer. He organized the shipment of 20,000 men, their artillery support, and 800 animals over a distance of 1,400 miles in eleven days. Unlike the transfer of Hooker's command, Schofield's required the use of both steamers and rail lines. About half the distance involved river travel, and the rest utilized five railroad companies. The most important difference lay in the mid-winter dangers of severely cold temperatures and ice gorges on the Ohio River. Despite these unusual difficulties, only one man died along the way. He jumped when it appeared his car might crash and was killed upon landing. The men who remained in the car were uninjured in the mishap. After enduring three weeks "of greater anxiety, suspense, and intense labor, I think, than I ever encountered before in my life," Parsons could console himself with the thought that he had personally managed "the most remarkable movement of a large body of Troops in the Annals of warfare."[44]

As with the shipment of the Eleventh and Twelfth Corps in 1863, the transfer of Schofield's Twenty-Third Corps seriously disrupted normal steamer and rail transport over a wide area of the West. This was another reason for placing so much emphasis on speed in shipping Schofield's men. Thomas had wanted to transfer the Fourth Corps to Eastport, Mississippi, but plans to do so had to be postponed. The transport of cavalry horses to Mississippi also had to be delayed for another day. Also, for Twenty-Third Corps men, the trip had its stresses and discomforts. In fact, the historian of Battery D, 1st Ohio Light Artillery, called it the "hardest, longest trip the Battery had ever taken."[45]

Schofield's men rested only a short while at Washington before coastal shipping transported them to the mouth of the Cape Fear River. Grant decided that the Twenty-Third Corps should reinforce Sherman's army group as it marched through the Carolinas rather than add more strength to the Army of the Potomac and the Army of the James along the Petersburg–Richmond lines. The strain of transporting and supplying Schofield's move, Terry's expedition against Fort Fisher, and preparing a fleet to deliver supplies to Sherman wherever he may require them stressed the coastal shipping system more than at any other period of the war. Meigs complained that all this activity had "occupied all the ocean steam vessels of the country, to the temporary interruption of most private lines. These movements have also exhausted the accumulated stock of coal at Fort Monroe, City Point, and Annapolis." Yet his quartermaster officers managed to struggle through the difficulties without causing undue suffering for anyone.[46]

As soon as the disruption to river traffic caused by Schofield's transfer began to subside, Union quartermasters were able to secure steamers for other needed shipments of troops. Smith's Right Wing of the Sixteenth Corps was headed for New Orleans from Eastport, Mississippi. Fairly typical of the units involved, the 32nd Iowa left Eastport on February 9 and steamed down the Tennessee River in very cold weather. It then traveled down the Ohio and into the Mississippi. Guerrillas shot at the steamer from the Arkansas shore, killing several men, but the rest arrived at New Orleans on February 21.[47]

The planned move of a Fourth Corps division from Huntsville, Alabama, to Eastport, Mississippi, in late January exhibits a typical way that quartermasters weighed options and planned a troop transfer. All wheeled vehicles and artillery were to march about 100 miles directly to Eastport. Meanwhile, the rest of the corps would be transported in railcars from Huntsville to Nashville, with 50 men in each car. Reaching Nashville, the troops would board steamers for the journey down the Cumberland and Ohio rivers, then ascend the Tennessee to Eastport. Quartermasters relied on rapid transit for the infantry and slow transit for the bulky equipment. They estimated it would take ten days for the wheeled vehicles to reach Eastport and that the infantry would arrive roughly at the same time or earlier.[48]

But this move was cancelled due to the demands of Schofield's and Smith's transfers, and the Fourth Corps continued to operate in the area of north Alabama and east Tennessee until it was needed elsewhere. The corps moved 373 miles from Carter's Station to Nashville near the end of the war. Quartermaster James F. Rusling managed the move and admitted to a good deal of worry. "It was no child's play," he told friends. "I watched the thing by telegraph, night and day; and you may believe I was 'mighty' glad when the thing was all over, without a man hurt or a mule injured. It was a great tax on the brain, and I sleep better now it is done."[49]

In fact, the end of the war accentuated the need for mass movement of men and material rather than ending it. With French intervention in the troubled affairs of Mexico, the Federal government was keen to shift troops to Texas. The all-black Twenty-Fifth Corps therefore moved from City Point, Virginia, to the Texas coast in May 1865. The transfer of 25,000 men, 200 wagons, and 2,000 horses and mules with forty days of rations and forage represented the most daunting assignment given coastal shipping in the Civil War.[50]

The logistical resources used in this grand troop transfer of the Twenty-Fifth Corps were enormous. Quartermaster officers gathered 57 ocean steamers totaling 56,987 tons for the 12-day trip. These steamers consumed 947 tons of coal every day, and the men and animals needed 50,000 gallons of fresh water daily. Ship owners constructed bunks for the troops and stalls for the animals on their vessels. It cost the government $33,300.91 per day, about $400,000 in all, to transport the Twenty-Fifth Corps to Texas. Although in Union hands, Mobile could not provide enough coal or fresh water quickly enough for a flotilla such as this, and it would take too much time to land the boats at the New Orleans levee. So Meigs arranged for the ships to stop at the mouth of the Mississippi River and for all needed resupplies to be shipped to that point from New Orleans. Meigs was motivated by a desire to lessen the discomfort of the men by shortening the trip as much as possible. He also wanted to reduce the cost to the government and release the steamers as soon as they deposited their men and cargo in Texas.[51]

Meigs felt keenly the need to release coastal steamers, not only to save money but to facilitate other logistical needs. At the same time that his subordinates were shipping the Twenty-Fifth Corps to Texas, they had to move 7,000 troops from Washington, D.C., to Savannah, Georgia, transport 3,000 Confederate prisoners from Point Lookout, Maryland, to Mobile, and handle the normal traffic of individual soldiers to and from their units for various purposes. Meigs estimated that more than 30,000 troops were in motion along the coast at any one time during May and June 1865.[52]

Meigs did not count many troops transfers that were taking place at the same time along the inland waterways and the railroads, some of which also utilized the coastal shipping system. The entire Fourth Corps moved from

Nashville to New Orleans in early June 1865. In order to shift it to the Texas coast, C. G. Sawtelle selected the best light draft steamers from among those returning from delivery of Twenty-Fifth Corps men and loaded Fourth Corps troops on board. He also shipped some units of the Thirteenth Corps from Mobile to Texas.[53]

Sawtelle also took responsibility for transporting an enormous cavalry force to Texas. Most of Philip Sheridan's troopers from the Army of the Potomac were transferred to the West after the war. By the time Sawtelle was given responsibility for them, these troopers were already at Memphis, Vicksburg, Baton Rouge, and New Orleans. Wesley Merritt's division of 4,500 men needed to move to Shreveport, Louisiana, and then to San Antonio, Texas; George Custer's division of 4,500 men was scheduled to go to Alexandria, Louisiana, before proceeding to Hempstead, Texas. Sawtelle chartered many river steamers to get both divisions to their Louisiana destinations and then provided wagons to support their march into Texas.[54]

The flurry of large-scale troop transfers at and after the war's end involved river and coastal steamers, but we must keep in mind that several important movements of men took place on foot during the war. William T. Sherman was responsible for two of the most impressive troop transfers by footpower. Following the Federal defeat at Chickamauga, he moved four divisions of the Army of the Tennessee from the Big Black River and Vicksburg toward Chattanooga. Starting on September 22, Fifteenth Corps men marched from the Big Black to Vicksburg and joined Seventeenth Corps troops on river steamers for a trip to Memphis. From there the Federals traveled by rail to and beyond Corinth, but everyone had to march the rest of the way. Sherman picked up 8,000 men of the Sixteenth Corps in northern Mississippi, but his progress was delayed by orders to repair the railroad as he went. Finally, while crossing the Tennessee River on steamers, Grant told Sherman to hurry his men as fast as feasible. An epic march followed across south Tennessee and north Alabama by way of Florence, Rogersville, Fayetteville, Winchester, Decherd, Stevenson, and Bridgeport. By November 23, most of Sherman's command (minus the Sixteenth Corps troops, who were left behind to work on the railroads) had assembled near Chattanooga. Roughly 20,000 men had moved nearly 900 miles in two months. They marched at least half of the way, traversing the Cumberland Plateau, improvising stream and river crossings, and relying heavily on foraging for food and fodder.[55]

Sherman also was responsible for the largest troop transfer of the war, although he rarely gets credit for it. Much has been made of the March to the Sea and through the Carolinas as an exercise in political strategy, and they certainly were campaigns designed in part to strike a blow to Confederate logistics, supply, and especially public morale. But Sherman's most fundamental and important goal in both campaigns was to shift 60,000 western veterans to aid Grant's campaign at Petersburg and overwhelm Lee's Army of Northern Virginia. All other benefits of this grand march were of secondary importance.[56]

But could Sherman have more efficiently moved his 60,000 men to Virginia by rail and river steamer? Parsons, who would have been responsible for this gargantuan move, had never attempted such an undertaking. The largest shipment by rail and river during the war was Schofield's Twenty-Third Corps shift from west Tennessee to Annapolis. That had involved 20,000 men, artillery, and animals making a distance of 1,400 miles in 11 days. The distance from Atlanta to Petersburg by way of Louisville, Northern railroads, and Washington, D.C., would have been about 1,300 miles, most of it by rail.

Parsons could not have done this in one movement, for even Union logistical capacity had its limits. Instead, he could have conducted the shift in three installments of 20,000 men each. That would have taken at least 33 days, but probably would have required a more extended time. It would probably have been impossible to tie up all the transportation needed to haul 60,000 men for 33 straight days. If Parsons could have devoted a couple of weeks to shipping each installment of 20,000 men, with a couple of weeks between each installment to allow for a temporary resumption of normal traffic, Sherman would have consumed close to three months to bring his men to Grant's aid, arriving by mid-February 1865. In contrast, after marching 300 miles from Atlanta to Savannah and then 475 miles from Savannah to Goldsborough, North Carolina, Sherman still was not within supporting distance of Grant even by the end of March. After necessary refitting, he was not ready to resume moving north until April 10 and still had 150 miles to march before reaching Petersburg. By then, however, it was no longer necessary to help Grant. Setting aside the other objectives of his two campaigns, Sherman could have delivered his 60,000 to Petersburg more efficiently by railroad than by walking and the war in Virginia might have been shortened by a few weeks.

In short, Federal quartermasters could have achieved their most important large-scale troop transfer of the war if Sherman had given them the opportunity to move his men to Virginia instead of marching them. It would have been a mighty testament to the administrative and fiscal power of the Federal government.

The cost of massive troop transfers was surprisingly low in many ways. Lewis B. Parsons estimated that by the latter part of the war it cost on average $1.05 per man to move soldiers from St. Louis to Memphis, a distance of 450 miles. To transport 20,000 men that distance would cost about $21,000. To ship a man from St. Louis to New Orleans, a distance he estimated at 1,250 miles, would have cost $3.62; 20,000 men could be shipped that distance for about $72,500. Never before had the U.S. government needed to move such masses of men, and never before could it have afforded to do so.[57]

The Confederate government also utilized the logistical system of the South to implement troop transfers, but on a far less intensive level. Because Richmond had no counterpart to Lewis B. Parsons, we have little in the way of reports detailing how it was done. The Confederate Quartermasters General were not the equal of Montgomery Meigs either, nor were the several Confederate secretaries of war the equal of Edwin M. Stanton. As seen in previous chapters, the Confederacy also did not have nearly as many river steamers available and its rail system was poor at best.

But a few significant troop transfers took place. After its defeat at the battle of Pea Ridge, Arkansas, Earl Van Dorn's Army of the West moved to Corinth to reinforce the Army of the Mississippi. Van Dorn received the order on March 25, 1862, along with an offer to send steamers to transport his 15,000 troops. The Army of the West marched from Van Buren to Des Arc, Arkansas, on the White River, where the troops boarded the boats. The first shipments left on April 7 and the last on April 25, far too late to participate in the battle of Shiloh.[58]

For Van Dorn's army, the trip down the narrow and winding White River was slow and tedious. In general, the steamers were large enough to accommodate one regiment. On reaching the Mississippi, the boats found a flooded stream and made good progress toward Memphis. From there the troops rode the rails to Corinth. Daniel Harris Reynolds's 1st Arkansas Mounted Rifles traveled from Des Arc to Corinth, a distance of about 300 miles, in ten days. A total of eight steamers were mentioned in extant sources, but it is possible that more were available for such a large shipment of troops. Some units were detained for quite some time in Memphis. Lucas's Missouri Battery, for example, spent a full month in the city before heading toward Corinth.[59]

Company D of the 2nd Missouri (C.S.) accompanied Van Dorn's army on its move to Corinth, and Corporal William O. Hedrick carefully recorded the details of travel. The company marched from Van Buren to Des Arc for 200 miles. Then it traveled 400 miles by boat to Memphis and 96 miles by rail to Corinth, for a total of 696 miles. Company D utilized rails for 13.7 percent of the journey, boats for 57.6 percent, and footed it for the rest (28.7 percent).[60]

The transfer of Braxton Bragg's Army of the Mississippi from Tupelo to Chattanooga in the late summer of 1862 was far larger and more ambitious than Van Dorn's move. It was prompted by a desire to secure Chattanooga from an approach by Don C. Buell's Army of the Ohio, and the most direct rail route was only 225 miles. But Federal forces already controlled portions of that rail link across northern Alabama, compelling Bragg to go by a roundabout way of 776 miles via Mobile and Atlanta. There was a shorter route through Selma and Montgomery, but it had gaps stemming from prewar construction plans that had never been realized.[61]

Bragg started the transfer with John P. McCown's division in July, utilizing 6 trains of 10 cars each to move 3,000 men. Upon arriving at Mobile, the men crossed Mobile Bay by boat and boarded cars for the trip to Montgomery. Daniel Harris Reynolds's 1st Arkansas Mounted Rifles was among those regiments taking part in this first shipment. Reynolds's men left Tupelo on June 29 and reached Chattanooga on July 5. There were layovers of two hours at West Point, Georgia, and nine hours at Atlanta, but in general the transfer proceeded smoothly and apparently with no accidents.[62]

The movement of McCown's division encouraged Bragg to commit fully to the transfer of 27,000 more troops along the same route. The six railroad companies involved in the transfer fulfilled their responsibilities commendably. This time there were some accidents, which was almost to be expected considering the size of the transfer. A train carrying the 18th Louisiana stopped at a bend in the track to take on more wood. The weather was "a little foggy" and the engineer of the next train, which carried the 19th Louisiana, ran into it. Several cars were wrecked and six men of the 18th Louisiana died in the mishap. One man of the 19th Louisiana also was mortally injured. Despite this deadly accident, the movement of Bragg's Army of the Mississippi from Tupelo to Chattanooga, the largest Confederate troop transfer of the war, continued relatively smoothly.[63]

As the Confederate rail system deteriorated, large transfers such as Bragg's became more problematic. When Carter L. Stevenson's division shifted from Murfreesboro, Tennessee, to Jackson, Mississippi, in December 1862, it took three weeks to make the move. Joseph E. Johnston, commander of Confederate forces in the West, worried about the delay. "Our disadvantage in this warfare is that the enemy can transfer an army from Mississippi to Nashville before we learn that it is in motion." In contrast, Confederate quartermasters could not move an equal number of troops the same distance "in less than six weeks."[64]

Bragg shifted another division, commanded by John C. Breckinridge, from middle Tennessee to Jackson, Mississippi, in May 1863. Daniel Harris Reynolds's 1st Arkansas Mounted Rifles once again participated in this movement. Reynolds packed his men on railroad cars at Wartrace on May 10; after delays of 5–6 hours each at Chattanooga and Atlanta, and 14 hours at West Point, the regiment arrived at Montgomery on May 13. Unlike Bragg's transfer the previous summer, Reynolds's men boarded boats and steamed for 110 miles along the Alabama River to Selma, Alabama, an 8-hour journey. They boarded cars again and headed west but were delayed several hours by a train wreck. For reasons unexplained, Reynolds used a steamer once again to travel from Demopolis to McDowell, where his men boarded cars for the journey to Meridian and Brandon. Reynolds's much-traveled regiment arrived at Jackson on the evening of May 19.[65]

The 1st Arkansas Mounted Rifles demonstrated that although deteriorating, the Southern rail system was still capable of fairly rapid movement of troops. But it has to be noted that other units involved in Breckinridge's transfer did not fare so well. Traveling 718 miles in seven days, William B. Lance of the 60th North Carolina was exhausted. "I assure you it was a tiresome trip certain," he told his wife and children. Several accidents occurred along the way, although none of them affected his regiment.[66]

That the 4th Kentucky (C.S.) survived the transfer of Breckinridge's trip was something akin to a miracle. John S. Jackman vividly remembered the early part of the journey years after the war. His regiment boarded "dilapidated freight cars" at Wartrace on May 25, packing 1,000 men on one train. After it passed Cowan and began to ascend the slope of the Cumberland Plateau, word circulated that only one car in the train had usable brakes. Passing through the tunnel, the train began a steep descent toward Stevenson, Alabama; its speed increased so rapidly that the engineer estimated his train traveled seven miles in just over four minutes, a speed of 105 miles per hour. When it reached the valley below, everyone suddenly realized the rear car was missing. Men who walked back found the car smashed, but all on board were uninjured. Another car was "disabled by having nearly half of one of the wheels broken off, and how it continued to stick to the track was a mystery." The soldiers of the 9th Kentucky declared that they preferred to risk the dangers of the battlefield rather than go through another harrowing experience such as this train ride.[67]

By the midpoint of the war, the Southern rail system produced one story of inefficiency after another. When Dabney Herndon Maury shifted his division to Vicksburg in late December 1862 he could get no more than 300 of his men to the battlefield of Chickasaw Bluffs in time to take part in the engagement. The problem was "vexatious delays and inefficiencies of the Rail Road people." A terrible collision compounded the problems; the 35th Mississippi reportedly lost 70 men. As a result of all these troubles, the division dribbled into Vicksburg over the course of several days after the battle ended.[68]

The transfer of Confederate troops south from Grenada, Mississippi, in late January 1863 conveniently illustrates the fact that Southern railroads suffered from much more than just hardware problems. The Confederate system of rail transportation was woefully lacking in modern, efficient methods of standard operation. Infantry officers insisted on controlling the loading process at Grenada, against the protests of railroad officials. As a result, they packed the cars with too many men, well over the 50 men per car that the general superintendent of the Virginia Central Railroad thought should be a standard ratio. Instead of three hours it took up to 36 hours to load at Grenada because of this interference, and the men suffered from exposure to cold winter winds while waiting to board the trains. Infantry officers once again interfered along the way when they insisted the trains stop due to the unusually cold weather—this was a legitimate concern because the Mississippi Central Railroad had obtained cars from other companies for this transfer and could only get flatcars, forcing many soldiers to ride in the open. Added to this problem, several engines derailed and caused even more delays. The normal running time between Grenada and Canton was 9 to 11 hours, but it took several days to deliver these troops between the two points because of the many administrative and hardware problems.[69]

At roughly the same time, States Rights Gist was ordered to take two regiments from Charleston to Wilmington in response to a Federal raid against Goldsborough, North Carolina, and he encountered nothing but trouble in making that relatively short rail journey. He was delayed by "overloading the trains, by the worn-out condition of the locomotives, want of wood and water at proper stations, and want of system in running the trains. I am convinced that no reliance can be placed upon the railroads for the transportation of troops to Wilmington in any reasonable time or from Wilmington to Charleston.[70]

Claudius C. Wilson discovered the truth of Gist's statement when he tried to move his brigade from Masonborough, North Carolina, to Savannah via Wilmington. It took three hours to load just one regiment at the Wilmington depot, and then the locomotive proved too weak to pull the train. Railroad men had to detach the last three cars. Every train carrying Wilson's troops experienced delays of several hours either in starting from Wilmington or in stopping at intermediate points on their journey to Savannah. The first train, which carried no more than eight companies of the 25th Georgia, was so slow that the second train caught up with and passed it even though it had started a full 17 hours after the first. Ironically, even though Gist and Wilson thoroughly documented the many problems in shifting their small commands short distances in the heart of the Confederacy, nothing was done to correct any of these factors that had begun to make a joke of Rebel logistical power only halfway through the war effort.[71]

Given this sorry state of logistical power, the successful transfer of two divisions from James Longstreet's corps from the Army of Northern Virginia to Braxton Bragg's Army of Tennessee in September 1863 stands out in Confederate history. Six railroad companies were involved in this movement, which totaled either 705 miles or 775 miles, depending on which of two routes used by Rebel quartermasters is counted. After moving the men from Orange Court House sixty miles to Richmond by rail, some trains went by way of Wilmington and others by way of Charlotte, North Carolina, to Atlanta. A much shorter route lay directly from Richmond to Bristol, Knoxville, and Chattanooga, a total of 540 miles, but Ambrose Burnside's occupation of Knoxville in early September prevented the Confederates from using it. Captain Frederick W. Sims managed the transfer.[72]

Lee issued orders for the move on September 6, and John B. Hood's division led the way two days later. The van of Hood's command reached Ringgold, Georgia, on September 16, eight days later. The rest of his men arrived in time to participate in the first day of fighting at Chickamauga on September 19. Longstreet and his staff, as well as two brigades of Lafayette McLaws's division, reached Bragg's headquarters that night. A total of five out of the nine brigades in Longstreet's two divisions participated in the bitter fighting of the second day, September 20, but none of his artillery arrived in time.[73]

The movement was delayed by the wretched state of the rail system. Soldiers often noted that their trains were forced to stop so engineers could adjust the engine. Long delays ensued as the troops stopped for meals. A variety of different cars carried the soldiers, and the men often broke holes in the sides to obtain ventilation. The last of the troops, E. Porter Alexander's artillery battalion, left Petersburg on September 17 and arrived at Ringgold on September 25.[74]

The late start of the movement and the fact that quartermasters could not utilize the shortest rail lines to Chattanooga greatly contributed to the fact that much of Longstreet's manpower and all of his artillery were unavailable to Bragg when needed. But the weaknesses of Southern railroad companies also greatly contributed to the failure to get all of the men and equipment into the zone of operations quickly enough to make a difference. In contrast, Federal quartermasters could have accomplished a move like this in time to make a difference in the fighting. Still, Longstreet's transfer overshadowed all other Confederate troop movements by rail. It seemed "to surpass them all in intense and dramatic interest, in hardiness, in secrecy, in success," according to Archer Anderson, one of Daniel H. Hill's staff officers. Years after the war, Alexander marveled that his artillery battalion managed to make it to Ringgold at all, considering the state of the Confederate rail system in late 1863.[75]

Two subsequent Rebel troop transfers lay in the shadows because of a shortage of documentation detailing how they were accomplished. Leonidas Polk moved two divisions from his Department of Mississippi and East Louisiana to join the Army of Tennessee in May 1864 and participate in the Atlanta campaign. The troops apparently used a combination of rail transport, walking, and perhaps some steamers along the Alabama River to shift from eastern Mississippi through northern Alabama until they joined Joseph E. Johnson's army at Resaca, Georgia. Daniel Harris Reynolds, who now led a brigade, participated in this transfer. He shifted his command from Pollard, Alabama, to Resaca from May 4 through 7, much faster than other units.[76]

The transfer of what was left of John B. Hood's Army of Tennessee from northern Mississippi to North Carolina following the disastrous Tennessee campaign was little short of a miracle. Hood had more than 17,000 men left by January 20, 1865. He was replaced first by Richard Taylor and later by Joseph E. Johnston, as Richmond officials decided that help was needed in North Carolina, where a growing concentration of Rebel manpower tried to stop Sherman's army group. Of 17,000 men, 4,000 were sent to defend Mobile and 6,000 other troops were retained in Mississippi, but the rest (7,000) started their long journey from Tupelo. Some went by the intermediate route via Selma and Montgomery to Macon, Milledgeville, and Augusta, but others took the longer route by way of Mobile. Therefore, the transfer took advantage of both rail and steamer transportation, and the troops walked whenever they encountered breaks in the rail system caused by Sherman's previous march through Georgia.[77]

Daniel Harris Reynolds participated in this troop transfer to North Carolina. He set out from West Point, Mississippi, on February 3, 1865, by rail to Mobile, where his men waited for 17 hours because of "want of transportation." By February 9 he boarded the cars for Midway, Georgia, near the state capital of Milledgeville. Here, Reynolds encountered the massive break in the Southern rail system caused by Sherman's men. His troops marched for four days before they found usable rail transportation at Mayfield and then rode to and beyond Augusta. Reynolds's men once again took to the road on February 16 and marched to Newberry, South Carolina, a total of about 80 miles. They rode the rails for a short distance, then resumed marching for many miles. The roads they encountered were "in a wretched condition" due to continual rains, but the brigade reached Chester by March 4. Once again the men boarded cars and traveled via Charlotte to Salisbury by March 7, although Reynolds found it "is slow business traveling on . . . railroad." The brigade continued to ride the rails to Raleigh and Goldsborough, reaching the latter place on March 11. Reynolds moved his men on the railroad and on foot for a total of 36 days to reach a place some 1,080 miles from West Point, Mississippi.[78]

By this stage of the war Federal quartermasters could have moved a brigade of troops more than 1,000 miles in almost any direction without giving the task much thought and in one-fourth of the time it took Reynolds to get to North Carolina. But for the Confederates, the movement of 7,000 men for more than 1,000 miles during the last two months before the war came crashing to an end was nothing less than a miracle. Moreover, the remnant of the once mighty Army of Tennessee, which Sherman had left for John Schofield and George H.

Thomas to deal with as he sliced in the opposite direction through the heart of the Confederacy, now appeared before him in North Carolina. These troops participated in the battle of Bentonville on March 19–21, 1865, the last major engagement of Sherman's command and one which temporarily halted his march through the Carolinas. They were included in Johnston's surrender to Sherman on April 26. The Rebel logistical system had delivered one final success in moving these men such a long distance and in time to participate in the final drama of the war. "No story of fiction could be more romantic than that fact of real war history," Schofield marveled after the conflict.[79]

9

TARGETING STEAMBOATS

Armies through the ages have attempted to strike at the logistical underpinnings of their enemies, and Union and Confederate forces were no exception. Rebel authorities spent a good deal of time and energy trying to develop an effective strategy to interrupt Federal shipment of goods and men on the western rivers. In addition, anti-Federal guerrillas acted on their own to fire at steamers and railroad trains. Cavalry raids against the rail-based network sometimes worked, but Confederate authorities had little opportunity to hit the coastal shipping system due to their lack of a powerful naval arm. Wagon trains were relatively safe even though they were in close proximity to enemy forces because they were escorted by friendly mounted troops or infantry.

Federal steamboats became a target soon after Union forces captured long stretches of the Mississippi River. Ironically, much of that Union success came with little fighting. Columbus fell without a battle, and the Federals captured New Madrid and Island No. 10 through maneuver rather than combat. Union troops occupied Helena, Arkansas, without a struggle by July of that year. At the same time, other Federal forces captured New Orleans with little bloodshed, occupied Baton Rouge, sailed past Port Hudson, and nearly secured Vicksburg by mid-summer of 1862. Northern armies captured most of the Confederate section of the Mississippi River faster and more easily than anyone could have guessed.

The Confederates began to strike back in small ways. By August 1862, individuals gathered in self-constituted guerrilla bands to take potshots at steamers in the vicinity of Memphis. William T. Sherman, the Federal commander in the city, was particularly keen for his people to possess and use "the great artery of America," the Mississippi River, because "whatever power holds it, holds the continent." He believed the free navigation of the Mississippi involved the destiny of the Northern people, a defense of their "self existence to push their power and Dominion so as to embrace the lands whose waters flow to the Mississippi. In this they must be despotic."[1]

Sherman became alarmed when guerrillas began to target steamboats. Federal troops captured 22 guerrillas who had fired at the *Champion* on the night of August 21, but the trouble only escalated after that capture. Shots were fired at the packet *Eugene* from Randolph, Tennessee, so Sherman sent the 46th Ohio to burn the town in retaliation. The *Eugene* carried passengers and private freight only, no military personnel or material. "So exposed are our frail boats, that we must protect them by all the terrors by which we can surround such acts of vandalism," Sherman explained. Women and children often rode the steamers, and some were on board the *Forest Queen* and *J. J. Roe* when guerrillas fired on them, leading Sherman to threaten the placement of captured guerrillas or the families of pro-Confederates from Memphis on board every riverboat.[2]

A new twist on the story began when the *Continental* and the *Dickey* were fired at by an artillery piece, signifying that regularly organized Confederate forces had begun to target the river-based system. Neither boat carried military supplies or personnel. On the *Gladiator,* two civilians were killed, several more were wounded, and the boat's crew barely managed to save the vessel when it caught fire due to an attack. Sherman responded by implementing his threat to evict pro-Confederate families from Memphis, randomly selecting the names of 40 people from a previously compiled list and escorting them at least 25 miles from the city. He continued to send the 46th Ohio to burn towns in retaliation for attacks on other boats as well. "How would they like it if we were to fire through the houses of their wives and families, as they do through the boats carrying our wives and families," Sherman wrote of the attackers.[3]

The Confederate government had nothing to do with the rise of guerrilla forces along the river, but it worked to create a viable strategy of harassing Union river travel. Naval Lieutenant Isaac N. Brown suggested that light artillery planted on the bank of the Mississippi could make life hazardous for boats and curtail the use of the stream. An anonymous contributor to the *Knoxville Register* argued that light cannon strapped to the backs of mules could provide an even more mobile artillery component to any small force of attackers along the river. Confederate authorities were aware of the rise of guerrilla groups along the Mississippi, but they never officially supported them. The Confederate Congress had passed a law authorizing the creation of partisan units (officially sanctioned by the army but operating independently behind Union lines). Some enterprising men wanted to create such units specifically for the purpose of harassing river traffic but argued their recruits needed the incentive of personal gain to risk their lives in capturing boats.[4]

General Samuel G. French thought a great deal about the prospects of attacking river steamers; having lived for years in the Mississippi delta as a planter, he was quite familiar with the river. Dense cane and timber crowded the banks of several bends where the main channel came close to the trees, providing good positions to conceal troops and artillery. The levees also could be used as parapets at key locations. He believed that six regiments and six batteries might essentially close navigation at many points. They would have to be highly mobile, moving from one point to another when necessary, and few good roads led from the interior to those places. The delta was rich with agricultural produce, and a force like this probably could live off the land. The Richmond authorities never moved forward to implement a plan like French's, probably due to the crushing demand for troops at many other locations.[5]

After Grant laid siege to Vicksburg, Confederate military authorities worked harder to devise an effective strategy for interrupting the flow of steamers downriver. Echoing French's concept, Secretary of War James L. Seddon thought special units of infantry or cavalry, with artillery pieces attached, should be created to move along the banks. Seddon recalled that two companies of a regularly organized battalion had operated from the Arkansas side of the river the previous winter with some success. The companies had pilots and rivermen in the ranks. Reports indicated they would have accomplished more if allowed, like partisan units, the opportunity to personally benefit from whatever material they captured on such duty. Seddon recognized that units operating in this fashion often lost their discipline and became dangerous to the local farmers, but he was desperate to help Vicksburg. Confederate generals stationed observers at key points along the Arkansas side to report on how many Federal transports made their way each day to Grant, and they often filled their reports with recommendations that a regiment of cavalry and a battery could so hamper river traffic at key points as to shut down the river-based system for at least a couple of days.[6]

Confederate attacks increased as the siege of Vicksburg progressed. John S. Marmaduke's division in Arkansas detailed 250 men and a section of artillery for that purpose below Memphis in June 1863. Guerrillas also added their contribution to the effort to hamper Grant's lifeline. Small arms and artillery fire riddled several boats. The *Prima Donna* carried 90 wagons and their accompanying mule teams; it was pummeled by artillery for one and a half hours before a gunboat came to its rescue. Nine horses and mules were killed, with another 17 badly injured. The boat displayed 42 holes made by artillery rounds and another 200 perforations made by small arms fire. Yet on some boats, little damage was done despite the hail of bullets that emerged from the timbered banks.[7]

"The difficulties of coming up or down the river are increasing," reported Sergeant William Taylor of the 100th Pennsylvania, part of Burnside's Ninth Corps contribution to Grant's army near Vicksburg, "and the rebels are firing on our boats more every day. . . . Few boats pass without being injured more or less." Fortunately for the Federals, most of the damage was minimal. A roving force of Union troops trying to track down the perpetrators of such attacks discovered that the levee near Island No. 83 had been carefully prepared for artillery, with three embrasures cut into the earthen bank. Another position had been prepared three miles farther down for two guns, and a military road had been cut to connect the two positions, enabling Confederate artillery to fire on the same boat from both places.[8]

Levees were larger in the lower Mississippi region, and Confederate officers took advantage of them. Captain T. A. Faries cut embrasures in a levee that stood 12 feet tall about a dozen miles south of Donaldsonville on the east bank of the Mississippi. He then fired on several boats on July 7–8, 1863. These steamers supported Nathaniel P. Banks's siege of Port Hudson. Faries cut more embrasures on July 9 and fired on nine gunboats and transports that night, suffering no damage because the levees so well protected his gun crews. He called "a 12-foot Mississippi River levee . . . the best of earthworks."[9]

Despite their opportunities, the Confederates never devoted enough manpower to riverboat duty to make a major impression on Grant's or Banks's logistical support. Vicksburg fell on July 4 and Port Hudson five days later. With the entire length of the Mississippi in Federal hands, one of the key war objectives of the northwestern states had been accomplished. Much fanfare accompanied the resumption of uninterrupted navigation on the Mississippi by producers and shippers of the North. Seddon was stung by how his enemy celebrated the opening of the great river "with the greatest possible ostentation, to produce effect both abroad and with their own people." For Seddon, it was imperative that Confederate troops close the stream "at least for trade" even if they could not prevent the Union army and navy from using it.[10]

Previously, it had been impossible for guerrillas and regularly organized Confederate units to distinguish between a steamer that was carrying military supplies and one that hauled only civilian freight. Now Seddon recognized that a mainly commercial targeting strategy was called for, and any scruples he or other Rebel authorities may have had about firing on boats containing women and children evaporated. "Great moral and political results must follow from thus practically exhibiting the impossibility of commanding the Mississippi," he told Edmund Kirby Smith, commander of the Trans-Mississippi Department. "The river may be as effectually closed to the enemy's trade, and they as much prevented from obtaining supplies of cotton, as if we had continued to hold Vicksburg." In Seddon's mind, harassing river traffic would demonstrate to northwesterners that they could never use "the Mississippi as an avenue of trade without peace and amity with the Confederate States."[11]

To achieve this goal required a greater commitment of manpower and artillery to the task than Rebel authorities had assembled prior to the fall of Vicksburg. To be sure, some Southern officers responded to the call with attempts to create special units for the purpose. In August 1863, Nathan Bedford Forrest, who already commanded a highly effective brigade of cavalry, proposed a new unit of men recruited from both banks of the Mississippi. After living along the river for 20 years, part of that time "engaged in buying and selling negroes," Forrest knew the country and the men. He believed he could raise a force of 5,000 to 10,000 men in two months. Jefferson Davis liked the idea but deferred to Forrest's superior, Braxton Bragg, who responded that he needed Forrest to support his own operations in Tennessee. As a result, Forrest did not receive permission to attempt his plan until late October 1863. When he did raise more troops, he employed them not for the purpose of hitting steamers on the Mississippi River but in raiding Union-occupied territory in west Tennessee and Kentucky. His capture of Fort Pillow in April 1864, and his temporary holding of that post, failed to seriously interrupt the flow of river traffic.[12]

The basic problem was that the Confederacy did not have enough manpower to handle all the various military needs imposed on it in the sprawling Western Theater of operations. When called on by Seddon to dispatch cavalry forces to river duty, Joseph E. Johnston admitted it was very difficult to find any that could be spared from other duties. Confederate officials talked big. "The benefits they expect from the fall of Vicksburg will not be reaped by them," John B. Magruder boastfully announced to the people of Texas. "Sharpshooters will line the banks of the Mississippi River, and their deadly volleys will be the only salute to the adventurous foe who may come to force trade over Southern waters." A group of Arkansas politicians urged their governor to depopulate the state's river counties to prevent people and resources from falling into Yankee hands. "Let that region become waste," they wrote, and suggested the Confederates aggressively attack Union river garrisons, fire on boats by the dozen, and "render the navigation of the Mississippi cumbersome and expensive, dangerous and practically useless for gain or advantage to the enemy, and thus increase the discontent and opposition to the war among the people of the Northwest."[13]

An entire field army would have had to be created to accomplish goals such as these, and there simply were not enough men left in the Confederate population. Seddon authorized the creation of at least two companies of 50 men each "for special service on the Mississippi River," but there is no record of whether it was done or the men accomplished anything. One can find documents in the *Official Records* of officers urging others to create such units, and very often recommending that they be recruited from among men with experience in the riverboat business before the war. When Leonidas Polk commanded the Department of Mississippi and East Louisiana, he had grandiose schemes to organize new units of mounted men, assign each unit a different sector of the east bank of the Mississippi, and charge them to prevent civilian trading with Yankee merchants as well as firing on steamboats. Polk indulged in dreaming when he envisioned a handful of daring men who could capture a steamer and use it to board and take a Federal gunboat, duplicating this fantastic plan until he had an entire fleet of river gunboats flying the Confederate flag. He believed that would enable him to recapture Vicksburg, Port Hudson, and New Orleans.[14]

Instead of an army and a fleet of gunboats (provided by the enemy), what the Confederacy did get after the fall of Vicksburg were a handful of small units detailed from other duty to fire on riverboats and a reliance on that uncontrollable element, the self-constituted band of guerrillas. There was nothing different in this than in the force that harassed Union river traffic before and during the siege of Vicksburg, and it does not seem to have been much larger in size. To be sure, quite a few steamboats were hit, some were sunk and some burned, but it was far from a war-winning strategy. In fact, it did not impede the Federal effort to support its invading army or its river garrisons even though the Rebel effort killed and wounded soldiers, crewmen, and civilian passengers without distinction.[15]

At the receiving end, it was difficult for those on board the boats to tell whether they were being fired at by regularly organized Confederate units or by guerrillas. The only real way to distinguish between the two lay in the presence of artillery. If the big guns were in action, the attacking force surely was a regularly organized unit. If only small arms fire was involved, it might well have been only guerrillas. This distinction made a difference because artillery fire was more deadly to river steamers than muskets; regularly organized units inflicted more damage and loss of life on the boats than did the roving bands of guerrillas. Occasionally guerrillas through some stratagem could capture a river steamer, but the most successful Rebel strategy for taking a toll on river traffic lay in securing a good position for artillery and waiting for the next boat to come up or down the river.

There is no definitive list of all the attacks on river steamers that took place from the fall of Vicksburg to war's end, but the existing information indicates that any attack using only small arms tended to annoy the boats rather than kill people or seriously damage vessels. Thirty guerrillas fired at the *South Western* on October 9, 1863, and killed a sutler but inflicted no other harm of note. Seventy-five guerrillas fired at the *Sir William Wallace* from behind a log breastwork. The captain estimated that about 100 rounds of small arms ammunition was fired, but only 27 hit the boat. Those rounds killed one person and wounded six others. As the *Alamo* steamed up the Arkansas River toward Fort Smith in November 1864, Confederate cavalry began firing at it and kept up the attack for six miles along the river. The Rebels had an estimated 300 men involved, but only 87 bullets hit the boat, producing no serious losses.[16]

Regularly organized Confederate troops inflicted more devastation with artillery. Captain William Edgar's battery fired 25 rounds at a Union transport on November 21, 1863, and damaged it so badly that the boat put ashore on the opposite bank. Edgar could see that many civilian passengers had been wounded and were taken off the boat. Two women were killed when the *Brazil* was riddled with both musketry and artillery fire on December 11. Although three artillery rounds went completely through the *Superior*, only one man was wounded by them. Five of 13 artillery rounds fired at the *White Cloud* hit the boat and produced little damage, but at least a handful of river steamers were destroyed by artillery fire that set the boats aflame.[17]

On occasion boats were put through a hellish experience by Confederate troops. The *Henry Von Phul* encountered heavy fire when nearing Morganza Bend from several pieces that had been previously planted at advantageous spots. A combination of smoothbore and rifled guns pounded the steamer, with 34 hits at comparatively short range. One-third of the pilot house was blown away, the captain died, and a steam pipe was cut, forcing the crew to steer toward the opposite bank even though only one of its side-wheels was still working. The timely arrival of gunboats saved the craft.[18]

Captain John Malloy also was killed at his post when the *Empress* was fired at by Rebel artillery in a narrow part of the Mississippi near Morganza Bend on August 10, 1864. Civilian passengers on board became panic stricken and demanded the boat surrender, but the crew and Union soldiers on board refused. They managed to compel the civilians to lie down quietly on the deck as they returned fire and tried to keep the boat moving upstream. It was making good progress when a solid shot smashed through the hull, cut a steam pipe, and neutralized all power to the wheel. From that point the *Empress* drifted, a sitting duck, until the timely arrival of gunboats saved it from destruction. Seven people were killed and 13 were wounded, a mixture of crew, military, and civilian passengers. A total of 62 rounds had hit the beleaguered vessel, wrecking the cabin and destroying both the bar and barbershop.[19]

The level of damage inflicted on the *Henry Von Phul* and the *Empress* by Confederate artillery, if duplicated 20 or 30 times, could have had a real impact on the river-based system, but Rebel authorities never devoted enough batteries to the task to achieve that kind of destruction. Some units, however, hit the enemy very hard on occasion. Colonel Colton Greene took one battery and two regiments from his cavalry brigade to operate for several days along the west bank of the Mississippi. According to his report, Greene fired at a total of 21 boats from May 24 to June 2, 1864. He lost only six men wounded while reportedly disabling five gunboats, damaging five transports, sinking one steamer, and capturing and burning two others. "These operations have demonstrated the practicability of blockading or seriously interrupting the navigation of the Mississippi with field artillery." He argued that by deploying heavier guns, such as 24-pounder rifles, "no boat could safely pass a battery, except an ironclad."[20]

Fortunately for Union logistics, the Confederates could not afford to detach many units that were as efficient as Greene's. It has to be pointed out, however, that even Green complained of problems attending his operations. He could spare only 275 men to support the guns, too few in his opinion. The gunners needed substantial infantry or cavalry support because of the large number of Union gunboats patrolling the river and the danger of Federal troops landing and attacking their improvised and temporary positions. Artillery officers complained of ammunition shortages as well; it was difficult to transport rounds along the long, muddy roads that gave access to remote points along both sides of the river. There were times when Federal gunboats pounded these artillery units and drove them away, and some levees were too small to afford much protection. Major T. A. Faries tangled with three Union gunboats on June 8, 1864, and paid a heavy price for it. With poor shelter and no infantry support, the Yankees damaged his guns and captured one when they landed soldiers on the bank.[21]

The attackers, in short, did not always have it their own way. The fact that Confederates planted at least one Quaker gun between Vicksburg and Natchez indicates that they were desperately short of real artillery to fire on river steamers. A lookout on the *Mollie Able* saw the gun, and the boat's pilot quickly steered a course away from it. Upon closer view it became obvious that the gun was really a barrel mounted on a portion of an ox wagon.[22]

Some harried Federal commanders viewed the strategic situation on the Mississippi with pessimism, but there was every reason for them to hope for the best. "It is supposed we hold the Mississippi River," gloomily commented Napoleon B. Buford. "It is true, no hostile vessel navigates its waters, but it is also true that the banks are lined with hostile people. Scarcely a week passes that a boat is not fired into, even though crowded with women and children." But Federal authorities and Northern civilians alike learned to adjust to this situation. All of the many gunboats available on the western rivers were devoted to escort or patrol duties; they sometimes ganged up on troublesome points along the Mississippi and engaged in fairly large-scale fights with Rebel batteries, often winning them, as we have seen. At times they lashed civilian steamers to their side and passed these batteries in the same manner as Grant passed the formidable heavy guns at Vicksburg in April 1863.[23]

Passengers on river steamers came to accept the fact that they may be fired on while traveling. Adjutant General Lorenzo Thomas did not think much of having the boat he rode on hit by a "few shots" now and then. When Matilda Gresham took her children to visit her husband at Vicksburg in early 1864, she fully expected an attack and was relieved when the steamer went through without incident. Guerrilla fire peppered the *C. E. Hillman* while steaming downriver between Cairo and Memphis in the fall of 1864. It shattered all the glass in the walls of the pilot house. "As the officers of the boat had become accustomed to be shot at by the guerrillas," recalled the pilot, "they did not seem to be excited or annoyed by such trifles." Smart captains and pilots could guess where guerrillas or Rebel artillery were likely to stage an attack and arranged their traveling schedule to pass those points at night so as to reduce their exposure to fire.[24]

Federal authorities had every incentive to meet the guerrillas and Confederate army units with force to maintain their control of the river system, and they were willing to devote more resources than the enemy as well. "The river Mississippi must be held sacred," Sherman declared in March 1864, "and any attempt of the enemy to make a lodgment anywhere on its banks must be prevented by any and all means; also its peaceful navigation must be assured." While capturing fortified posts along the river from 1861 to 1863 was the major military effort, protecting navigation from 1863 to 1865 was imperative but comparatively minor as far as the deployment of military resources was concerned. Unlike their opponents, the Federals could spare enough manpower to guard the river and more or less protect navigation while still pursuing important strategic goals elsewhere.[25]

That is not to say that the Union effort to protect the river was minor. In fact, a large administrative structure was involved because the great length of the Mississippi embraced several military departments. With Sherman conducting the campaign against Atlanta, Edward R. S. Canby was given control over resources on both sides of the Mississippi so he could better coordinate efforts to protect steamers. "As long as we can all pull together, it makes little difference who commands," Sherman thought. He also outlined the essential Union strategy for protecting navigation: maintain adequate garrisons to hold key towns along both sides of the river, rely on gunboats to hit temporary positions held by guerrillas and enemy artillery, and encourage packet travel because it "increases a feeling of security. It brings private enterprise to the aid of the general purpose." A total of 71 armed vessels were available for use on the Mississippi River system, and army commanders readily called on them for help when they needed to send detachments of troops from garrisons to threatened points. The detailed log of the USS *Rattler* indicates that the boat fired on enemy troops, guns, and positions on a total of 21 days from June 23 to December 31, 1864, or about one out of every 10 days. It also sent a landing party to deal with the enemy on nine days of that time period.[26]

Sherman supported the idea of making civilians play a role in combating attacks on river steamers. He thought the army should compel the rich planters who remained within Union lines to pay cash as compensation for those who suffered in attacks and in his more heated moments condoned rather brutal retaliation. "For every bullet shot at a steam-boat, I would shoot a thousand 30-pounder Parrotts into even helpless towns," he wrote in December 1863. "To secure the safety of the navigation of the Mississippi River I would slay millions. On that point I am not only insane, but mad. Fortunately the Great West is with me there."[27]

Of course the Federals never adopted the more radical of Sherman's suggestions, but the general did convince Admiral David D. Porter to compile lists of damages to steamers so he could press compensation from civilians living along the river, in cotton if not in cash. "I think we can make People feel that they must actively prevent Guerillas from carrying out their threat." This was actually done in at least one case, when Federal authorities seized 1,000 bales of cotton to provide compensation for the owners of the *Allen Collier*, which was burned by guerrillas. During the early months of 1864, Sherman pushed for harsh measures against civilians as the best way to deal with guerrillas, and that included widespread confiscation of horses, mules, food, and other resources as a way to pressure them into becoming friends of the Union and stripping away their support for guerrillas. He even thought about depopulating the counties that lined both banks of the Mississippi and repeopling them with sturdy and loyal Northerners. There is little doubt that one result of Confederate attacks on river steamers was at least a light increase in the hard war attitude among Northerners that had already been developing from many other sources.[28]

The navy had much to do with protecting river navigation, but Porter, who was in charge of the gunboats on the western rivers, never went as far as Sherman in his thinking about how to do it. Porter concentrated mostly on coordinating his vessels, establishing patrol protocol, convoying steamers on occasion, and restricting all riverboats to stopping only at protected points along the bank. One danger was that anytime a boat put in at an isolated private landing, guerrillas could be lurking in the nearby woods. Porter was willing to use some gunboats to protect woodyards as well. He estimated that the enemy could devote 20,000 men to attacking river steamers (much more than they actually committed), yet he thought his gunboats could handle such a large force. To reduce the cover afforded by levees, Federal authorities forbade the reconstruction or building of new levees along the Mississippi River for the duration of the war.[29]

The Federals also made efforts to arm civilian transports for self-defense. Samuel R. Curtis had advocated such a plan as early as August 1862. He estimated that 150 small guns would not cost over $150,000, which he considered a small amount compared to the potential losses of government property on those transports. The plan never went anywhere because the army had no guns to spare and it did not consider the plan important enough to justify the cost of acquiring new ones. Suggestions to plate transports with iron for protection also were never realized because of the cost and the great need for iron plating by navy gunboats. On only a few occasions did steamboat owners manage to acquire iron plates. Each vessel in a fleet bearing supplies for Rosecrans's army had their pilot house "covered with boiler iron on each side, and the sides were boarded up with heavy plank" in January 1863. Coal bags, bales of hay or cotton, and grain sacks were more readily available as temporary protection for important elements of the steamers, such as the pilot house, and this was done more widely. Some steamers supporting Grant's siege of Vicksburg also used iron plating as well as planks two inches thick and even a small howitzer or two. It is not known how many boat owners fortified or armed their vessels, but in the District of Central Missouri all boats plying the Missouri River were required by general orders to protect their engine rooms and pilot houses. Owners were threatened with punishment if they failed to obey. Protecting key components of the boat made great sense, but there is no evidence that small guns on board, manned by inexperienced gunners, were ever actually employed in a fight with the enemy.[30]

Confederate authorities initiated a new twist in the river war when they recruited special agents to act as saboteurs. The Engineer Bureau lined up at least seven men who were willing to plant explosives on river steamers in return for the value of half the property they destroyed plus all the guns and munitions they captured through the use of "their new inventions." Seddon approved this scheme in late August 1863. An additional nine men were soon added to the list. Exactly what these 16 agents did is unclear, but the Richmond government was keen to use subterfuge as a weapon against Mississippi River shipping. Jefferson Davis suggested planting submarine torpedoes in the river to blow up civilian boats. A shadowy plot supported by a judge named Tucker led to some activity even before the fall of Vicksburg, supported by $20,000 drawn from the Confederate Treasury and urged on by Governor John J. Pettus of Mississippi. Exactly who these men were and what they did is obscure, but by October 1863 they were claiming great success and Joseph E. Johnston supported those claims.[31]

We do know that several river steamers were torched by agents beginning in August 1863. The *Ruth* went up in flames at Columbus, Kentucky, destroying $2.5 million in cash belonging to army paymasters. Federal authorities believed it was set deliberately by someone. William Murphy was identified as the perpetrator behind the burning of the *Champion* later in August as it lay at the Memphis levee. The Confederate government reportedly paid him $3,000 for the deed.[32]

The pace of attacks increased in September when four boats burned at the St. Louis levee, consuming more than $200,000 worth of property. It started on the *Imperial* and spread to the *Hiawatha*, the *Post Boy*, and then the *Jesse K. Bell*. The ropes burned and caused all four boats to drift together downstream. Local fishermen saw what appeared to be a black man setting fire to the *Imperial*. A man named Frazer was later identified as the ringleader of the group that accomplished this destruction. The *Imperial* had a significant history; Grant had ordered it to make the first trip from Vicksburg to New Orleans after the fall of Port Hudson "to demonstrate that the navigation of the Mississippi had been restored," according to the *St. Louis Missouri Democrat*. The *Hiawatha* also made a trip from St. Louis to New Orleans soon after the opening of the river. Whether the shadowy Frazer and his mates knew of the symbolic nature of their attacks on these boats is unknown.[33]

Confederate agents continued their assault with the *Capt. Campbell* burning at Milliken's Bend. The perpetrator reportedly was a passenger "disguised as a Negro." Frazer and his confederates were again identified as the agents who torched three boats at St. Louis in early October 1863. A large crowd gathered to see the conflagration and became angry at the agents and the government for letting them burn private property with impunity. Rebel agents burned two boats at Louisville in February 1864 and, in the biggest boat burning of the war, torched six vessels at St. Louis in July of that year. This last incident involved close to half a million dollars' worth of property. Saboteurs initially started a fire on the *E. F. Dix*, and it spread to five other craft. The commander of the post at St. Louis had received some warning of trouble a few days before and increased the number of guards along the levee, but some of the boats had only two watchmen on board in violation of standing orders earlier issued by headquarters, Department of the Missouri. The St. Louis newspapers admitted that there was no conclusive proof the trouble had been caused by saboteurs, but all indications pointed to it.[34]

Lewis B. Parsons carefully tabulated all steamboat losses during the course of the Civil War and noted how they were destroyed. Out of 327 boats that were lost, he attributed 29 (8.8 percent) to Confederate agents. Accidents took a far higher toll on shipping, with 155 boats (47.4 percent) lost to an array of causes that normally afflicted river shipping even in peacetime.[35]

The boat burning incidents began in August 1863 and seem to have ended by July 1864. They consumed only a small proportion of boats plying the rivers—29 out of some 350 available at any one time to Federal quartermasters. But these incidents made spectacular headlines in the newspapers and angered people far more deeply than accidental losses to snags or groundings on sandbars. "The continued destruction of steamboats by fire, on these waters is assuming a very alarming feature," Robert Allen told Halleck. He had no doubt that "an organized band of incendiaries" was at work, infiltrating the crews of various boats.[36]

Halleck agreed something had to be done. He suggested placing detectives on each boat and offering a reward of $10,000 for information leading to a conviction. Halleck also wanted to try suspects by military tribunal, not civilian court, with the death penalty serving as an appropriate punishment. Various commanders issued orders laying out protocol for safeguarding against saboteurs. Porter mandated that all watchmen be armed and stop anyone who approached a boat at night. No rowboats were allowed on the river near major ports at night, and the levees had to be thoroughly patrolled. Porter also wanted two tugs to keep up steam so as to pull a burning boat from the levee as quickly as possible before the fire spread to its neighbors. Canby in New Orleans also ordered that barrels filled with water should be kept at all times on every boat, and that each vessel should have up to half a dozen watchmen on board every night.[37]

The Federals mounted a major effort to defend boats against agents and to find the saboteurs. Canby discovered evidence that a former lawyer from

Shreveport and current lieutenant in the Rebel army, T. F. Beall, had joined the "rebel secret service." Beall led a group of 10 men with plans to burn boats at all the major river ports. They operated in squads of two to three men each, dressed as civilians. Porter compiled a list of names and residences of several men suspected of acting as agents for the Confederate government, while the provost marshal of the Department of the Missouri accumulated quite a bit of evidence to prove that organized bands of incendiaries were supported by the Richmond authorities. He gathered information through detectives and actually arrested some men who had smuggled gold currency through the lines near Memphis to pay these agents, who had their headquarters at St. Louis.[38]

Sherman's reaction to the incendiaries was predictable. He thought Federal authorities should "drop them overboard and let them find the bottom in their own way." He did not want to clog the court system with such cases because "It is not war," meaning that these incidents were not part of civilized warfare and did not need to be treated as such.[39]

The situation was worse than Sherman realized, for these men were active agents of the Richmond government. The attacks seemed to have ended by mid-summer of 1864, and that worried some Rebel politicians. Senator Williamson S. Oldham of Texas and Senator Waldo P. Johnson of Missouri consulted with Jefferson Davis about it in February 1865 and all agreed that the incendiary program had to be rejuvenated. Oldham even brought up the prospect of setting fire to Northern cities. He assured Davis that an agent could carry combustible material without being detected; a Professor Richard S. McCulloch was working on a plan to accomplish that goal. Oldham did not favor the use of military personnel. He wanted to hire civilians who could not only burn river steamers but ocean transports sailing from Europe. Davis endorsed all these ideas and urged cooperation with the secretary of state.[40]

Lewis B. Parsons was mostly right when he reported that "the rebel Government have had an extended and effective organization under the direction of a cabinet officer for the sole purpose of the destruction of our transports, offering unparalleled rewards for the success of miscreants in this nefarious business." Fortunately for the Federals it was short-lived. Oldham was unable to restart the process early in 1865 and, as we have seen, the total losses did not amount to more than a severe annoyance.[41]

The level of damage and destruction of western riverboats was accomplished mostly by attacks conducted by guerrillas, organized Confederate units with artillery, and secret agents. But some Rebels managed also to capture river steamers. Confederate cavalrymen under Phillip D. Roddey caught two steamers while they were exchanging cargo at the junction of the Duck River with the Tennessee River in August 1862. The Rebels paroled the crew members and then burned the boats. When guerrillas managed to capture a vessel, they also burned it and just as likely killed at least some of the crew members. A large group of guerrillas nabbed two steamers on the Cumberland River in April 1863 and killed eight black crew members. When the captain of one of the boats protested this action, the guerrillas killed him as well.[42]

Several Confederates hatched schemes to capture and then use a steamer, often bragging that it could be easily done "with a dozen determined men," as one of them put it. In some cases Rebel plotters contacted the captain or crew members on board a particular steamer who were loyal to the Confederate cause. Through contacts such as these they were able to obtain information and work out plans for the boat to be placed in a vulnerable position for waiting guerrillas.[43]

This is similar to what happened to the *Belle of St. Louis* when it innocently landed near Randolph, Tennessee, on October 27, 1864. A passenger on board convinced the captain to tie up for a while so he could load some cotton from a nearby warehouse. As soon as the boat lowered its ramps and a few hands walked onto the levee, 40 guerrillas burst from the warehouse and ran for the steamer. Captain Zeigler immediately called for the pilot, Sam McPheeters, to back off, but a handful of guerrillas managed to jump on board before he could do so. Most of them, driven by greed, began to rob the passengers, but two of them made their way to the pilot house, where they forced McPheeters at gunpoint to steam back to the levee. The boat was saved by the brave action of two army paymasters, who ran to the pilot house with their pistols. An ugly shoot-out occurred. Both of the guerrillas were killed, but they managed to mortally wound both paymasters. McPheeters now sheered the boat away from the levee just in time, with the other guerrillas on the bank shouting and firing furiously at the boat. The guerrillas who had been robbing passengers lost their nerve and swam to the bank. The *Belle of St. Louis* had $40,000 in cash, which the guerrillas did not touch. It had been a perilously close call for everyone on board, and the two paymasters were hailed as heroes.[44]

There is not a single instance in the war when a river steamer was captured and then used in service of the Confederate cause. In every case, the captors were compelled by circumstances to burn the craft. They really sought its contents rather than the boat itself. Without trustworthy crew members and with Federal domination of the river system, any scheme to take and use a steamer had little chance of success.[45]

In the same vein, every Rebel scheme to recapture a river town ended in a fizzle. As early as June 1863, there was some discussion about retaking Helena, Arkansas, in order to choke off Grant's logistical support during the siege of Vicksburg, although the cost in blood was keenly known to the officers in gray. A fantastic scheme to purchase Helena somehow was floated as well, which received the strong support of Jefferson Davis, who authorized funds to be transferred from the Confederate treasury to Commodore Samuel Barron for the deal. Nothing came of it. In another instance, Colton Greene fired a few rounds of six-pounder artillery into Memphis from the Arkansas side of the Mississippi, but that had no effect.[46]

Actually, it made some sense to attack river towns during the hectic logistical effort to supply Grant's troops in the trenches at Vicksburg. Napoleon B. Buford reported that Cairo, Illinois, one of the key river ports in the Mississippi Valley, was sadly vulnerable. Only 284 troops were available in the city during July 1863, and they were parolees with inadequate arms. Buford thought a mere 1,000 Rebel cavalry could take the city and that "would cripple the entire flotilla below, and cut off all communication with the Ohio and Mississippi above." He also worried about Confederate loyalists on board any number of river steamers who could cooperate with Rebel efforts to attack the city, which served as one of many important links between the river-based system and the rail-based system of the Northern war effort.[47]

Fortunately for the worried Buford, Rebel authorities never mounted an effort against Cairo. Their attack on Helena, which took place on the same day that Vicksburg fell, July 4, 1863, ended in bloody failure. Not until March 1864 did anyone in gray propose another scheme to recapture river towns from the Yankees. In a proposal already discussed, Leonidas Polk dreamed up a plan to secretly purchase a steamer at St. Louis and arrange to have it land someplace where Confederate soldiers could easily take possession of it. He thought they would then use it to capture other civilian steamers. With guns mounted on this new fleet, Polk would retake New Orleans and other towns until the entire length of the Mississippi was restored to Confederate control. For once Jefferson Davis hesitated to endorse such a plan. Instead, he referred it to Braxton

Bragg, then serving as the president's military advisor. Bragg did not take the proposal seriously, pointing out that at best it might lead to a handful of boats falling into Confederate possession before the weight of Union naval power on the western waters would have its effect.[48]

Other Confederates offered plans for the recapture of river towns as impractical as Polk's. One such proposer argued that a mere 1,000 men could make a quick dash and take Vicksburg, given that the town was held by a small garrison of black troops. Such a move could be the start of a general offensive to reclaim the entire Mississippi River, and accomplishing that "would of itself end the war." Jefferson Davis did not respond to this pie-in-the-sky idea. Such schemes were woefully lacking in an appreciation of Union resources and will power to hold the Mississippi. "Of course the possession of Vicksburg is a *sine qua non*," Sherman told Adjutant General Lorenzo Thomas. "We don't want the task of taking it again."[49]

Unable to close down Mississippi River navigation by guerrilla attacks, the Confederates also could not rely on regularly organized troops even with effective artillery support, boat burners, or grandiose plans to retake towns. But there was a chance Confederate authorities could sneak supplies from the Trans-Mississippi across the river between Union gunboat patrols and continue to some degree their supply network for troops operating east of the great river.

Rebel quartermasters and commissaries had steadily shipped food and other supplies from the Trans-Mississippi to the east side during the first half of the Civil War, and they intensified those efforts during the twin sieges of Vicksburg and Port Hudson. They swam herds of beef cattle across narrow points of the river and assigned army personnel to superintend and protect the crossings. Soon after the fall of Vicksburg, Grant sent Brigadier General Thomas E. G. Ransom's brigade to Natchez in order to intercept the herds that were reportedly crossing near that city. Ransom captured 5,000 Texas cattle and sent them to Vicksburg for Grant's army.[50]

The Confederates tried very hard to send weapons across the river from east to west to supply Edmund Kirby Smith's isolated Department of the Trans-Mississippi after both Vicksburg and Port Hudson fell. There were many problems. One attempt to shuffle close to 30,000 small arms fell apart in January 1864 because bad roads prevented wagons from hauling them to the riverbank on the east side. Members of Lawrence S. Ross's cavalry brigade carried 1,500 of them for 15 miles on foot. When they managed to get 600 guns over the river, there were no Confederate troops from the Trans-Mississippi Department there to take possession of them due to a breakdown in coordinating the transfer. The guns lay on the bank for two days with no one in charge of them. Making matters worse, Ross unwisely ordered his artillery to fire on a steamer that approached the crossing point, alerting nearby gunboats. That ended any hope of moving more weapons across the river even if the onset of cold weather had not created frozen, muddy conditions on the poor roads leading to the stream. Chunks of ice were seen floating down the current.[51]

Moving troops and other personnel across the Mississippi after the fall of Vicksburg and Port Hudson seemed to be impractical. But dispatches could be taken by small parties who quietly made their way to the river and secured small boats and canoes, swimming their horses alongside. Jefferson Davis admitted that sizeable troop transfers were impossible; only individuals and small groups could evade Union gunboat patrols.[52]

In short, Federal control of the Mississippi River after July 1863 was not an illusion, it was a fact tempered only by the limited assaults on shipping that failed to curtail or even seriously impair Yankee logistical support. It was not a simple matter of too few resources; the Confederate government, without explicitly stating it, had made a decision that protecting Richmond and the Central Theater of operations in middle Tennessee and northwest Georgia was more important than maintaining control of the Mississippi River. Whether that was a wise decision is debatable; it certainly led to the collapse of Confederate positions in the Mississippi Valley faster than Rebel defenses crumbled elsewhere, sealed the satisfaction of northwestern merchants and farmers who were desperate to regain control of the great river, and started a process that eventually led to ultimate Confederate defeat. Efforts to interrupt Northern use of the river after July 1863 were too feebly supported to have a dramatic effect, and dreams of recapturing the river could not be taken seriously. The Confederacy lost the Mississippi and with it took a giant step toward losing the war.

The Rebel flag had one last hurrah on the Mississippi. The *William H. Webb* had been constructed in New York in 1856 as an ocean vessel but was used as an ice breaker in coastal ports. Purchased before the war by New Orleans merchants who later used it as a privateer, capturing several river steamers, the boat fled New Orleans before its fall and was converted into a side-wheel ram of wood and iron called the CSS *Webb* at Shreveport and Alexandria. Armed with six guns, a spar, and five torpedoes, the boat posed a serious threat to

Union shipping. Lieutenant Charles W. Read placed cotton bales for added protection and then steamed down the Red River on April 23, 1865. The boat avoided Union patrols and entered the Mississippi, steaming as fast as it could go for New Orleans. Read stopped every 15 miles to cut telegraph lines and flew the U.S. flag and used Federal signals as he approached the Crescent City. Gunboat commanders were aware of his effort and managed to damage the *Webb* with gunfire but could not stop the fast-moving vessel on April 24. Two Federal warships gave chase and caught up with Read about 25 miles south of New Orleans. Read ran the *Webb* aground on the east bank and some of his crew escaped into the countryside, but 45 members of the 200-man crew were killed and 34 were captured. Exactly what Read intended to do once he reached the Gulf of Mexico is unclear. The voyage of CSS *Webb* may well have been little more than an emotional response to Confederate defeat, similar to the desire of some former Rebels to escape the United States for South America, Europe, or Canada.[53]

Federal authorities had little opportunity to target Confederate steamboats because the Southern river-based system was never very large or prominently vulnerable to them. Grant attempted to reach Confederate river transports during the Vicksburg campaign and succeeded to a limited degree. He sent Major General Francis J. Herron's division to Yazoo City right after the fall of Vicksburg because most of the river steamers used in the Mississippi delta operated out of that town several miles up the Yazoo River from the Mississippi. The transports fled Yazoo City on Herron's approach, but Union cavalry hounded their journey upriver so closely that the crews set fire to and then abandoned five boats. Federal troopers managed to capture another steamer. Ironically, the Confederates inflicted more damage on their river-based system than did the Yankees. They destroyed 12 of their own transports in Mississippi during Grant's approach to Vicksburg in May 1863, and another dozen when he moved troops to various points in the state in July after the fall of the city. According to Parsons's tabulation, these two dozen boats are the sum total of Confederate river craft destroyed as the indirect result of action by Federal forces during the Civil War.[54]

10

TARGETING RAILROADS, COASTAL VESSELS, AND WAGON TRAINS

The Federals managed to keep their river-based system of military transportation intact and operable despite many attempts to disrupt it by a desperate foe. But the rail-based system was much more vulnerable to enemy attack than the riverboats. Trains were exposed nearly through the entire length of their journey across the Southern countryside. It was impossible for Federal troops to guard every mile of track, and the problem dramatically increased every time the army made another campaign into Confederate territory. Guerrillas or regularly organized Rebel troops could disrupt the system merely by tearing up a few rails. In contrast, they could not redirect the flow of western rivers or affect the water level needed by steamers to operate. They also could fire into railroad cars, block their progress, and burn the track, train, and bridges. Attacks on railroads began very early in the conflict and escalated with the increasing tempo of Union military operations. All types of attacks took place, conducted by a variety of civilian and Confederate personnel, and the Federals were forced to adopt extraordinary measures in an attempt to keep the trains rolling.

As early as July 1861, civilians began to interfere with rail transport of Federal forces in the border state of Missouri. Saboteurs fired into trains running along the North Missouri Railroad, and Brigadier General John Pope, commander of the District of North Missouri, announced a plan to make all civilians living within five miles of both sides of the track responsible for it. If they did not cooperate by giving information, he would levee payments of cash or property to compensate for the damage. Pope sent 600 troops into Marion County, the center of this activity, and they created a good deal of anger among the neutral elements through wanton destruction of property. Locally prominent citizens talked with Pope to ameliorate the depredations. Pope was

235

convinced his policy worked; by mid-August he announced that his actions had quelled attacks on the railroad. "That order seems to have united all responsible persons who have anything to lose in efforts to preserve the peace, and they have organized for that purpose."[1]

Pope may have won the first battle with guerrillas who targeted the railroad, but other Federal officers in Missouri enjoyed less success. Ulysses S. Grant sent detachments of troops to chase guerrillas who fired into the cars, and they could only find men who seemed innocent of any wrong. Armed and mounted parties burned railroad bridges and escaped before troops could arrive on the scene. Henry W. Halleck ordered that anyone caught in the act should be shot on sight, considering them "guilty of the highest crime known to the code of war." Halleck also mandated impressment of property from civilians near the burned bridges to compensate for the damage. Thomas Ewing, William T. Sherman's foster father, pointed out to Halleck that Confederate authorities had hanged several loyalists who burned railroad bridges in east Tennessee and the Federals therefore had every right to do the same.[2]

If Union logistical arrangements had remained as simple as operating a few miles of track in Missouri, the guerrilla problem also would have remained small. But after Grant's capture of Fort Donelson in February 1862, Federal troops moved on to occupy a large tract of Confederate territory that included western and central Tennessee and parts of northern Mississippi. Don Carlos Buell's Army of the Ohio moved east in an attempt to take Chattanooga, rebuilding the railroads along the way, and the track became vulnerable to Rebel cavalry strikes. At times the force was merely a handful of companies that targeted trestles. Guerrillas also became very active, firing into trains, loosening rails so that engines ran off the track, and killing and wounding train crew members. By late July 1862, Buell ordered his chief engineer to construct small earthworks and timber stockades at the more important bridges along his rail network; some of them were large enough to hold two companies of troops. This was the beginning of what would evolve into a massive system of railroad defenses, but at this stage of the conflict they represented a tiny effort to protect the vulnerable logistical network. Because Braxton Bragg took the offensive into Kentucky, forcing Buell to give up his advance on Chattanooga, the defenses were not completed or really tested. When the Federals returned to the area later in the war they found the timber works all burned, but the earthen fortifications remained more or less intact. While the Confederates occupied portions of Kentucky during the fall of 1862 they did so much destruction to the Louisville and Nashville Railroad that the company spent more money to repair the damage than it received in revenue from hauling government freight for that period of time.[3]

Attacks on railroads in the Virginia theater of operations were less serious due to the shorter lines of Federal supply, but John Pope transferred his Missouri policies to the East when he took command of the Army of Virginia in the summer of 1862. Pope threatened to hold all civilians living near his rail lines responsible for attacks on the trains, confiscating not only their property but pressing them to do the work of repair. Robert E. Lee also applied large parts of the Army of Northern Virginia to railroad wrecking duties in October 1862, following his failed invasion of Maryland. He tore up stretches of the Winchester and Harper's Ferry Railroad and the Baltimore and Ohio Railroad to the extent possible without provoking a major battle with the Army of the Potomac.[4]

Following Bragg's retreat from Kentucky, William S. Rosecrans was charged with the responsibility of restoring the Union offensive in middle Tennessee. First, he had to oversee the reconstruction of many parts of the Louisville and Nashville Railroad that had been cut by Rebel cavalry raids during the past several months. John Hunt Morgan's destruction of two bridges near Elizabethtown and Muldraugh's Hill in Kentucky took more than a month to repair. Troops had to improvise methods of wagon transport to bypass breaks in the line and an accelerated program of building stockade defenses at key points was put into gear.[5]

Soon after this activity, Abraham Lincoln suggested to Rosecrans that he play the same game as the enemy, sending mounted forces behind Rebel lines to tear up their rail network. Rosecrans experimented with this strategy by dispatching a brigade of infantry mounted on mules with orders to burn all types of resources (food, tanneries, and factories) along the way. Colonel Abel D. Streight led the effort with 1,700 men, riding through north Alabama and northwest Georgia, but hard-riding Confederate troops under Nathan Bedford Forrest surrounded and captured Streight's men early in May 1863.[6]

Despite the dismal failure of Rosecrans's effort, the pace of attacks on railroads increased and the type and size of forces dedicated to the task changed and grew as well. In the wake of Vicksburg's fall in July 1863, Grant sent Sherman with a large force to deal with Joseph E. Johnston's concentration of Rebel troops at Jackson. Sherman began on this campaign to develop his strategic focus on railroads—protecting his own and attacking his enemy's line of transport. After compelling Johnston to evacuate Jackson without a battle, Sherman devoted considerable time to wrecking railroads around the Mississippi state capital. His troops destroyed the lines for 40 miles north of the city, 60 miles south of it, and 10 miles east. His men had destroyed another 10 miles west of Jackson back in May 1863, and it was still not repaired. "Jackson ceases to be a place for the enemy to collect stores and men from which to threaten our great river," he reported to David D. Porter. Sherman saw railroads in their full strategic significance and targeted them as a way to limit the enemy's choice of movement. His men also destroyed all the rolling stock they could lay their hands on and worked with "a right good will, and most thoroughly" in the words of a division commander, burning the cross ties and heating the rails so that they left "nothing but the road-bed."[7]

The destruction wrought by Sherman's men around Jackson was immense, to be sure; in fact, it was the largest destruction of rail resources to date in the conflict. But Sherman evacuated the Jackson area immediately after doing this work because the Federals did not see possession of the city as fitting into their strategic plans. Confederate troops came back to occupy Jackson and the work of reconstruction commenced. The same was true of Sherman's next great railroad raid, against Meridian, Mississippi, in February 1864. His men drove away the Confederate army and wrecked about 80 miles of track along several lines connecting at the city, and destroyed about 60 bridges and trestles. In addition, they burned 19 locomotives and 28 cars. Sherman retired to bases along the Mississippi River, and the Confederates immediately began to rebuild the rail network around Meridian. Despite straitened resources, Rebel authorities managed to get virtually all the destroyed sections repaired and back in operation within two months.[8]

The Confederates also saw destruction of rail lines as an increasingly important element in strategy by 1863. Robert E. Lee dedicated his army to tearing up in a thorough manner the Orange and Alexandria Railroad from a point near Manassas Junction to Rappahannock Station during the Bristow Station campaign of October 1863. He could not stay in the region due to food shortages and wanted to retire, but wasted the logistical capacity of the line so as to create a kind of no-man's land between the Army of Northern Virginia and the Army of the Potomac. "A more complete piece of destruction I have never seen," commented Virginia artilleryman John Walters. Rebel troops took up and burned all the ties, heated the rails in the middle and bent them double, burned bridges, partly filled up cuts with timber and dirt, and tore down water tanks.[9]

Confederate authorities in Texas conducted a similar scorched earth policy when they destroyed the line between Lavaca and Victoria in March 1864. As a Federal general put it, the destruction approached "more nearly to annihilation" than the limited work Confederates normally applied to railroad wrecking. Not only did the Rebels tear up the track thoroughly, they used sledge hammers to break up locomotives and burned freight and passenger cars until nothing was left of them except the iron frames.[10]

By 1863 the Confederates dedicated larger resources to railroad destruction than ever before, but the Federals also dedicated more resources to repair damages and construct fortifications for defending rail lines. The railroad war heated up as Union forces continued to penetrate Rebel territory and lengthen their rail networks. Sherman was not the only Federal general who saw that attacking Confederate rail lines could offer strategic benefits of one kind or another.

Trains well behind the developing front lines continued to be harassed by small parties of guerrillas and small cavalry detachments. Captain T. Henry Hines of the 9th Kentucky Cavalry (C.S.) led 14 of his men in a raid behind Union lines in February 1863, ranging across middle Tennessee and into Kentucky. The group traveled for 21 days and destroyed a train of 21 cars, plus a steamer and a depot. Hines estimated his men burned half a million dollars' worth of property without meeting any Federal troops.[11]

As Hines demonstrated, small parties of men, either guerrillas or regularly organized cavalry sent as detachments behind Union lines, could be very effective precisely because of their small size. They could annoy rail traffic with relatively little effort. Some officers thought there was no need to tear up track; simply firing into cars as they passed by would be as effective in disrupting traffic. But stopping the train was preferable to merely firing into it. A guerrilla gang of 75 men out for plunder rather than patriotism stopped a train near Franklin, Kentucky, in March 1863. They robbed the passengers and stole the case belonging to express agents on board. A detachment of the 129th Illinois came on the scene in time to disperse the guerrillas and recovered much of the loot. Just as with river steamers, guerrillas tended to target civilians more than military personnel in their train attacks.[12]

The procedure for stopping a train, whether by guerrillas or detailed cavalrymen, was a minor science. The best way to do so was to choose a spot where the track made a sharp curve and remove the outside rail. That was guaranteed to produce a wreck. Some saboteurs removed a rail from the inside curve near Burke's Station in Virginia in July 1863; this stopped the train but did not throw it off the track. A dozen men tried to capture the stalled cars, but the train guard drove them off. Some smart saboteurs near Trenton, Tennessee, set fire to both ends of the ties along a short stretch of the track. That caused the ties to expand and threw the entire track out of joint, wrecking the next train to drive over it.[13]

As attacks on trains escalated, Union policies against saboteurs of all kinds became harsher. Federal generals increasingly tried to pressure civilians along the lines to help Union authorities or risk punishment. When 50 citizens encouraged some guerrillas to burn a cattle guard and tear up miles of track near Gallatin, Tennessee, the local Union commander vowed "to make an example of some of them." Stephen Hurlbut deported 10 secessionist families from Memphis in retaliation for a guerrilla attack on a train outside the city that resulted mostly in the robbing of civilians on board. Many commanders resorted to pressing property and cash from wealthy, pro-secessionist families in their area of occupation for such attacks. When guerrilla assaults of all kinds heated up in Kentucky during 1864, authorities shot those they could capture, deported Rebel sympathizers, and suspended the writ of habeas corpus in the state.[14]

The scale of railroad defenses increased as the war progressed. During 1861–1863 they tended to be small, simple blockhouses designed for infantrymen and placed within musket range of railroad bridges. Such works could not stand bombardment by field artillery, so Union engineer officer William E. Merrill developed a larger, stronger blockhouse design. The structure incorporated a wall made of two layers of logs, a second floor, and a roof. Many of these Merrill blockhouses were constructed in the West during 1864 in rectangular and octagonal shapes. The number of blockhouses depended on the number and size of bridges along a particular route. For example, 54 blockhouses (most with double walls) were strung along 200 miles of line between Nashville, Tennessee, and Decatur, Alabama. Officers urged garrisons to depend only on their own resources to hold the position until help arrived.[15]

The improved railroad defense system was in place to support Sherman's operations against Atlanta in 1864. In fact, the most intense railroad targeting of the war took place during the course of this important four-month campaign for Atlanta. The Federals relied on a rail line from Louisville that was 350 miles long, surely a record for any campaign by that point in global military history. Sherman, the consummate logistician among Civil War generals, warned Montgomery Meigs to expect "heavy losses of stores this year," for the enemy was bound to "make heavy swoops at our lines of communication." Just before the campaign kicked off a Rebel officer proposed a plan to use agents for the destruction of Sherman's accumulated supplies at Nashville. Predictably, Jefferson Davis liked the idea, but it never seems to have been implemented. As early as May 10, one week into the campaign, guerrillas began firing into trains and removing rails in Tennessee and north Alabama, well to the rear of Sherman's advancing army. (His logistical network for the campaign included nearly all rail lines in the general area from Louisville to Nashville, Decatur, Stevenson, and Chattanooga, exposing a huge rail target.) Guerrillas also took shots at trains even a few miles behind the advancing Union army.[16]

Joseph E. Johnston, whose Army of Tennessee opposed Sherman, authorized the dispatch of cavalry detachments from his army to bypass the Federals and strike at the rails linking the enemy with Chattanooga. Frank C. Armstrong picked 505 men of his Mississippi cavalry brigade and led them behind Union lines early in June. They hit the railroad near the Etowah River, capturing 40 Federals and tearing up track. Part of his force rode into Calhoun on June 10, burned five cars, and planted a torpedo on the track that blew up when an empty train steaming northward hit it. How long Armstrong's men hovered around the rail lines is difficult to ascertain, but they apparently remained only a short while. Yet the scattered attacks continued, at least one of them involving a torpedo. Cars continued to be torched and small bridges burned. Defending Federals tried to place small squads of troops at every vulnerable point, but it was impossible to find enough men to do this thoroughly. Officers arranged for regular patrols along the rail line and ordered planks to be nailed to the tops of cars so guards could have some kind of slim fortification from which to return fire on attackers. "The country around here is full of bushwhackers," reported George C. Rogers from Allatoona on June 27. "I am taking measures to drive them out of the country, and am sending suspicious families away from the line of the railroad. Many others are going north voluntarily."[17]

Federal guards engaged in a mini-war of small parties along the rail line linking Sherman's army group with Chattanooga throughout the Atlanta campaign. Their measures tended to limit the destruction but never eliminated the problem. In groups as small as 25 men and as large as 300, the Confederates tore up rails and fired into cars. The scouts normally used by cavalry commanders to gather information took part in this war of small parties; they roamed behind Union lines not only to find out what the Yankees were doing, but to harass their shipping during the campaign. Roving Union patrols often foiled their plans to ambush the next train, but at other times the waiting Rebels succeeded in hurting train crews and burning cars. The Federals continued to construct fortifications at bridges along the line between Chattanooga and Sherman's army as the campaign progressed. Sherman took the time to write specific instructions about turning Marietta into a fortified town after it was occupied by his troops. He advised cutting loopholes in the walls of the courthouse and other buildings and constructing covered positions on the roofs for infantrymen. "A few hours' work will convert any good brick or stone house into a citadel," he argued.[18]

"The whole country between this post and the front is infested with guerrilla bands," reported James B. Steedman from Chattanooga. It often was next to impossible for the Federals to tell whether the men were true guerrillas or regularly organized Confederate soldiers, but at times they gathered surprisingly accurate information about their opponents, identifying Rebel cavalry scouts as the saboteurs. They also knew that these bands sneaked through the countryside in small groups and rendezvoused at prearranged assembly points near the railroad, making it very difficult to find and capture them. At times they did catch such bands and even found them equipped with tools handy for dismantling tracks.[19]

All the Unionists could do was to carry on. Sherman detached a full division to guard the rail line south of Chattanooga, and he called on the governors of several western states for militia troops to protect the extensive rail system running through Kentucky and Tennessee so that better troops could be shifted south to more threatened areas. Sherman's main reliance was on his efficient railroad construction crew to quickly repair the damage these small parties were able to inflict on the track. These breaks often were no more than 40 yards of line and disrupted transportation for only a few hours. Other breaks, such as those that required clearing away the wreckage of an entire train, took a couple of days to repair.[20]

The attacks by small parties failed to seriously interrupt Sherman's logistical support and spurred increasingly harsh measures by the Federals on the local citizens. After July 7, James B. Steedman began deporting all civilians within three miles of the railroad who could not clearly prove that they were loyal to the U.S. government in some way. News of this policy spread widely and caused "quite a stir among the citizens." Sherman fully supported Steedman's policy. "The country behind us now should be cleaned out of all the elements out of which guerrillas and loafers are made up, and we should appropriate and put in store all forage and produce within reach." Sherman instructed another officer to send any family away on a mere suspicion of disloyalty and to shoot on sight anyone found tampering with the track or the telegraph wire that ran along it. "Make somebody suffer for the break," Sherman told the commander of occupied Marietta in mid-August. An enterprising officer in Tennessee also ordered that all fences near the railroad should be dismantled by landowners so as not to provide a ready source of fuel for guerrillas to start fires on the track. If owners failed to do so, Union patrols would burn the fences.[21]

The Atlanta campaign devastated the region for a few miles along both sides of the Western and Atlantic Railroad that linked Chattanooga with Atlanta. Not only did the armies eat their way south and civilians flee before their farms became battle zones, but even after Sherman pushed south the citizens were not safe. Guerrillas and small parties of Confederate cavalrymen brought the war back to their counties, and frustrated Federal officers sent patrols through the area, eventually sending away many families and indirectly causing many more to flee on their own accord. By the time the campaign came to an end in September (and the region along the rail road was further devastated by John Bell Hood's subsequent campaign northward along roughly the same route in October), the area was a wasteland.[22]

Sherman accepted the fact that he could not eliminate the small parties making war on his logistics. He advised officials of the U.S. Military Railroad in the West to be ready for the loss of half a dozen trains every month in Georgia, for it "cannot be prevented." But he compensated for this by stockpiling supplies at various depots along the way and devoting more resources to repairing the breaks than one can see in any other campaign of the Civil War. In the end, these small parties stopped rail traffic a total of 20 days during the 120-day Atlanta campaign. At most, repair crews had to rebuild a total of only 10 miles of track destroyed by these small parties during four months of campaigning. Once again, the Confederates devoted enough resources to the task of targeting railroads to annoy the enemy, but not enough to influence the course of the fighting. Superior resources, a higher degree of ability in managing those resources, and most of all a fierce determination to press on with the campaign no matter what happened spelled success for Sherman. His men contained the threat posed by these small parties, quickly repaired the damage they inflicted, and kept the trains rolling 83.3 percent of the time covered by the campaign for Atlanta. That was an impressive accomplishment.[23]

There was another aspect of the railroad war associated with the Atlanta campaign—the desire by Sherman to target the Confederate rail system as a key element of his strategy for capturing the city. His modus operandi during the campaign was to threaten Johnston's rail link with Atlanta, thereby forcing the Confederates from one strongly held position to another. Before crossing the Chattahoochee River, he planned not to directly attack the strong earthworks defending Atlanta but "to make a circuit, destroying all its railroads. This is a delicate movement and must be done with caution." In addition to doing this with his large infantry force, Sherman tried to get cavalry onto that rail system. He arranged for a mounted force of some 3,000 men under Lovell H. Rousseau to enter Alabama from middle Tennessee and wreck sections of the rail line east of Montgomery in mid-July. Rousseau tore up about 30 miles of track without opposition (the Confederates in Alabama were taken completely by surprise and responded too late to interfere), but Rebel engineers managed to repair the damage in two weeks.[24]

Sherman tried the largest mounted raid of the campaign when he sent two divisions of cavalry from his army group to bypass Atlanta and hit the railroad south of the city on July 28. Army of Tennessee cavalry forces, energetically led by Joseph Wheeler, immediately gave chase and in a series of running battles prevented any serious damage to the track. In fact, Wheeler administered a severe defeat on the Federals, capturing hundreds of them in the process. Two-thirds of Sherman's mounted force was decimated, with nothing to show for it.[25]

Despite the dismal failure of his big raid, Sherman continued to think that even small breaks of 10 or 15 miles in the Confederate rail system would threaten the Army of Tennessee's stand in Atlanta. He apparently did not assume that John Bell Hood, who replaced Johnston in late July, would have his own engineers ready to repair any damage as quickly as possible. Sherman's experience at dealing with small parties, which created small breaks in his own rail line, also should have disabused him of any idea that minor interruptions could bring strategic results.[26]

The Confederate generals also had longed for a cavalry raid against Sherman's line ever since the Atlanta campaign began. Johnston had consistently urged the Richmond authorities to send Nathan Bedford Forrest, who had ample experience raiding railroads behind enemy lines, to middle Tennessee to lay waste to the tracks. Jefferson Davis refused because Sherman had sent several major expeditions from Memphis and other Mississippi River garrisons into central Mississippi, forcing the Confederates to keep Forrest there to aid in protecting the agricultural regions Rebel commissaries depended on to feed the army. It must be pointed out as well that in all of his mounted raids on Union railroads, even Forrest had never achieved decisive results that determined the result of a campaign. The rail system that Forrest would have targeted was more heavily defended in 1864 than ever before; whether he could have achieved anything more than to annoy the enemy is an open question.[27]

Johnston tried to use his own cavalry force to interrupt Federal supply. While he normally used his mounted troops to skirmish, collect information, and hold trenches as a way to extend his infantry line, Johnston briefly allowed Wheeler to take a brigade of cavalry a short distance behind Union positions in late May. Wheeler managed to catch a Union supply train near Cassville, burn 20 wagons, and carry away 20 more before the Federals responded. Sherman became increasingly worried that Johnston would try this with a much larger force by early July, based apparently on the testimony of a Confederate officer who deserted and told the Yankees that Johnston planned to send 10,000 Rebel cavalry on "a big raid" north along the railroad.[28]

By late July, after Hood replaced Johnston, something like this was in the works. Soon after assuming command, Hood struck at Sherman's army group with large numbers of his infantry force, losing close to 12,000 men in failed assaults at Peach Tree Creek north of Atlanta on July 20, in the battle of July 22 east of the city, and at Ezra Church west of Atlanta on July 28. Jefferson Davis now cautioned him not to attack fortified positions and approved Hood's suggestion to send most of his cavalry force under Wheeler to tear up the railroad south of Chattanooga. "We are in a state of siege," reported Colonel Ellison Capers of the 24th South Carolina in Hood's army, and the only prospect of relief seemed to be Wheeler's planned expedition to destroy Sherman's line of communication.[29]

Wheeler left with 4,000 men, carrying Hood's instructions to strike the railroad between Chattanooga and Marietta and then to cross the Tennessee River and hit the road between Nashville and Chattanooga. He accomplished little in the first phase of his mission, hitting the railroad north of Marietta, near Cassville, and then near Calhoun. His men could only tear up short stretches of rails before moving on so as not to be caught by aroused Union officers. After the war Hood told an inquiring newspaper reporter that Wheeler was surprised to find the rail line so heavily fortified, with blockhouses of a superior design. "The cavalry could do nothing with them," Hood recalled. Wheeler captured a small detachment near Tilton, took more than 1,000 beef cattle and some wagons, but failed to reduce any significant post or blockhouse. Although heavily outnumbering the garrison of Dalton (which consisted of less than 500 men), Wheeler could not compel the commanding officer to surrender and he judged the losses incumbent on attacking the place to be too high to justify the effort.[30]

As soon as word of Wheeler's raid became known, the ample force Sherman had detached to guard his communications went into action. Steedman arranged for converging columns to intercept Wheeler and personally led a force south from Chattanooga that began to pressure the Confederates and precipitate their withdrawal from the Dalton area. After his failure there, Wheeler broke away from the rail line and headed northeast on August 15. Steedman saved the tunnel at Tunnel Hill and drove the Rebel cavalry away from the railroad. Wheeler managed to tear up a total of two miles of track, separated into several small sections, as well as two bridges and two water tanks. He killed, wounded, or captured 200 Federals but lost about that number of his own men, according to Steedman's estimate. Wheeler left behind 200 men to continue harassing the railroad and claimed they ran 20 trains off the track, stopping rail travel for two weeks. But Steedman made no mention of these actions and reported that Union repair crews got the railroad fully working by August 18. Wheeler with his 4,000 men had done little more in August than the small parties had accomplished in June and July.[31]

Sherman did not worry much about what Wheeler might do during the second phase of his mission, hitting Union logistics in middle Tennessee. It took a while for the Confederate cavalry to get there, for Wheeler was compelled to ride deep into east Tennessee to find a suitable place to ford the Tennessee River. But he accomplished more destruction on the line between Nashville and Chattanooga than south of the latter place. His men thoroughly tore up a section near Smyrna and wrecked eight miles of track between Murfreesboro and La Vergne. The blockhouses held up well to artillery fire, although the garrison of one blockhouse surrendered and allowed Wheeler's men to burn a bridge. Defense troops once again compelled the Rebel cavalry to leave the area and ride into north Alabama, horses and men alike exhausted by their long journey and unable to return to Hood's army in time to aid in the final stages of the struggle for Atlanta.[32]

Far from a decisive, campaign-winning move, Wheeler's August raid failed to do more than inconvenience the Yankees. "The enemy care nothing for Wheeler and his seven thousand [sic] cavalry in the rear," concluded Robert Toombs after reading reports of the raid in newspapers. "They did not obstruct his trains more than four days, if that." Wheeler's men tended to retain faith in their ability to hurt Union logistics, despite the relative lack of accomplishment, but little import could be placed in such faith. While Wheeler's men lived on roasting ears for three or four days during the raid, Federal troops with Sherman suffered little more than an interruption in their mail.[33]

Sherman was almost ready to conclude that cavalry raids were the biggest humbug of the war, but he wanted to try just one more. The alternative to mounted strikes was to move most of his large infantry force south to cut the last rail line feeding Hood's army in Atlanta, but such a move involved a good deal of risk—breaking contact with his own line of communication, living off rations carried in wagon trains, and hoping to decisively shape the campaign in a few days so that the Confederates were forced out of the city. He preferred to send Judson Kilpatrick's division of cavalry to hit Confederate tracks before putting that complicated infantry move into action. "It is not a raid," Sherman wrote of Kilpatrick's move, "but a deliberate attack for the purpose of so disabling that road that the enemy will be unable to supply his army in Atlanta." Sherman wanted the horsemen to hit the Atlanta and West Point Railroad between Red Oak and Fairburn before that line joined the Macon and Western Railroad at East Point a few miles south of Atlanta. Then they were to ride to the latter road near Jonesborough. For Sherman, this was an acid test to determine whether cavalry had the capacity to decisively break an enemy railroad. If the tracks were obstructed for at least 10 days, Hood probably would have to leave Atlanta. If not, "we must then go out in force" with most of the infantry to do the job.[34]

Kilpatrick set out with 4,700 horsemen on the evening of August 18. Hood immediately sent cavalry to pursue and infantry to hold Jonesborough. Kilpatrick did not pass Sherman's test. He tore up small sections of track on both roads, captured Jonesborough, but fled upon word that several Rebel columns were converging on his location. He rode back to Sherman's army reporting that his men had torn up 14 miles of track, enough to break Rebel communications for at least 10 days. But more objective evidence would indicate the level of destruction was far lower; Confederate trains rolled into Atlanta by August 21. Sherman was finally convinced. "Cavalry usually do so little damage to a road that it can be repaired faster than they damage it," he told one of his officers.[35]

On August 26, Sherman set out with six of his seven corps, breaking contact with the railroad and heading toward the exact spots on both railroads that Kilpatrick failed to break. With a couple of days' head start on Hood, the Federal infantry descended on the Atlanta and West Point Railroad by the thousands and systematically wrecked it beyond hope of immediate repair. They dismantled the track, burned the ties, and heated, bent, and twisted the rails so that it would take a rolling mill to restore them for use. They filled in cuts with timber and dirt, creating a break stretching for many miles near Red Oak and Fairburn. Then Sherman led them to Jonesborough, where the last battle of the Atlanta campaign took place. Hood shifted two of his three corps to that town by August 31; they attacked Sherman's men and were easily repulsed. Upon receiving word that other Federals were hitting the track between Atlanta and Jonesborough, Hood pulled one corps away, allowing Sherman to attack the lone corps left at Jonesborough and drive it away on September 1. Hood lost the struggle for Confederate communications and with it the city of Atlanta. Six corps of infantry succeeded where brigades and divisions of cavalry failed; only massive force and permanent occupation of a rail line could decisively cut rail-based communications and alter the course of a campaign.[36]

Logistics continued to play a major role in the objectives of both armies after the fall of Atlanta. Hood launched a strike against Sherman's railroad beginning in late September when he moved the Army of Tennessee northward across the Chattahoochee River, sending divisions to tear up track along the Western and Atlantic Railroad in an effort to force Sherman to fall back northward from Atlanta. A fierce attack on the huge depot at Allatoona was repulsed in heavy fighting on October 5, but Dalton, which had held out against Wheeler's cavalry, was compelled to surrender by an overwhelming force of Confederate infantry. Hood made no attempt to strike Chattanooga, but veered westward into north Alabama to rest his army near Florence for several weeks before invading middle Tennessee. He had disrupted the flow of supplies for a couple of weeks but failed to compel Sherman to give up Atlanta.[37]

Forrest also accomplished more in the way of destroying Federal logistics in the fall of 1864 than earlier in the conflict. He raided through north Alabama and into middle Tennessee in late September as an adjunct to Hood's drive across the Chattahoochee River, captured the Union garrison at Athens, Alabama, and destroyed a large railroad bridge called the Sulphur Springs trestle. To support Hood's invasion of middle Tennessee, Forrest hit the large Union complex at Johnsonville on the east bank of the Tennessee River, a junction of the river-based and rail-based systems, and destroyed (or compelled the Federals to self-destroy) an estimated $2.2 million in government property. The Federals mounted several raids on Confederate logistics in Mississippi that supported Hood's presence in middle Tennessee in November and December 1864. The largest raid, led by Benjamin Grierson, destroyed a lot of track and rolling stock between Tupelo and Okolona.[38]

Grant also targeted Lee's logistics to a limited degree during the Virginia campaigns in 1864 and 1865. He tried several cavalry raids, as did Sherman, but none of them succeeded in a decisive way. The Wilson-Kautz raid against the Danville Railroad in mid-June 1864 cut the road for 23 days and strained the Confederate supply system, but Rebel engineers repaired the damage. Intense guerrilla attacks on the Manassas Gap Railroad in the fall campaign through the lower Shenandoah Valley led Union authorities to order subordinates to burn houses within five miles of the track and send the citizens away. This created a no-man's zone along the rail line where Union forces had authority to consider anyone they found a bushwhacker, but how thoroughly this was done is unclear. When Philip Sheridan led the bulk of his cavalry force from the Shenandoah Valley to join Grant's concentration at Petersburg and Richmond in March 1865, he targeted all the Confederate transportation resources possible along the way. Essentially unopposed, the Union horsemen wreaked enormous destruction on the James River and Kanawha Canal for 98 miles, thoroughly tore up 3 miles of the Virginia Central Railroad, and blew up or burned 8 major railroad bridges.[39]

By the last year of the war, the process of wrecking railroads had been honed to a science. "It is more work to destroy a R.R. than one would imagine," reported a Union commissary officer named Cyrus Clay Carpenter. It was not easy to remove the spikes and crack the rails from the ties. Along the roadbeds

10.1. Federal Troops Destroying a Southern Railroad. This image illustrates the most efficient way that Sherman's troops destroyed long stretches of railroad during the last half of the Civil War. Entire units arrayed along one side of the track lifted and turned it upside down, then dismantled the rails from the ties. (Johnson and Buel, *Battles and Leaders*, 4:684)

of older lines the ties tended to settle over time into the raw earth and it was difficult to pry them out. Soldiers often had to find some combustible material to place among the ties when making bonfires of them because they had become damp through contact with the earth. If the ties were made of pine, as often was the case in the Deep South, they burned well once started. Heating a rail in the middle allowed men to take hold of both ends and twist it round any nearby tree or telegraph pole. A member of the 14th Wisconsin devised a cant hook useful in catching both ends of the rail and twisting it, doing even more damage to the rail than wrapping it around a tree. As Hosea Rood of the 12th Wisconsin put it, destroying railroads "came to be a skilled labor with us."[40]

Some Southern rail lines were put together more strongly than others. Federal troops assigned to tear up tracks near Jackson in July 1863 found that the ends of the rails were fastened together with plates secured by bolts and it was more than doubly difficult to take this track apart. Federal cavalry who hit the Weldon Railroad in Virginia during December 1864 encountered a similar problem. Even when they turned the entire track over they could not break the connection between rails.[41]

But most Southern railroad companies did not go to such lengths when they constructed their lines before the war. It was comparatively easy to tear these lines apart. Sherman's army group conducted the most thorough destruction of railroads during its famous march through Georgia in November and December 1864, and through the Carolinas in February and March 1865. Sherman's chief engineer laid out a protocol for the task, instructing infantry commanders to tear off the rails, build a crib work of the ties, stuff kindling material inside, and place the rails so the middle would receive the hottest flames. Each pile was to be placed 35 feet from its neighbor, and engineer troops would twist the heated rails. Sherman wanted the job to be done well. Upon inspecting the work of Twentieth Corps troops near Graham's Station, South Carolina, he lectured Henry W. Slocum that "the bars are not twisted; better do half the quantity, but do it thoroughly; unless there is a warp, the bar can be straightened again." Sherman's men wrecked an estimated 200 miles of track in South Carolina alone.[42]

Sherman focused on long-term disabling of Southern lines, seared by the repeated failures of his cavalry during the Atlanta campaign to deliver anything other than a pinprick to Confederate logistics. He studied the problem and identified proper remedies that could cripple enemy transportation for a long time after his men had departed. Herman Haupt also applied his fertile mind to the problems associated with tearing up enemy railroads and rebuilding Federal lines wrecked by the Confederates. After Lee's army tore up 10 miles of the Cumberland Valley Railroad and the Franklin Railroad near Chambersburg, Pennsylvania, during the Gettysburg campaign, Haupt experimented with rehabilitating the bent rails. He found that his operatives could straighten three-fourths of them without heating and estimated it took only one-tenth as much time to do so as the enemy had invested in bending them. If bent "with a curve of one foot or more radius," his men could straighten it in two to four minutes. More damage than that required heating.[43]

Haupt devoted more time and thought to methods of destruction than repair. He knew what Sherman came to realize, that a twisted rail was more difficult to reuse than a bent rail. His operative, E. C. Smeed, devised a tool capable of twisting rails and small enough to be carried by cavalrymen. Haupt estimated, on the basis of needing five minutes to loosen one rail, that 2,200

10.2. Workers Demonstrate How to Loosen Rails. In this image by Andrew J. Russell, exposed sometime in 1862 or 1863, "contraband" laborers illustrate a different method of separating the rails from the ties using a heavy timber as a lever with a cant hook attached to one end. The upturned rail laying on the track appears to be hollow inside. (Library of Congress, LC-DIG-ppmsca-10396)

troopers could destroy five miles of line in one hour. Haupt argued against Sherman's contention that the credit for devising this tool belonged to Orlando Poe rather than to Smeed. But as we have seen, even a private in the 14th Wisconsin developed such a tool; it was a simple device that many men thought of simultaneously. In addition to cant hooks, Haupt pushed for the use of torpedoes to bring down railroad bridges quickly and thoroughly. He told his assistant engineer exactly how to conduct experiments testing explosive devices that could collapse bridges. The method involved boring a hole with an augur in the most important supporting timber, pushing the torpedo in, and lighting the fuse. It is not known how often torpedoes were used in this way, if ever.[44]

Federal officers and enlisted men pursued their war against Southern railroads with persistence and achieved an incredibly high level of destruction by the end of the war, wrecking hundreds of miles of track. Just as railroad

10.3. Smeed's Cant Hooks for Dismantling Railroads. E. C. Smeed, an engineer working for the U.S. Military Railroad, developed a cant hook to loosen rails from their ties and to twist them so that they would not be readily available for use. He probably is the civilian on the left in this photograph by Andrew J. Russell taken in 1862 or 1863. The upturned rail in this photo appears to be solid rather than hollow. (Library of Congress, LC-DIG-ppmsca-10393)

use was far higher in the American Civil War than in any previous conflict in global history, railroad destruction was the highest thus far as well. Given time and without interference from defending troops, large forces of blue-coated infantrymen demonstrated to the world how to devastate an enemy's rail-based lines of transportation in a thorough and lasting way. Cavalry raids had been incapable of achieving this level of destruction. Ironically, if large infantry forces could destroy with impunity, then the need to destroy seemed less urgent. Possession of the rail line in itself denied its use to the enemy. But, as in the case of

Sherman's marches, if the infantrymen intended to move away, then the need to destroy very thoroughly was quite high.

The Confederates had very little opportunity to target the third important system of Union military transportation, coastal shipping. They did not possess the naval resources to challenge Union control of the shipping routes and used very few coastal vessels in their own logistical efforts. Lee tried to hit McClellan's shipping after the Seven Days campaign. In late July 1862 he sent 50 field pieces supported by infantry to take up a position from which they could fire at the vessels at anchor in the James River. "I know of no heavier blow that could be dealt General McClellan's Army than to cut off his communication," Lee told the Confederate secretary of war. That would either force the Federals to pull away farther down the James or intimidate them into not resuming the On to Richmond drive that Lee had decisively stopped in the Seven Days fighting.[45]

The effort failed to cut McClellan's supply line. Daniel H. Hill, who was in charge of the expedition, could place only 43 guns on the south side of the river, and they were supplied with no more than 30 rounds each. Confederate gunners planted their pieces on the night of July 31 and opened fire just after midnight, creating a good deal of surprise and alarm on the boats. While Hill claimed to inflict much damage, the truth was that only 10 Federals were killed, 12 wounded, and 6 horses injured. No appreciable damage occurred to the ships. McClellan positioned troops on the south side of the river and cut timber at key points to deny the enemy cover for their guns, and that ended the scheme. Lee wanted Hill to try again, but these simple Union countermeasures prevented him from attempting a second strike.[46]

The next Rebel attack on Union coastal shipping took place during the Petersburg campaign, when two agents planted a torpedo with a timed detonation device on board a barge at City Point, the logistical nerve center of Grant's position at Petersburg and Richmond. The device exploded on August 9, 1864, killed 250 soldiers and civilian workers, and destroyed 600 feet of warehouse and 180 feet of wharf. The damages amounted to over $2 million, and Federal authorities assumed it was due to an accident until just after the war, when information became available that the Confederate torpedo service had been responsible for it. Two days after the explosion, Jefferson Davis was presented with a plan to more widely use such devices, planting them on dozens of ships employed by the Federals in order to strike at the coastal shipping system in a more systematic way. The plan apparently was never implemented.[47]

Late in the war, Lee once again tried to hit the coastal shipping system. Captain Thaddeus Fitzhugh of the 5th Virginia Cavalry identified several fast steamers in Union employment that could be captured and used to attack other vessels, but Lee suggested that instead he capture a vessel laden with supplies and bring its cargo in to be used by his starving men in the Petersburg trenches. Fitzhugh handpicked 28 men of his company, gathered three boats, and worked his way up the Potomac River with his men disguised as civilian workers. They chose the *Harriet De Ford*, a 149-ton screw steamer only one year old, boarding her while docked at Fair Haven, Maryland, 30 miles down from Annapolis on the Potomac River. The Confederates easily took possession of the ship. Unfortunately for Fitzhugh, the captain told him that news of Richmond's fall had been broadcast to the nation. There was no point to the plan now, but Fitzhugh could not turn back; he compelled the crew to steam toward the mouth of the Rappahannock River and a distance up the stream before setting the *Harriet De Ford* on fire. His men got away just before seven Federal gunboats caught up with him and shelled the woods along the bank. Some of Fitzhugh's men had told *Harriet De Ford* crew members of their captain's hopes to capture other steamers and "to burn and pillage generally," but the end of the war ended all such dreams.[48]

The Confederates had little hope to impair their enemy's use of coastal shipping, given their lack of resources to contend with the Federal navy, but Rebel troops had some opportunity to hit Union wagon trains. Ironically, even though operating closer to major concentrations of Confederate troops, wagon trains were the least vulnerable of all military transportation systems in the Civil War. They were of the most immediate value to commanders of field armies and closest to their own concentration of friendly troops—therefore, wagon trains were usually more thoroughly guarded than river steamers, railroads, or coastal ships. Only on occasion could the Confederates manage by circumstance to throw a large force of cavalry against a Federal wagon train that happened to be vulnerable at the right time. When that happened, the Confederates could inflict serious damage.

Braxton Bragg wanted to use the large mounted arm attached to the Army of Tennessee to hit William S. Rosecrans's logistics during the Stones River campaign. Dependent on a wagon link to Nashville as he advanced 30 miles toward Murfreesboro in late December 1862, Rosecrans's communications were vulnerable. Acting on Bragg's order, Joseph Wheeler led his brigade on a ride around the Federal army and hit two large wagon trains in a circuit around Rosecrans on December 30–31. Bragg sent him out again on January 1, accompanied by John Wharton's cavalry brigade. They hit a large train near La Vergne but were called back, only to mount a third effort on January 2. This time, near Cox's Hill, the Federals were ready for the Rebel horsemen. A large number of Union infantrymen defended their train and saved it from capture. Wheeler succeeded because he took the enemy by surprise in his first two forays but failed when the Federals devoted more manpower to logistical defense. In all, Confederate cavalrymen burned 250 Union wagons and severely hurt Rosecrans's ability to feed his men. Many of them resorted to cutting off chunks of horses killed in the fierce fighting outside Murfreesboro, roasting them over fires, and devouring the meat. However, the Unionists were never forced to retreat because of these attacks on their logistical system; Bragg fell back on the night of January 3 and gave up the field.[49]

Wheeler had another chance to burn Federal wagons in the aftermath of Bragg's victory at Chickamauga. Taking refuge in newly acquired Chattanooga, Rosecrans's defeated army dug in and relied on a tenuous wagon link with middle Tennessee that snaked across the Cumberland Plateau. Bragg sent Wheeler's division of 5,000 troopers to cut that link. Wheeler managed to get 1,500 men into the Sequatchie River Valley that drained the middle of the plateau by October 1, 1863; those troopers happened to find several wagon trains the next day that were guarded by small forces of Union cavalry and infantry, easily drove off the guards, and then lay waste to the trains. They burned 350 wagons plus 40 sutler's wagons and captured 1,800 mules. Federal cavalry units gave chase and in a running fight lasting two days recaptured 800 mules, but the destruction of wagons severely strained Rosecrans's already precarious supply arrangement. Once again, the Federals held on, more or less compensated for the losses, and eventually secured control of Chattanooga with Grant's victory over Bragg's "besieging" army at the end of November.[50]

But a campaign-clinching destruction of wagon trains took place in April 1864 during Frederick Steele's expedition to Camden, Arkansas. Perched 100 miles from his base at Little Rock and heavily dependent on wagon train shipments because the area around Camden was largely devoid of food and forage, Steele devoted considerable strength to guarding his trains. But he did not do enough. Samuel Bell Maxey's Confederate division came upon one of Steele's trains near Poison Springs on April 18, 1864, fought a fierce battle with 2,500

10.4. "Wheeler's Cavalry Destroying Rosecrans's Wagon-Train in Sequatchie Valley." Confederate Major General Joseph Wheeler destroyed 350 Federal wagons in a large raid on Major General William S. Rosecrans's supply line in October 1863 following the Rebel victory at Chickamauga. It was one of the few examples of a successful mounted raid on wagon trains in the Civil War. (Dodson, *Campaigns of Wheeler*, 1)

defending Federals, and severely defeated them. The entire train fell into Confederate hands. Maxey burned 30 wagons on the battlefield because they were too damaged to be moved and secured the remaining 170 for Confederate use. This Rebel victory convinced Steele to evacuate Camden and conduct a perilous retreat to Little Rock in foul weather. Hounded by Rebel forces, he barely made it to safety.[51]

Whether attacking riverboats, trains, coastal ships, or wagons, the key to success as in many military operations lay in bringing a large enough force to a key point to overwhelm outnumbered defenders and effect some result that went beyond merely inconveniencing the enemy. That ideal rarely happened in the Civil War. Confederate authorities were limited in the number of men and resources they could afford to send on risky ventures behind Union lines, and Federal authorities gradually invested a great deal of their available resources in defending important lines of communication. As a result, the overwhelming majority of Rebel attacks (whether by regularly organized forces or by self-constituted guerrilla bands) failed to make much of a dent in Union transportation.

There were a handful of unusually effective strikes against logistics in the war. John Hunt Morgan inflicted more than normal damage on the Federals when his cavalry captured Gallatin, Tennessee, on August 12, 1862, and then destroyed the Big South Tunnel by piling combustibles on flatcars, setting it afire, and rolling the cars into the tunnel. The resulting conflagration burned the timbered supports and parts of the tunnel collapsed. It took Union engineers nearly three months to repair the damage and get the Louisville and Nashville Railroad fully operational. But even this spectacular act of destruction failed to cut the line completely. The Federals organized a wagon train around the tunnel to keep some degree of supplies rolling along the railroad.[52]

Forrest achieved more destruction than normal when his men burned the Sulphur Springs trestle north of Athens, Alabama, in September 1864. He placed artillery on good ground to dominate the area around the trestle and the fort and two block houses the Federals held near it. This fire compelled the garrison to surrender. The trestle was 300 feet long and 72 feet high, an imposing structure that required many weeks to replace. But the bridge was on the Central Alabama Railroad, which was used as a secondary line of supply for Sherman's army group in Georgia, and thus Federal quartermasters could get by without using it. Nevertheless, the lesson was clear: destroying a key link such as a tunnel or an unusually large bridge was far more serious for the Federals than merely tearing up a few miles of track that could easily be relaid.[53]

Another campaign-turning act of destruction, similar to Maxey's capture of the wagon train at Poison Springs, can be found in Earl Van Dorn's capture of Holly Springs, Mississippi. To counter Grant's drive south along the Mississippi Central Railroad against Vicksburg, John C. Pemberton dispatched Van Dorn with a large cavalry force to bypass Grant and strike at his rail line of communications with west Tennessee. Van Dorn hit Holly Springs on December 20, 1862, captured 1,500 prisoners in a short fight, and then destroyed $400,000 worth of Federal property. Grant felt he did not have enough troops to adequately guard the line, so he decided to retire, placing his hopes on a cooperating column of Federal troops under Sherman that had set out from Memphis by river steamer to attack Vicksburg. In short, Grant decided that relying on the river-based network was preferable to the rail-based system in this case, and he was right.[54]

The highest level of success in targeting enemy logistics was achieved by Sherman in the last year of the Civil War, when he essentially used his entire army group to not only pursue strategic movements but tear up the transportation infrastructure of the South in a systematic way. By 1864 the opportunity presented to a single brigade or division of roaming cavalry to decisively influence the course of a campaign had vanished; only large-scale troop deployment on logistical targets could change the way the war went, and no one in either army understood that better than did Sherman, who not only was more keen than anyone else to protect Union riverboats but more desperate than anyone else to wreck his enemy's military transportation system. The Federals won the struggle to see which side could achieve more success in destroying their opponent's logistics, and that was an important factor in their winning the war.

CONCLUSION

As early as January 1862, Thomas Bragg detected hopeful signs that the Federal war effort might collapse under its own weight. A brother of Confederate general Braxton Bragg and currently serving as attorney general in the Rebel cabinet, Thomas read reports that Lincoln's government would accrue a debt of $900 million by the middle of 1863. "*Their* system will not stand it," he confided to his diary, "and will probably topple and fall. They have raised so large a force that they cannot wield it. It takes more money than they can raise & to advance with such immense armies requires more transportation than they can procure & manage—they cannot keep them supplied, when they leave their shipping on the coast, or their depots when in the interior."[1]

Bragg severely underestimated the financial and logistical power of the Northern government. He could not foresee that his enemy would meet the challenge of moving men and supplies for their already large army or that the size of that army would nearly double within a year. The Civil War witnessed the largest military forces ever raised in the Western Hemisphere, and it also witnessed the most impressive triumph of military transportation thus far in world history.

"When we remember the size of the army, it is wonderful how thoroughly the wants of its members were supplied from the very beginning of the war," commented Richard W. Johnson as he praised Union logistical success in his memoirs. "If subsistence stores were at any time scarce, it was not for the want of them, but for the temporary derangement of our modes of transportation, which could not be foreseen or guarded against."[2]

By the spring of 1864, Federal officers were operating under the need to provide for 1 million men under arms. Transportation officers worked overtime to provide modes of shifting thousands of those men over hundreds of miles at almost a moment's notice. Lewis B. Parsons carefully tabulated the statistics that demonstrate the logistical power of the Northern government. Federal quartermasters moved a grand total of 3,982,438 people during the last fiscal year of the war (ending June 30, 1865). Of that number, 3,376,610 were soldiers under orders from their commanders to go from one point to another. Additionally, 201,106 were soldiers going to or from their homes on furlough. Another 256,693 men were prisoners of war. In addition, army quartermasters moved 148,629 civilians who elected to travel on government transport. Parsons also moved 716,420 animals during the last fiscal year of the war. That included 407,848 horses, 123,448 mules, and 185,124 cattle.[3]

Parsons also kept records of the mountains of supplies moved by military transport during the last fiscal year of the war. More than 4.1 million tons of food for soldiers, over 3.7 million tons of quartermaster stores, 1.3 million tons of ordnance stores, nearly 90,000 tons of medical stores, and 127,000 tons of miscellaneous material found their way by steamer, rail, and coastal shipping to military destinations. That amounted to a grand total of 9,458,871 tons of material transported across the country during the final months of the war. Ironically, feeding animals tended to take up the lion's share of transport to areas that had little forage. Fifty percent of the shipments along the railroad from Aquia Creek Landing to the Army of the Potomac near Fredericksburg during the early months of 1863 consisted of forage, in contrast to the next largest contingent of material, commissary stores for army personnel, which represented 25 percent of the daily shipments.[4]

As Bragg knew, the cost of transporting all these men, animals, and material was staggering. Parsons reported that the government expended $8,724,230 to move people during the last fiscal year of the conflict. By that time quartermasters were paying on average one-third of a cent per man for each mile. At that rate, a trip from St. Louis to New Orleans (which Parsons calculated at 1,250 miles) amounted to only $3.625 per soldier. Moving a force of 20,000 men that distance cost the government about $85,000. In contrast, Federal authorities spent a grand total of over $21 million to transport all varieties of freight during the last fiscal year of the war.[5]

Northern quartermasters utilized a triad system of transportation to construct their impressive network of strategic lines of communication, knitting together the advantages of riverboats, railroads, and coastal freighters. Comparisons of their relative importance founder on the fact that each of the three systems played a unique role that neither of the other two could fill.

Everyone, however, had their own opinion as to the relative worth of these national lines of supply. "Steamboats were more generous transports than rail road trains," concluded John Levering, a quartermaster who served on the division staff of Joseph J. Reynolds at the time of the Stones River campaign. He considered the rail line toward Nashville a "slender thread" in comparison. Many officers recognized that while railroads could be torn up, the river was a natural highway normally impervious to impediment in any thorough way. "I am never easy with a railroad," William T. Sherman confessed to David D. Porter while moving several divisions from Memphis to Chattanooga in the fall of 1863. Railroads required "a whole army to guard, each foot of rail being essential to the whole, whereas they cannot stop the Tennessee [River], and each boat can make its own game."[6]

Charles Parsons compiled a list of the transportation he furnished for the fiscal year ending June 30, 1863, which compared how much movement took place by water and rail. In many categories the amounts were about even. While moving 34,718 horses and mules by steamer, for example, he shipped 47,963 by railroad. Parsons moved many more cattle by river (23,353) than he did by rail (2,196) and quite a bit more wagons and ambulances by steamer than by cars. More than double the number of cannon and caissons went by rail compared to the number shipped on the rivers. The railroads transferred 193,023 men compared to 135,909 troops moved by river steamers. But more than twice as much food, ordnance, and quartermaster stores were shipped by steamboats (337,912,363 pounds) as by rail (153,102,100 pounds). There is no clear pattern in these numbers; one mode of transportation was generally about as useful as the other, and much depended on the needs of various army units operating along the river (to be served by steamboats) as compared to operating in the hinterland (to be served by railroads).[7]

There also is no clear evidence concerning the relative importance of steamers versus railroads in terms of moving personnel, except in circumstantial need. The overwhelming majority of all Union and Confederate soldiers traveled far more extensively during their army service than previously in their civilian lives. Moving vast distances within relatively short periods of time fascinated many of them and led to records of how far their units moved and what conveyance took them from one point to another. Charles Wills of the 103rd Illinois believed that he personally traveled at least 3,000 miles during the course of the war. Battery L of the 2nd New York Artillery (which was reborn as the 34th New York Battery early in 1864) moved a total of 18,758 miles because it saw service in both the East and West.[8]

Other soldiers recorded how much of their wartime travel took place on different logistical venues. The Chicago Board of Trade Battery traveled 5,368 miles on foot and 1,231 miles (or 18.7 percent of its total wartime travel) by rail. Through a series of movements, the 32nd Iowa started from Columbus, Kentucky, in January 1864 and wound up in Montgomery, Alabama, by April 1865. It moved a total of 6,668 miles during that period, 65.1 percent of those miles by river steamer, 30.9 percent on foot, and only 3.8 percent by rail.[9]

As the story of the 32nd Iowa indicates, those regiments serving primarily along the western river system used steamers more often than railroads when they moved long distances. The 83rd Ohio served essentially its entire career along the Mississippi River. It rode on river steamers a total of 7,130 miles (or 74.5 percent of its wartime travel distance), while marching on foot only 19.1 percent and moving by railroad a mere 6.4 percent of the time. The 15th Missouri served in the Trans-Mississippi, along the rail line penetrating the southeastern Confederacy during the war, and along the coast of Texas after the conflict. It utilized rails for only 22.9 percent of its wartime travel in comparison to river and coastal steamers for 44.7 percent and foot power for 32.4 percent of its travel distance.[10]

Interestingly, the only regiments that left behind a detailed calculation of the distance moved during the war were those Union and Confederate units that served at least part of their time in the Western Theater. That theater was enormously expansive in geographic extent, and many units traveled across its wide breadth, impressing members with the experience of moving on multiple transportation systems over thousands of miles of varied terrain.

More Union units than Confederate ones kept detailed data of movement, but Company D, 2nd Missouri (C.S.), was an exception. Corporal William O. Hedrick maintained a record of all company movements up to March 3, 1865, when the regiment wound up defending Mobile. By that time, Hedrick noted a grand total of 4,536 miles of travel by the company. That amounted to 67 percent conducted on foot, 24.1 percent by rail, and only 8.8 percent by river steamer.[11]

Confederate soldiers tended to travel by rail and steamer in lesser proportion than their Federal counterparts. This was mostly the result of the lower
capacity, reliability, and availability of military transportation in the South. Two
contrasting personal stories help to illustrate the difference between Confederate and Union transport in the Civil War.

One story involved the initial movement of Company D, 8th Texas Cavalry,
from its origin point at Bastrop, Texas, to Bowling Green, Kentucky, in the fall
of 1861. The recruits rode their horses 60 miles to Alleyton, the nearest railroad
head, and boarded the cars for Houston. There they were forced to wait several
hours at Pierce Junction because no train was immediately available. The men,
who had given up their horses at Alleyton, decided to walk the nine remaining
miles to Houston. From there, it took nearly an entire day to ride the rails 80
miles to Beaumont, where the company boarded a river steamer that moved
up the Neches River and the Sabine River to Niblett's Bluff. Then the troops
walked another 100 miles before they were supplied with civilian carts from the
local area to carry their baggage. These carts were huge affairs, with wheels six
feet tall and pulled by two oxen. Each cart carried up to eight men in addition
to their baggage, but the troopers had to stand as Creole drivers pushed the
slow-moving oxen forward for 40 miles. At New Iberia, the company boarded
boats and steamed along Bayou Teche to Brasher and New Orleans. By this
time, the company had been on the road for a full week. It boarded railroad cars
that had recently been used to haul cattle and were still dirty, but in 20 hours
the men reached Nashville and within another day arrived at Bowling Green.[12]

The odyssey of Company D, 8th Texas Cavalry, came about mostly because
of the frontier state of transportation in Texas; once east of the Mississippi
River, the journey might have been dirty but it was swift. However, one must
contrast this story with that of a Federal soldier named August Bondi of the
5th Kansas Cavalry, who also traveled in the Trans-Mississippi region. The
difference was he traveled by way of the transportation system provided by
the Federal government. Bondi was recovering from a wound and his term
of enlistment had expired. Leaving Pine Bluff, Arkansas, in an ambulance on
November 10, 1864, he reached Little Rock and caught the railroad to Duvall's
Bluff. From there he boarded a river steamer for Memphis, where he took a
regular packet boat headed for St. Louis, reaching the Missouri city by November 18. Another steamer took him to Hannibal the next day, and from there
he rode the rails to St. Joseph by November 20. Another steamer took him to

Fort Leavenworth, where he stayed over two days before taking a buggy ride to Greeley, Kansas, arriving November 24.[13]

The Texas troopers traveled about 1,000 miles by horse, foot, ox cart, railroad, and river steamer to reach Bowling Green early in the war. August Bondi traveled 1,345 miles to go home late in the conflict. He smoothly used the rail and river system available to Federal quartermasters in a part of the country that had comparatively limited transportation facilities. His trip was conducted in a leisurely fashion with deliberate stopovers and he did not have to resort to improvised means of getting from one point to another along the way. One wonders how much more difficult the Texans' trip would have been if they had essayed their journey late in the war.

Although Erna Risch categorically states that river-based transport held "a decided advantage over railroads" in the West, the statistics provided by all of the sources noted thus far fail to support that conclusion. River steamers were in general less vulnerable to guerrilla attacks than railroads, but that does not mean quartermasters used them more than the trains. Historians of transportation tend to see the relationship between riverboats and trains as a struggle by the middle decades of the nineteenth century, with the railroad steadily winning. Louis Hunter believes the railroads turned the corner in this competition during the Civil War and that the steamboat industry steadily declined after that. More recent historians have argued that this decline was less steep, and that the riverboats continued to play a major role in the economy of the Mississippi Valley compared to railroads well into the latter decades of the century.[14]

As a new technology, railroads proved their worth for military purposes in the Civil War. This was true not only of the American experience but of world experience. Railroads played an important but somewhat limited role in troop mobilization during the Second War of Italian Unification, a short conflict little more than one major campaign in length that tested the new transportation system only to a limited extent.

Daniel McCallum was keenly aware that the Federal government conducted the first massive use of trains for making war in world history. In fact, he identified Sherman's Atlanta campaign as the most severe test of the entire conflict. After the war, McCallum heard from Southern railroad officials that Rebel officers were impressed "at the rapidity with which railroad breaks were repaired and the regularity with which trains were moved to the front; and it was only when the method of operating was fully explained that it could be comprehended."[15]

Despite having no prior plans for the military use of railroads before the firing on Fort Sumter, the U.S. government quickly improvised a system to do so. The Federals innovated, experimented, and continually adjusted that system, expanding it many times over as needed, until it produced a stunning success. Edwin Pratt, an English historian who wrote the first scholarly study of railroads at war, credited Lincoln's administration with this little-recognized achievement in his 1915 book. Pratt argued, however, that prewar planning was essential if European nations were to effectively use railroads for war, because of the close proximity of potential enemies and the need to mobilize a huge number of men very quickly.[16]

The Federal accomplishment was impressive enough in the East, but vastly more so in the West, a theater of operations featuring expansive territory, rugged mountains, and wide rivers. William Logan Rand of the 118th Illinois grew irritated on repeatedly reading of reverses suffered by the Army of the Potomac. "The eastern army is near at home," he wrote his father, "and has had all the men and supplies that they have asked for while the western army is very remote from civilization . . . and its supplies are limited and we have driven the enemy at every point." Quartermaster S. B. Holabird fully agreed, noting that the huge territorial expanse of the Western Theater lent itself to the development of "a prodigious development of river, rail, and land transportation" skillfully managed by both quartermasters and army commanders. In other words, the logistical triumph of the Union was to a very large degree a triumph of Federal officers in the West rather than in the East. Quartermasters, engineers, and generals in the West faced far larger supply challenges than their counterparts in the East and generally met those challenges in brilliant fashion.[17]

As the war drew to a close, quartermasters were eager to highlight their logistical success and lend some brilliance to a department that often languished in the shadows of public awareness. Robert Allen noted that everyone was keen to criticize the quartermaster, making a scapegoat of him for the failure of a campaign, but ignorant of his work when everything needed was supplied. He asserted that no other war witnessed such large armies moving over such huge expanses of territory, and yet in general they were abundantly supplied with all they needed.[18]

Lewis B. Parsons correctly pointed out that the "application of steam to land and water transportation" altered the nature of warfare as much as it changed the nature of civilian commerce. By allowing for "more rapid concentration of troops and supplies at distant points" it lent "greater vigor to a campaign and vast advantage to the party having superiority in this respect." Parsons theorized that with only 24 hours' notice a good quartermaster could move an army the size of Napoleon's from Boston or Baltimore by rail to Cairo in three days, then put the men onto a fleet of riverboats and have them in New Orleans in four more days. That represented a journey of some 2,200 miles in little more than a week. Actually, Parsons exaggerated the speed of such a hypothetical movement, but he was not far off the mark. Quartermaster Frederick S. Winslow thought the new age of steam transportation enabled an army to change its location "with almost the facility a family changes [its] residence," and to feed the men "with the promptness found in a well regulated household."[19]

Most observant Confederates realized just how far the Union army surpassed them in logistical power. "In every form of contest in which mechanical instruments requiring skill and heavy machinery to make them, can be used, the Federals are our superiors," concluded William J. Hardee halfway through the war. Grant knew that point well. While commanding the expansive Military Division of the Mississippi, he relied on steam transportation to go everywhere needed and the telegraph to keep in touch with his subordinates. "I can command whilst traveling and visiting about as well as by remaining" in one place he wrote. When Sherman penned his memoirs, he devoted a good deal of space to logistical matters, which greatly pleased Lewis B. Parsons. The retired army quartermaster read the book page by page to his family and only wished Sherman could have given even more attention to logistics. Another quartermaster, serving at a fort in Texas, thought Sherman's "estimate of measures, your lessons in logistics and strategy," were important to all professional army officers.[20]

Army quartermasters who missed the Civil War but studied its logistical history in the late nineteenth century were mightily impressed. They were especially interested in how Grant supplied his men during the Vicksburg and Overland campaigns and how quartermasters supported Sherman's army while driving toward Atlanta. They also found it instructive to understand how the various depots were constantly changed to provide the most forward supply points for advancing armies. Of course, the use of railroads dominated their study because it represented the only new feature of logistics in the Civil War.[21]

While Northern quartermasters and the generals they served had ample reason to be proud of their logistical success, their Confederate counterparts had little to say about their own logistical experience during the war. The Union had all the advantages and the Confederates had all the limitations when it came to moving men and material. Most of the western riverboats were constructed and owned by Northerners, most of them were in Northern rivers when the war broke out, and all of the owners were eager to do work for the U.S. government. That eagerness stemmed in part from patriotism, but more importantly from the faith they had in the financial stability of the government in Washington. Most Northern quartermasters developed a working relationship with those owners so as to offer them financial incentives to do army work without gouging the government too badly. The Confederates never were able to utilize a large fleet of river transports due to shortages of boats. They never appointed a transportation officer to supervise all river traffic and left behind far too few records to document what they actually did accomplish in the way of river transportation. Moreover, they felt compelled to destroy dozens of their riverboats to keep them from falling into Union hands when Grant penetrated central Mississippi during the Vicksburg campaign.

The Confederate failure to transform its rail system into an effective logistical support for the army is more widely documented. Southern railroads were still catching up with Northern lines when Fort Sumter was fired upon, and they never rose to the challenges imposed on them by the war. Southern railroads managed fairly well for the first few months of the conflict and then declined rapidly. There were too few engineers and mechanics, too little iron, too little money, and too few plants capable of building engines and cars. The Confederate government failed to compensate for these problems. As its financial status declined, the Richmond government became a poor customer for the railroad companies, who preferred to ship private freight and passengers. Everyone from Jefferson Davis down was loath to seize railroad companies and run them with army personnel. The failure of Confederate railroads was multifaceted; it represented a failure of technology, industrial capacity, financial power, and the assertion of government control. In every way, the Northern railroad situation was virtually the opposite of the Southern.

While the Confederates at least had a slim chance at making their railroads work for their war needs, they had no hope of using coastal shipping. The Northern naval blockade of the Southern coast negated that prospect. Davis's government had no hope of controlling the coastal shipping lanes, and the few bits of evidence that Rebel quartermasters used a coastal ship now and then represents nothing more than a furtive effort. Given its long coastline and numerous coastal fortifications, the Confederate army could have benefitted from coastal shipping, but it had no real opportunity to try.

Of course the Confederates knew how to make and use wagons, but they often suffered from shortages because of limited production facilities. When the Army of the Mississippi finally left the area around Corinth and retreated to Tupelo in late May 1862, it found itself for the first time needing significant numbers of wagons to support long-distance movement. Braxton Bragg had to scramble for weeks to round them up from civilian farms and plantations in Mississippi, delaying his planned movement to Chattanooga. That army and Lee's Army of Northern Virginia constantly suffered wagon shortages throughout the war. The problem was not nearly as severe as with river-based, rail-based, and coastal shipping, but the Federals generally were better supplied with land transportation than their opponents throughout the conflict.

When the war ended, the Northern government was in possession of far more transportation than it had ever owned or contracted. Officials now had to develop a strategy for getting rid of it. The standard freight and passenger rate worked out with railroads early in 1862 continued in effect until March 1867, but the government divested itself of most of the hardware it had acquired much earlier. In June 1865 Meigs instructed his subordinates to invoice all quartermaster stores that were no longer needed and prepare them for public sale. Soon after, government officials began to work out the details for transferring control of Southern railroads back to their original owners. They preferred to give the railroad to a state government board of public works if possible or to the original privately owned company if its executives took an oath of allegiance to the U.S. government. The company could not file a claim for damages or to recover profits the government accrued while it controlled the facility. Excess equipment and material could be auctioned off by the government or in some cases sold directly to the rejuvenated company. In many cases the government charged the company for the immense outlay expended in improving their track for military use, but it was repaid on lenient credit terms over long periods of time.[22]

The last spurt of military railroad construction took place in Georgia in an effort to avert starvation in the spring of 1865. Federal authorities were compelled to rebuild the Western and Atlantic Railroad at the end of the war in order to rush food to the starving population around Atlanta. Workers relaid 140 miles of track and constructed 16 bridges and 20 water tanks at a cost of more than $2.3 million.[23]

By June 30, 1866, every line operated by the U.S. Military Railroad had been given back to civilian control. Most of the excess rolling stock, equipment, and supplies had been sold. It took another 20 years for the Federal government to collect the debts owed to it by Southern railroad companies.[24]

At the same time that Federal authorities divested themselves of railroad property, they were selling canal boats, barges, river steamers, and coastal ships. Entrepreneurs saw in this an opportunity to buy them cheaply if they could organize united efforts to drive down the prices. Initially Meigs wanted to sell boats through advertising and sealed bids. He was careful to mandate that the sale price had to fall within 25 percent of the valuation of the craft. This was not very successful, resulting in the sale of barely half of the first round of boats offered by quartermasters. Meigs was then forced to sell at public auction. The government barely recovered fair value for most of the vessels, but it managed to sell about 200 boats in the West by April 1866.[25]

From being the biggest shipper in U.S. history during the war, the Federal government deflated into just one more customer in the civilian transportation economy. Stanton was not concerned. He pointed out to Andrew Johnson that the army could just as easily enter that economy and buy, contract, or charter any kind of transportation on land, river, rail, or sea to meet any need at any time. Civilian transportation "remains in this country, and can answer any exigency."[26]

Did the European powers pay attention to the immense experiment in military use of riverboats, railroads, and coastal shipping in the American war? The answer is a qualified no. Prussian officials were mostly concerned with prewar planning, cooperation between the military and civilian sector, and the repairing and maintaining of railroad systems to keep pace with advancing armies. The Americans conducted no prewar planning, but their conflict offered immense opportunities to study military-civilian cooperation during wartime. The details of that important subject, however, were not readily available to an outsider and there is no evidence that the Prussians or anyone else in Europe paid attention to it. After their war with Austria in 1866, Prussian officials became aware of Daniel McCallum's final report and had it translated into German for distribution in an effort to improve the operation of their small railroad construction corps.[27]

Although the American Civil War was the first true railroad war, and despite the fact that Northern and Southern quartermasters utilized both riverboats and coastal shipping on an unusually large scale, European military use of modern transportation spun out along its own course of development with precious little in the way of lessons learned from the American experience. Prussia conducted a small, short war with Denmark in the early months of 1864 over control of two provinces, Schleswig and Holstein. By all accounts the movement of troops by rail proceeded smoothly, but the size of these troop transfers was small. German quartermasters shifted more than 15,000 men, plus 4,500 animals and 377 vehicles, a distance of 175 miles in five days early in the conflict.[28]

Prussia's war with Austria in 1866 was a more severe test of its plans for mobilizing a large army quickly against a dangerous enemy. Moltke factored in the rail systems of both countries in his planning for the campaign against Austria and realized he could count on five major rail lines to move troops to the theater of operations while his opponent had but one. He estimated Prussia could concentrate most of its army where it needed to fight the war in only three weeks and that Austria would need twice as much time. Soon after war broke out, Prussian quartermasters were smoothly moving troops at a massive rate as they shifted four corps (40 trains per day) from May 23 to June 5, 1866. Austrian quartermasters could manage only 20 trains per day. Ironically, the Prussians had devoted immense planning to moving troops and little prewar thinking about how to supply them. The men got to their destination well but suffered because the shipment of food and supplies was improvised on the spot. They had to live off the land as much as possible and do without on occasion. This problem did not prevent Prussia from winning a dramatic victory over its larger opponent in a campaign that lasted only a few weeks.[29]

Prussia's Eisenbahntruppe units, only three in number and with no more than 100 men in each unit, were overwhelmed by the problem of repairing railroads within the theater of operations. The units were too few in number and not adequately supported with material and prewar training. Prussian authorities learned a lesson from this experience; they studied McCallum's report and increased the size to five units with 200 men each by the time of their war with France in 1870.[30]

The Prussian army also became more focused after 1866 on tighter military-civilian cooperation in preparation for war, extending to the level of military input when new civilian lines were proposed for construction. They also added a new administrative bureau to more closely supervise the supply of troops after they arrived in the theater of operations.[31]

France was a more formidable opponent than Austria, with four strategic rail lines (60 percent of the route double-tracked), leading to the potential theater of operations with Prussia. The Germans still held an advantage in their six strategic lines, most of which also were double-tracked. They also had more experience and more thorough prewar planning on their side. When war broke out in the summer of 1870, Prussia quickly took the lead in logistics. Moving 50 trains each day compared to France's 12 trains, Prussian quartermasters shoved a large army into battle. While German troop movements went smoothly, the French transfer was attended with a good deal of confusion, especially at the destination.[32]

Despite improvements in handling supplies, the Prussians once again experienced logistical difficulties in 1870–1871. Lower-level quartermasters tended to use railroad cars for storage rather than unloading them quickly and sending them back for more, a common problem in the Civil War as well. Work details often were slow to unload cars; land transportation to convey the food from railheads to the advancing troops also was in short supply. As a result, Prussian armies were compelled to live off the land a good deal.[33]

The Prussians also experienced problems in their efforts to repair and maintain railroads in occupied French territory, despite the expansion of their Eisenbahntruppe units. French destruction of the abandoned lines proved to be more extensive than anticipated, and the continued resistance of several fortresses through which some railroads ran compelled costly efforts to construct new lines around them. Prussian workers were barely able to establish rail support for the German siege of Paris by late 1870. They used a total of 2,000 miles of French railways and had to deploy 100,000 troops to protect them from guerrilla attacks.[34]

As Northern quartermasters found, it was comparatively easy to conduct massive troop transfers by rail as long as the companies controlling lines were cooperative and possessed adequate rolling stock. But the Americans did a better job of supplying those troops once they reached their destination than did the Prussians. The real answer as to why lay in time and experience; Prussia's strategy was quick mobilization, decisive operations in the field, and a fast victory. America's military policy was very different, with the maintenance of a small professional army and reliance on untrained recruits improvised into volunteer armies to meet national emergencies as they developed. The United States was therefore destined to get started slowly to fight major wars and had a longer trial time to work out supply problems. No amount of prewar planning could hope to eliminate all the small and unexpected difficulties associated with shifting mountains of equipment and supplies to a moving mass of troops; only experience could work out such problems as they arose. Despite the problems, the Prussian use of railroads in the war with France was a resounding triumph of logistics. The rail-based system worked brilliantly in moving troops, and the problems involved in shipping supplies did not prevent the armies from winning victories.[35]

By the time the United States fought its short war with Spain in 1898, the rail system of the country had greatly expanded and was in the process of consolidating into truly national companies. This relatively small war placed limited demands on the country's railroads. Army quartermasters worked out arrangements to move men and supplies at lower rates than those charged civilian customers and without government interference or military administration. Troops traveled in coaches and sleeping cars, not boxcars as in the Civil War. One infantry regiment needed six trains as a result, but the demand for space was easily met by the large railroad industry of the day. Altogether, some 435,000 men and 17,000 officers were transported by rail during the war with no serious mishaps. All of this took place within the United States; American troops used little if any rail transport in the theaters of operations.[36]

The government needed long-range sea transport in 1898 and initially chartered ships before supplementing that strategy by purchasing vessels. Eventually quartermasters spent more than $16 million to buy seagoing ships, the largest capable of carrying up to 1,000 men and 1,000 animals. The worst logistical problems of the war were those associated with supplying William Shafter's campaign in Cuba. It started with congestion in the single rail line leading to Tampa, Florida, the point of debarkation, and continued with faulty planning as to what type of supplies and clothing the American troops needed in a tropical climate. At the destination, Shafter had no real port facilities until Santiago fell.[37]

Administrative problems during the Spanish American War led to a major overhaul of the military structure in the early twentieth century. Congress merged the Quartermaster, Subsistence, and Pay Departments into the new Quartermaster Corps in 1912. It was headed by an officer given the title of

Quartermaster General of the Army two years later, and by 1916 the new corps was supported by 369 officers and 6,000 enlisted men. For the first time ever, the U.S. Army had the services of specially organized enlisted men to do quartermaster work. Thomas S. Jesup had proposed the enlistment of quartermaster troops well before the Civil War, and Montgomery C. Meigs had suggested the creation of a Transportation Corps, but Congress listened to neither man. The chief quartermaster had to rely on enlisted personnel detailed from the ranks to handle a wide range of duties before 1912.[38]

Using preexisting rail lines continued to absorb the attention of engineers and quartermasters in all countries, but small experiments continued to be made in terms of constructing entirely new rail lines specifically for military purposes during the course of a conflict. The British had pioneered in this during the siege of Sebastopol with their short rail line linking the siege works with their base at Balaclava. The best example of it in the Civil War was Grant's military railroad at Petersburg. The British constructed a military railroad during their small campaign in Abyssinia during 1867–1868. It was 12 miles long and used 4 engines and 60 cars. The Germans constructed a 22-mile military railroad during the Franco-Prussian War of 1870–1871 by employing 4,000 men for 50 days. The Russian government planned the largest military railroad construction to date to support their war with the Ottoman Empire in 1877–1878. They managed to finish 229 miles of it before the war ended. The new track mileage was located within the Russian Empire rather than directly in the theater of operations.[39]

By 1914, most of the problems associated with railroad use in war had been worked out to a remarkable degree. The size of armies had grown to gargantuan proportions, and logistical demands increased many times. Compared to nineteenth-century wars, World War I represented a decisive watershed in the development of military logistics. In troop movements and in moving a bewildering variety and quantity of equipment, food, and supplies, the Great War simply dwarfed all previous conflicts. Logistical problems tended to occur only during the initial mobile phase of the campaign in 1914. When that phase ended by October with the construction of a nearly continuous line of earthworks across northeastern France and western Belgium, the static nature of military operations along the Western Front allowed quartermasters to build new military railroads and keep each sector of the front well supplied, shifting reinforcements quickly as needed to contain breakthroughs.[40]

In the sweep of modern military history, the American Civil War played an important role in pointing toward the extensive use of railroads, river transport, coastal shipping, and land transportation. Northern and Southern quartermasters faced the same kinds of problems that their predecessors and those who followed them would encounter in these four areas. Unfortunately, few of their contemporaries and even fewer of those who followed paid much attention to their work.

NOTES

AAS	American Antiquarian Society, Worcester, Massachusetts
ADAH	Alabama Department of Archives and History, Montgomery
AHC	Atlanta History Center, Atlanta, Georgia
ALPL	Abraham Lincoln Presidential Library, Springfield, Illinois
AM	Archives of Michigan, Lansing
AU	Auburn University, Special Collections and Archives, Auburn, Alabama
BC	Bowdoin College, Special Collections, Brunswick, Maine
BHL-UM	University of Michigan, Bentley Historical Library, Ann Arbor
BPL	Boston Public Library, Boston, Massachusetts
CCNMP	Chickamauga and Chattanooga National Military Park, Fort Oglethorpe, Georgia
CHM	Chicago History Museum, Chicago, Illinois
CHS	Connecticut Historical Society, Hartford
CWM	College of William and Mary, Special Collections, Williamsburg, Virginia
CU	Cornell University, Division of Rare and Manuscript Collections, Ithaca, New York
DU	Duke University, Rubenstein Rare Book and Manuscript Library, Durham, North Carolina
EU	Emory University, Manuscript, Archives, Rare Book Library, Atlanta, Georgia
FHS	Filson Historical Society, Louisville, Kentucky
GLIAH	Gilder Lehrman Institute of American History, New York
IHS	Indiana Historical Society, Indianapolis
KHS	Kansas Historical Society, Topeka
LC	Library of Congress, Manuscript Division, Washington, D.C.
LMU	Lincoln Memorial University, Abraham Lincoln Library and Museum, Harrogate, Tennessee
LSU	Louisiana State University, Louisiana and Lower Mississippi Valley Collection, Special Collections, Baton Rouge
MaryHS	Maryland Historical Society, Baltimore
MDAH	Mississippi Department of Archives and History, Jackson
MHM	Missouri History Museum, St. Louis

MassHS	Massachusetts Historical Society, Boston
MHS	Minnesota Historical Society, St. Paul
NARA	National Archives and Records Administration, Washington, D.C.
N-YHS	New-York Historical Society, New York, New York
NYSL	New York State Library, Albany
OR	*War of the Rebellion: A Compilation of the Official Records of the Union and Confederate Armies.* 70 vols. in 128. Washington, D.C.: Government Printing Office, 1880–1901. (Unless otherwise cited, all references are to Series 1.)
ORN	*Official Records of the Union and Confederate Navies in the War of the Rebellion.* 30 vols. Washington, D.C.: Government Printing Office, 1894–1922.
SHSM-RCC	State Historical Society of Missouri, Research Center, Columbia
SOR	*Supplement to the Official Records of the Union and Confederate Armies.* 100 vols. Wilmington, N.C.: Broadfoot, 1993–2000.
SRNB	Stones River National Battlefield, Murfreesboro, Tennessee
TAM	Texas A&M University, Special Collections, College Station
TSLA	Tennessee State Library and Archives, Nashville
UA	University of Alabama, W. Stanley Hoole Special Collections Library, Tuscaloosa
UAF	University of Arkansas, Special Collections, Fayetteville
UC	University of Chicago, Special Collections Research Center, Chicago, Illinois
UCB	University of Colorado, Special Collections, Boulder
UF	University of Florida, Special and Area Studies Collections, Gainesville
UM	University of Mississippi, Special Collections, Oxford
UNC	University of North Carolina, Southern History Collection, Chapel Hill
UND	University of Notre Dame, Rare Books and Special Collections, South Bend, Indiana
UTK	University of Tennessee, Special Collections, Knoxville
UVA	University of Virginia, Special Collections, Charlottesville
UW	University of Washington, Special Collections, Seattle
UWyo	University of Wyoming, American Heritage Center, Laramie
VTU	Virginia Tech, Special Collections, Blacksburg
WHS	Wisconsin Historical Society, Madison
WCL-UM	University of Michigan, William L. Clements Library, Ann Arbor
YU	Yale University, Sterling Memorial Library, New Haven, Connecticut

PREFACE

1. https://en.oxforddictionaries.com/definition/logistics.

2. See for example Waddell, *United States Army Logistics,* 1–3, 57–85.

3. Scott, *Military Dictionary,* 393; Halleck, *Elements,* 88.

4. Halleck to McClellan, December 19, 1861, *OR,* vol. 8, 449; Williams, ed., *Wild Life of the Army,* 256.

5. Gabel, *Railroad Generalship,* 2–4.

6. Luttwak, "Logistics and the Aristocratic Idea," 3–4.

7. Van Creveld, *Supplying War,* 2–3.

8. See for example the essays in Pryor, ed., *Logistics of Warfare,* including Guilmartin, "Logistics of Warfare at Sea," and Lazenby, "Logistics in Classical Greek Warfare," in addition to Erdkamp, *Hunger and the Sword*; Wheeler, "Logistics of the Cromwellian Conquest"; Crowell, "Logistics in the Madras Army"; Bachrach, "Military Logistics"; Harari, "Strategy and Supply."

9. Gibson, "Military Transports," 4; Fuller, "Study of Mobility," 266; Browning, *From Cape Charles to Cape Fear,* 167–99; Grimsley, *Hard Hand of War,* 162–63; Hess, *Civil War in the West,* 307–19.

10. Pratt, *Rise of Rail-Power,* x.

11. Ibid.

12. Ibid. iv

13. Van Creveld, *Supplying War,* 94–95, 102, 104–5; Pratt, *Rise of Rail-Power,* 56–57, 110–12.

14. Hess, *Civil War in the West,* 247, 317–19.

15. Sharpe, "Art of Supplying Armies," 45, 94; Furse, *Provisioning Armies in the Field,* 17.

1. THE LOGISTICAL HERITAGE

1. Lynn, "History of Logistics and Supplying War," 11–13, 20–22. The persistent flaw of Martin Van Creveld's pioneering study *Supplying War* is that he tends to see the history of logistics as a choice between methods of supply rather than as commanders adopting a multifaceted approach to the problem that mixed several different methods of feeding and moving armies. See pages 12–13, 19, 33–34.

2. Lazenby, "Logistics in Classical Greek Warfare," 10; Roth, *Logistics of the Roman Army,* 156, 189, 192–93, 197; Erdkamp, *Hunger and the Sword,* 55–56, 59–60.

3. Roth, *Logistics of the Roman Army,* 5; Erdkamp, *Hunger and the Sword,* 18, 46–47, 73, 82, 297–98.

4. Roth, *Logistics of the Roman Army,* 329–30; Lazenby, "Logistics in Classical Greek Warfare," 3–4.

5. Bachrach, "Military Logistics," 425, 439.

6. Runyan, "Naval Logistics," 79–84, 90, 92–93.

7. Harari, "Strategy and Supply," 312–14.

8. Ibid., 308–11, 314, 317–18, 321–23, 325–26.

9. Wheeler, "Logistics of the Cromwellian Conquest," 2–13.

10. Lynn, *Giant of the Grand Siècle,* 118, 129, 134–42; Lynn, "Food, Funds, and Fortresses," 140–41.

11. Bowler, "Logistics and Operations," 63–64; Bowler, *Logistics,* 6, 9, 239–41.

12. Bowler, *Logistics,* 65–66.

13. Ibid., 243, 247, 255, 259, 260, 263.

14. Spring, *With Zeal and With Bayonets,* 33–37, 41–42.

15. Syrett, *Shipping,* vii–viii, 183, 185, 190–91, 245, 248.

16. Ibid., 61, 77–78, 107, 109–10, 114–15, 245, 248–50.

17. Shy, "Logistical Crisis," 163–64, 166; Huston, *Logistics of Liberty,* 145–47; Carp, *To Starve the Army,* 5, 55–73, 77–98, 221; Bowler, "Logistics and Operations," 55–56, 59, 62.

18. Risch, *Quartermaster Support,* 1, 19, 21–22.

19. Huston, *Logistics of Liberty,* 27–63, 79–143, 163–218, 256–78; Spring, *With Zeal and With Bayonets,* 38, 42; Bowler, "Logistics and Operations," 70; Syrett, *Shipping,* 122, 124–26, 128.

20. Van Creveld, *Supplying War,* 35–36, 40–61; Moore, "Mobility and Strategy," 69, 77.

21. Greenhous, "Note on Western Logistics," 41–44; Risch, *Quartermaster Support,* 155, 162–63, 207, 230–33; Waddell, *United States Army Logistics,* 33, 42.

22. Crowell, "Logistics in the Madras Army," 1, 3, 20–23, 25.

23. Watson, *Jackson's Sword*, 228, 232, 234–35, 237, 243–44, 256, 261–62; Waddell, *United States Army Logistics*, 37–38, 50.

24. Risch, *Quartermaster Support*, 243–45.

25. Ibid., 258–59, 261, 262–263, 268.

26. Ibid., 269–71.

27. Ibid., 284, 287, 289, 291–92, 294; Johnson, *A Gallant Little Army*, 17, 36–37, 108–9, 120, 124; Scott, *Memoirs*, 2:419; Smith, *War with Mexico*, 1:493n and 2:38, 422n.

28. Risch, *Quartermaster Support*, 296.

29. Ibid., 306–9, 312; Waddell, *United States Army Logistics*, 53–54.

30. Pratt, *Rise of Rail-Power*, 1–3, 8–9, 27; Van Creveld, *Supplying War*, 82.

31. Delafield, *Art of War*, 63–64, 66–67; *Instruction for Field Artillery*, 61–62.

32. Delafield, *Art of War*, 58, 97–107.

33. Sweetman, "Military Transport," 81–82, 87, 90–91; Sweetman, *War and Administration*, 42–45, 50–52, 54–55.

34. Pratt, *Rise of Rail-Power*, 206–8, 210; Delafield, *Art of War*, 58.

35. Schneid, "A Well-Coordinated Affair," 395–98, 408, 410–12, 414; Schneid, *French-Piedmontese Campaign*, 43; Pratt, *Rise of Rail-Power*, 9.

36. Pratt, *Rise of Rail-Power*, 10–12; Schneid, *French-Piedmontese Campaign*, 50–52, 72–75; Schneid, "A Well-Coordinated Affair," 415–17, 419; Showalter, *Railroads and Rifles*, 48.

37. Showalter, *Railroads and Rifles*, 19, 21, 25, 27, 33–34, 36–37.

38. Ibid., 38–40, 44–46.

2. QUARTERMASTERS NORTH AND SOUTH

1. Report of Special Committee, C.S. Congress, January 29, 1862, *OR*, ser. 4, vol. 1, 884.

2. Ingalls to Meigs, September 28, 1863, *OR*, vol. 19, pt. 1, 100; Weigley, *Quartermaster General*, 204; Stewart Van Vliet to Stanton, September 27, 1862, Edwin McMasters Stanton Papers, LC.

3. Meigs to Stanton, November 18, 1862, *OR*, ser. 3, vol. 2, 789. For insight into the varied duties of the Civil War quartermaster, see Meigs to Stanton, November 8, 1865, *OR*, ser. 3, vol. 5, 213; Donaldson to Allen, March 8, 1865, *OR*, vol. 49, pt. 1, 870–71; Donaldson to Whipple, April 2, 1865, *OR*, vol. 49, pt. 2, 186.

4. Weigley, *Quartermaster General*, 216–17, 219, 223; Wilson, *Business of Civil War*, 35, 57–58; Lewis B. Parsons to Trumbull, June 30, 1864, Lyman Trumbull Correspondence, LC; *Report of the Quartermaster General*, 199; Risch, *Quartermaster Support*, 428, 430.

5. Risch, *Quartermaster Support*, 347, 390–93; draft of Metzgar to Quartermaster General, August 22, 1864, John J. Metzgar Papers, UNC.

6. Risch, *Quartermaster Support*, 332–33, 335–36; Weigley, *Quartermaster General*, 19, 30, 44, 52.

7. Weigley, *Quartermaster General*, 165, 214, 223.

8. Ibid., 229–31; Meigs to Stanton, November 18, 1862, *OR*, ser. 3, vol. 2, 789. For insight into the paperwork performed by quartermasters, see Taylor, "Supply for Tomorrow," 110.

9. Meigs to Stanton, November 18, 1862, *OR*, ser. 3, vol. 2, 789–90; Weigley, *Quartermaster General*, 224, 235.

10. General Orders No. 18, Headquarters, Middle Military Division, September 10, 1864, *OR*, vol. 43, pt. 2, 63.

11. Swords to Meigs, October 6, 1863, *OR*, vol. 52, pt. 1, 467; Weigley, *Quartermaster General*, 234–35; Gibson and Gibson, *Dictionary of Transports*, x.

12. Wilson, *Business of Civil War*, 2; Beaudoin, "Union Victory," 38. For information about the process of procuring quartermaster material, see Wilson, *Business of Civil War*, 108–15, 135, 138–39; Gates, *Agriculture and the Civil War*, 132–35; Swords to Meigs, October 6, 1863, *OR*, vol. 52, pt. 1, 468.

13. Rusling, "A Word for the Quartermaster's Department," 57–59.

14. Symonds, *Report of a Commissary* 70 71, Lewis B. Parsons to Trumbull, June 30, 1864, Lyman Trumbull Correspondence, LC; Taylor, "Supply for Tomorrow," 7, 9–10; Sheridan, *Personal Memoirs*, 1:127–128; Rusling, *Men and Things*, 166, 174.

15. Wilson, *Business of Civil War*, 60; Haupt, *Reminiscences*, 147.

16. Leib, *Nine Months*, 18, 20–24.

17. Circular, Headquarters, Army of the Potomac, March 10, 1863, *OR*, vol. 25, pt. 2, 563; Rosecrans to Meigs, March 8, 1863, *OR*, vol. 23, pt. 2, 119.

18. *Report of the Quartermaster General*, 199.

19. Alexander Bliss to mother, May 10, 1865, Bancroft-Bliss Family Papers, LC; Rusling, *Men and Things*, 348, 350.

20. Henry H. Howland to mother, March 6, 1862, Walter M. Howland Papers, DU; Baxter to Parsons, January 21, 1862, *OR*, vol. 8, 512.

21. LeDuc, *Recollections*, 123–24.

22. Rusling, *Men and Things*, 312, 322.

23. Sawtelle to Meigs, December 13, 1865, *OR*, vol. 53, 608.

24. Dana to Ord, January 22, 1864; Holabird to Stone, January 30, 1864, *OR*, vol. 34, pt. 2, 166, 185.

25. Rusling, *Men and Things*, 175; Warner, *Generals in Blue*, 3–4.

26. Allen to Meigs, July 1, 1865, *OR*, vol. 52, pt. 1, 691; Sherman to Allen, June 18, 1864, *OR*, vol. 38, pt. 4, 515; William T. Sherman to William Myers, November 4, 1865, William T. Sherman Letters, GLIAH; Rusling, *Men and Things*, 184, 189; Warner, *Generals in Blue*, 4.

27. Dodge to Rochester, July 8, 1862; Parsons to General, December 20, 1862, *OR*, vol. 17, pt. 2, 81, 441; Major and Fitch, *Supply of Sherman's Army*, 26; Warner, *Generals in Blue*, 127.

28. Meigs to Blair, August 28, 1861, *OR*, vol. 3, 464–65; Halleck to McClellan, December 6, 1861, *OR*, vol. 8, 409.

29. Clark to Meigs, September 26, 1863, *OR*, vol. 52, pt. 1, 453–54.

30. Bahde, ed., *Story of My Campaign*, 94; Meigs to Stanton, November 8, 1865, *OR*, ser. 3, vol. 5, 218; Leib, *Nine Months*, 63–69.

31. Leib, *Nine Months*, 24–26; Clubb to Anne, August 24, 1863, Henry Clubb Collection, UM. The perception of corruption could be as harmful to quartermasters as the reality. Stanton had the sense that the Cincinnati Depot was riddled with it but had to wait until just after the war ended before instituting a board to investigate. After six months of work the board came to the conclusion that nothing unusual was happening, frustrating Stanton enormously. See Brinkerhoff, *Recollections*, 177–78.

32. Parker, "William J. Kountz," 238–39, 241, 245, 247, 251–54.

33. Ingalls to Meigs, September 28, 1863, *OR*, vol. 19, pt. 1, 105; Alexander Bliss, "Narrative," Bancroft-Bliss Family Papers, LC.

34. Risch, *Quartermaster Support*, 346–47; Wilson, *Business of Civil War*, 189.

35. Parsons to Meigs, October 6, 1863, *OR*, vol. 52, pt. 1, 459; Lewis B. Parsons to Trumbull, June 29, 30, 1864, Lyman Trumbull Correspondence, LC; Pratt, "Lewis B. Parsons," 350–52; Schottenhamel, "Lewis Baldwin Parsons," 109, 111; Grant to Parsons, May 20, 1865, *OR*, vol. 47, pt. 3, 539.

36. Wilson, *Business of Civil War*, 1, 57.

37. Ibid., 191–92; Sherman to William Myers, November 4, 1865, William T. Sherman Letters, GLIAH; Ingalls to Meigs, September 28, 1863, *OR*, vol. 19, pt. 1, 100; Beaudoin, "Union Victory," 36–37; Weigley, *Quartermaster General*, 350.

38. Wilson, *Confederate Industry*, 4–6, 85, 88–89; Nichols, *Confederate Quartermaster*, 3–4.

39. Circulars, March 4, April 6, 1863, Headquarters, Wheeler's Cavalry Corps, box 130, Joseph Wheeler Family Papers, ADAH.

40. Ruffin, "Chapter of Confederate History," 109; Northrop to Benjamin, January 18, 1862, *OR*, ser. 4, vol. 1, 872.

41. Ruffin, "Chapter of Confederate History," 110; Northrop to Davis, April 21, 1878, in Rowland, ed., *Jefferson Davis*, 8:182.

42. Clark, *Railroads in the Civil War*, 224–26; Goff, *Confederate Supply*, 243, 251.

3. THE RIVER-BASED SYSTEM

1. Parsons to Meigs, October 15, 1865, *OR*, vol. 52, pt. 1, 708; Haites, Mak, and Walton, *Western River Transportation*, 12–13.

2. Saxon, *Father Mississippi*, 253–54.

3. Ibid., 257, 261, 263.

4. Hunter, *Steamboats*, 5, 12–13, 15, 24, 63, 106–7; Haites, Mak, and Walton, *Western River Transportation*, 48–49.

5. Hunter, *Steamboats*, 33; Haites, Mak, and Walton, *Western River Transportation*, 61.

6. Haites, Mak, and Walton, *Western River Transportation*, 59, 61, 69.

7. Ibid., 163.

8. Ibid., 108–9.

9. Hunter, *Steamboats*, 72, 76, 78, 81–82, 167.

10. Ibid., 100–101.

11. Ibid., 307–8.

12. Ibid., 311, 360–61.

13. Ibid., 362–63, 443, 446, 448; Haites, Mak, and Walton, *Western River Transportation*, 141.

14. Hunter, *Steamboats*, 317–20, 342–47, 381–82, 390, 663.

15. Sharpe, "Art of Supplying Armies," 63; Hunter, *Steamboats*, 568–69, 571–72, 574, 576, 579.

16. Hunter, *Steamboats*, 240.

17. Saxon, *Father Mississippi*, 249.

18. Ibid., 246–47; Hess, "Mississippi River and Secession," 188; Hunter, *Steamboats*, 490–91, 493.

19. Hunter, *Steamboats*, 218–19, 498; Haites, Mak, and Walton, *Western River Transportation*, 10–11, 120, 124–25, 127.

20. Sherman, *Memoirs*, 1:289; Scott to McClellan, May 3, 1861, *OR*, vol. 51, pt. 1, 369–70.

21. Mansfield to Totten, June 4 and 7, 1861; Totten memorandum, June 3, 1861, *OR*, vol. 52, pt. 1, 157–58, 160, 164–65; Haites, Mak, and Walton, *Western River Transportation*, 130–31. For differing

statistics on the number of steamers available, see Lee, "Siege of Vicksburg," 70, and Hunter, *Steamboats,* 664.

22. Hunter, *Steamboats,* 548–50; Parsons to Meigs, October 6, 1863, *OR,* vol. 52, pt. 1, 462.

23. Warner, *Generals in Blue,* 360–61.

24. Parsons to Meigs, October 15, 1865, *OR,* vol. 52, pt. 1, 704–5; Parsons to Allen, June 23, 1863, *OR,* ser. 3, vol. 3, 407.

25. Parsons to Allen, June 23, 1863, *OR,* ser. 3, vol. 3, 407; Halleck to McClellan, December 19, 1861, *OR,* vol. 8, 449; Parsons to Meigs, October 15, 1865, *OR,* vol. 52, pt. 1, 704–5.

26. Grant to McKeever, October 4, 1861, *OR,* vol. 3, 520; Foote to Meigs, January 4, 1862, *OR,* vol. 8, 488.

27. Winslow to Parsons, February 13, 1865, in Parsons, *Reports to the War Department,* 44.

28. Parsons to Meigs, October 6, 1863, *OR,* vol. 52, pt. 1, 462–64.

29. Ibid., 463–64.

30. Parsons to Allen, June 23, 1863, *OR,* ser. 3, vol. 3, 408–9; Parsons to Meigs, October 6, 1863, *OR,* vol. 52, pt. 1, 464; Special Orders No. 39, Headquarters, Armies of the United States, February 25, 1865, *OR,* vol. 46, pt. 2, 688.

31. Parsons to Meigs, October 15, 1865, *OR,* vol. 52, pt. 1, 705–6.

32. Ibid., 706.

33. Parsons to Meigs, October 6, 1863; Parsons to Meigs, October 15, 1865, *OR,* vol. 52, pt. 1, 462, 707.

34. Parsons to Meigs, October 15, 1865, *OR,* vol. 52, pt. 1, 707; Schottenhamel, "Lewis Baldwin Parsons," 113.

35. Schottenhamel, "Lewis Baldwin Parsons," 95, 97–99.

36. Parsons to Meigs, October 6, 1863; Parsons to Meigs, October 15, 1865, *OR,* vol. 52, pt. 1, 465, 707.

37. Parsons to Meigs, October 6, 1863, *OR,* vol. 52, pt. 1, 465; Schottenhamel, "Lewis Baldwin Parsons," 84; Warden and Company to Charles Parsons, June 1, 1863; A. Phillips to Charles Parsons, June 1, 5, 1863; C. Faris to Charles Parsons, June 4, 1863; and C. B. Greeley and John Head to Robert Allen, June 13, 1863, all in box 39, folder 7, Charles Parsons Papers, MHM; Joseph Walton to not stated, January 17, 1863, box 39, folders 3 and 4, Charles Parsons Papers, MHM.

38. Gaines, *Encyclopedia,* 163; invoice for *Thomas E. Tutt,* 1862, box 23, folder 15, Charles Parsons Papers, MHM. The *Thomas E. Tutt* met an untimely end. It was captured by Confederate cavalry at Cumberland City, Tennessee, on December 9, 1864, used to transport more than 3,000 Rebels over the Cumberland River, and then burned.

39. Pass number 41799, for John Montgomery and three men, September 9, 1862, box 23, folder 15, Charles Parsons Papers, MHM.

40. George W. Neare to A. C. Woolfolk, December 13, 1862, box 39, folders 3 and 4, Charles Parsons Papers, MHM; R. E. Clary to Robert Allen, June 16, 1863, box 39, folder 7, Charles Parsons Papers, MHM.

41. Grant to Allen, July 25, 1863, in Simon, ed., *Papers of Ulysses S. Grant,* 9:121, 121n; Grant to Meigs, August 10, 1863, in Simon, ed., *Papers of Ulysses S. Grant,* 9:162–63.

42. Alexander Bliss to mother, January 30, 1865, Bancroft-Bliss Family Papers, LC; Donaldson to Whipple, April 2, 1865, *OR,* vol. 49, pt. 2, 185.

43. Schottenhamel, "Lewis Baldwin Parsons," 144.

44. Ibid., 121.

45. "Contract for Transportation of Freight Between St. Louis and Memphis" and "Contract for all Government Transportation Between St. Louis and New Orleans," in Parsons, *Reports to the War Department*, 57–64.

46. Parsons to Meigs, October 15, 1865, *OR*, vol. 52, pt. 1, 707; Haites, Mak, and Walton, *Western River Transportation*, 162. Faced with the prospect of paying his own transportation to go home to Ohio on furlough from Vicksburg, Joseph P. Van Nest hesitated when he discovered it would cost an estimated $30. Van Nest to wife, July 29, 1863, Joseph P. Van Nest Letters, FHS.

47. Schottenhamel, "Lewis Baldwin Parsons," 102; Ulysses S. Grant to C. A. Reynolds, February 16, 1863, Ulysses S. Grant Letters, GLIAH; General Orders No. 61, Headquarters, Military Division of West Mississippi, October 11, 1864, *OR*, vol. 41, pt. 3, 775; Parsons to Canby, June 3, 1864, *OR*, vol. 34, pt. 4, 187; Reeder to Allen, February 20, 1863, *ORN*, vol. 24, 450.

48. Parsons to Meigs, October 6, 1863, *OR*, vol. 52, pt. 1, 464.

49. Grant to McKeever, October 9, 17, 1861, *OR*, vol. 3, 529, 536; Reeder to Allen, February 20, 1863, *ORN*, vol. 24, 450; Dudley, *Autobiography*, 44; Noble Walter Wood Diary, June 16, 19, 1863, UCB.

50. McGregor, *History of the Fifteenth Regiment*, 590, 593; "The Civil War Diary of Charles Henry Snedeker," June 27–30, 1864, AU; General Orders No. 52, Headquarters, Third Division, Fourth Corps, June 18, 1865, *OR*, vol. 49, pt. 2, 1009; Special Orders No. 125, Headquarters, First Division, Sixteenth Corps, September 2, 1864, *OR*, vol. 41, pt. 3, 27.

51. Hunter, *Steamboats*, 264–65, 267–69.

52. Hogan, ed., *General Reub Williams's Memories*, 94, 111.

53. Eaton, *Grant, Lincoln, and the Freedmen*, 133, 138.

54. Ibid., 139–40; invoice, October 10, 1863; C. M. Jarman to Charles Parsons, May 8, 1863, box 23, folder 15, Charles Parsons Papers, MHM.

55. J. W. McClurg to Charles Parsons, December 10, 1862, box 39, folders 3 and 4, Charles Parsons Papers, MHM.

56. Hunter, *Steamboats*, 240–47; General Orders No. 10, Headquarters, Department of the Mississippi, March 28, 1862, *OR*, vol. 8, 834; General Orders No. 4, Headquarters, Military Division of the Mississippi, February 6, 1864, *OR*, vol. 32, pt. 2, 346–47; Gibson, "Military Transports," 11, 16.

57. Grant to Scott, March 18, 1865, in Simon, ed., *Papers of Ulysses S. Grant,* 17:392–393; Josyph, ed., *Wounded River,* 52.

58. James F. Luker certificate, December 23, 1863, box 23, folder 15, Charles Parsons Papers, MHM; Cobb to Parsons, September 2, 1863, *OR*, vol. 52, pt. 1, 466–67; Foote to Sanford, January 30, 1862, *OR*, vol. 8, 537; Curtis to Rosecrans, June 7, 1864, *OR*, vol. 34, pt. 4, 259.

59. Henry W. Tisdale Dairy, June 8, 1863, BPL.

60. "Instructions to Officers in Charge of Troops on Board Transports," November 15, 1863, Zebediah W. Marsh Papers, MHM.

61. Slack to father and mother, January 31, 1863, Albert L. Slack Letters, EU; Charles Parsons to Capt. Metcalfe, June 3, 1863, box 39, folder 7, Charles Parsons Papers, MHM; Kent to Dornblaser, November 6, 1864, *OR*, vol. 41, pt. 4, 450; Rogers to Read, April 16, 1864, *OR*, vol. 34, pt. 1, 386.

62. Shepard to parents, brothers, and sisters, August 8, 1863, Irwin Shepard Papers, BHL-UM; Charles J. Obriham to Lavinia, January 6, 1865, June and Gilbert Krueger Civil War Letters, CU.

63. Henry W. Tisdale Diary, June 9–11, 18, 1863, BPL.

64. Hogan, ed., *General Reub Williams's Memories,* 86–89.

65. Ibid., 90.

66. Bering and Montgomery, *History of the Forty-Eighth Ohio,* 69–70; Lougheed to Jennie, December 20, 1862, Samuel D. Lougheed Papers, UW; Throne, ed., *Civil War Diary,* 112–14; Porter to Canby, June 9, 1864, *OR,* vol. 34, pt. 4, 275.

67. General Orders No. 52, Headquarters, Third Division, Fourth Corps, June 18, 1865, *OR,* vol. 49, pt. 2, 1009–10; Timothy Phillips Diaries, June 11, July 12, 26, 1863, WHS; Hoadley to cousin, May 29, 1863, Robert Bruce Hoadley Papers, DU; Anonymous Civil War Diary, June 13, 1863, LSU; Hogan, ed., *General Reub Williams's Memories,* 97.

68. Hunter, *Steamboats,* 272–73, 287, 291, 521, 539, 542–43, 545. See also Gould, *Fifty Years on the Mississippi,* 431–33, 438.

69. Reid to Sherman, November 17, 1863, *OR,* vol. 31, pt. 3, 180; *St. Louis Daily Missouri Democrat,* October 28, 1862.

70. Meredith to Morton, January 27, 1865, *OR,* vol. 49, pt. 1, 600; Slack to Kuhn, September 11, 1864, *OR,* vol. 41, pt. 3, 152–53.

71. Shepard to parents, brothers, and sisters, August 8, 1863, Irwin Shepard Papers, BHL-UM; *Story of the Fifty-Fifth,* 44–47.

72. I. I. Drake to Charles Parsons, January 18, 1863, box 39, folders 3 and 4, Charles Parsons Papers, MHM; "Wreck of the *James Watson,*" 213, 227–28; diary entry, September 28, 1863, Wayne Johnson Jacobs Diaries and Lists, LSU.

73. Shepard to parents, brothers, and sisters, August 8, 1863, Irwin Shepard Papers, BHL-UM; diary entries, September 28–29, 1863, and October 1–3, 1863, Wayne Johnson Jacobs Diaries and Lists, LSU; "List of Boats destroyed on the Mississippi River and its tributaries from May 1st 1861 to the surrender of Genl. Kirby Smith's Army and the cessation of hostilities, June 2d 1865," oversize folder 7, Lewis Baldwin Parsons Papers, ALPL; E. M. Schofield to Lewis B. Parsons, December 29, 1862, box 39, folders 3 and 4, Charles Parsons Papers, MHM; Hunter, *Steamboats,* 250–56.

74. Lee to Welles, January 18, 1865, *ORN,* vol. 26, 769; Livingston to Richmond, February 4, 1864, *OR,* vol. 34, pt. 2, 241–42.

75. A. C. Woolfolk to Charles Parsons, January 5, 1863; Charles Parsons to Spencer Ball, January 6, 1863; Spencer Ball to Charles Parsons, January 9, 12, 1863; and Lysander J. Ball to Charles Parsons, January 12, 1863, all in folders 3 and 4, box 39, Charles Parsons Papers, MHM.

76. McAlester memorandum, October 4, 1864, *OR,* vol. 41, pt. 3, 599–600.

77. Merrick, *Old Times,* 206–10.

78. Little and Maxwell, *History of Lumsden's Battery,* 6–7.

79. Parsons to Meigs, October 15, 1865, *OR,* vol. 52, pt. 1, 706, 708–9.

80. "List of Boats destroyed on the Mississippi River and its tributaries from May 1st 1861 to the surrender of Genl. Kirby Smith's Army and the cessation of hostilities, June 2d 1865," oversize folder 7, Lewis Baldwin Parsons Papers, ALPL; William G. Christie to brother, August 20, 1863, Christie Family Letters, MHS; Dudley, *Autobiography,* 80–81.

81. "List of Boats destroyed on the Mississippi River and its tributaries from May 1st 1861 to the surrender of Genl. Kirby Smith's Army and the cessation of hostilities, June 2d 1865," oversize folder 7, Lewis Baldwin Parsons Papers, ALPL; Parsons to Meigs, October 15, 1865, *OR,* vol. 52, pt. 1, 714. For a vivid description of the inside of a sunken riverboat only a month after it settled on the river bottom, see Fayette Clapp Diary, May 24, 1863, SHSM-RCC.

82. Aten, *History of the Eighty-Fifth,* 70; Henry W. Tisdale Diary, June 12, 1863, BPL; Stevens, *History of the Fiftieth Regiment,* 222.

83. Parsons to Allen, June 23, 1863: General Orders No. 22 1/2, U.S. Quartermaster Department, December 9, 1863, *OR,* ser. 3, vol. 3, 408, 1161; Schottenhamel, "Lewis Baldwin Parsons," 198, 200–201, 203, 207.

84. Parsons to Meigs, October 6, 1863, *OR,* vol. 52, pt. 1, 465; Gibson and Gibson, *Dictionary of Transports,* xi; Schottenhamel, "Lewis Baldwin Parsons," 270.

85. Schottenhamel, "Lewis Baldwin Parsons," 358–78; Brayman to not stated, May 2, 1864, *OR,* vol. 32, pt. 1, 513.

86. Schottenhamel, "Lewis Baldwin Parsons," 151–55; Parsons to Meigs, October 15, 1865, *OR,* vol. 52, pt. 1, 714–15; General Orders No. 17, Quartermaster General's Office, March 16, 1865, *Report of the Quartermaster General,* 150.

87. Saxon, *Father Mississippi,* 250; Haites, Mak, and Walton, *Western River Transportation,* 123, 130–31.

88. Gaines, *Encyclopedia,* 1–193.

89. Bliss to mother, December 30, 1861, Robert Lewis Bliss Papers, ADAH; Pettus to wife, February 16, 1862, Edmund Winston Pettus Family Papers, ADAH; diary, March 24, 26, May 8–11, 1862, William Lewis Roberts Papers, ADAH; Christopher C. Pearson to cousin, June 10, 1862, Pearson and Danielly Family Papers, ADAH.

90. Goodloe, *Confederate Echoes,* 160–62.

91. Brown, ed. *Journey to Pleasant Hill,* 215. Brief references to steamboats under Confederate employment can be found in Martin L. Smith telegram to Ruggles, October 6, 1862, and Thomas H. Rosser telegram to Ruggles, June 3, 1862, both in Daniel Ruggles Papers, DU; Nichols, *Confederate Quartermaster,* 10–11; Gray to Polk, October 16, 1861, *OR,* vol. 3, 720–21; Reed to Key, November 27, 1862, *OR,* vol. 17, pt. 2, 764; Johnson to Jones, January 21, 1863; Ferguson to Pemberton, February 3, 1863; Reed to Johnston, February 12, 1863; Ferguson to [Stevenson], April 18, 1863; Pemberton to Featherston, April 20, 1863, *OR,* vol. 24, pt. 3, 593, 615, 624, 762, 771; Jones to Bullock, April 16, 1865, *OR,* vol. 49, pt. 2, 1245.

92. Claud McGiven to M. M. Kimmel, July 21, 1862, Robert A. Smith Papers, MDAH.

93. Gaines, *Encyclopedia,* 1–193.

94. Parsons to Meigs, October 15, 1865, *OR,* vol. 52, pt. 1, 714; "List of steamers and other vessels at Mobile, and on the Mississippi river and tributaries, belonging to the United States, June 30, 1865," *Report of the Quartermaster General,* 125.

4. THE RAIL-BASED SYSTEM

1. Stover, *American Railroads,* 2–3, 12–14.

2. Ibid., 16, 19–20.

3. Ibid., 26, 28–30; Meyer, *History of Transportation,* 502; Black, *Railroads of the Confederacy,* 42–45.

4. Stover, *American Railroads,* 36, 43.

5. Ibid., 35–36.

6. Ibid., 24, 43; Weber, *Northern Railroads,* 8.

7. Weber, *Northern Railroads,* 55, 72, 74, 98; Stover, *American Railroads,* 51.

8. Summers, *Baltimore and Ohio*, 15, 17–19, 43–44.

9. Cotterill, "Louisville and Nashville," 700–701; Stover, *American Railroads*, 42.

10. Turner, *Victory Rode the Rails*, 30–33; Black, *Railroads of the Confederacy*, 4, 294; Pickenpaugh, *Rescue by Rail*, 19–20.

11. Thomas, *Iron Way*, 28, 215; Gabel, *Rails to Oblivion*, 2.

12. Asa Whitney quoted in Thomas, *Iron Way*, 1; "Railroads," Albert N. Ames Papers, NYSL.

13. Thomas, *Iron Way*, 9–10; "Distances and Times By Railroad from New York to the following places," in diary, 1864, William Penn Lloyd Diary and Notebooks, UNC; diary, July 15, 1863, Henry Boydon Blood Papers, LC.

14. Haupt to Watson, August 23, 1862, *OR*, vol. 12, pt. 3, 635; Black, *Railroads of the Confederacy*, 16–17; Williams, ed., *Wild Life of the Army*, 256; Wright to McCallum, May 20, 1865, *OR*, ser. 3, vol. 5, 34.

15. Black, *Railroads of the Confederacy*, 24, 32; Weber, *Northern Railroads*, 12.

16. Black, *Railroads of the Confederacy*, 15; Weber, *Northern Railroads*, 10, 56; Stover, *American Railroads*, 25, 44.

17. Weber, *Northern Railroads*, 9, 19–11; Black, *Railroads of the Confederacy*, 18–19.

18. Turner, *Victory Rode the Rails*, 40; "Distances and Times By Railroad from New York to the following places," in diary, 1864, William Penn Lloyd Diary and Notebooks, UNC; Stover, *American Railroads*, 48.

19. Black, *Railroads of the Confederacy*, 17, 31–32; Balloch to wife, October 15, 1863, George Williamson Balloch Papers, DU

20. Black, *Railroads of the Confederacy*, 13–14; Weber, *Northern Railroads*, 6–7, 63–64; Stover, *American Railroads*, 21.

21. Black, *Railroads of the Confederacy*, 14.

22. Smith to Haupt, October 11, [1862], *OR*, vol. 19, pt. 2, 411–12; Lash, "Joseph E. Johnston," 9; *History of the Fourth Maine Battery*, 13.

23. McCallum to Meigs, May 26, 1866, *OR*, ser. 3, vol. 5, 982.

24. Scott to Stanton, October 4, 1863, *OR*, vol. 29, pt. 1, 188–89.

25. Haupt, *Reminiscences*, 148.

26. Adolph Engelmann to Mina, September 25, 1862, Engelmann-Kircher Collection, ALPL; Howard to mother, October 11, 1863, Charles Henry Howard Collection, BC; Edward C. Dale to son, August 7, 1864, Dale-Holt-Hensley Family Papers, MHM; Quint, *Record*, 196; Sherman, *Memoirs*, 1:341.

27. Black, *Railroads of the Confederacy*, 21–22; McPherson to Logan, April 2, 1864, *OR*, vol. 32, pt. 3, 229; Cotterill, "Louisville and Nashville," 711.

28. Thomas B. House to Quintard, July 4, 1895, Charles Todd Quintard Papers, DU; Haupt, *Reminiscences*, 296.

29. Meyer, *History of Transportation*, 570, 577–79; Black, *Railroads of the Confederacy*, 35–36, 39.

30. Risch, *Quartermaster Support*, 363–64.

31. Ibid., 365; Clark, *Railroads in the Civil War*, 35–36, 38.

32. Clark, *Railroads in the Civil War*, 36; Schottenhamel, *Lewis Baldwin Parsons*, 66. An unusual case of delayed compensation occurred for the Illinois Central Railroad, which hauled more than 43,000 passengers and nearly 12 million pounds of freight for the government from April 24, 1861, to December 31, 1862. Parsons denied close to $5,000 from its bill of $130,061, and paperwork problems caused the bill not to be fully paid until 1865. Schottenhamel, *Lewis Baldwin Parsons*, 69–76, 81.

33. Parsons to Meigs, October 15, 1865, *OR*, vol. 52, pt. 1, 715; *Report of the Quartermaster General*, 21.

34. Parsons to Meigs, October 6, 1863, *OR*, vol. 52, pt. 1, 460.

35. Stover, *American Railroads*, 31; Black, *Railroads of the Confederacy*, 37; Thomas, *Iron Way*, 219; Schottenhamel, "Lewis Baldwin Parsons," 152–53.

36. Boughton to Friends at Home, June 25, 1863, Clement Abner Boughton Papers, WCL-UM; Weber, *Northern Railroads*, 61–62, 220–21.

37. Weber, *Northern Railroads*, 67–68, 221.

38. Ibid., 221–22.

39. Herman Haupt to Montgomery Meigs, November 11, 1862, Herman Haupt Letter Book, Lewis Muhlenberg Haupt Family Papers, LC; Gardner, "First Kansas Battery," 265; Schottenhamel, "Lewis Baldwin Parsons," 67. A rare case of a soldier (a quartermaster officer) who had the opportunity to ride in a sleeping car during the war can be found in Sawin to wife, July 31, 1863, George Sawin Papers, CHM. "You could hardly tell that you was on a rail road Car, so smoothly it glided along," he wrote.

40. Goodman to Pemberton, February 14, 1863, *OR*, vol. 24, pt. 3, 628; General Orders No. 214, Department of the Missouri, November 29, 1864, *OR*, vol. 41, pt. 4, 714.

41. Herman Haupt to Montgomery Meigs, November 11, 1862, Herman Haupt Letter Book, Lewis Muhlenberg Haupt Family Papers, LC.

42. Herman Haupt to J. H. Devereux, February 10, 1863, Herman Haupt Letter Book, Lewis Muhlenberg Haupt Family Papers, LC.

43. C. M. Stein to Herman Haupt, December 24, 1862, and Herman Haupt to P. H. Watson, February 2, 1863, both in Herman Haupt Letter Book, Lewis Muhlenberg Haupt Family Papers, LC.

44. Stover, *American Railroads*, 40.

45. Devereux to Ingalls, January 14, 1864; McCrikett to Williams, April 18, 1864, *OR*, vol. 33, 378, 899.

46. Devereux to Ingalls, January 14, 1864, *OR*, vol. 33, 377–78.

47. Circular No. 4, Headquarters, Fifth Corps, January 18, 1864, *OR*, vol. 33, 390–91.

48. Stover, *American Railroads*, 45; Julius E. Thomas Civil War Diary, May 25, 1864, UTK; Bliss to mother November 9, 1862, Robert Lewis Bliss Papers, ADAH.

49. Henry H. Belfield to James H. Trowbridge, July 25, 1864, Henry H. Belfield and Belfield Family Papers, UC; Weber, *Northern Railroads*, 225–28; Turner, *Victory Rode the Rails*, 297–309.

50. Risch, *Quartermaster Supply*, 362, 395.

51. Weber, *Northern Railroads*, 135; Pickenpaugh, *Rescue by Rail*, 20.

52. Weber, *Northern Railroads*, 99; McCallum to Meigs, May 26, 1866, *OR*, ser. 3, vol. 5, 976–77.

53. Stanton to Vanderbilt, November 20, 1863, *OR*, ser. 3, vol. 3, 1083.

54. Summers, *Baltimore and Ohio*, 203–5; Garrett to Stanton, September 7, 1862, *OR*, vol. 19, pt. 2, 208–9; Smith to McCallum, September 25, 1863, *OR*, vol. 29, pt. 1, 158; Ingalls to Rawlins, May 24, 1865, in Simon, ed., *Papers of Ulysses S. Grant*, 15:485.

55. Cotterill, "Louisville and Nashville," 708, 713–14; Fitch, *Annals of the Army of the Cumberland*, 268.

56. Turner, *Victory Rode the Rails*, 311; Weber, *Northern Railroads*, 5, 59–60, 71, 74.

57. Weber, *Northern Railroads*, 44–46.

58. Parsons to Meigs, October 15, 1865, *OR*, vol. 52, pt. 1, 714–15.

59. McCallum to Meigs, May 26, 1866, *OR*, ser. 3, vol. 5, 974; Weber, *Northern Railroads*, 137.

60. Wright to McCallum, April 24, 1866; McCallum to Meigs, May 26, 1866, *OR*, ser. 3, vol. 5, 968; 977; Weber, *Northern Railroads*, 192–93.

61. McCallum to Meigs, May 26, 1866, *OR*, ser. 3, vol. 5, 1000.

62. Ibid.

63. Ibid., 1003–4; Army, *Engineering Victory*, 133–44.

64. McCallum to Meigs, May 26, 1866, *OR*, ser. 3, vol. 5, 1000–1001, 1005.

65. Stevens to McCallum, [July 1, 1865], *OR*, ser. 3, vol. 5, 85; Haupt, *Reminiscences*, 294; Lee to Smith, September 24, 1862, *OR*, vol. 19, pt. 2, 625.

66. J. H. Devereux to W. W. Beckwith, February 3, 1864, W. W. Beckwith Correspondence, LC; Haskell and Barker to Parsons, December 29, 1862, box 39, folders 3 and 4, Charles Parsons Papers, MHM; Schottenhamel, "Lewis Baldwin Parsons," 61–65; McCallum to Meigs, May 26, 1866, *OR*, ser. 3, vol. 5, 992.

67. Parsons to Meigs, October 6, 1863, *OR*, vol. 52, pt. 1, 461.

68. Herman Haupt to Daniel McCallum, April 29, 1863, Herman Haupt Letter Book, Lewis Muhlenberg Haupt Family Papers, LC; McCallum to Meigs, May 26, 1866, *OR*, ser. 3, vol. 5, 996–98.

69. J. H. Devereux to W. W. Beckwith, February 3, 8, 1864, W. W. Beckwith Correspondence, LC.

70. Stevens to McCallum, [July 1, 1865], *OR*, ser. 3, vol. 5, 87–88; McPherson to Halleck, August 24, 1862, *OR*, vol. 17, pt. 2, 185.

71. Wright to McCallum, April 24, 1866, *OR*, ser. 3, vol. 5, 968.

72. Crane to Meigs, September 1, 1864, *OR*, vol. 52, pt. 1, 613–14; McCallum to Meigs, May 26, 1866, *OR*, ser. 3, vol. 5, 979–80, 991, 993; Stevens to McCallum, [July 1, 1865], *OR*, ser. 3, vol. 5, 87.

73. Ingalls to Rawlins, May 24, 1865; Rawlins to Hancock, May 30, 1865; Emory to King, July 7, 1865, *OR*, vol. 46, pt. 3, 1203, 1239, 1312; Parsons to Meigs, October 15, 1865, *OR*, vol. 52, pt. 1, 713.

74. Clark, *Railroads in the Civil War*, 63; Weigley, *Quartermaster General*, 331; McCallum to Meigs, May 26, 1866, *OR*, ser. 3, vol. 5, 999, 1004.

75. Wilson to Winslow, June 2, 1865; Wilson to Thomas, June 4, 1865; Thomas to Whipple, June 10, 1865, *OR*, vol. 49, pt. 2, 950, 955, 976–77.

76. Grant to Meade, April 20, 1865; Dodamead to Meade, April 24, 1865; Meigs to Halleck, May 3, 1865; Peebles to Halleck, May 26, 1865, *OR*, vol. 46, pt. 3, 849, 917, 1074, 1217.

77. Weber, *Northern Railroads*, 222–23.

78. Clark, *Railroads in the Civil War*, 72; Amasa Stone Jr. to Stanton, November 4, December 10, 1863, Edwin McMasters Stanton Papers, LC.

79. Clark, *Railroads in the Civil War*, 62.

80. Wright to McCallum, May 20, 1865, *OR*, ser. 3, vol. 5, 37.

81. Meigs to Stanton, November 8, 1865, *OR*, ser. 3, vol. 5, 214.

82. Report of Special Committee, Confederate Congress, January 19, 1862, *OR*, ser. 4, vol. 1, 885.

83. Cooper to Bragg, July 10, 1862, *OR*, vol. 17, pt. 2, 644. Some historians have stated that the Confederate government actually seized a line or two temporarily, but they really are referring only to quartermaster officers being able to talk the lines into setting aside private business for a few days in favor of government business. That did not constitute the taking and operation of the rolling stock by army officials. For example, see Moore, *Confederate Commissary General*, 249–50.

84. Davis to Bragg, March 20, 1863, and Davis to Letcher, March 25, 1863, in Rowland, ed., *Jefferson Davis*, 5:453–54; Goff, *Confederate Supply*, 215.

85. Northrop to Benjamin, January 18, 1862, *OR*, ser. 4, vol. 1, 872; Northrop to Breckinridge, February 9, 1865, *OR*, vol. 46, pt. 2, 1213.

86. Black, *Railroads of the Confederacy*, 65, 107–10, 121–22, 164, 167; Turner, *Victory Rode the Rails*, 245–46; Pickenpaugh, *Rescue by Rail*, 24–25; Randolph to Lee, November 14, 1862, *OR*, vol. 19, pt. 2, 717; Gabel, *Rails to Oblivion*, 7.

87. Black, *Railroads of the Confederacy*, 80–82, 104–5.

88. Black, *Railroads of the Confederacy*, 110–12. A railroad executive had suggested a through freight schedule to link New Orleans with Richmond early in the war, but the Confederate government was not interested. See Ruffin, "Chapter of Confederate History," 109.

89. Black, *Railroads of the Confederacy*, 114, 119–20.

90. Ibid., 172, 218; Rives to Meriwether, December 5, 1863, *OR*, vol. 31, pt. 3, 787.

91. Hardee to Ives, December 24, 1863, *OR*, vol. 31, pt. 3, 860.

92. Report of Special Committee, Confederate Congress, January 19, 1862, *OR*, ser. 4, vol. 1, 885.

93. [Bragg] to Cooper, June 26, 1862; Randolph to Bragg, June 30, 1862; Jordan to Tate, July 4, 1862, *OR*, vol. 17, pt. 2, 624, 629, 637; Black, *Railroads of the Confederacy*, 148–59; Turner, *Victory Rode the Rails*, 237–39.

94. Turner, *Victory Rode the Rails*, 234–37; Morehead to [Ruffin], December 4, 1861, and Ashe to [Ruffin], February 8, 1862, in Hamilton, ed., *Papers of Thomas Ruffin*, 3:200–201, 213.

95. Seddon to Vance, January 31, 1865, *OR*, vol. 46, pt. 2, 1166–67; Goff, *Confederate Supply*, 225–26; Black, *Railroads of the Confederacy*, 227–29. Efforts to widen the gauge of the Piedmont Railroad had been instituted as early as November 1863, with no success. See Harvie to Ruffin, November 28, 1863, in Hamilton, ed., *Papers of Thomas Ruffin*, 3:346–47.

96. Taylor, *Destruction and Reconstruction*, 247–48; Daniel to Seddon, August 1, 1863, *OR*, vol. 51, pt. 2, 747; Goodman to Pemberton, February 14, 1863, *OR*, vol. 17, pt. 3, 628; St. John to Davis, July 14, 1873, in Rowland, ed., *Jefferson Davis*, 7:353.

97. Jewett, ed., *Rise and Fall*, 59, 97.

98. Mallet, "Work of the Ordnance Bureau," 13–14.

99. Ashe to [Ruffin], December 8, 1861, in Hamilton, ed., *Papers of Thomas Ruffin*, 3:203; Fleece to Smith, January 2, 1862, *OR*, vol. 7, 818.

100. Fleece to Smith, January 2, 1862, *OR*, vol. 7, 818.

101. Wallace to Kirby Smith, November 17, 1862, *OR*, vol. 20, pt. 2, 406.

102. Black, *Railroads of the Confederacy*, 126–27.

103. Daniel Harris Reynolds Diary, January 13, 1863, UAF; Wright to McCallum, May 20, 1865, *OR*, ser. 3, vol. 5, 34–35.

104. Hughes, ed., *Civil War Memoir*, 101; Black, *Railroads of the Confederacy*, 217–18.

105. Lash, "Joseph E. Johnston," 11, 27; McCardle to Davis, August 26, 1878, in Rowland, ed., *Jefferson Davis*, 8:261.

106. Clark, *Railroads in the Civil War*, 39–40, 72; French to Northrop, January 12, 1864, *OR*, vol. 46, pt. 2, 1223, 1225.

107. Rowan to Johnston, April 10, 1864, quoted in Ritter, "Sketches of the Third Maryland Artillery," 436; Loring to Benjamin S. Ewell, December 17, 1863, William Wing Loring Letter Book, UF.

108. F. Molloy to Ruggles, [June] 1, 1862; E. D. Frost to Ruggles, June 1, 1862; B. Desha Harman to Ruggles, June 1, 1862; and W. Goodman to Ruggles, June 9, 1862, all in Daniel Ruggles Papers, DU.

109. Goodloe, *Confederate Echoes*, 163; Stiles, *Four Years*, 45; Hughes, ed., *Civil War Memoir*, 101.

110. Diary, December 31, 1863–January 6, 1864, G.W.F. Harper Papers, UNC.

111. Bradford Nichol Memoir, 215, TSLA.

112. Black, *Railroads of the Confederacy,* 294.

113. Ibid., 64–65, 172; Turner, *Victory Rode the Rails,* 244; Clark, *Railroads in the Civil War,* 27, 40, 73, 219.

114. Black, *Railroads of the Confederacy,* 295; Stover, *American Railroads,* 55, 59–60.

5. THE COASTAL SHIPPING SYSTEM

1. Albion, *Square-Riggers,* 49.

2. Haites, Mak, and Walton, *Western River Transportation,* 5, 6n; Albion, *Square-Riggers,* 50, 253–56.

3. Albion, *Square-Riggers,* 80, 98, 130, 274, 286–95, 299–300, 326–27.

4. Ibid., 317; Martin, *Standard,* 256–57

5. Wise to Meigs, August 31, 1865, *OR,* ser. 3, vol. 5, 289.

6. Gibson and Gibson, *Dictionary of Transports,* x–xi; Wise to Meigs, August 31, 1865, *OR,* ser. 3, vol. 5, 289.

7. Risch, *Quartermaster Support,* 368–69, 372; *Report of the Quartermaster General,* 19.

8. Risch, *Quartermaster Support,* 372; *Report of the Quartermaster General,* 19.

9. Wise to Meigs, August 31, 1865, *OR,* ser. 3, vol. 5, 290; Risch, *Quartermaster Support,* 372, 415.

10. Gibson and Gibson, *Dictionary of Transports,* viii, xx.

11. Weigley, *Quartermaster General,* 245–47.

12. Clarke to Williams, February 1, 1863, *OR,* vol. 11, pt. 1, 175.

13. Meigs to Ingalls, July 12, 1862; Meigs to Tompkins, August 12, 1862, *OR,* vol. 11, pt. 3, 318, 371–72.

14. Meigs to Wise, April 16, 1864, *OR,* vol. 33, 886.

15. Wise to Meigs, April 19, 1864, *OR,* vol. 33, 915.

16. Ingalls to Meigs, July 28, 1864, *OR,* vol. 40, pt. 3, 555; Halleck to Banks, January 28, 1864, *OR,* vol. 34, pt. 2, 171; Meigs to Foster, July 28, 1864, *OR,* vol. 35, pt. 2, 196.

17. Meigs to Foster, July 28, 1864, *OR,* vol. 35, pt. 2, 196; Herman Haupt to T. E. Hall, May 5, 1863, Herman Haupt Letter Book, Lewis Muhlenberg Haupt Family Papers, LC.

18. Wise to Meigs, August 31, 1865, *OR,* ser. 3, vol. 5, 287–88; Grant to Stanton, July 22, 1865, *OR,* vol. 34, pt. 1, 44.

19. Ingalls to Rucker, March 20, 1865, *OR,* vol. 46, pt. 3, 52; Meigs to Halleck, December 20, 1862, *OR,* vol. 21, 868; Butler to Farragut, October 25, 1862, *OR,* vol. 53, 540–41.

20. Clark, *One Hundred and Sixteenth,* 50–51; McGregor, *History of the Fifteenth Regiment,* 187; Edwards to Maria, June 4, 1863, Marianne Edwards Letters, LSU.

21. Fessenden to parents, January 23, 1863, Anson D. Fessenden Papers, LSU.

22. McGregor, *History of the Fifteenth Regiment,* 162, 164, 166; Beecher, *History of the First Light Battery,* 1:323, 325.

23. Stevens, *History of the Fiftieth Regiment,* 43–44, 47, 49, 51–52; Irwin, *History of the Nineteenth Army Corps,* 57.

24. Stevens, *History of the Fiftieth Regiment,* 15–16, 18, 22.

25. Holbrook, *Narrative,* 2–4.

26. McGregor, *History of the Fifteenth Regiment,* 194–95; Keyes to sister, November 29, 1862, Charles L. Keyes Letters, LSU; Peter Eltinge to father, December 4, 1862, and sister, December 7,

1862, Eltinge-Lord Family Papers, DU; Cox, *Military Reminiscences*, 2:399–400; diary, January 7, 1865, Montgomery C. Meigs Papers, LC.

27. Wise to Meigs, August 31, 1865, *OR*, ser. 3, vol. 5, 290.

28. Beecher, *History of the First Light Battery*, 1:322; Crowell, "Logistics in the Madras Army," 3, 20.

29. Miller to wife, March 19, 1865, Monroe Joshua Miller Papers, MHM; *Twenty-Fifth Regiment Connecticut*, 12–14; Evans to mother, March 5, 1862, Simeon A. Evans Letters, LSU; Solomon Nelson Journal, December 10–11, 16, 27, 1862, LSU; Fuller to Shaffer, June 21, 1864, *OR*, vol. 40, pt. 2, 289; diary, March 8, 1863, Anson D. Fessenden Papers, LSU.

30. *Twenty-Fifth Regiment Connecticut*, 57–58; McGregor, *History of the Fifteenth Regiment*, 197; Moors, *History of the Fifty-Second Regiment*, 25; Beecher, *History of the First Light Battery*, 1:324; Blake, *Succinct History*, 48.

31. McGregor, *History of the Fifteenth Regiment*, 168; Stevens, *History of the Fiftieth Regiment*, 23, 26; Moors, *History of the Fifty-Second Regiment*, 18–19, 24, 26–27; Noyes, ed., *Jesse Macy*, 64–65.

32. Fessenden to parents, January 23, 1863, Anson D. Fessenden Papers, LSU; Stevens, *History of the Fiftieth Regiment*, 24; Evans to mother, March 5, 1862, Simeon A. Evans Letters, LSU; Blake, *Succinct History*, 45, 47–48.

33. Stevens to Molly, February 1, 1862 [1863], William H. Stevens Letters, UNC; Watkins to John, March 1, 1865, John Watkins Papers, UTK.

34. Record of events, Company G, 128th New York, *SOR*, pt. 2, vol. 46, 676; Brett, ed., *Letters and Diary*, 24.

35. Moors, *History of the Fifty-Second Regiment*, 22–23, 26; Solomon Nelson Journal, January 10, 1863, LSU; Fessenden to parents, January 23, 1863, Anson D. Fessenden Papers. LSU.

36. Clark, *One Hundred and Sixteenth*, 189–90; William Shelly Diary, February 12, 1863, LSU.

37. Hecht, ed., *Echoes*, 182–83.

38. Brett, ed., *Letters and Diary*, 20.

39. Ibid., 18; Wise to Meigs, August 31, 1865, *OR*, ser. 3, vol. 5, 290–91.

40. Cox, *Military Reminiscences*, 2:401.

41. Delafield, *Art of War*, 63–64, 66–67.

42. Stevens to Molly, February 3, 1863, William H. Stevens Letters, UNC; Beecher, *History of the First Light Battery*, 1:68, 71, 73–74, 77, 83.

43. Royce to Carter, January 1, 1865, *OR*, vol. 42, pt. 1, 987; Stevens to Molly, February 1, 1862 [1863], William H. Stevens Letters, UNC.

44. Watkins to John, March 1, 1865, John Watkins Papers, UTK; *Military Record*, 194.

45. Chase, *Battery F*, 26.

46. Hearn, *When the Devil Came Down to Dixie*, 153; Farragut to Butler, May 7, 1862, *OR*, vol. 53, 525; Smith to brother, June 30, 1862, William H. Smith Letters, LSU.

47. Brett, ed., *Letters and Diary*, 18; father to Whitney, April 12, 1863, Henry Mitchell Whitney Correspondence, MassHS; Hanaburgh, *History of the One Hundred and Twenty-Eighth Regiment*, 18.

48. Irwin, *History of the Nineteenth Army Corps*, 6, 58–59; Record of Events, 114th New York, *SOR*, pt. 2, vol. 46, 242–43.

49. Brett, ed., *Letters and Diary*, 15–16, 19–20; McGregor, *History of the Fifteenth Regiment*, 168, 170, 173, 178, 180–81, 184, 162, 164, 186–89, 191–97; Peter Eltinge to father, December 11, 1862, Eltinge-Lord Family Papers, DU; Chadbourne to father, December 12, 1862, Danville S. Chadbourne

Letters, LSU; Stevens to Molly, February 1, 1862 [1863], February 3, 1863, William H. Stevens Letters, UNC.

50. "War Record of Henry Barstow of Newbury, Mass.," not paginated, Henry Barstow War Record and Letters, LSU; William Shelly Diary, January 13–19, February 14, 19, 1863, LSU; Stevens, *History of the Fiftieth Regiment,* 23–26, 30–31, 33, 35–36, 54; Fessenden to parents, January 29, [1863], Anson D. Fessenden Papers, LSU; Smith to brother, January 1, 1863, William H. Smith Letters, LSU.

51. Butler, *Private and Official Correspondence,* 3:22.

52. Beckwith to Banks, October 24, 1863, *OR,* ser. 3, vol. 3, 926–27.

53. Grant to Stone, July 21, 1863, in Simon, ed., *Papers of Ulysses S. Grant,* 9:92; Banks to Grant, July 18, 1863; Grant to Halleck, August 11, 1863, *OR,* vol. 24, pt. 3, 527, 587; Banks to Porter, August 28, 1863, David D. Porter Papers, MHM.

54. Goodell to not stated, August 3, 1863, Henry H. Goodell Letter, CHS.

55. Gile to friends, July 16, 1863, David Herrick Gile Correspondence, YU; Moors, *History of the Fifty-Second Regiment,* 210–12, 214.

56. McGregor, *History of the Fifteenth Regiment,* 587–91, 593, 600.

57. Stevens, *History of the Fiftieth Regiment,* 222–25, 228–30; record of events, Company H, 4th Massachusetts, *SOR,* pt. 2, vol. 27, 586.

58. Edwards to Maria, August 6, 1863, Marianne Edwards Letters, LSU.

59. Dinges, and Leckie, eds., *Just and Righteous Cause,* 323–24.

60. Fisher, "Union Combined Operations," 62, 68–69.

61. Washburn to Banks, January 1, 12, 1864; Washburn to Stone, January 4, 1864; Dana to Ord, January 22, 1864; Holabird to Stone, January 30, 1864, *OR,* vol. 34, pt. 2, 3–5, 17–18, 63, 165–66, 185; Irwin, *History of the Nineteenth Army Corps,* 268, 272.

62. Washburn to Banks, January 1, 1864, *OR,* vol. 34, pt. 2, 4.

63. Holabird to Stone, January 3, 1864, *OR,* vol. 34, pt. 2, 11–12; Fisher, "Union Combined Operations," 70–71.

64. Beecher, *History of the First Light Battery,* 1:322, 326, 330–33.

65. Clark, *One Hundred and Sixteenth,* 187–90.

66. Fonvielle, *Wilmington Campaign,* 109; Royce to Carter, January 1, 1865, *OR,* vol. 42, pt. 1, 987–88; Goulding, "A Month on a Transport," 82–83, 87–94.

67. Grover to Forsyth, January 11, 1865; Morgan to Rawlins, January 12, 1865; Newport to Thomas, January 12, 1865, *OR,* vol. 46, pt. 2, 104, 106, 112.

68. Canby to Halleck, February 28, 1865, *OR,* vol. 49, pt. 1, 789; Miller to wife, March 19, 1865, Monroe Joshua Miller Papers, MHM.

69. Scott, *Story of the Thirty-Second Iowa,* 330–31; Job H. Yaggy Diary, March 16, 1865, ALPL.

70. Smith to Taylor, March 26, 1862, *OR,* vol. 11, pt. 3, 400.

71. Browning, *From Cape Charles to Cape Fear,* 307–8; Gaines, *Encyclopedia,* 173–93.

72. Wise to Meigs, August 31, November 8, 1865, *OR,* ser. 3, vol. 5, 288–89, 291–93; *Report of the Quartermaster General,* 19, 101, 103, 105, 107, 109, 110–11; Gibson and Gibson, *Dictionary of Transports,* viii.

73. *Report of the Quartermaster General,* 18; Weigley, *Quartermaster General,* 248.

74. Comstock to Grant, February 1, 1866, in Simon, ed., *Papers of Ulysses S. Grant,* 16:454; Wise to Meigs, August 31, 1865, *OR,* ser. 3, vol. 5, 288; Gibson and Gibson, *Dictionary of Transports,* viii, xx.

75. Goulding, "A Month on a Transport," 94.

6. WAGON TRAINS

1. Sweetman, "Military Transport," 81–82, 87, 90–91.

2. Ingalls to Meigs, August 28, 1864, *OR*, vol. 40, pt. 1, 39.

3. Billings, *Hardtack and Coffee*, 352–53; Risch, *Quartermaster Support*, 373; Balloch to mother, August 11, 1864, George Williamson Balloch Papers, DU.

4. Ingalls to Williams, November 18, 1863, *OR*, vol. 29, pt. 2, 473; Williams to commanding officer, Cavalry Corps, April 17, 1863; Dana to Ingalls, May 24, 1863, *OR*, vol. 25, pt. 2, 222, 547; Special Field Orders No. 85, Headquarters, Army of the Tennessee, April 8, 1865, *OR*, vol. 47, pt. 3, 131; Purington to Evans, April 27, 1865, *OR*, vol. 46, pt. 1, 1232; Ingalls to Williams, April 13, 1864, *OR*, vol. 33, 855. Many estimates of the capacity of army wagons are too high. See Hagerman, *American Civil War*, 45, and Grabau, *Ninety-Eight Days*, 32–33.

5. Ludington to Meigs, September 9, 1865, *Report of the Quartermaster General*, 809; Easton to Meigs, March 16, 1865, *OR*, ser. 3, vol. 5, 396; Batchelder to Meigs, September 15, 1863, and September 15, 1864, *OR*, vol. 51, pt. 1, 103, 1223. Poteete notes in "Military Mules" (50) that a brake was developed for the army wagon in the latter part of the war, but he provides no details.

6. Billings, *Hardtack and Coffee*, 282–83; Castle, "Some of the Army Mules," 463–78.

7. Swords to Meigs, October 6, 1863, *OR*, vol. 52, pt. 1, 467–68; General Orders No. 18, Headquarters, Middle Military Division, September 10, 1864, *OR*, vol. 43, pt. 2, 63.

8. Draper, *Recollections*, 107.

9. Van Vliet to Marcy, August 2, 1862, *OR*, vol. 11, pt. 1, 159; Sherman, *Memoirs*, 2:389–90. For a detailed breakdown of the weight of army rations and consequent wagon capacity to haul them, see Ingalls to Williams, November 18, 1863, *OR*, vol. 29, pt. 2, 472, and Ingalls to Williams, April 13, 1864, *OR*, vol. 33, 855.

10. Halleck to Stanton, November 25, 1862, *OR*, vol. 19, pt. 1, 6; Halleck to Meade, August 7, 1863, *OR*, vol. 29, pt. 2, 13; Sherman, *Memoirs*, 2:403; Stevens, *Three Years*, 223–24; [Wilson], "Feeding a Great Army," 149–50.

11. Alexander Bliss, "Narrative," Bancroft-Bliss Family Papers, LC; Rusling, *Men and Things*, 263–67.

12. Roth, *Logistics of the Roman Army*, 68, 79–83, 86, 200, 331.

13. Wheeler, "Logistics of the Cromwellian Conquest," 12.

14. Holabird, "Army Wagon Transportation," 21.

15. Hogan, ed., *General Reub Williams's Memories*, 229; Halleck to McKean, December 12, 1861, *OR*, vol. 8, 430; Van Vliet to Marcy, August 2, 1862, *OR*, vol. 11, pt. 1, 157.

16. Ingalls to Marcy, February 17, 1863, *OR*, vol. 11, pt. 1, 165; Ingalls to Meigs, July 18, 1862; General Orders No. 153, Headquarters, Army of the Potomac, August 10, 1862, *OR*, vol. 11, pt. 3, 326–27, 365–66; Ingalls to Marcy, February 17, 1863, *OR*, vol. 19, pt. 1, 95; Meigs to Halleck, August 18, 1862, *OR*, vol. 12, pt. 3, 596–97.

17. Granger testimony, Buell Commission, *OR*, vol. 16, pt. 1, 437–38; Taylor, *"Supply for Tomorrow,"* 84.

18. Sherman to Guthrie, August 14, 1864, *OR*, vol. 39, pt. 2, 248; Granger testimony, Buell Commission, *OR*, vol. 16, pt. 1, 432; Bragg to wife, September 18, 1862, Braxton Bragg Papers, MHM.

19. Stevens, *Three Years*, 224; Meigs to Halleck, August 18, 1862, *OR*, vol. 12, pt. 3, 597; Hagerman, *American Civil War*, 60–64; Halleck to Stanton, November 25, 1862, *OR*, vol. 19, pt. 1, 6.

20. Meigs to Stanton, October 9, 1862, *OR*, ser. 3, vol. 2, 654–55; Huston, "Logistical Support," 37.

21. General Orders No. 130, War Department, Adjutant General's Office, September 14, 1862; Meigs to Stanton, October 9, 1862; General Orders No. 160, War Department, Adjutant General's Office, October 18, 1862, *OR*, ser. 3, vol. 2, 544, 655, 671–72; General Orders No. 153, Headquarters, Army of the Potomac, August 10, 1862, *OR*, vol. 11, pt. 3, 365.

22. Circular, Headquarters, Army of the Potomac, March 10, 1863, *OR*, vol. 25, pt. 2, 562–63; "Recapitulation of the number of officers and enlisted men, cavalry and artillery horses, wagons, and means of transportation in the Army of the Potomac," May 1–June 1, 1863; Ingalls to Williams, July 11, 1863, *OR*, vol. 27, pt. 3, 213, 652–53; Ingalls to Meigs, September 28, 1863, *OR*, vol. 19, pt. 1, 101; Hagerman, *American Civil War*, 71, 74, 77; Daniel, *Days of Glory*, 227; Special Orders No. 15, Headquarters, Department of the Tennessee, January 15, 1863, *OR*, vol. 17, pt. 2, 565–66.

23. Fitch, *Annals of the Army of the Cumberland*, 267; Halleck to Meade, August 7, 1863; General Orders No. 274, War Department, Adjutant General's Office, August 7, 1863, *OR*, vol. 29, pt. 2, 13–15.

24. Batchelder to Meigs, September 15, 1863, *OR*, vol. 51, pt. 1, 103.

25. General Orders No. 83, Headquarters, Army of the Potomac, August 21, 1863; General Orders No. 100, Headquarters, Army of the Potomac, November 5, 1863, *OR*, vol. 29, pt. 2, 85–87, 420–22; Batchelder to Meigs, September 15, 1864, *OR*, vol. 51, pt. 1, 1220–21; Ingalls to Williams, April 13, 1864, *OR*, vol. 33, 852–54.

26. Meade endorsement, April 14, 1864, on Ingalls to Williams, April 13, 1864, *OR*, vol. 33, 855; Billings, *Hardtack and Coffee*, 361–63; "Report of the means of transportation in the Army of the Potomac, as reported this the 3d day of May, 1864, Major-General Burnside's command excepted," *OR*, vol. 36, pt. 2, 355; Special Orders No. 44, Headquarters, Armies of the United States, June 28, 1864, *OR*, vol. 40, pt. 1, 40–41; General Orders No. 2, Headquarters U.S. Forces at Harper's Ferry, August 7, 1864, *OR*, vol. 43, pt. 1, 721.

27. Sherman to Thomas, April 11, 1864; General Orders No. 7, Headquarters, Military Division of the Mississippi, April 18, 1864, *OR*, vol. 32, pt. 3, 323, 408; Hagerman, *American Civil War*, 279; General Orders No. 56, Headquarters, First Division, Fourteenth Corps, April 16, 1864, Order Book, Company I, 78th Pennsylvania Regimental File, SRNB; Sherman to Meigs, May 3, 1864, *OR*, vol. 38, pt. 4, 20.

28. Sherman to Meigs, May 3, 1864, *OR*, vol. 38, pt. 4, 20.

29. Easton to Meigs, March 16, 1865; Fort to Meigs, January 26, 1865, *OR*, ser. 3, vol. 5, 394, 404; Easton to Meigs, August 8, 1865, *OR*, vol. 52, pt. 1, 702.

30. Remington to [Meigs], July 1, 1865, *OR*, ser. 3, vol. 5, 420; Geary to Perkins, March 26, 1865, *OR*, vol. 47, pt. 1, 697.

31. Hagerman, *American Civil War*, 155, 181, 191; General Orders No. 2, Headquarters, Arkansas Expedition, August 5, 1863, *OR*, vol. 22, pt. 2, 433; General Orders No. 76, Headquarters, Military Division of West Mississippi, December 1, 1864, *OR*, vol. 41, pt. 4, 733–34; Smith to Osterhaus, March 23, 1865, *OR*, vol. 49, pt. 2, 69; General Orders No. 11, Headquarters, Department of Arkansas, April 21, 1864, *OR*, vol. 34, pt. 3, 245; Pope to Sibley, February 17, 1863, *OR*, vol. 22, pt. 2, 115–16.

32. General Orders No. 109, 117, Headquarters, Department No. 2, August 8, 16, 1862, *OR*, vol. 17, pt. 2, 672, 680–81; General Orders No. 2, Headquarters, Army of Tennessee, November 24, 1862, *OR*, vol. 20, pt. 2, 425; General Orders No. 182 and 17, Headquarters, Army of Tennessee, September 24, 1863, and January 28, 1864, Orders and Circulars, Army of Tennessee and Subordinate Commands, 1862–1864, Chapter II, Vol. 53, RG 109, NARA; Hagerman, *American Civil War*, 277; "Armament and

ammunition of the Army of Tennessee, commanded by General Joseph E. Johnston, for the week ending June 19, 1864," *OR*, vol. 38, pt. 4, 782.

33. Lee to Jackson, October 1, 1862, *OR*, vol. 19, pt. 2, 641; General Orders No. 77, Headquarters, Army of Northern Virginia, July 16, 1863, *OR*, vol. 37, pt. 3, 1015; Hagerman, *American Civil War*, 115, 128; General Orders No. 27, Headquarters, Army of Northern Virginia, April 5, 1864, *OR*, vol. 33, 1262–64; General Orders No. (not stated), Headquarters Valley District, June 27, 1864, *OR*, vol. 37, pt. 1, 768.

34. General Orders No. 1, [Beauregard's headquarters], January 3, 1864, *OR*, vol. 28, pt. 2, 428–29; General Orders No. 19, Headquarters, Trans-Mississippi Department, May 6, 1864, *OR*, vol. 34, pt. 3, 809; Harvie to Fauntleroy, January 18, 1863; Maury to Waddy, January 19, 1863, *OR*, vol. 17, pt. 2, 844–45; Barbour to Breckinridge, June 14, 1863, *OR*, vol. 24, pt. 3, 964.

35. Weigley, *Quartermaster General*, 269; Holabird, "Army Wagon Transportation," 2–4; Holabird, "Transport of Troops," 494.

36. *Report of the Quartermaster General*, 31–32; Purington to Evans, April 27, 1865, *OR*, vol. 46, pt. 1, 1233.

37. Twitchell, *History of the Seventh Maine*, 52; Blanton et al., eds. *I Must Tell*, 88.

38. Redfield, "Characteristics," 362–63.

39. Joseph E. Johnston to Jefferson Davis, February 16, 1864, "Records Cleburnes Div Hardees Corps A of Tenn," Chapter II, No. 265, RG 109, NARA; Cox to Fremont, May 2, 1862, *OR*, vol. 12, pt. 3, 128; Sherman to McPherson, June 20, 1862, *OR*, vol. 17, pt. 2, 20; Van Vliet to Meigs, May 23, 1862, *OR*, vol. 11, pt. 1, 162; McClellan to Halleck, October 7, 1862, *OR*, vol. 19, pt. 1, 11; Mackall journal, June 4, 1864, *OR*, vol. 38, pt. 3, 991; Stevenson to Stanton, September 25, 1864, *OR*, vol. 43, pt. 2, 174.

40. Easton to Meigs, September 21, 1863, *OR*, vol. 53, 570–71; Denver to assistant adjutant general, Department of the Mississippi, April 2, 1862, *OR*, vol. 8, 654.

41. Bowles to Meigs, September 24, 1863, *OR*, vol. 52, pt. 1, 451–52; Githins to wife, September 30, 1863, William Harrison Githins Letters, Gail and Stephen Rudin Collection of Civil War Letters, CU; Risch, *Quartermaster Support*, 423; Sherman to Kelton, June 23, 1862, *OR*, vol. 17, pt. 2, 28; LeDuc to Ingalls, May 25, 1863, *OR*, vol. 25, pt. 2, 557; diary, March 27–28, 1865, Alexander Miller Ayers Papers, EU.

42. Grant to Butler, August 27, 1861, *OR*, vol. 3, 463; Ingalls to Williams, September 10, 1862, *OR*, vol. 19, pt. 2, 235.

43. Circular, Headquarters, Department of the Cumberland, November 5, 1863, *OR*, vol. 31, pt. 3, 53–54; General Orders No. 155, Headquarters, Army of the Potomac, August 14, 1862, *OR*, vol. 11, pt. 3, 376–77; Orders, [no number], Headquarters, Twentieth Corps, May 22, 1864: Special Field Orders No. 7, Headquarters, Left Wing Sixteenth Corps, May 22, 1864: Special Field Orders No. 15, Headquarters, Fifteenth Corps, May 25, 1864, *OR*, vol. 38, pt. 4, 291–92, 315; Risch, *Quartermaster Support*, 425–26.

44. LeDuc to Ingalls, May 25, 1863, *OR*, vol. 25, pt. 2, 557.

45. General Orders No. 24, Headquarters, Army of the Ohio, June 15, 1862, *OR*, vol. 16, pt. 2, 26; Carr to assistant adjutant general, District of Southwest Missouri, January 3, 1862, *OR*, vol. 8, 483.

46. General Orders No. 35, Headquarters, Porter's Division, Third Corps, April 3, 1862, *OR*, vol. 51, pt. 1, 566; Hazen to Woodhull, February 1, 1865: Special Orders No. 32, Headquarters, Fifteenth Corps, February 1, 1865, *OR*, vol. 47, pt. 2, 196.

47. Easton to Meigs, August 8, 1865, *OR*, vol. 52, pt. 1, 703; Dunbar to Meigs, January 19, 1865; Remington to [Meigs], July 1, 1865, *OR*, ser. 3, vol. 5, 404, 420.

48. Byrne, ed., *Uncommon Soldiers,* 226.

49. Patrick and Willey, eds., *Fighting for Liberty and Right,* 323; William Merrell, "Personal Memoirs of the Civil War," LMU; Smith to Woodhull, March 11, 1865, *OR,* vol. 47, pt. 2, 782

50. Ebenezer W. Wells Narrative, 18–19, N-YHS; Garber to Meigs, July 10, 1865, *OR,* vol. 53, 52–53.

51. Ingalls to Meigs, September 28, 1863, *OR,* vol. 19, pt. 1, 104; Wild, *Memoirs,* 78.

52. Batchelder to Meigs, September 15, 1863, *OR,* vol. 51, pt. 1, 102; Alexander Bliss, "Narrative," Bancroft-Bliss Family Papers, LC.

53. Gibson and Gibson, *Dictionary of Transports,* x; Nichols, *Confederate Quartermaster,* 85; Windham, "Problem of Supply," 156, Ramsdell, "General Robert E. Lee's Horse Supply," 776.

54. Weigley, *Quartermaster General,* 269.

7. PACK TRAINS, CATTLE HERDS, AND FOOT POWER

1. Essin, *Shavetails and Bell Sharps,* 1, 9, 13–15; Billings, *Hardtack and Coffee,* 290; General Orders No. 1, Headquarters, Fourth Corps, January 12, 1865, *OR,* vol. 45, pt. 2, 574.

2. Holabird, "Army Wagon Transportation," 17, 19.

3. Leib, *Nine Months,* 109–12, 119.

4. Ingalls to Meigs, May 29, 1863, *OR,* vol. 25, pt. 2, 545; Holabird, "Army Wagon Transportation," 19; Metzgar to Quartermaster General, August 22, 1864, John J. Metzgar Papers, UNC.

5. Butterfield to commanding officer, Third Corps, April 30, 1863; Dana to Ingalls, May 24, 1863; Caslow to Ingalls, May 25, 1863, *OR,* vol. 25, pt. 2, 314, 547, 552.

6. Alexander Bliss, "Narrative," Bancroft-Bliss Family Papers, LC.

7. Dana to Ingalls, May 24, 1863; Rusling to Ingalls, May 24, 1863, *OR,* vol. 25, pt. 2, 548, 551.

8. LeDuc to Ingalls, May 25, 1863, *OR,* vol. 25, pt. 2, 556–57.

9. Ingalls to Meigs, May 29, 1863, *OR,* vol. 25, pt. 2, 546–47; Circular, Headquarters, [Army of the Potomac], June 4, 1863, *OR,* vol. 27, pt. 3, 7; Sharpe, "Art of Supplying Armies," 78.

10. Williams to commanding officer, Cavalry Corps, April 22, 1863; Butterfield to Meigs, May 13, 1863; Sawtelle to Ingalls, May 24, 1863, *OR,* vol. 25, pt. 2, 244, 487, 561–62.

11. General Orders No. 274, War Department, Adjutant General's Office, August 7, 1863; General Orders No. 100, Headquarters, Army of the Potomac, November 5, 1863, *OR,* vol. 29, pt. 2, 14–15; 420–22; Special Orders No. 44, Headquarters, Armies of the United States, June 28, 1864, *OR,* vol. 40, pt. 1, 40; Ludington to Meigs, September 9, 1865, *Report of the Quartermaster General,* 806.

12. Sheridan to Rawlins, July 16, 1865; Merritt to Forsyth, May 7, 1865, *OR,* vol. 46, pt. 1, 475–76, 485, 488.

13. General Orders No. 2, Headquarters, Army of Tennessee, November 24, 1862, "Records Cleburnes Div Hardees Corps A of Tenn," Chapter 2, No. 265, RG 109, NARA.

14. Holabird, "Army Wagon Transportation," 16.

15. Billings, *Hardtack and Coffee,* 281–81; Van Vliet to Meigs, April 28, 1862, *OR,* vol. 11, pt. 1, 161; *Report of the Quartermaster General,* 32; Holabird, "Transport of Troops," 497.

16. Cook and Benton, eds., *"Dutchess County Regiment,"* 154; William Merrell, "Personal Memoirs of the Civil War," LMU.

17. Billings, *Hardtack and Coffee,* 369–70. Oxen trains were used successfully during the Civil War on the frontier. Wagons pulled by steers transported supplies to Fort Gibson, although it took a long

time compared to those pulled by mules. Thayer to Wattles, November 28, 1864, *OR*, vol. 41, pt. 4, 706.

18. Holabird, "Army Wagon Transportation," 12–13; Billings, *Hardtack and Coffee*, 282.

19. Billings, *Hardtack and Coffee*, 282; Gardner, "First Kansas Battery," 238.

20. Gardner, "First Kansas Battery," 239.

21. Orders No. 54, Headquarters, Fifth Division, July 19, 1862, *OR*, vol. 17, pt. 2, 106; Ingalls to Meigs, September 28, 1865, *OR*, vol. 51, pt. 1, 253.

22. Taylor to Meigs, April 27, 1863, *OR*, vol. 23, pt. 2, 282.

23. *Report of the Quartermaster General*, 26; Green, *Horses at Work*, 127, 129, 134; Essin, *Shavetails and Bell Sharps*, 69.

24. Meigs to Rosecrans, May 1, 1863, *OR*, vol. 23, pt. 2, 301; Fitch, *Annals of the Army of the Cumberland*, 268; Meigs to Stanton, November 8, 1865, *OR*, ser. 3, vol. 5, 220–21; Sawers, "U.S. Army Procurement of Draft and Pack Animals," 59–67.

25. *Report of the Quartermaster General*, 26–28; Fitch, *Annals of the Army of the Cumberland*, 267–68; Green, *Horses at Work*, 135.

26. Dunbar to Meigs, January 19, 1865, *OR*, ser. 3, vol. 5, 404.

27. Sharrer, "Great Glanders Epizootic," 80, 82, 84, 86, 89–90; Green, *Horses at Work*, 143; Ingalls to Marcy, February 17, 1863, *OR*, vol. 19, pt. 1, 95.

28. Fitch, *Annals of the Army of the Cumberland*, 267; Green, *Horses at Work*, 161; Samuel R. Curtis to Sheridan, February 18, 1862, Philip Henry Sheridan Papers, LC.

29. Throne, ed., "A Commissary in the Union Army," 73.

30. Miller to wife, May 4, 1864, Marshall Mortimer Miller Papers, LC; Jones, *An Artilleryman's Diary*, 152.

31. *Report of the Quartermaster General*, 809; Green, *Horses at Work*, 144.

32. Meigs to Scott, October 25, 1863, *OR*, vol. 31, pt. 1, 729; Meigs to Thomas, April 20, 1864, *OR*, vol. 32, pt. 3, 423.

33. Easton to Meigs, March 16, 1865, *OR*, ser. 3, vol. 5, 395; Garber to Meigs, July 10, 1865, *OR*, vol. 53, 50–51.

34. Easton to Meigs, March 16, 1865: Whittelsly to Easton, January 20, 1865: Remington to [Meigs], July 1, 1865, *OR*, ser. 3, vol. 5, 397–98, 417.

35. Meigs to Stanton, November 8, 1865, *OR*, ser. 3, vol. 5, 221; Ramsdell, "General Robert E. Lee's Horse Supply," 772–73.

36. Meigs to Stanton, November 8, 1865, *OR*, ser. 3, vol. 5, 221; Essin, *Shavetails and Bell Sharps*, 1, 89–121, 150–51, 158–88, 190–95, 200–202.

37. Billings, *Hardtack and Coffee*, 321–22, 324.

38. Ibid., 324; [Wilson], "Feeding a Great Army," 150; Benham to Woodward, June 17, 1864; Williams to Sheridan, July 2, 1864, *OR*, vol. 40, pt. 2, 121, 592–93.

39. Edward C. Dale to wife, June 18, 1864, Dale-Holt-Hensley Family Papers, MHM; Jones to father and mother, July 18, 1864, James H. Jones Papers, IHS.

40. Wilson, *Reminiscences*, 36–37.

41. Spence, *Diary*, 80–81.

42. Goodloe, *Confederate Echoes*, 167–69.

43. "Military History of Captain Thomas Sewell, Co. G, 127th Ill. Vol. Inf. During the War of the Rebellion, 1861 to 1865," Thomas Sewell Papers, DU; Prokopowicz, *All for the Regiment*, 160–61.

44. Bennett and Haigh, *History of the Thirty-Sixth Regiment Illinois*, 198–202.

45. Sherman, *Memoirs*, 2:184.

46. Diary, May 27, 1862, Thomas Bragg Papers, UNC.

47. Merritt James Symonds Diary, May 17, 1863, CCNMP.

48. Sherman, *Memoirs*, 2:390.

49. Meigs to not stated, January 2, 1862, *OR*, vol. 25, pt. 2, 489; Hagerman, *American Civil War*, 71–73.

50. General Orders No. 15, Headquarters, Fifth Corps, April 27, 1863; Ingalls to Meigs, May 29, 1863, *OR*, vol. 25, pt. 2, 269, 545; Hagerman, *American Civil War*, 71–73.

51. Ingalls to Meigs, August 28, 1864, *OR*, vol. 40, pt. 1, 39.

52. Dana to Ingalls, May 24, 1863; Batchelder to Ingalls, May 23, 1863; Caslow to Ingalls, May 25, 1863, *OR*, vol. 25, pt. 2, 547–49, 552.

53. LeDuc to Ingalls, May 24, 25, 1863, *OR*, vol. 25, pt. 2, 55–556.

54. Ingalls to Meigs, May 29, 1863; Dana to Ingalls, May 24, 1863; LeDuc to Ingalls, May 25, 1863, *OR*, vol. 25, pt. 2, 545–46, 548, 557.

55. Meigs to Butterfield, May 11, 1863; Butterfield to Meigs, May 13, 1863; Special Orders No. 65, Headquarters, Army of the Potomac, March 7, 1863, *OR*, vol. 25, pt. 2, 486–89.

56. Meigs to Stanton, November 18, 1862, *OR*, ser. 3, vol. 2, 804–5.

57. Cross to wife, August 14, 1864, Joseph Cross Civil War Letters, AAS.

58. Cutrer, ed., "'We Are Stern and Resolved,'" 210; W. E. Preston Reminiscences, 34, L. B. Williams Papers, AU; Bennett and Haigh, *History of the Thirty-Sixth Regiment Illinois*, 357–58; Wild, *Memoirs*, 69. It must be noted that even Northern civilians living near Gettysburg descended on the battlefield to scrounge government property before the army could stop them. See Rankin to Ingalls, July 15, 1863, *OR*, vol. 27, pt. 3, 706, and Blood diary, July 6, 8–11, 16–18, 21, 1863 Henry Boyden Blood Papers, LC.

59. Graham to Copeland, October 22, 1864, *OR*, vol. 43, pt. 1, 339; General Orders No. 114, War Department, Adjutant General's Office, June 15, 1865, *OR*, vol. 46, pt. 3, 1279.

60. McPherson to Sherman, April 2, 1864, *OR*, vol. 32, pt. 3, 229; Banks to McDowell, July 21, 1862, *OR*, vol. 12, pt. 3, 493.

61. McCloskey, "History of Military Road Construction," 354–55.

62. Bahde, ed., *Story of My Campaign*, 72, 74–75.

63. Merdinger, "Roads," pt. 1, 273; Edward C. Dale to son, August 7, 1864, Dale-Holt-Hensley Family Papers, MHM; Round, "Telegraph Road," 45; Warren to Hancock, May 4, 1864, *OR*, vol. 36, pt. 2, 375.

64. Jackson, *Time Exposure*, 66–67; Bennett and Haigh, *History of the Thirty-Sixth Regiment Illinois*, 323; Brinkerhoff, *Recollections*, 143; Smith and Baker, eds., *"Burning Rails as We Pleased,"* 10; Francis, *Narrative*, 95; Byrne, ed., *Uncommon Soldiers*, 11; Hight, *History of the Fifty-Eighth Regiment*, 277.

65. Hamilton, ed., *Papers of Randolph Abbott Shotwell*, 1:499.

66. Freeman, "Eighteenth U.S. Infantry," 120; Gates, ed., *Rough Side of War*, 309; Miller to wife, September 3, 1864 [1862], Marshall Mortimer Miller Papers, LC; Wagner to [Hascall], January 16, 1863, *OR*, vol. 20, pt. 1, 985; "History of the Chicago Board of Trade Battery," 15, John A. Nourse Papers, CHM.

67. Doyle, Smith, and McMurry, eds., *This Wilderness of War*, 51; Chamberlain to not stated, January 29, 1863, Joseph Wright Chamberlain Papers, IHS; unsigned letter to editor, February 19, 1863, in *Belmont Chronicle*, March 5, 1863; Funk to brother, February 9, 1863, Kaufman Funk Letter, UND.

68. Smith to Thomas, December 30, 1864, *OR*, vol. 45, pt. 2, 427; Cox to Fremont, March 31, 1862, *OR*, vol. 12, pt. 3, 34.

69. Banks to McClellan, February 11, 1862, *OR*, vol. 51, pt. 1, 529; Van Vliet to Meigs, April 28, 1862, *OR*, vol. 11, pt. 1, 161, 163–64.

70. Alexander to Barnard, November 27, 1862, *OR*, vol. 21, 1117–20.

71. Cox to Fremont, April 5, 1862, *OR*, vol. 12, pt. 3, 47.

72. Githens to wife, September 11, 1863, William Harrison Githens Letters, Gail and Stephen Rudin Collection of Civil War Letters, CU; Simmons, *History of the 84th Reg't*, 71–72.

73. Fout, *Dark Days*, 236; Cox, *Military Reminiscences*, 2:78–80, 83–84.

74. Edward C. Dale to son, August 7, 1864, Dale-Holt-Hensley Family Papers, MHM; Sherman to Porter, November 8, 1863, *ORN*, vol. 25, 540; Huntington to Stewart, October 15, 1863, *OR*, vol. 30, pt. 4, 388–89.

75. Sherman to Halleck, June 21, 1864, *OR*, vol. 38, pt. 4, 544; Hazen to Woodhull, February 1, 1865; Everts to Adams, January 29, 1865; Howard to Blair, January 16, 1865, *OR*, vol. 47, pt. 2, 64, 159–60, 196; Cox, *Military Reminiscences*, 2:72; Circular, Headquarters, Army of the Potomac, December 3, 1863, *OR*, vol. 29, pt. 2, 540; Rucker to mother, March 31, 1863, R. M. Rucker Letter, UA; Mechling to Debray, January 29, 1864, *OR*, vol. 34, pt. 2, 927.

76. Whittelsey to not stated, January 19, 1865; Dunbar to Meigs, January 19, 1865, *OR*, ser. 3, vol. 5, 401–3.

77. Diary, February 24, 28, March 2, 1865, Alexander Miller Ayers Papers, EU; Morgan to McClurg, March 2, 1865; Williams to Dayton, March 10, 1865; Logan to [Van Dyke], March 11, 1865, *OR*, vol. 47, pt. 2, 650, 765, 780.

78. Michie, "American Military Roads," 621; James M. Snook Diary, May 23, 1864, MaryHS.

79. Fry to Wood, January 16, 1862, *OR*, vol. 7, 556; Hartpence, *History of the Fifty-First Indiana*, 14.

80. Rosecrans to Hooker, October 10, 1863, *OR*, vol. 30, pt. 4, 262–63; Smith, *On Wheels*, 104–5.

81. "Army Life in the 12th and 20th Corps: The Story of the Campaigns of the 12th Corps with the Army of the Potomac and of the 20th Corps with the Left Wing of Sherman's Army together with a Complete History of the 20th Regiment Connecticut Volunteer Infantry," 59, Philo Beecher Buckingham Papers, AAS; Stevens, *Three Years*, 222; William Merrell, "Personal Memoirs of the Civil War," LMU; Smith to Woodhull, March 26, 1865, *OR*, vol. 47, pt. 1, 325; Sherman to Terry, March 21, 1865, *OR*, vol. 47, pt. 2, 945.

82. Osborn, "Sherman's Carolina Campaign," 115; Smith to Woodhull, March 26, 1865; Force to Cadle, March 28, 1865, *OR*, vol. 47, pt. 1, 325, 411; Poe to Chief Engineer, October 8, 1865, *OR*, ser. 3, vol. 5, 199.

83. Remington to [Meigs], July 1, 1865, *OR*, ser. 3, vol. 5, 417; Crosman endorsement, November 9, 1862, on Thomas to Rucker, October 29, 1862, *OR*, vol. 19, pt. 2, 505.

84. Cox, *Military Reminiscences*, 2:111; Tyler to Rosecrans, August 11, 1861, *OR*, vol. 51, pt. 1, 444; LeDuc, *Recollections*, 123.

85. *Atlanta Journal*, December 7, 1901.

86. General Orders No. 47, Headquarters, Right Wing, Army of Northern Virginia, November 7, 1862, *OR*, vol. 52, pt. 2, 642.

87. Halleck, *Elements*, 348; Haupt, *Military Bridges*, iii.

88. Michie, "American Military Roads," 622.

89. Ibid., 622, 624–25.

90. Haupt, *Military Bridges,* 188–91; Herman Haupt to Joseph Hooker, February 7, 1863, Herman Haupt Letter Book, Lewis Muhlenberg Haupt Family Papers, LC.

91. W. G. Buck to friend and cousin, December 2, 1863, W. G. Buck Letter, VTU; Harry Stanley Diary, July 19, 1864, AHC; Sherman, *Memoirs,* 2:184.

92. [Rood], *Story of the Service,* 413–14; Poe to Chief Engineer, October 8, 1865, *OR,* ser. 3, vol. 5, 199–200.

93. Haupt, *Military Bridges,* iii–iv, 95–106; Halleck, *Elements,* 350–51, 353.

94. Morton, *Artillery of Nathan Bedford Forrest's Cavalry,* 218.

95. Hess, *Knoxville Campaign,* 181, 185, 190; Sheridan, *Personal Memoirs,* 1:333.

8. TROOP TRANSFERS

1. Daniel to Randolph, April 26, 1862, *OR,* ser. 4, vol. 1, 1094.

2. Parsons to Meigs, October 15, 1865, *OR,* vol. 52, pt. 1, 709–12.

3. Van Vliet to Marcy, August 2, 1862, *OR,* vol. 11, pt. 1, 158; Rucker to Meigs, September 19, 1863, *OR,* vol. 51, pt. 1, 1095; Risch, *Quartermaster Support,* 416–17; Rusling, *Men and Things,* 235.

4. Stanton to Halleck, June 28, 30, 1862; Halleck to Stanton, June 30, 1862; Lincoln to Halleck, July 4, 1862; Halleck to Lincoln, July 5, [1862], *OR,* vol. 17, pt. 2, 42–43, 52, 70–72; Halleck to Buell, July 12, 1862, *OR,* vol. 16, pt. 2, 128.

5. Burnside to Parke, March 18, 1863, *OR,* vol. 25, pt. 2, 148; Roemer, *Reminiscences,* 287; Parsons to Meigs, October 6, 1863 and October 15, 1865, *OR,* vol. 52, pt. 1, 460, 710–11.

6. Diary, August 4–11, 1863, George Benton Arnold Collection, AM.

7. George M. Kirkpatrick to friend, July 31, 1863, Wright Family Papers, AU.

8. Niven, ed., *Salmon P. Chase Papers,* 1:450–52.

9. Green, "Movement of the 11th and 12th Army Corps," 112–13; Haupt, *Reminiscences,* 289; Halleck to McCallum, September 24, 1863; McCallum to Stanton, September 24, 1863; Smith to McCallum, September 24, 1863; McCallum to Smith, September 24, 1863, *OR,* vol. 29, pt. 1, 153–55.

10. Stanton to Meigs, September 24, 1863; Stanton to not stated, September 24, 1863; Garrett to Stanton, September 24, 1863, *OR,* vol. 29, pt. 1, 150–52; Green, "Movement of the 11th and 12th Army Corps," 113–14.

11. Halleck to Rosecrans, September 24, 1863, 2:30 A.M. and 10 A.M.; Rosecrans to Halleck, September 24, 1863, *OR,* vol. 29, pt. 1, 150–51.

12. Smith to McCallum, September 25, 1863; Garrett to Hooker, September 25, 1863; Smith to McCallum, September 25, 1863; Devereux to Smith, September 25, 1863, *OR,* vol. 29, pt. 1, 157–59.

13. Stanton to Bowler, September 24, 1863; Bowler to Stanton, September 24, 1863; Smith to Stanton, September 26, 1863; Smith to McCallum, September 26, 1863; Stanton to Scott, September 27, 1863; McCallum to Smith, September 27, 1863; Devereux to Smith, September 27, 1863, *OR,* vol. 29, pt. 1, 153, 161, 164–65, 171; Pickenpaugh, *Rescue by Rail,* 73, 131; Thayer, "Railroad Feat," 229.

14. Smith to Stanton, September 27, 1863; Stanton to Smith, September 27, 1863; Schurz to Stanton, October 1, 1863, *OR,* vol. 29, pt. 1, 167, 169–70, 181–83.

15. Scott to Hooker, September 26, 1863; Smith to Stanton, September 27, 1863, *OR,* vol. 29, pt. 1, 163, 167.

16. Balloch to wife, September 28, 1863, George Williamson Balloch Papers, DU; Wheeler, *Letters,* 425.

17. Smith to Stanton, September 28, 1863; Smith to Stanton, October 1, 1863; Scott to Stanton, October 5, 1863, *OR*, vol. 29, pt. 1, 173, 183, 191; Thayer, "Railroad Feat," 230.

18. Scott to Stanton, September 28, 1863, *OR*, vol. 29, pt. 1, 175.

19. Stanton to Stone, September 25, 26, 1863; Stone to Stanton, September 25, 26, 1863; Watson to Allen, September 28, 1863, *OR*, vol. 29, pt. 1, 157, 163, 176; Stanton to John B. Anderson, September 28, 1863, Anderson Family Papers, KHS.

20. Smith to Stanton, September 28, 1863; Stanton to Smith, September 28, 1863, *OR*, vol. 29, pt. 1, 173.

21. Henry E. Ellis to sis, October 15, 1863, C. Eugene Southworth Papers, DU; Scott to Stanton, September 29, 1863, 10:15 A.M., *OR*, vol. 29, pt. 1, 178–79.

22. Green, "Movement of the 11th and 12th Army Corps," 115; Scott to Rosecrans, September 29, 1863; Scott to Stanton, September 29, 1863, *OR*, vol. 29, pt. 1, 178, 181.

23. Scott to Stanton, September 30, 1863; Scott to Lincoln, October 1, 1863; Smith to Stanton, October 1, 1863, *OR*, vol. 29, pt. 1, 180, 183–84.

24. Scott to Stanton, October 2, 1863, 10 P.M., *OR*, vol. 29, pt. 1, 185.

25. Scott to Stanton, October 2, 1863, 10 P.M.; Meigs to Stanton, October 3, 1863, *OR*, vol. 29, pt. 1, 185–86.

26. Garrett to Stanton, October 4, 1863; Rucker to Hodges, October 9, 1863; Smith to McCallum, October 5, 1863; McCallum to Koontz, October 5, 1863; Smith to Stanton, October 6, 1863; Garrett to Cole, no date; Garrett to Stanton, October 12, 1863, *OR*, vol. 29, pt. 1, 188, 190, 192–95.

27. Howard, *Autobiography*, 1:452–58; Green, "Movement of the 11th and 12th Army Corps," 115–16; Taylor, *"Supply for Tomorrow,"* 162, 164.

28. Wheeler, *Letters*, 424–25; Charles H. Howard to mother, October 7, 1863, Charles Henry Howard Collection, BC; Meigs to Stanton, October 17, 1863, *OR*, vol. 29, pt. 1, 195; Pickenpaugh, *Rescue by Rail*, 92–93.

29. Sawtelle to Meigs, December 13, 1865, *OR*, vol. 53, 605; Irwin, *History of the Nineteenth Army Corps*, 353–54.

30. Metcalf to Parsons, October 25, 1865, in Parsons, *Reports to the War Department*, 52; General Orders No. 62, Headquarters, First Division, Sixteenth Corps, November 26, 1864; General Orders No. 23, Headquarters, Third Division, Sixteenth Corps, November 28, 1864, *OR*, vol. 41, pt. 4, 707.

31. Metcalf to Parsons, October 25, 1865, in Parsons, *Reports to the War Department*, 53; General Orders No. 18, Headquarters, Right Wing, Sixteenth Corps, November 26, 1864, *OR*, vol. 41, pt. 4, 693; "Itinerary of the First Division, Brig. Gen. John McArthur, U.S. Army, commanding," *OR*, vol. 41, pt. 1, 903.

32. Circular, Headquarters, Provisional Division, Army of the James, November 7, 14, 1864; Hawley to Gordon, November 10, 1864; Hawley to Puffer, November 14, 1864, *OR*, vol. 43, pt. 2, 570, 600, 628–30.

33. Schofield to Grant, December 27, 1864, *OR*, vol. 45, pt. 2, 377–78; Grant to Sherman, January 21, 1865, *OR*, vol. 47, pt. 2, 101.

34. Dana to Parsons, January 11, 1865, box 17, folder 1, Lewis Baldwin Parsons Papers, ALPL.

35. Parsons to Stanton, February 2, 1865, in Parsons, *Reports to the War Department*, 23; Parsons to J. A. Potter, January 11, 1865, and Potter to Parsons, January 12, 1865, in "Journal and Record of Proceedings of Col. Lewis B. Parsons, Chief of Rail, and River Transportation, under Order of the Asst Secty of War, To transport the Army of the Ohio General Schofield Comd'g, from Eastport Miss. to *Annapolis, Md*," box 20, folder 2, Lewis Baldwin Parsons Papers, ALPL.

36. Parsons to Stanton, February 2, 1865, in Parsons, *Reports to the War Department*, 23–24; "Journal and Record of Proceedings of Col. Lewis B. Parsons, Chief of Rail, and River Transportation, under Order of the Asst Secty of War, To transport the Army of the Ohio General Schofield Comd'g, from Eastport Miss. to *Annapolis, Md*," box 20, folder 2, Lewis Baldwin Parsons Papers, ALPL. See also Allen to McKim, January 13, 1865; McKim to Allen, January 14, 1865; Allen to Adin, January 13, 1865; Allen to Woolfolk, January 13, 14, 1865; Woolfolk to Allen, January 13, 1865; and Parsons to Schofield, January 16, 1865, all in ibid.

37. "Journal and Record of Proceedings of Col. Lewis B. Parsons, Chief of Rail, and River Transportation, under Order of the Asst Secty of War, To transport the Army of the Ohio General Schofield Comd'g, from Eastport Miss. to *Annapolis, Md*," box 20, folder 2, Lewis Baldwin Parsons Papers, ALPL; Parsons to Stanton, February 2, 1865, *OR*, vol. 47, pt. 2, 215; *Military Record*, 192.

38. Parsons to Burr, January 21, 1865; Lough to Parsons, January 21, 1865, *OR*, vol. 47, pt. 2, 248, 250; "Journal and Record of Proceedings of Col. Lewis B. Parsons, Chief of Rail, and River Transportation, under Order of the Asst Secty of War, To transport the Army of the Ohio General Schofield Comd'g, from Eastport Miss. to *Annapolis, Md*," box 20, folder 2, Lewis Baldwin Parsons Papers, ALPL.

39. "Journal and Record of Proceedings of Col. Lewis B. Parsons, Chief of Rail, and River Transportation, under Order of the Asst Secty of War, To transport the Army of the Ohio General Schofield Comd'g, from Eastport Miss. to *Annapolis, Md*," box 20, folder 2, Lewis Baldwin Parsons Papers, ALPL.

40. Ibid.; journal, 24–25, Tilghman Blazer Collection, UTK.

41. Allen to Halleck, January 27, 1865, *OR*, vol. 49, pt. 1, 595–96.

42. "Journal and Record of Proceedings of Col. Lewis B. Parsons, Chief of Rail, and River Transportation, under Order of the Asst Secty of War, To transport the Army of the Ohio General Schofield Comd'g, from Eastport Miss. to *Annapolis, Md*," box 20, folder 2, Lewis Baldwin Parsons Papers, ALPL.

43. Ibid.; Stevenson to Seward, January 22, 1865; Garrett to Stanton, January 29, 1865, *OR*, vol. 46, pt. 2, 204, 296.

44. "Journal and Record of Proceedings of Col. Lewis B. Parsons, Chief of Rail, and River Transportation, under Order of the Asst Secty of War, To transport the Army of the Ohio General Schofield Comd'g, from Eastport Miss. to *Annapolis, Md*," box 20, folder 2, Lewis Baldwin Parsons Papers, ALPL. The five railroad companies involved in the Twenty-Third Corps' transfer included the Little Miami Railroad, the Hamilton and Dayton Railroad, the Steubenville and Indiana Railroad, the Ohio Central Railroad, and the Baltimore and Ohio Railroad. See Parsons to Stanton, February 2, 1865, in Parsons, *Reports to the War Department*, 25–28

45. Chambliss to Wilson, January 27, 1865; Donaldson to Ramsey, January 31, 1865, *OR*, vol. 49, pt. 1, 597, 617; *Military Record*, 194.

46. Meigs to Ingalls, January 30, 1865, *OR*, vol. 46, pt. 2, 298.

47. Field Orders No. 2, Headquarters, First Division, Detachment, Army of the Tennessee, February 5, 1865, *OR*, vol. 49, pt. 1, 655; Scott, *Story of the Thirty-Second Iowa*, 329.

48. Orders, no number, Headquarters, Third Division, Fourth Corps, January 31, 1865, *OR*, vol. 49, pt. 1, 618.

49. Ramsey to Stanley, February 2, 1865, *OR*, vol. 49, pt. 1, 629; McCallum to Meigs, May 26, 1866, *OR*, ser. 3, vol. 5, 1005; Rusling, *Men and Things*, 345–46.

50. Rawlins to Meigs, May 17, 1865, *OR*, vol. 46, pt. 3, 1162.

51. Wise to Meigs, August 31, 1865, *OR*, ser. 3, vol. 5, 289; *Report of the Quartermaster General*, 18;

Meigs to Grant, June 7, 1865; Weitzell to Forsyth, June 15, 1865, *OR*, vol. 48, pt. 2, 802–3, 890; Sawtelle to Meigs, December 13, 1865, *OR*, vol. 53, 607.

52. *Report of the Quartermaster General*, 19.

53. Sawtelle to Meigs, December 13, 1865, *OR*, vol. 53, 607–8.

54. Ibid., 608.

55. Sherman to Rawlins, December 19, 1863, *OR*, vol. 31, pt. 2, 569–72.

56. Hess, *Civil War in the West*, 263.

57. Parsons to Meigs, October 15, 1865, *OR*, vol. 52, pt. 1, 706–7.

58. Shea and Hess, *Pea Ridge*, 288–89.

59. Daniel Harris Reynolds Diary, April 16–19, 25, 1862, UAF; Fitzhugh, ed., *Cannon Smoke*, 178–80; record of events, Lucas-Lowe Missouri Battery, C.S., *SOR*, pt. 2, vol. 38, 360.

60. Record of events, Company D, 2nd Missouri Infantry (C.S.), *SOR*, pt. 2, vol. 38, 421.

61. Clark, *Railroads in the Civil War*, 30.

62. Ibid., 30n; Daniel Harris Reynolds Dairy, June 28–July 5, 1862, UAF.

63. Harris to wife and family, August 11, 1862, John A. Harris Letters, LSU; Brown to wife, July 25, 1862, Edward Norphlet Brown Letters, ADAH; Black, *Railroads of the Confederacy*, 180–81.

64. Johnston to Jefferson Davis, April 10, 1863, Joseph E. Johnston Papers, DU.

65. Daniel Harris Reynolds Diary, May 10–17, 19, 1863, UAF; William B. Lance to Delia and children, May 31, 1863, Samuel J. Lance Papers, LSU.

66. William B. Lance to Delia and children, May 31, 1863, Samuel J. Lance Papers, LSU; record of events, Company A, 60th North Carolina, *SOR*, pt. 2, vol. 49, 450.

67. Jackman, "A Railroad Adventure," 109–12.

68. Maury to Sterling Price, January 19, 1863, Dabney Herndon Maury Letter, GLIAH.

69. Goodman to Pemberton, February 14, 1863, *OR*, vol. 24, pt. 3, 627–28; Whitcomb to Seddon, May 8, 1864, *OR*, vol. 52, pt. 2, 903.

70. Gist to Jordan, January 3, 1863, *OR*, vol. 14, 741.

71. Wilson to Jordan, February 12, 1863, *OR*, vol. 14, 774–75. For another insight into the administrative inefficiency of Confederate rail transport, see Bird to Randolph, June 13, 1862, *OR*, vol. 11, pt. 3, 598.

72. Black, *Railroads of the Confederacy*, 185; Pickenpaugh, *Rescue by Rail*, 28.

73. Pickenpaugh, *Rescue by Rail*, 27, 29, 32, 42–43.

74. Ibid., 33–35.

75. Anderson, "Campaign and Battle of Chickamauga," 400; Alexander, "Longstreet at Knoxville," 746. Northern railroad executive John Kimber Jr. did not believe the Confederates were capable of shifting 20,000 men in three weeks from Richmond to Murfreesboro, Tennessee, when rumors circulated that Lee was sending reinforcements to Bragg's army in January 1863. Kimber assumed the reinforcements would be moving on the most direct line, through east Tennessee, a route denied Longstreet by September. His conclusion further enhances the unexpected success of Confederate railroad men in getting Longstreet to the Chattanooga area. See Kimber to Stanton, January 5, 1863, *OR*, vol. 20, pt. 2, 302.

76. Daniel Harris Reynolds Diary, May 4–7, 1864, UAF; Connelly, *Autumn of Glory*, 332, 334–35, 341.

77. Connelly, *Autumn of Glory*, 514; Black, *Railroads of the Confederacy*, 271–73, 277; Whitfield to Harvie, January 16, 1865, *OR*, vol. 45, pt. 2, 786–87; Brent to Beauregard, March 4, 1865, *OR*, vol. 47, pt. 2, 1322–23.

78. Daniel Harris Reynolds Diary, February 3–9, 11–14, 16–19, 21–23, 26–28, March 2–11, 1865, UAF.

79. Schofield, *Forty-Six Years,* 335.

9. TARGETING STEAMBOATS

1. Sherman to Ellen, June 10, 1862, and Sherman to Ewing, August 10, 1862, in Simpson and Berlin, eds., *Sherman's Civil War,* 248, 262.

2. Sherman to Ellen, August 20, 1862, in Simpson and Berlin, eds., *Sherman's Civil War,* 282; Quinby to Grant, August 23, 1862; Sherman to Walcutt, September 24, 1862; Sherman to Grant, October 4, 1862, *OR,* vol. 17, pt. 2, 184, 235–36, 261; Sherman to Rawlins, September 26, 1862, *OR,* vol. 17, pt. 1, 144–45.

3. Sherman to Carr, October 17 1862; Sherman to Hindman, October 17, 1862, *OR,* vol. 13, 742–43; Special Orders No. 283, Headquarters, First Division, District of West Tennessee, October 18, 1862; Sherman to Hurlbut, November 7, 1862, *OR,* vol. 17, pt. 2, 280–81, 860; Sherman to Stanton, December 16, 1862, in Simpson and Berlin, eds., *Sherman's Civil War,* 347.

4. Brown to Ruggles, June 20, 1862, *OR,* vol. 17, pt. 2, 615; correspondence of *Knoxville Register* reported in *Memphis Daily Appeal,* January 12, 1863; Barton to Hindman, February 28, 1863, *OR,* vol. 22, pt. 2, 792.

5. French to Seddon, March 10, 1863, *OR,* vol. 24, pt. 3, 660–61.

6. Seddon to Kirby Smith, June 3, 1863; Pritchard to Maclean, June 18, 1863, enclosing L. L. Moore report, June 16, 1863, *OR,* vol. 22, pt. 2, 852–53, 877.

7. Moore to Maclean, June 13, 23, 1863; [Price] to [Holmes], June 15, 1863, *OR,* vol. 22, pt. 2, 867, 869, 882; Brown to Baker, July 6, 1863; Asboth to Halleck, June 18, 1863, *OR,* vol. 24, pt. 2, 290, 507; Merrill to Grant, June 17, 1863, in Simon, ed., *Papers of Ulysses S. Grant,* 8:560–61; Ebenezer W. Wells Narrative, 13–15, N-YHS; Barnard to father and mother, June 19, 22, 1863, William A. Barnard Collection, AM.

8. Taylor to Jane, June 25, 1863, William Taylor Letters, CWM; Nasmith to Rawlins, July 1, 1863, *OR,* vol. 24, pt. 2, 516.

9. Faries to Wade, July 10, 1863, *OR,* vol. 26, pt. 1, 220–22.

10. Seddon to Kirby Smith, August 3, 1863, *OR,* vol. 22, pt. 2, 952.

11. Seddon to Kirby Smith, August 3, 1863; Seddon to Johnston, August 19, 1863, *OR,* vol. 22, pt. 2, 953, 971.

12. Forrest to Cooper, August 9, 1863, *OR,* vol. 30, pt. 4, 508–9.

13. Watkins, Johnston, Garland, and Danley to Flanagin, July 26, 1863; Johnston to Seddon, September 2, 1863, *OR,* vol. 22, pt. 2, 946, 988; Magruder to People of Texas, July 16, 1863, *OR,* vol. 26, pt. 2, 114.

14. Kay to Polk, January 14, 1864; Seddon to not stated, March 14, 1864, *OR,* vol. 52, pt. 2, 599–601, 638–39; Polk to Davis, March 21, 1864, *OR,* vol. 34, pt. 2, 1065–67.

15. Boggs to Holmes, November 8, 1863, *OR,* vol. 22, pt. 2, 1063.

16. Walker to not stated, October 10, 1863, *OR,* vol. 30, pt. 4, 240; Moore to Comstock, February 1, 1864, *OR,* vol. 32, pt. 1, 156–57; Fry to Duncan, November 30, 1864, *OR,* vol. 41, pt. 1, 947.

17. Edgar to French, November 21, 1863, *SOR,* pt. 1, vol. 4, 841–42; Greer to Porter, December 22,

1863, *ORN*, vol. 25, 624; Parkhurst to Sayles, April 23, 1864, *OR*, vol. 34, pt. 1, 473–74; "List of Boats destroyed on the Mississippi River and its tributaries from May 1st 1861 to the surrender of Genl. Kirby Smith's Army and the cessation of hostilities, June 2d 1865," oversize folder 7, Lewis Baldwin Parsons Papers, ALPL; Andrews to Lawler, August 29, 1864, *OR*, vol. 41, pt. 1, 301.

18. Girtman to French, December 8, 1863; Daniel to French, December 9, 1863, *SOR*, pt. 1, vol. 6, 42–43, 46–48; Ferris, ed., "Captain Jolly in the Civil War," 24–26; Brooks to Foster, December 12, 1863, *ORN*, vol. 25, 625–26.

19. General Orders No. 152, Headquarters, Department of the Missouri, August 19, 1864, *OR*, vol. 41, pt. 2, 773; Perry, *Recollections*, 35–40, 42.

20. Greene to Ewing, June 8, 1864, *OR*, vol. 34, pt. 1, 951–52.

21. Greene to Ewing, May 30, 1864; Faries to Moncure, June 9, 1864, *OR*, vol. 34, pt. 1, 949–50, 987–88.

22. Ferris, ed., "Captain Jolly in the Civil War," 28.

23. Buford to Chase, March 1, 1864, in Niven, ed., *Salmon P. Chase Papers*, 4:312; "Abstract from Record of Events on Return of the Military Division of West Mississippi for June, 1864"; Scott to Adams, June 19, 1864, *OR*, vol. 34, pt. 1, 953, 1014.

24. Thomas to Stanton, September 11, 1864, *OR*, ser. 3, vol. 4, 709; Gresham, *Life of Walter Quintin Gresham*, 1:282–83; Ferris, ed., "Captain Jolly in the Civil War," 29; Frazer, "Reminiscences of the Mississippi Squadron," 259.

25. Sherman to McPherson, March 7, 1864, *OR*, vol. 32, pt. 3, 34.

26. Sherman, *Memoirs*, 1:388; Canby to Slocum, May 27, 1864, *OR*, vol. 34, pt. 4, 59; Canby to Sherman, September 11, 1864, *OR*, vol. 39, pt. 2, 363; Sherman to Halleck, August 20, 1864, *OR*, vol. 38, pt. 5, 609; Sherman to Porter, October 25, 1863, *OR*, vol. 31, pt. 1, 737; List of Vessels, December 1, 1863, *ORN*, vol. 25, 609–10; Nathaniel P. Banks to Porter, August 28, 1863, David D. Porter Papers, MHM; General Orders No. 6, Headquarters, Military Division of West Mississippi, May 27, 1864, *OR*, vol. 34, pt. 4, 60; McPherson to Leggett, January 9, 1864, *OR*, vol. 32, pt. 2, 55; Canby to Porter, June 3, 1864, *OR*, vol. 39, pt. 2, 77; Abstract Log, USS *Rattler*, June 3 to December 31, 1864, *ORN*, vol. 26, 794–97.

27. Sherman to Hill, September 7, 1863, *OR*, vol. 30, pt. 3, 402; Sherman to Grant, December 29, 1863, *OR*, vol. 31, pt. 3, 527; Sherman to Logan, December 21, 1863, *OR*, vol. 31, pt. 3, 459.

28. Sherman to Porter, December 21, 1863; Sherman to Grant, December 29, 1863, *OR*, vol. 31, pt. 3, 460–61, 527; Sherman to Hurlbut, October 24, 1863, *OR*, vol. 31, pt. 1, 719; Sherman to Owen, January 30, 1864, *OR*, vol. 32, pt. 1, 185; Sherman to Smith, January 6, 1864: Sherman to Banks, January 16, 1864, *OR*, vol. 32, pt. 2, 36, 115; Special Field Orders No. 25, Headquarters, Department of the Tennessee, March 7, 1864, *OR*, vol. 32, pt. 3, 36; Sherman to Porter, November 8, 1863, *ORN*, vol. 25, 540; Sherman to John Sherman, December 29, 1863, and April 11, 1864, in Simpson and Berlin, eds., *Sherman's Civil War*, 577, 620.

29. Porter to Sherman, October 29, 1863, *OR*, vol. 31, pt. 1, 780–81; Rawlins to McPherson, November 2, 1863, *OR*, vol. 31, pt. 3, 22; General Orders No. 121, U.S. Mississippi Squadron, November 12, 1863, *ORN*, vol. 26, 705; Townsend to Smith, October 28, 1864, *OR*, vol. 39, pt. 3, 493; Townsend to Mitchell, October 29, 1864, *ORN*, vol. 26, 704.

30. Curtis to Fisk, January 7, 1863; Halleck to Curtis, January 8, 1863, *OR*, vol. 22, pt. 2, 25–26; Meigs to Rosecrans, January 19, 1863, *OR*, vol. 20, pt. 2, 338–39; High, *History of the Sixty-Eighth Regiment*, 27–28; Sauers, ed., *Civil War Journal*, 122; Winther, ed., *With Sherman to the Sea*, 59; Sherman to Porter, October 25, 1863, *OR*, vol. 31, pt. 1, 737; General Orders No. 7, Headquarters, District of Central

Missouri, February 14, 1864, *OR*, vol. 34, pt. 2, 327; Curtis to captain of *Emilie*, October 8, 1864, *OR*, vol. 41, pt. 3, 718.

31. Rives to Kirby Smith, August 20, 1863; Davis to Kirby Smith, November 19, 1863, *OR*, vol. 22, pt. 2, 973, 1072; Johnston to Seddon, January 31, 1864, *OR*, vol. 24, pt. 3, 1066.

32. "List of Boats destroyed on the Mississippi River and its tributaries from May 1st 1861 to the surrender of Genl. Kirby Smith's Army and the cessation of hostilities, June 2d 1865," oversize folder 7, Lewis Baldwin Parsons Papers, ALPL.

33. *St. Louis Daily Missouri Democrat*, September 14, 1863; "List of Boats destroyed on the Mississippi River and its tributaries from May 1st 1861 to the surrender of Genl. Kirby Smith's Army and the cessation of hostilities, June 2d 1865," oversize folder 7, Lewis Baldwin Parsons Papers, ALPL.

34. "List of Boats destroyed on the Mississippi River and its tributaries from May 1st 1861 to the surrender of Genl. Kirby Smith's Army and the cessation of hostilities, June 2d 1865," oversize folder 7, Lewis Baldwin Parsons Papers, ALPL; *St. Louis Daily Missouri Democrat*, October 5, 1863, and July 16, 1864.

35. "List of Boats destroyed on the Mississippi River and its tributaries from May 1st 1861 to the surrender of Genl. Kirby Smith's Army and the cessation of hostilities, June 2d 1865," oversize folder 7, Lewis Baldwin Parsons Papers, ALPL.

36. Allen to Halleck, October 5, 1863, *OR*, vol. 22, pt. 2, 607.

37. Halleck to Allen, October 8, 1863, *OR*, vol. 22, pt. 2, 618; General Orders No. 105, U.S. Mississippi Squadron, October 10, 1863, *ORN*, vol. 25, 463; General Orders No. 4, Headquarters, Military Division of the Mississippi, February 6, 1864, *OR*, vol. 32, pt. 2, 347–48; General Orders No. 15, Headquarters, Military Division of West Mississippi, July 1, 1864, *OR*, vol. 41, pt. 2, 4.

38. Canby to Rosecrans, June 19, 1864; Special Orders No. 185, Headquarters, U.S. Mississippi Squadron, March 21, 1864, *OR*, vol. 34, pt. 4, 456, 480; Baker to Parsons, March 29, 1865, *OR*, vol. 48, pt. 1, 1291–92.

39. Sherman to Rosecrans, April 23, 1864, *OR*, vol. 32, pt. 3, 463–64.

40. Oldham to Davis, February 11, 1865, in Crist, ed., *Papers of Jefferson Davis*, 11:398–99.

41. Parsons to Meigs, October 15, 1865, *OR*, vol. 52, pt. 1, 708.

42. "List of Boats destroyed on the Mississippi River and its tributaries from May 1st 1861 to the surrender of Genl. Kirby Smith's Army and the cessation of hostilities, June 2d 1865," oversize folder 7, Lewis Baldwin Parsons Papers, ALPL; Pool to Porter, November 7, 1863, *ORN*, vol. 25, 536–37.

43. Phelps to Steele, February 27, 1864, *OR*, vol. 34, pt. 2, 432; Greene to Ewing, May 30, 1864, *OR*, vol. 34, pt. 1, 949.

44. "Thrilling Times on the River," in *St. Louis Daily Missouri Republican*, November 7, 1885; Jameson to Adjutant General, U.S. Army, October 29, 1864; Kent to Townsend, October 29, 1864, *OR*, vol. 39, pt. 1, 880–81.

45. "List of Boats destroyed on the Mississippi River and its tributaries from May 1st 1861 to the surrender of Genl. Kirby Smith's Army and the cessation of hostilities, June 2d 1865," oversize folder 7, Lewis Baldwin Parsons Papers, ALPL; Cooper to Scott, June 17, 1864; Watie to [Cooper], June 17, 27, 1864, *OR*, vol. 34, pt. 1, 1011–13.

46. Holmes to Price, June 13, 1863, *OR*, vol. 22, pt. 2, 866; Greene to Ewing, June 19, 1863, *OR*, vol. 24, pt. 2, 507–8; Davis to Johnston, June 25, 1863; Johnston to Davis, June 28, 1863, *OR*, vol. 24, pt. 1, 197.

47. Buford to Asboth, July 15, 1863, *OR*, vol. 23, pt. 2, 533–34.

48. Polk to Davis, March 21, 1864, and Bragg endorsement, April 26, 1864, *OR*, vol. 34, pt. 2, 1064–67.

49. Jefferies to Davis, December 20, 1864, *OR*, vol. 52, pt. 2, 799–800; Sherman to Thomas, April 12, 1864, *OR*, ser. 3, vol. 4, 225.

50. Taylor to Boggs, June 11, 1863; Ransom to Clark, July 16, 1863, *OR*, vol. 24, pt. 2, 461, 681.

51. Vick to Mouton, January 9, 1864, *OR*, vol. 53, 925–26.

52. Claiborne to "Genl," August 21, 1899, folder 10, Thomas Claiborne Papers, UNC; Davis to Oldham, June 10, 1864, *OR*, vol. 53, 1000; Douglas, ed., *Douglas's Texas Battery*, 82–83.

53. Gaines, *Encyclopedia*, 75; Pinkerton to Wood, April 25, 1865, *OR*, vol. 48, pt. 1, 203–5.

54. Herron to Rawlins, July 25, 1863, *OR*, vol. 24, pt. 2, 667–68; Gaines, *Encyclopedia*, 82–89; James and Whitehead, "Civil War Steamboat Wrecks," 140–41, 145–63; "List of Boats destroyed on the Mississippi River and its tributaries from May 1st 1861 to the surrender of Genl. Kirby Smith's Army and the cessation of hostilities, June 2d 1865," oversize folder 7, Lewis Baldwin Parsons Papers, ALPL.

10. TARGETING RAILROADS, COASTAL VESSELS, AND WAGON TRAINS

1. Pope to Charles, July 21, 1861; Pope to Kelton, August 17, 1861; Hayward to Brooks, August 13, 14, 1861, *OR*, vol. 3, 403–4, 447, 458–60.

2. Grant to Butler, August 27, 1861, *OR*, vol. 3, 463; Halleck to McClellan, December 26, 1861; General Orders No. 32, Headquarters, Department of the Missouri, December 22, 1861; Ewing to Halleck, January 5, 1862, *OR*, vol. 8, 463–64, 824.

3. Roddey to not stated, August 8, 1862; Morrison to Scott, September 10, 1862, *SOR*, pt. 1, vol. 3, 233–34, 243–44; McPherson to Halleck, August 24, 1862, *OR*, vol. 17, pt. 2, 185; Morton to Skinner, no date, 1863, *OR*, vol. 16, pt. 1, 722; Cotterill, "Louisville and Nashville," 710.

4. General Orders No. 7, Headquarters, Army of Virginia, July 10, 1862, *OR*, vol. 12, pt. 2, 51; Lee to Davis, October 22, 1862, *OR*, vol. 19, pt. 2, 675.

5. Boyle to Rosecrans, January 3, 1863; Rosecrans to Boyle, January 6, 1863, *OR*, vol. 20, pt. 2, 296, 303; Daniel J. Prickitt Diary, February 8, 1863, 3rd Ohio Cavalry Regimental File, SRNB.

6. Lincoln to Rosecrans, February 17, 1863, in Basler, ed., *Collected Works*, 6:108; Streight to Garfield, April 9, 1863, *OR*, vol. 23, pt. 2, 224; Streight to Whipple, August 22, 1864, *OR*, vol. 23, pt. 1, 285, 287–89, 292–93.

7. Sherman to Porter, July 19, 1863, *OR*, vol. 24, pt. 3, 531; Sherman to Rawlins, July 28, 1863; Benton to Scates, July 27, 1863, *OR*, vol. 24, pt. 2, 536, 609.

8. Black, *Railroads of the Confederacy*, 241.

9. Lee to Seddon, October 16, 1863, *OR*, vol. 29, pt. 1, 407; Wiley, ed., *Norfolk Blues*, 98–99.

10. Dana to Banks, March 7, 1864, *OR*, vol. 34, pt. 2, 521–22.

11. Hines to Breckinridge, March 3, 1863, *SOR*, pt. 1, vol. 4, 185–86; Maxwell to Semple, July 6, 1863, *OR*, vol. 23, pt. 1, 821. See also Dodge to Grant, December 15, 1863, *OR*, vol. 31, pt. 3, 412.

12. Jordan to Porter, June 23, 1862, *OR*, vol. 17, pt. 2, 621; Sherwood to Kise, March 21, 1863, *OR*, vol. 23, pt. 1, 149–50.

13. Brayman to Harris, March 22, 1863; Chalmers to Pemberton, March 28, 1863, *OR*, vol. 24, pt. 1, 470–71; Haupt to Ingalls, July 27, 1863, *OR*, vol. 27, pt. 3, 774; Davies to Halleck, December 27, 1862, *OR*, vol. 17, pt. 2, 493–94.

14. Paine to Goddard, February [1], 1863, *OR*, vol. 23, pt. 2, 33; Special Orders No. 52, Headquarters, Sixteenth Corps, March 20, 1863, *OR*, vol. 24, pt. 3, 154; Special Orders No. 217, Headquarters, Sixteenth Corps, September 10, 1863, *OR*, vol. 30, pt. 3, 506; General Orders No. 59, Headquarters, District of Kentucky, July 16, 1864; General Orders No. 233, Adjutant General's Office, War Department, July 19, 1864, *OR*, vol. 39, pt. 2, 174, 180–82.

15. Curtis to Kelton, December 29, 1861, *OR*, vol. 8, 472; Gilmer to Presstman, December 5, 1863, *OR*, vol. 31, pt. 3, 786–87; Willett, *Rambling Recollections*, 5; Merrill, "Block-Houses," 441, 443–47, 452–53; Orders No. 28, Headquarters, District of Tennessee, June 27, 1864, in *Nashville Daily Times and True Union*, July 27, 1864.

16. Sherman to Meigs, April 26, 1864, *OR*, vol. 32, pt. 3, 504; Davis to Polk, May 3, 1864, *OR*, vol. 52, pt. 2, 665; Hequembourg to Crane, May 10, 1864, *OR*, vol. 39, pt. 2, 20; Van Dyne to Smith, May 19, 1864, *OR*, vol. 38, pt. 4, 259; Leonard Eicholtz Diaries, May 21, 1864, UWyo.

17. Champion to wife, June 11, 1864, Sidney S. Champion Papers, DU; Mackall to wife, June 14, 1864, William Whann Mackall Papers, UNC; Deupree, "Noxubee Squadron," 98–99; Lowe to Elliott, June 10, 1864, *OR*, vol. 38, pt. 2, 865; Lowe to Elliott, June 11, 1864: Milward to Moe, June 23, 24, 1864; Sherman to Thomas, June 24, 1864; Steedman to Dayton, June 24, 1864; Rogers to Cadle, June 27, 1864, *OR*, vol. 38, pt. 4, 457, 580–82, 587, 624; Julius E. Thomas Civil War Diary, June 19, 20–23, 1864, UTK; Shannon, "'Infernal Machines,'" 458.

18. Hambright to Whipple, June 2, 1864; Van Duzer to Dayton, June 18, 1864, *OR*, vol. 38, pt. 4, 387, 517; Leonard Eicholtz Diaries, June 20, 1864, UWyo; Wright, *History of the Eighth Regiment*, 252; Raum to Shite, July 5, 1864; Vandever to Smith, July 5, 1864; Laiboldt to Steedman, July 6, 1864; Wolfley to Steedman, July 7, 1864; Sherman to commanding officer, Marietta, July 14, 1864, *OR*, vol. 38, pt. 5, 63–64, 71, 83, 141–42; Wiley N. Nash account, folder 30, J.F.H. Claiborne Papers, UNC; Childress, "Scouts for Gen. Sul Ross," 466; Wever to Nichelson, July 12, 1864, *OR*, vol. 38, pt. 3, 273; Julius E. Thomas Civil War Diary, June 19, July 7, 9, 24–25, 1864, UTK.

19. Garrard to Sherman, July 10, 1864; Steedman to Whipple, July 10, 1864, *OR*, vol. 38, pt. 5, 111, 113; Lowe to Sherman, July 9, 1864, *OR*, vol. 38, pt. 2, 866.

20. McArthur to Sherman, August 13, 1864; Sullivan to Van Dyne, no date; Van Dyne to Sherman, August 13, 18, 1864, *OR*, vol. 38, pt. 5, 486–87, 591; Sherman to governors of Indiana, Illinois, Iowa, and Wisconsin, May 23, 1864; Sherman to Thomas, June 20, 1864, *OR*, vol. 38, pt. 4, 294–95, 533–34.

21. General Orders No. 2, Headquarters, District of the Etowah, June 28, 1864, *OR*, vol. 38, pt. 4, 634–35; *Chattanooga Daily Gazette*, July 8, 1864; Julius E. Thomas Civil War Diary, July 9, 1864, UTK; Sherman to Steedman, July 10, 1864; Sherman to Smith, July 14, 1864; Sherman to McArthur, August 13, 1864, *OR*, vol. 38, pt. 5, 112, 141, 486–87; Polk to Milroy, September 25, 1864, *OR*, vol. 39, pt. 2, 472.

22. Holmes, *52d O.V.I.*, 263–64.

23. Sherman to Anderson, July 1, 1864, *OR*, vol. 38, pt. 5, 4; Wright to McCallum, April 24, 1866, *OR*, ser. 3, vol. 5, 950, 952; Easton to Meigs, August 18, 1865, *OR*, vol. 52, pt. 1, 697.

24. Sherman to Halleck, July 6, 1864; Sherman to Canby, July 7, 1864, *OR*, vol. 38, pt. 5, 66, 85; Black, *Railroads of the Confederacy*, 251–52.

25. Evans, *Sherman's Horsemen*, 208–376; Castel, *Decision in the West*, 437–40.

26. Sherman to Thomas, August 16, 1864, *OR*, vol. 38, pt. 5, 524–25.

27. Johnston to Lee, June 11, 1864; Johnston to Bragg, June 13, 1864; Johnston to Bragg, June 27, 1864, *OR*, vol. 38, pt. 4, 769, 772, 795–96.

28. Hambright to Whipple, May 24, 1864, *OR*, vol. 38, pt. 4, 306; Sherman to Garrard, July 4, 1864; Whipple to Steedman, July 5, 1864, *OR*, vol. 38, pt. 5, 48, 63.

29. Hood to Seddon, July 30, 1864, *OR*, vol. 38, pt. 5, 930; Castel, *Decision in the West*, 448, 450–51; Hood, *Advance and Retreat*, 198; Capers to wife, August 11, 1864, Ellison Capers Papers, DU.

30. Smith to Moe, September 14, 1864; Wheeler to Mason, October 9, 1864, *OR*, vol. 38, pt. 3, 268, 957–58; Connelly, *Autumn of Glory*, 457; Castel, *Decision in the West*, 466; article by correspondent of *Montreal Gazette*, reprinted in unidentified newspaper clipping, John B. Hood Papers, NARA; Wheeler to Shoup, August 16, 1864, *OR*, vol. 38, pt. 5, 967; Steedman to assistant adjutant general, Department of the Cumberland, September 11, 1864, *OR*, vol. 38, pt. 2, 496; Laiboldt to assistant adjutant general, District of the Etowah, August 18, 1864, *OR*, vol. 38, pt. 1, 323–25.

31. Steedman to assistant adjutant general, Department of the Cumberland, September 11, 1864, *OR*, vol. 38, pt. 2, 495–96; Steedman to Thomas, August 17, 1864; Wheeler to Shoup, August 16, 1864, *OR*, vol. 38, pt. 5, 563, 967; Wheeler to Mason, October 9, 1864, *OR*, vol. 38, pt. 3, 958.

32. Sherman to Steedman, August 21, 1864, *OR*, vol. 38, pt. 5, 626; Boone to Otis, September 13, 1864, *OR*, vol. 38, pt. 2, 507–8; Merrill, "Block-Houses," 448.

33. Phillips, ed., *Correspondence*, 2:651; Smith to Lue, September 9, 1864, J. M. Smith Letters, TAM; Pruitt to daughter, September 13, 1864, Samuel W. Pruitt Papers, FHS.

34. Sherman to Thomas, August 15, 16, 17, 1864; Thomas to Sherman, August 16, 1864; Thomas to Stanley, August 18, 1864; Sherman to Howard, August 17, 1864; Sherman to Schofield, August 18, 1864, *OR*, vol. 38, pt. 5, 506, 524, 548, 551, 557, 574, 582.

35. Thomas to Sherman, August 22, 1864; Sherman to Steedman, August 22, 1864; Sherman to Thomas, August 23, 1864; Sherman to Granger, August 24, 1864, *OR*, vol. 38, pt. 5, 629, 634, 639, 652; Sherman to Halleck, September 4, 1864, in Simpson and Berlin, eds., *Sherman's Civil War*, 698; Castel, *Decision in the West*, 469–73.

36. Ramsey to Le Favour, August 28, 1864; Sherman to Schofield, August 29, 1864, *OR*, vol. 38, pt. 5, 692, 705; Castel, *Decision in the West*, 407–522.

37. Hess, *Civil War in the West*, 249–52.

38. Forrest to Ellis, October 17, 1864; Sinclair to Hardie, January 7, 1865, *OR*, vol. 39, pt. 1, 542–48, 862; Black, *Railroads of the Confederacy*, 266–67.

39. Humphreys to Wilson, June 21, 1864, *OR*, vol. 40, pt. 2, 285; Ruffin, "Chapter of Confederate History," 109; Halleck to McCallum, October 12, 1864; Stevenson to Stanton, October 14, 1864, *OR*, vol. 43, pt. 2, 348, 368–69; "Schedule of property and public works captured and destroyed by the First Cavalry Division from February 27 to March 18, 1865," *OR*, vol. 46, pt. 1, 494.

40. Throne, ed., "Commissary in the Union Army," 77; [Rood], *Story of the Service*, 409–10.

41. Fullerton to Scates, July 20, 1863, *OR*, vol. 24, pt. 2, 577; Gregg to Warren, December 8, 1864, *OR*, vol. 42, pt. 3, 885.

42. Poe to Logan, February 7, 1865; Sherman to Slocum, February 9, 1865, *OR*, vol. 47, pt. 2, 331, 364; Black, *Railroads of the Confederacy*, 273.

43. Haupt, *Reminiscences*, 255.

44. Ibid., 197–98, 200, 294; Haupt to Julius Moore, November 26, 1862, Herman Haupt Letter Book, Lewis Muhlenberg Haupt Family Papers, LC; Haupt, *Military Bridges*, 124–25.

45. Lee to Randolph, July 28, 1862, *OR*, vol. 11, pt. 2, 936.

46. Hill to Chilton, no date, 1862; McClellan to Halleck, August 1, 1862; Lee to Hill, August 2, 1862; Pendleton to French, August 9, 1862, *OR*, vol. 11, pt. 2, 934–35, 939–40, 945–56.

47. Ingalls to Meigs, September 28, 1865, *OR*, vol. 51, pt. 1, 253; Gaines, *Encyclopedia*, 183–84; Ingalls to Williams, August 10, 1864, *OR*, vol. 42, pt. 2, 102; Wright to Davis, August 11, 1864, in Crist, ed., *Papers of Jefferson Davis*, 10:608.

48. Fitzhugh to Payne, April 16, 1865, *OR*, vol. 46, pt. 1, 1305–7; Gaines, *Encyclopedia*, 182; Dornin to Welles, April 5, 1865; Parker to Tole, April 5, 1865; Sewall to Taylor, April 5, 1865; Parker to Welles, April 7, 1865, *OR*, vol. 46, pt. 3, 588–90, 618.

49. "Statement of public animals and means of transportation captured by the enemy, killed in battle, and lost and destroyed from December 26, 1862, until January 16, 1863"; Wheeler to Brent, January 16, 1863, *OR*, vol. 20, pt. 1, 226–29, 958–59.

50. Daniel, *Days of Glory*, 341; diary, October 2, 1863, Montgomery C. Meigs Papers, LC; Meigs to Stanton, October 3, 1863, *OR*, vol. 29, pt. 1, 186.

51. Maxey to Belton, April 23, 1864, *OR*, vol. 34, pt. 1, 841–42.

52. Hess, *Banners to the Breeze*, 12.

53. Forrest to Ellis, October 17, 1864, *OR*, vol. 39, pt. 1, 542, 544–45.

54. Grant to Kelton, December 25, 1863; Van Dorn to Pemberton, December 20, 1862, *OR*, vol. 17, pt. 1, 478, 503.

CONCLUSION

1. Diary, January 13, 1862, Thomas Bragg Papers, UNC.

2. Johnson, *A Soldier's Reminiscences*, 187–88.

3. Stanton to Johnson, November 22, 1865, *OR*, ser. 3, vol. 5, 496; "Summary Statement of Transportation furnished during the Fiscal Year ending June 30, 1865," in Parsons, *Reports to the War Department*, 54.

4. "Summary Statement of Transportation furnished during the Fiscal Year ending June 30, 1865," in Parsons, *Reports to the War Department*, 55; Gable, *Railroad Generalship*, 8.

5. "Summary Statement of Transportation furnished during the Fiscal Year ending June 30, 1865," in Parsons, *Reports to the War Department*, 56; Parsons to Meigs, October 15, 1865, *OR*, vol. 52, pt. 1, 707.

6. John Levering, "Recollections of the Civil War, 1861–1866," 259, UVA; Culbertson to wife, January 7, 1863, William Culbertson Papers, DU; Sherman to Porter, October 25, 1863, *OR*, vol. 31, pt. 1, 737.

7. "Statement of the amount of transportation furnished by Office of Transportation at St. Louis, fiscal year ending June 30, 1863," *OR*, vol. 52, pt. 1, 466.

8. Wills, *Army Life*, 353; Roemer, *Reminiscences*, 317.

9. *Historical Sketch of the Chicago Board of Trade Battery*, 6; Scott, *Story of the Thirty-Second Iowa*, unpaginated.

10. Marshall, *History of the Eighty-Third Ohio*, 9–14; Marcoot, *Five Years*, unpaginated preface.

11. Record of events, Company D, 2nd Missouri Infantry (C.S.), *SOR*, pt. 2, vol. 38, 424.

12. Giles, *Terry's Texas Rangers*, 12–16.

13. Reminiscences, unpaginated, August Bondi Papers, KHS.

14. Risch, *Quartermaster Support*, 406; Hunter, *Steamboats*, 565–66, 585, 588; Haites, Mak, and Walton, *Western River Transportation*, 123, 130–31.

15. McCallum to Meigs, May 26, 1866, *OR*, ser. 3, vol. 5, 1001; Weber, *Northern Railroads*, 207.

16. Pratt, *Rise of Rail-Power*, 98, 103–4.

17. William Logan Rand to father, June 1, 1863, Rand Family Papers, ALPL; Holabird, "Army Wagon Transportation," 9.

18. *Report of the Quartermaster General*, 23; Allen to Meigs, July 1, 1865, *OR*, vol. 52, pt. 1, 692–93.

19 Parsons to Meigs, October 6, 1863, *OR*, vol. 52, pt. 1, 459; Winslow to Parsons, February 13, 1865, in Parsons, *Reports to the War Department*, 44.

20. Hardee to Brent, February 28, 1863, *OR*, vol. 20, pt. 1, 778; Grant to father, March 1, 1864, in Simon, ed., *Papers of Ulysses S. Grant*, 10:183; Thomas M. Anderson to Sherman, June 21, 1875, and Lewis B. Parsons to Sherman, July 29, 1875, William T. Sherman Papers, LC.

21. Chester, "Art of Subsisting Armies," 1319–21; Sharpe, "Art of Supplying Armies," 94; Michie, "American Military Roads," 619.

22. Risch, *Quartermaster Support*, 460–62; General Orders No. 13, War Department, Adjutant General's Office, June 15, 1865, *OR*, vol. 46, pt. 3, 1279; Weber, *Northern Railroads*, 217; Weigley, *Quartermaster General*, 331–32; Thomas, *Iron Way*, 186; *Report of the Quartermaster General*, 406–7.

23. Thomas, *Iron Way*, 184.

24. Risch, *Quartermaster Support*, 461.

25. *Report of the Quartermaster General*, 18; Schottenhamel, "Lewis Baldwin Parsons," 336–38, 343–44, 349–52.

26. Stanton to Johnson, November 22, 1865, *OR*, ser. 3, vol. 5, 512.

27. Luvaas, *Military Legacy*, 226–28; Pratt, *Rise of Rail-Power*, 50–53, 127.

28. Showalter, *Railroads and Rifles*, 49–52; Van Creveld, *Supplying War*, 83.

29. Showalter, *Railroads and Rifles*, 54–61, 66–68, 70–71, 78–80, 84.

30. Pratt, *Rise of Rail-Power*, 122, 127–28, 132; Van Creveld, *Supplying War*, 91–92.

31. Showalter, *Railroads and Rifles*, 221–22.

32. Wawro, *Franco-Prussian War*, 74; Van Creveld, *Supplying War*, 86; Pratt, *Rise of Rail-Power*, 140, 145, 147, 149–74.

33. Pratt, *Rise of Rail-Power*, 110–12; Van Creveld, *Supplying War*, 94.

34. Van Creveld, *Supplying War*, 95, 102, 104–5; Pratt, *Rise of Rail-Power*, 56–57.

35. Showalter, *Railroads and Rifles*, 222–23.

36. Cosmas, *Army for Empire*, 167–168.

37. Ibid., 209–12, 218–20; Waddell, *United States Army Logistics*, 100–101.

38. Waddell, *United States Army Logistics*, 94, 104–5.

39. Pratt, *Rise of Rail-Power*, 210, 212–13, 215–16, 218–19.

40. Van Creveld, *Supplying War*, 109–13, 139–40.

BIBLIOGRAPHY

ARCHIVES

Abraham Lincoln Presidential Library, Springfield, Illinois
    Engelmann-Kircher Collection
    Lewis Baldwin Parsons Papers
    William Logan Rand Letters, Rand Family Papers
    Job Yaggy Diary
Alabama Department of Archives and History, Montgomery
    Robert Lewis Bliss Papers
    Edward Norphlet Brown Letters
    Pearson and Danielly Family Papers
    Edmund Winston Pettus Family Papers
    William Lewis Roberts Papers
    Joseph Wheeler Family Papers
American Antiquarian Society, Worcester, Massachusetts
    Philo Beecher Buckingham Papers
    Joseph Cross Civil War Letters
Archives of Michigan, Lansing
    George Benton Arnold Collection
Atlanta History Center, Atlanta, Georgia
    Harry Stanley Diary
Auburn University, Special Collections and Archives, Auburn, Alabama
    W. E. Preston Reminiscences, L. B. Williams Papers
    "The Civil War Diary of Charles Henry Snedeker"
    Wright Family Papers
Boston Public Library, Boston, Massachusetts
    Henry W. Tisdale Diary

Bowdoin College Library, Special Collections and Archives, Brunswick, Maine
    Charles Henry Howard Collection
Chicago History Museum, Chicago, Illinois
    John A. Nourse Papers
    George Sawin Papers
Chickamauga and Chattanooga National Military Park, Fort Oglethorpe, Georgia
    Merritt James Symonds Diary
College of William and Mary, Special Collections, Williamsburg, Virginia
    William Taylor Letters
Connecticut Historical Society, Hartford
    Henry H. Goodell Letter
Cornell University, Rare and Manuscript Collections, Ithaca, New York
    William Harrison Githens Letters, Gail and Stephen Rudin Collection of Civil War
        Letters
    Charles J. Obriham Letters, June and Gilbert Krueger Civil War Letters
Duke University, Rubenstein Rare Book and Manuscript Library, Durham, North Carolina
    George Williamson Balloch Papers
    Ellison Capers Papers
    Sidney S. Champion Papers
    William Culbertson Papers
    Peter Eltinge Letters, Eltinge-Lord Family Papers
    Robert Bruce Hoadley Papers
    Walter M. Howland Papers
    Joseph E. Johnston Papers
    Charles Todd Quintard Papers
    Daniel Ruggles Papers
    Thomas Sewell Papers
    C. Eugene Southworth Papers
Emory University, Manuscript, Archives, Rare Book Library, Atlanta, Georgia
    Alexander Miller Ayers Papers
    Albert L. Slack Letters
Filson Historical Society, Louisville, Kentucky
    Samuel W. Pruitt Papers
    Joseph P. Van Nest Letters
Gilder Lehrman Institute of American History, New York, New York
    Ulysses S. Grant Letters
    Dabney Herndon Maury Letter
    William T. Sherman Letters

Indiana Historical Society, Indianapolis
    Joseph Wright Chamberlain Papers
    James H. Jones Papers
Kansas Historical Society, Topeka
    Anderson Family Papers
    August Bondi Papers
    John R. Graton Correspondence
Library of Congress, Manuscript Division, Washington, D.C.
    Bancroft-Bliss Family Papers
    W. W. Beckwith Correspondence
    Henry Boyden Blood Papers
    Lewis Muhlenberg Haupt Family Papers
    Montgomery C. Meigs Papers
    Marshall Mortimer Miller Papers
    Philip Henry Sheridan Papers
    William T. Sherman Papers
    Edwin McMasters Stanton Papers
    Lyman Trumbull Correspondence
Lincoln Memorial University, Abraham Lincoln Library and Museum, Harrogate, Tennessee
    William Merrell, "Personal Memoirs of the Civil War."
Louisiana State University, Louisiana and Lower Mississippi Valley Collections, Special Collections, Baton Rouge
    Anonymous Civil War Diary
    Henry Barstow War Record and Letter
    Danville S. Chadbourne Letters
    Marianne Edwards Letters
    Simeon A. Evans Letters
    Anson D. Fessenden Papers
    John A. Harris Letters
    Wayne Johnson Jacobs Diaries and Lists
    Charles L. Keyes Letters
    Samuel J. Lance Papers
    Solomon Nelson Journal
    William Shelly Diary
    William H. Smith Letters
Maryland Historical Society, Baltimore
    James M. Snook Papers

Massachusetts Historical Society, Boston
    Henry Mitchell Whitney Correspondence
Minnesota Historical Society, St. Paul
    Christie Family Letters
Mississippi Department of Archives and History, Jackson
    Robert A. Smith Papers
Missouri History Museum, St. Louis
    Braxton Bragg Papers
    Dale-Holt-Hensley Family Papers, Alphabetical Files
    Zebediah W. Marsh Papers
    Monroe Joshua Miller Papers
    Charles Parsons Papers
    David D. Porter Papers
National Archives and Records Administration, Washington, D.C.
    John B. Hood Papers, RG 109
    Orders and Circulars, Army of Tennessee and Subordinate Commands, 1862–1864,
        Chapter 2, Vol. 53, RG 109
    "Records Cleburnes Div Hardees Corps A of Tenn," RG 109, Chapter 2, No. 265
New-York Historical Society, New York, New York
    Ebenezer W. Wells Narrative
New York State Library, Albany
    Albert N. Ames Papers
State Historical Society of Missouri, Research Center, Columbia
    Fayette Clapp Diary
Stones River National Battlefield, Murfreesboro, Tennessee
    Order Book, Company I, 78th Pennsylvania Regimental File
    Daniel J. Prickitt Diary, 3rd Ohio Cavalry Regimental File
Tennessee State Library and Archives, Nashville
    Bradford Nichol Memoir
Texas A&M University, Special Collections, College Station
    J. M. Smith Letters
University of Alabama, Special Collections, Tuscaloosa
    R. M. Rucker Letter
University of Arkansas, Special Collections, Fayetteville
    Daniel Harris Reynolds Diary
University of Chicago, Special Collections Research Center, Chicago, Illinois
    Henry H. Belfield and Belfield Family Papers

University of Colorado, Special Collections, Boulder
  Noble Walter Wood Diary
University of Florida, Special and Area Studies Collections, Gainesville
  William Wing Loring Letter Book
University of Michigan, Bentley Historical Library, Ann Arbor
  Erwin Shepard Papers
University of Michigan, William L. Clements Library, Ann Arbor
  Clement Abner Boughton Papers
University of Mississippi, Special Collections, Oxford
  Henry Clubb Collection
University of North Carolina, Southern Historical Collection, Chapel Hill
  Thomas Bragg Papers
  J.F.H. Claiborne Papers
  Thomas Claiborne Papers
  G.W.F. Harper Papers
  William Penn Lloyd Diary and Notebooks
  William Whann Mackall Papers
  John J. Metzgar Papers
  William H. Stevens Letters
University of Notre Dame, Rare Books and Special Collections, Notre Dame, Indiana
  Kaufman Funk Letter
University of Tennessee, Special Collections, Knoxville
  Tilgham Blazer Collection
  Julius E. Thomas Civil War Diary
  John Watkins Papers
University of Virginia, Special Collections, Charlottesville
  John Levering, "Recollections of the Civil War, 1861–1866."
University of Washington, Special Collections, Seattle
  Samuel W. Lougheed Papers
University of Wyoming, American Heritage Center, Laramie
  Leonard Eicholtz Diaries
Virginia Tech, Special Collections, Blacksburg
  W. G. Buck Letter
Wisconsin Historical Society, Madison
  Timothy Phillips Diaries
Yale University, Sterling Memorial Library, New Haven, Connecticut
  David Herrick Gile Correspondence, Civil War Manuscripts Collection

NEWSPAPERS

Atlanta Journal
Belmont Chronicle
Chattanooga Daily Gazette
Knoxville Register
Memphis Daily Appeal
Nashville Daily Times and True Union
St. Louis Daily Missouri Democrat
St. Louis Daily Missouri Republican

WEBSITES

https://en.oxforddictionaries.com/definition/logistics

ARTICLES, BOOKS, THESES, AND DISSERTATIONS

Albion, Robert Greenhalgh. *Square-Riggers on Schedule: The New York Sailing Packets to England, France, and the Cotton Ports.* Hamden, Conn.: Archon Books, 1965.

Alexander, E. Porter. "Longstreet at Knoxville." *Battles and Leaders of the Civil War,* vol. 3. Edited by Robert Underwood Johnson and Clarence Clough Buel, 745–51. New York: Thomas Yoseloff, 1956.

Anderson, Archer. "Campaign and Battle of Chickamauga." *Southern Historical Society Papers* 9 (1881): 385–418.

Army, Thomas F., Jr. *Engineering Victory: How Technology Won the Civil War.* Baltimore, Md.: Johns Hopkins Univ. Press, 2016.

Aten, Henry J. *History of the Eighty-Fifth Regiment, Illinois Volunteer Infantry.* Hiawatha, Kans.: N.p., 1901.

Bachrach, David Stewart. "Military Logistics During the Reign of Edward I of England, 1272–1307." *War in History* 13, no. 4 (2006): 423–40.

Bahde, Thomas, ed. *The Story of My Campaign: The Civil War Memoir of Captain Francis T. Moore, Second Illinois Cavalry.* DeKalb: Northern Illinois Univ. Press, 2011.

Basler Roy P., ed. *Collected Works of Abraham Lincoln.* 8 vols. New Brunswick, N.J.: Rutgers Univ. Press, 1953.

Beaudoin, Frederic J. "Union Victory: Manpower, Management of Resources, or Generalship?" *Naval War College Review* 25, no. 4 (March–April 1973): 36–40.

Beecher, Herbert W. *History of the First Light Battery Connecticut Volunteers, 1861–1865,* vol. 1. New York: A. T. De La Mare, 1901.

Bennett, L. G., and William M. Haigh. *History of the Thirty-Sixth Regiment Illinois Volunteers, During the War of the Rebellion.* Aurora, Ill.: Knickerbocker and Hodder, 1876.

Bering, John A., and Thomas Montgomery. *History of the Forty-Eighth Ohio Vet. Vol. Inf.* Hillsboro, Ohio: Highland News Office, 1880.

Billings, John D. *Hardtack and Coffee: Or The Unwritten Story of Army Life.* Boston: George M. Smith, 1887.

Black, Robert C., III. *The Railroads of the Confederacy.* Chapel Hill: Univ. of North Carolina Press, 1952.

Blake, E. E. *A Succinct History of the 28th Iowa Volunteer Infantry.* Belle Plaine, Iowa: Union Press, 1896.

Blanton, Leonard L., Jessie E. Summers, and Carl Summers Jr., eds. *I Must Tell: An Autobiography, Benjamin F. McPherson, 1825–1909.* Valley, Ala.: Chattahoochee Valley Historical Society, 1998.

Bowler, R. Arthur. "Logistics and Operations in the American Revolution." In *Reconsiderations on the Revolutionary War: Selected Essays,* edited by Don Higginbotham, 54–71. Westport, Conn.: Greenwood Press, 1978.

———. *Logistics and the Failure of the British Army in America, 1775–1783.* Princeton, N.J.: Princeton Univ. Press, 1975.

Brett, Alden Chase, ed. *The Letters and Diary of Captain Jonathan Huntington Johnson.* N.p: n.p., 1961.

Brinkerhoff, Roeliff. *Recollections of a Lifetime.* Cincinnati: Robert Clarke, 1900.

Brown, Norman D., ed. *Journey to Pleasant Hill: The Civil War Letters of Captain Elijah P. Petty, Walker's Texas Division CSA.* San Antonio: University of Texas Institute of Texan Cultures, 1982.

Browning, Robert M. Jr. *From Cape Charles to Cape Fear: The North Atlantic Blockading Squadron During the Civil War.* Tuscaloosa: Univ. of Alabama Press, 1993.

Butler, Benjamin. *Private and Official Correspondence of Gen. Benjamin F. Butler During the Period of the Civil War.* 5 vols. Norwood, Mass.: Plimpton Press, 1917.

Byrne, Frank L., ed. *Uncommon Soldiers: Harvey Reid and the 22nd Wisconsin March with Sherman.* Knoxville: Univ. of Tennessee Press, 2001.

Carp, E. Wayne. *To Starve the Army at Pleasure: Continental Army Administration and American Political Culture, 1775–1783.* Chapel Hill: Univ. of North Carolina Press, 1984.

Castel, Albert. *Decision in the West: The Atlanta Campaign of 1864.* Lawrence: Univ. Press of Kansas, 1992.

Castle, Henry A. "Some of the Army Mules Esteemed Contemporaries." In *Glimpses of the Nation's Struggle: Sixth Series, Papers Read Before the Minnesota Commandery of the Military Order of the Loyal Legion of the United States, January, 1903–1908, 463–78.* Wilmington, N.C.: Broadfoot Publishing, 1992.

Chase, Philip S. *Battery F, First Regiment Rhode Island Light Artillery, in the Civil War, 1861–1865.* Providence. R.I.: Snow and Farnham, 1892.

Chester, James. "The Art of Subsisting Armies in War." *Journal of the Military Service Institution of the United States* 14 (1893): 1319–21.

Childress, R. G. "Scouts for Gen. Sul Ross." *Confederate Veteran* 14 (1906): 466.

Clark, John E., Jr. *Railroads in the Civil War: The Impact of Management on Victory and Defeat.* Baton Rouge: Louisiana State Univ. Press, 2001.

Clark, Orton S. *The One Hundred and Sixteenth Regiment of New York State Volunteers.* Buffalo: Matthews and Warren, 1868.

Connelly, Thomas Lawrence. *Autumn of Glory: The Army of Tennessee, 1862–1865.* Baton Rouge: Louisiana State Univ. Press, 1971.

Cook, S. G., and Charles E. Benton, eds. *The "Dutchess County Regiment," (150th Regiment of New York State Volunteer Infantry) in the Civil War: Its Story as Told by Its Members.* Danbury, Conn.: Danbury Medical Printing, 1907.

Cosmas, Graham A. *An Army for Empire: The United States Army in the Spanish-American War.* Columbia: Univ. of Missouri Press, 1971.

Cotterill, R. S. "The Louisville and Nashville Railroad, 1861–1865." *American Historical Review* 29. no. 4 (July 1924): 700–715.

Cox, Jacob D. *Military Reminiscences of the Civil War.* 2 vols. New York: Scribner's Sons, 1900.

Crist, Lynda Lasswell, ed. *The Papers of Jefferson Davis.* 14 vols. Baton Rouge: Louisiana State Univ. Press, 1971–2015.

Crowell, Lorenzo M. "Logistics in the Madras Army circa 1830." *War and Society* 10, no. 1 (October 1992): 1–33.

Cutrer, Thomas W., ed. "'We Are Stern and Resolved:' The Civil War Letters of John Wesley Rabb, Terry's Texas Rangers." *Southwestern Historical Quarterly* 91, no. 2 (October 1987): 185–226.

Daniel, Larry J. *Days of Glory: The Army of the Cumberland, 1861–1865.* Baton Rouge: Louisiana State Univ. Press, 2004.

Delafield, Richard. *Report on the Art of War in Europe in 1854, 1855, and 1856.* Washington, D.C.: George W. Bowman, 1860.

Deupree, J. G. "The Noxubee Squadron of the First Mississippi Cavalry, C.S.A., 1861–1865." *Publications of the Mississippi Historical Society.* Centenary Series, vol. 2 (1918): 12–143.

Dinges, Bruce J., and Shirley A. Leckie, eds. *A Just and Righteous Cause: Benjamin H. Grierson's Civil War Memoir.* Carbondale: Southern Illinois Univ. Press, 2008.

Douglas, Lucia Rutherford, ed. *Douglas's Texas Battery, CSA.* Tyler, Tex.: Smith County Historical Society, 1966.

Doyle, Julie A., John David Smith, and Richard M. McMurry, eds. *This Wilderness of War: The Civil War Letters of George W. Squier, Hoosier Volunteer.* Knoxville: Univ. of Tennessee Press, 1998.

Draper, William F. *Recollections of a Varied Career.* Boston: Little, Brown, 1908.

Dudley, Henry Walbridge. *Autobiography.* Menasha, Wisc.: George Banta, [1914].

Eaton, John. *Grant, Lincoln, and the Freedmen: Reminiscences of the Civil War.* New York: Longmans, Green, 1907.

Erdkamp, Paul. *Hunger and the Sword: Warfare and Food Supply in Roman Republican Wars (264–30 B.C.).* Amsterdam: J. C. Gieben, 1998.

Essin, Emmett M. *Shavetails and Bell Sharps: The History of the U.S. Army Mule.* Lincoln: Univ. of Nebraska Press, 1997.

Evans, David. *Sherman's Horsemen: Union Cavalry Operations in the Atlanta Campaign.* Bloomington: Indiana Univ. Press, 1996.

Ferris, Ruth, ed. "Captain Jolly in the Civil War." *Bulletin of the Missouri Historical Society* 22, no. 1 (October 1965): 14–31.

Fisher, John P. "Union Combined Operations on the Texas Coast, 1863–64." In *Union Combined Operations in the Civil War,* edited by Craig L. Symonds, 56–73. New York: Fordham Univ. Press, 2010.

Fitch, John. *Annals of the Army of the Cumberland.* Philadelphia: J. B. Lippincott, 1864.

Fitzhugh, Lester Newton, ed. *Cannon Smoke: The Letters of Captain John J. Good, Good-Douglas Texas Battery, CSA.* Hillsboro, Tex.: Hill Junior College Press, 1971.

Fonvielle, Chris E., Jr. *The Wilmington Campaign: Last Rays of Departing Hope.* Mechanicsburg, Pa.: Stackpole Books, 2001.

Fout, Frederick W. *The Dark Days of the Civil War, 1861 to 1865.* N.p.: F. A. Wagenfeuhr, 1904.

Francis, Charles Lewis. *Narrative of a Private Soldier in the Volunteer Army of the United States.* Brooklyn, N.Y.: William Jenkins, 1879.

Frazer, Persifor. "Reminiscences of the Mississippi Squadron in 1864–65." In *Military Essays and Recollections of the Pennsylvania Commandery, Military Order of the Loyal Legion of the United States,* vol. 1, 255–88. Wilmington, N.C.: Broadfoot Publishing, 1995.

Freeman, H. B. "Eighteenth U.S. Infantry from Camp Thomas to Murfreesboro and the Regular Brigade at Stone River." In *Glimpses of the Nation's Struggle: Third Series, Papers Read Before the Minnesota Commandery of the Military Order of the Loyal Legion of the United States, 1889–1892,* 106–31. Minneapolis: D. D. Merrill, 1893.

Fuller, J.F.C. "A Study of Mobility in the American Civil War." *Army Quarterly* 29 (1935): 261–69.

Furse, George Armand. *Provisioning Armies in the Field.* London: William Clowes and Sons, 1899.

Gabel, Christopher R. *Railroad Generalship: Foundations of Civil War Strategy.* Fort Leavenworth, Kans.: U.S. Army Command and General Staff College Press, 1997.

———. *Rails to Oblivion: The Decline of Confederate Railroads in the Civil War.* Fort Leavenworth, Kans.: U.S. Army Command and General Staff College Press, 2002.

Gaines, W. Craig. *Encyclopedia of Civil War Shipwrecks.* Baton Rouge: Louisiana State Univ.
Press, 2008.

Gardner, Theodore. "The First Kansas Battery: An Historical Sketch, with Personal Reminiscences of Army Life, 1861–'65." *Collections of the Kansas State Historical Society* 14
(1915–1918): 235–82.

Gates, Arnold, ed. *The Rough Side of War: The Civil War Journal of Chesley A. Mosman.*
Garden City, N.Y.: Basin Publishing, 1987.

Gates, Paul W. *Agriculture and the Civil War.* New York: Knopf, 1965.

Gibson, Charles Dana. "Military Transports, Civilian Crews, During the Civil War." *Pe-
riodical Journal of the Council on America's Military Past* 16, no. 1 (April 1989): 3–20.

Gibson, Charles Dana, and E. Kay Gibson. *Dictionary of Transports and Combatant Vessels,
Steam and Sail, Employed by the Union Army, 1861–1868.* Camden, Maine: Ensign Press,
1995.

Giles, L. B. *Terry's Texas Rangers.* Austin, Tex.: Pemberton Press, 1967.

Goff, Richard D. *Confederate Supply.* Durham, N.C.: Duke Univ. Press, 1969.

Goodloe, Albert Theodore. *Confederate Echoes: A Voice from the South in the Days of Secession and of the Southern Confederacy.* Nashville: Smith and Lamar, 1907.

Gould, E. W. *Fifty Years on the Mississippi.* St. Louis: Nixon-Jones, 1889.

Goulding, Joseph H. "A Month on a Transport." In *Vermont War Papers and Miscellaneous
States Papers and Addresses for Military Order of the Loyal Legion of the United States,*
79–97. Wilmington, N.C.: Broadfoot Publishing, 1994.

Grabau, Warren E. *Ninety-Eight Days: A Geographer's View of the Vicksburg Campaign.* Knoxville: Univ. of Tennessee Press, 2000.

Green, Ann N. *Horses at Work: Harnessing Power in Industrial America.* Cambridge, Mass.:
Harvard Univ. Press, 2008.

Green, John P. "The Movement of the 11th and 12th Army Corps from the Potomac to
the Tennessee." In *Military Essays and Recollections of the Pennsylvania Commandery,
Military Order of the Loyal Legion of the United States,* vol. 1, 107–22. Wilmington, N.C.:
Broadfoot, 1995.

Greenhous, Brereton. "A Note on Western Logistics in the War of 1812." *Military Affairs*
34, no. 2 (April 1970): 41–44.

Gresham, Matilda. *Life of Walter Quintin Gresham, 1832–1895.* 2 vols. Chicago: Rand Mc-
Nally, 1919.

Grimsley, Mark. *The Hard Hand of War: Union Military Policy Toward Southern Civilians,
1861–1865.* New York: Cambridge Univ. Press, 1995.

Guilmartin, John F., Jr. "The Logistics of Warfare at Sea in the Sixteenth Century: The

Spanish Perspective." In *Feeding Mars: Logistics in Western Warfare from the Middle Ages to the Present,* edited by John A. Lynn, 109–36. Boulder, Colo.: Westview Press, 1993.

Hagerman, Edward. *The American Civil War and the Origins of Modern Warfare: Ideas, Organization, and Field Command.* Bloomington: Indiana Univ. Press, 1988.

Haites, Erik F., James Mak, and Gary M. Walton. *Western River Transportation: The Era of Early Internal Development, 1810–1860.* Baltimore: Johns Hopkins Univ. Press, 1975.

Halleck, H. Wager. *Elements of Military Art and Science: or, Course of Instruction in Strategy, Fortification, Tactics of Battles.* New York: D. Appleton, 1862.

Hamilton, J. G. De Roulhac, ed. *The Papers of Randolph Abbott Shotwell.* 3 vols. Raleigh: North Carolina Historical Commission, 1929.

———, ed. *The Papers of Thomas Ruffin.* 4 vols. Raleigh: Edwards and Broughton, 1920.

Hanaburgh, D. H. *History of the One Hundred and Twenty-Eighth Regiment, New York Volunteers (U.S. Infantry) in the Late War.* Pokeepsie, N.Y.: Enterprise Publishing, 1894.

Harari, Yuval Noah. "Strategy and Supply in Fourteenth-Century Western European Invasion Campaigns." *Journal of Military History* 64, no. 2 (April 2000): 297–333.

Hartpence. William R. *History of the Fifty-First Indiana Veteran Volunteer Infantry.* Cincinnati, Ohio: Robert Clarke, 1894.

Haupt Herman. *Military Bridges: With Suggestions of New Expedients and Constructions for Crossing Streams and Chasms.* New York: D. Van Nostrand, 1864.

———. *Reminiscences of General Herman Haupt.* Milwaukee, Wisc.: Wright and Joys, 1901.

Hearn, Chester G. *When the Devil Came Down to Dixie: Ben Butler in New Orleans.* Baton Rouge: Louisiana State Univ. Press, 1997.

Hecht, Lydia P., ed. *Echoes from the Letters of a Civil War Surgeon.* N.p.: Bayou Publishing, 1996.

Hess, Earl J. *Banners to the Breeze: The Kentucky Campaign, Corinth, and Stones River.* Lincoln: Univ. of Nebraska Press, 2000.

———. *The Civil War in the West: Victory and Defeat from the Appalachians to the Mississippi.* Chapel Hill: Univ. of North Carolina Press, 2012.

———. *The Knoxville Campaign: Burnside and Longstreet in East Tennessee.* Knoxville: Univ. of Tennessee Press, 2012.

———. "The Mississippi River and Secession, 1862: The Northwestern Response." *Old Northwest* 10, no. 2 (summer 1984): 187–207.

High, Edwin W. *History of the Sixty-Eighth Regiment Indiana Volunteer Infantry, 1862–1865.* N.p.: Sixty-Eighth Indiana Infantry Association, 1902.

Hight, John J. *History of the Fifty-Eighth Regiment of Indiana Volunteer Infantry.* Princeton, Ill.: Clarion, 1895.

Historical Sketch of the Chicago Board of Trade Battery, Horse Artillery, Illinois Volunteers. Chicago: Henneberry, 1902.

History of the Fourth Maine Battery Light Artillery in the Civil War, 1861–65. Augusta, Maine: Burleigh and Flynt, 1905.

Hogan, Sally Coplen, ed. *General Reub Williams's Memories of Civil War Times: Personal Reminiscences of Happenings That Took Place from 1861 to the Grand Review.* Westminster, Md.: Heritage Books, 2004.

Holabird, S. B. "Army Wagon Transportation." *Ordnance Notes* 6, no. 189 (April 15, 1882): 1–30.

———. "The Transport of Troops and Supplies." In *Operations of the Division of Military Engineering of the International Congress of Engineers, Held in Chicago Last August, Under the Auspices of the World's Congress Auxiliary of the Columbian Exposition,* 489–98. Washington, D.C.: Government Printing Office, 1894.

Holbrook, William C. *A Narrative of the Services of the Officers and Enlisted Men of the 7th Regiment of Vermont Volunteers (Veterans), From 1862 to 1866.* New York: American Bank Note, 1882.

Holmes, J. T. *52d O.V.I.: Then and Now.* Columbus, Ohio: Berlin Printing, 1898.

Hood, J. B. *Advance and Retreat: Personal Experiences in the United States and Confederate States Armies.* Philadelphia: Burk and M'Fetridge, 1880.

Howard, Oliver Otis. *Autobiography of Oliver Otis Howard.* 2 vols. New York: Baker and Taylor, 1907.

Hughes, Nathaniel Cheairs, Jr., ed. *The Civil War Memoir of Philip Daingerfield Stephenson, D. D.* Conway: Univ. of Central Arkansas Press, 1995.

Hunter, Louis C. *Steamboats on the Western Rivers: An Economic and Technological History.* Cambridge, Mass.: Harvard Univ. Press, 1949.

Huston, James A. "Logistical Support of Federal Armies in the Field." *Civil War History* 7, no. 1 (March 1961): 36–47.

———. *Logistics of Liberty: American Services of Supply in the Revolutionary War and After.* Newark: Univ. of Delaware Press, 1991.

Instruction for Field Artillery. Philadelphia: J. B. Lippincott, 1860.

Irwin, Richard B. *History of the Nineteenth Army Corps.* New York: Putnam's Sons, 1892.

Jackman, J. S. "A Railroad Adventure." *Southern Bivouac* 1, no. 3 (November 1882): 109–12.

Jackson, William Henry. *Time Exposure: The Autobiography of William Henry Jackson.* New York: Putnam's Sons, 1940.

James, Stephen R., Jr., and Alan Whitehead. "Civil War Steamboat Wrecks of the Upper Yazoo River." *Mississippi Archaeology* 39, no. 2 (winter 2004): 125–68.

Jewett, Clayton E., ed. *Rise and Fall of the Confederacy: The Memoir of Senator Williamson S. Oldham, CSA.* Columbia: Univ. of Missouri Press, 2006.

Johnson, R. W. *A Soldier's Reminiscences in Peace and War.* Philadelphia: J. B. Lippincott, 1886.

Johnson, Timothy D. *A Gallant Little Army: The Mexico City Campaign.* Lawrence: Univ. Press of Kansas, 2007.

Jones, Jenkin Lloyd. *An Artilleryman's Diary.* [Madison, Wisc.:] Democrat Printing, 1914.

Josyph, Peter, ed. *The Wounded River: The Civil War Letters of John Vance Lauderdale, M.D.* East Lansing: Michigan State Univ. Press, 1993.

Lash, Jeffrey N. "Joseph E. Johnston and the Virginia Railways, 1861–62." *Civil War History* 35, no. 1 (March 1989): 5–27.

Lazenby, J. F. "Logistics in Classical Greek Warfare." *War in History* 1, no. 1 (1994): 3–18.

LeDuc, William G. *Recollections of a Civil War Quartermaster.* St. Paul, Minn.: North Central Publishing, 1963.

Lee, Stephen D. "The Siege of Vicksburg." *Publications of the Mississippi Historical Society* 3 (1900): 55–71.

Leib, Charles. *Nine Months in the Quartermaster's Department: Or, The Chances for Making a Million.* Cincinnati: Moore, Wilstach, Keyes, 1862.

Little, George, and James R. Maxwell. *A History of Lumsden's Battery, C.S.A.* Tuscaloosa, Ala.: R. E. Rhodes Chapter, United Daughters of the Confederacy, n.d.

Luttwak, Edward N. "Logistics and the Aristocratic Idea of War." In *Feeding Mars: Logistics in Western Warfare from the Middle Ages to the Present,* edited by John A. Lynn, 3–7. Boulder, Colo.: Westview Press, 1993.

Luvaas, Jay. *The Military Legacy of the Civil War: The European Inheritance.* Chicago: Univ. of Chicago Press, 1959.

Lynn, John A. "Food, Funds, and Fortresses: Resource Mobilization and Positional Warfare in the Campaigns of Louis XIV." In *Feeding Mars: Logistics in Western Warfare from the Middle Ages to the Present,* edited by John A. Lynn, 137–59. Boulder, Colo.: Westview Press, 1993.

———. *Giant of the Grand Siècle: The French Army, 1610–1715.* New York: Cambridge Univ. Press, 1997.

———. "The History of Logistics and Supplying War." In *Feeding Mars: Logistics in Western Warfare from the Middle Ages to the Present,* edited by John A. Lynn, Boulder, 9–27. Colo.: Westview Press, 1993.

Major, Duncan K., and Roger S. Fitch. *Supply of Sherman's Army During the Atlanta Campaign.* Fort Leavenworth, Kans.: [Army Service Schools Press], 1911.

Mallet, J. W. "Work of the Ordnance Bureau." *Southern Historical Society Papers* 37 (1909): 1–20.

Marcoot, Maurice. *Five Years in the Sunny South: Reminiscences of Maurice Marcoot, Late of Co. "B," 15th Reg. Missouri Veteran Volunteer Infantry from 1861 to 1866.* N.p.: N.p., n.d.

Marshall, T. B. *History of the Eighty-Third Ohio Volunteer Infantry: The Greyhound Regiment.* Cincinnati: Gibson and Perin, 1913.

Martin, Edgar W. *The Standard of Living in 1860: American Consumption Levels on the Eve of the Civil War.* Chicago: Univ. of Chicago Press, 1942.

McCloskey. Joseph F. "History of Military Road Construction." *Military Engineer* 41 (1949): 353–56.

McGregor, Charles. *History of the Fifteenth Regiment New Hampshire Volunteers, 1862–1863.* N.p.: N.p., 1900.

Merdinger, Charles J. "Roads Through the Ages: Part I, Early Developments." *Military Engineer* 44 (1952): 268–73.

Merrick, George Byron. *Old Times On the Upper Mississippi: The Recollections of a Steamboat Pilot from 1854 to 1863.* Cleveland, Ohio: Arthur H. Clark, 1909.

Merrill, W. E. "Block-Houses, Etc.: The Engineer Service in the Army of the Cumberland." In *History of the Army of the Cumberland*, vol. 2, by Thomas B. Van Horne, 439–58. Cincinnati: Robert Clarke, 1875.

Meyer, Balthasar Henry. *History of Transportation in the United States Before 1860.* Washington, D.C.: Carnegie Institution of Washington, 1917.

Michie, P. S. "American Military Roads and Bridges." In *Operations of the Division of Military Engineering of the International Congress of Engineers, Held in Chicago Last August, Under the Auspices of the World's Congress Auxiliary of the Columbian Exposition,* 615–25. Washington, D.C.: Government Printing Office, 1894.

A Military Record of Battery D, First Ohio Veteran Volunteers Light Artillery. Oil City, Pa.: Derrick Publishing, 1908.

Moore, Jerrold Northrop. *Confederate Commissary General: Lucius Bellinger Northrop and the Subsistence Bureau of the Southern Army.* Shippensburg, Pa.: White Mane Publishing, 1996.

Moore, John G. "Mobility and Strategy in the Civil War." *Military Affairs* 24, no. 2 (summer 1960): 68–77.

Moors, J. F. *History of the Fifty-Second Regiment Massachusetts Volunteers.* Boston: George H. Ellis, 1893.

Morton, John Watson. *The Artillery of Nathan Bedford Forrest's Cavalry.* Nashville: M. E. Church Publishing House, 1909.

Nichols, James L. *The Confederate Quartermaster in the Trans-Mississippi.* Austin: Univ. of Texas Press, 1964.

Niven, John, ed. *The Salmon P. Chase Papers.* 5 vols. Kent, Ohio: Kent State Univ. Press, 1993–1998.

Noyes, Katharine Macy, ed. *Jesse Macy: An Autobiography.* Springfield, Ill.: Charles C. Thomas, 1933.

Official Records of the Union and Confederate Navies in the War of the Rebellion. 30 vols. in 2 series. Washington, D.C.: Government Printing Office, 1894–1922.

Osborn, Hartwell. "Sherman's Carolina Campaign." *Western Reserve University Bulletin* 15, no. 8 (November 1912): 101–19.

Parker, Theodore R. "William J. Kountz, Superintendent of River Transportation Under McClellan, 1861–62." *Western Pennsylvania Historical Magazine* 21, no. 4 (December 1938): 237–54.

Parsons, Lewis B. *Reports to the War Department, by Brev. Maj. Gen. Lewis B. Parsons, Chief of Rail and River Transportation.* St. Louis: George Knapp, 1867.

Patrick, Jeffrey L., and Robert J. Willey, eds. *Fighting for Liberty and Right: The Civil War Diary of William Bluffton Miller, First Sergeant, Company K, Seventy-Fifth Indiana Volunteer Infantry.* Knoxville: Univ. of Tennessee Press, 2005.

Perry, Oran. *Recollections of the Civil War,* 2nd ed. Indianapolis: Historical Bureau of the Indiana Library and Historical Department, 1928.

Phillips, Ulrich B., ed. *Correspondence of Robert Toombs, Alexander H. Stephens, and Howell Cobb: Annual Report of the American Historical Association for the Year 1911.* 2 vols. Washington, D.C.: Government Printing Office, 1913.

Pickenpaugh, Roger. *Rescue by Rail: Troop Transfer and the Civil War in the West, 1863.* Lincoln: Univ. of Nebraska Press, 1998.

Poteete, Tim. "Military Mules, 1785–1925." Master's thesis, Northeastern Oklahoma State University, 1994.

Pratt, Edwin A. *The Rise of Rail-Power in War and Conquest, 1833–1914.* London: P. S. King and Son, 1915.

Pratt, Harry E. "Lewis B. Parsons: Mover of Armies and Railroad Builder." *Journal of the Illinois State Historical Society* 44. no. 4 (winter 1951): 349–54.

Prokopowicz, Gerald J. *All for the Regiment: The Army of the Ohio, 1861–1862.* Chapel Hill: Univ. of North Carolina Press, 2001.

Pryor, John H., ed. *Logistics of Warfare in the Age of the Crusades.* Aldershot, Hampshire, England: Ashgate, 2006.

Quint, Alonzo H. *The Record of the Second Massachusetts Infantry, 1861–65.* Boston: James P. Walker, 1867.

Ramsdell, Charles W. "General Robert E. Lee's Horse Supply, 1862–1865." *American Historical Review* 35, no. 4 (July 1930): 758–77.

Redfield, H. V. "Characteristics of the Armies." In *Annals of the War Written by Leading Participants North and South Originally Published in the Philadelphia Weekly Times,* 357–71. Edison, N.J.: Blue and Gray Press, 1996.

Report of the Quartermaster General of the United States Army to the Secretary of War, for the Year Ending June 30, 1865. Washington, D.C.: Government Printing Office, 1865.

Risch, Erna. *Quartermaster Support of the Army: A History of the Corps, 1775–1939.* Washington, D.C.: Center of Military History, 1989.

Ritter, William L. "Sketches of the Third Maryland Artillery." *Southern Historical Society Papers* 11 (1883): 433–42.

Roemer, Jacob. *Reminiscences of the War of the Rebellion, 1861–1865.* Flushing, N.Y.: Estate of Jacob Roemer, 1897.

[Rood, Hosea W.] *Story of the Service of Company E, and of the Twelfth Wisconsin Regiment, Veteran Volunteer Infantry, in the War of the Rebellion.* Milwaukee, Wisc.: Swain and Tate, 1893.

Roth, Jonathan P. *The Logistics of the Roman Army at War (264 B.C.–A.D. 235).* Leiden, The Netherlands: Brill, 1999.

Round, Harold F. "The Telegraph Road." *Civil War Times Illustrated* 6, no. 3 (June 1967): 42–45.

Rowland, Dunbar, ed. *Jefferson Davis, Constitutionalist: His Letters, Papers and Speeches.* 10 vols. New York: J. J. Little and Ives, 1923.

Ruffin, F. G. "A Chapter of Confederate History." *North American Review* 134, no. 302 (January 1882): 97–110.

Runyan, Timothy J. "Naval Logistics in the Late Middle Ages: The Example of the Hundred Years' War." In *Feeding Mars: Logistics in Western Warfare from the Middle Ages to the Present,* edited by John A. Lynn, 79–107. Boulder, Colo.: Westview Press, 1993.

Rusling, James F. "A Word for the Quartermaster's Department." *United States Service Magazine* 3, no. 1 (January 1865): 57–67.

———. *Men and Things I Saw in Civil War Days.* New York: Eaton and Mains, 1899.

Sauers, Richard A., ed. *The Civil War Journal of Colonel William J. Bolton, 51st Pennsylvania.* Conshohocken, Pa.: Combined Books, 2000.

Sawers, Larry. "U.S. Army Procurement of Draft and Pack Animals in the Civil War Era." *Eastern Economic Journal* 29, no. 1 (winter 2003): 59–67.

Saxon, Lyle. *Father Mississippi.* Gretna, La.: Pelican Publishing, 2006.

Schneid, Frederick C. *The French-Piedmontese Campaign of 1859.* Rome: Stato Maggiore Dell'Esercito Ufficio Storico, 2014.

———. "A Well-Coordinated Affair: Franco-Piedmontese War Planning in 1859." *Journal of Military History* 76, no. 2 (April 2012): 395–425.

Schofield, John M. *Forty-Six Years in the Army.* New York: Century, 1897.

Schottenhamel, George Carl. "Lewis Baldwin Parsons and Civil War Transportation." Ph.D. diss., University of Illinois, 1954.

Scott, H. L. *Military Dictionary.* New York: D. Van Nostrand, 1861.

Scott, John. *Story of the Thirty-Second Iowa Infantry Volunteers.* Nevada, Iowa: John Scott, 1896.

Scott, Winfield. *Memoirs of Lieut. General Scott, LL.D.* 2 vols. New York: Sheldon, 1864.

Shannon, I. N. "'Infernal Machines' Described." *Confederate Veteran* 13 (1905): 458.

Sharpe, Henry G. "The Art of Supplying Armies in the Field as Exemplified During the

Civil War." *Journal of the Military Service Institution of the United States* 18 (January 1896): 45–95.

Sharrer, G. Terry. "The Great Glanders Epizootic, 1861–1866." *Agricultural History* 69, no. 1 (winter 1995): 79–97.

Shea, William L., and Earl J. Hess. *Pea Ridge: Civil War Campaign in the West.* Chapel Hill: Univ. of North Carolina Press, 1992.

Sheridan, P. H. *Personal Memoirs.* 2 vols. New York: Charles L. Webster, 1888.

Sherman, William T. *Memoirs.* 2 vols. New York: D. Appleton, 1875.

Showalter, Dennis E. *Railroads and Rifles: Soldiers, Technology, and the Unification of Germany.* Hamden, Conn.: Archon Books, 1975.

Shy, John. "Logistical Crisis and the American Revolution: A Hypothesis." In *Feeding Mars: Logistics in Western Warfare from the Middle Ages to the Present,* edited by John A. Lynn, 161–79. Boulder, Colo.: Westview Press, 1993.

Simmons, L. A. *The History of the 84th Reg't Ill. Vols.* Macomb, Ill.: Hampton Brothers, 1866.

Simon, John Y., ed. *The Papers of Ulysses S. Grant.* 32 vols. Carbondale: Southern Illinois Univ. Press, 1967–2012.

Simpson, Brooks D., and Jean V. Berlin, eds. *Sherman's Civil War: Selected Correspondence of William T. Sherman, 1860–1865.* Chapel Hill: Univ. of North Carolina Press, 1999,

Smith, Barbara Bentley, and Nina Bentley Baker, eds. *"Burning Rails as We Pleased": The Civil War Letters of William Garrigues Bentley, 104th Ohio Volunteer Infantry.* Jefferson, N.C.: McFarland, 2004.

Smith, Justin H. *The War with Mexico.* 2 vols. New York: Macmillan, 1919.

Smith, W. B. *On Wheels and How I Came There.* New York: Hunt and Eaton, 1893.

Snell, Mark A. "Union Lifeline." In *The Ongoing Civil War: New Versions of Old Stories,* edited by Herman Hattaway and Ethan S. Rafuse, 74–97. Columbia: Univ. of Missouri Press, 2004.

Spence, John C. *A Diary of the Civil War.* Murfreesboro, Tenn.: Rutherford County Historical Society, 1993.

Spring, Matthew H. *With Zeal and With Bayonets Only: The British Army on Campaign in North America, 1775–1783.* Norman: Univ. of Oklahoma Press, 2008.

Stevens, George T. *Three Years in the Sixth Corps: A Concise Narrative of Events in the Army of the Potomac, From 1861 to the Close of the Rebellion, April, 1865.* Albany: S. R. Gray, 1866.

Stevens, William B. *History of the Fiftieth Regiment of Infantry, Massachusetts Volunteer Militia, in the Late War of the Rebellion.* Boston: Griffith-Stillings, 1907.

Stiles, Robert. *Four Years Under Marse Robert.* New York: Neale, 1903.

Story of the Fifty-Fifth Regiment Illinois Volunteer Infantry in the Civil War, 1861–1865. Clinton, Mass.: W. J. Coulter, 1887.

Stover, John F. *American Railroads,* 2nd ed. Chicago: Univ. of Chicago Press, 2008.

Summers, Festus P. *The Baltimore and Ohio in the Civil War.* New York: G.P. Putnam's Sons, 1939.

Supplement to the Official Records of the Union and Confederate Armies. 100 vols. Wilmington, N.C.: Broadfoot, 1993–2000.

Sweetman, John. "Military Transport in the Crimean War, 1854–1856." *English Historical Review* 88, no. 346 (January, 1973): 81–91.

———. *War and Administration: The Significance of the Crimean War for the British Army.* Edinburgh: Scottish Academic Press, 1984.

Symonds, H. C. *Report of a Commissary of Subsistence, 1861–65.* Astor Place, N.Y.: J. J. Little, [1888].

Syrett, David. *Shipping and the American War, 1775–83.* London: Athlone Press, 1970.

Taylor, Lenette S. *"The Supply for Tomorrow Must Not Fail": The Civil War of Captain Simon Perkins Jr., a Union Quartermaster.* Kent, Ohio: Kent State Univ. Press, 2004.

Taylor, Richard. *Destruction and Reconstruction: Personal Experiences of the Late War.* New York: Longmans, Green, 1955.

Thayer, George A. "A Railroad Feat of War." In *Sketches of War History, 1861–1865: Papers Prepared for the Ohio Commandery of the Military Order of the Loyal Legion of the United States, 1890–1896,* vol. 4, 214–34. Wilmington, N.C.: Broadfoot Publishing, 1991.

Thomas, William G. *The Iron Way: Railroads, the Civil War, and the Making of Modern America.* New Haven, Conn.: Yale Univ. Press, 2011.

Throne, Mildred, ed. *The Civil War Diary of Cyrus F. Boyd, Fifteenth Iowa Infantry, 1861–1863.* Baton Rouge: Louisiana State Univ. Press, 1998.

———, ed. "A Commissary in the Union Army: Letters of C. C. Carpenter." *Iowa Journal of History* 53, no. 1 (January 1955): 59–88.

Turner, George Edgar. *Victory Rode the Rails: The Strategic Place of the Railroads in the Civil War.* Indianapolis: Bobbs-Merrill, 1953.

The Twenty-Fifth Regiment Connecticut Volunteers in the War of the Rebellion. Rockville, Conn.: Rockville Journal, 1913.

Twitchell, A. S. *History of the Seventh Maine Light Battery, Volunteers in the Great Rebellion.* Boston: E. B. Stillings, 1892.

Van Creveld, Martin. *Supplying War: Logistics from Wallenstein to Patton,* 2nd ed. Cambridge, UK: Cambridge Univ. Press, 2004.

Waddell, Steve R. *United States Army Logistics: From the American Revolution to 9/11.* Santa Barbara, Calif.: Praeger Security International, 2010.

War of the Rebellion: A Compilation of the Official Records of the Union and Confederate Armies. 70 vols. in 128. Washington, D.C.: Government Printing Office, 1880–1901.

Warner, Ezra J. *Generals in Blue: Lives of the Union Commanders.* Baton Rouge: Louisiana State Univ. Press, 1964.

Watson, Samuel J. *Jackson's Sword: The Army Officer Corps on the American Frontier, 1810–1821*. Lawrence: Univ. Press of Kansas, 2012.

Wawro, Geoffrey. *The Franco-Prussian War: The German Conquest of France in 1870–1871*. New York: Cambridge Univ. Press, 2003.

Weber, Thomas. *The Northern Railroads in the Civil War, 1861–1865*. New York: Columbia Univ. Press, 1952.

Weigley, Russell F. *Quartermaster General of the Union Army: A Biography of M. C. Meigs*. New York: Columbia Univ. Press, 1959.

Wheeler, James Scott. "The Logistics of the Cromwellian Conquest of Scotland, 1650–1651." *War and Society* 10, no. 1 (May 1992): 1–18.

Wheeler, William. *Letters of William Wheeler of the Class of 1855, Y.C.* Riverside, Cambridge, Mass.: H. O. Houghton, 1875.

Wild, Frederick W. *Memoirs and History of Capt. F. W. Alexander's Baltimore Battery of Light Artillery, U.S.V.* Loch Raven, Md.: Maryland School for Boys, 1912.

Wiley, Kenneth, ed. *Norfolk Blues: The Civil War Diary of the Norfolk Light Artillery Blues*. Shippensburg, Pa.: Burd Street Press, 1997.

Willett, James R. *Rambling Recollections of a Military Engineer*. Chicago: J. Morris, 1888.

Williams, Frederick D., ed. *The Wild Life of the Army: Civil War Letters of James A. Garfield*. Lansing: Michigan State Univ. Press, 1964.

Wills, Charles W. *Army Life of an Illinois Soldier*. Washington, D.C.: Globe Printing, 1906.

Wilson, Harold S. *Confederate Industry: Manufacturers and Quartermasters in the Civil War*. Jackson: Univ. Press of Mississippi, 2002.

Wilson, Mark R. *The Business of Civil War: Military Mobilization and the State, 1861–1865*. Baltimore: Johns Hopkins Univ. Press, 2006.

[Wilson, Thomas]. "Feeding a Great Army." *United Service* 2, no. 2 (February 1880): 149–59.

Wilson, Thomas B. *Reminiscences of Thomas B. Wilson*. N.p.: N.p., n.d.

Windham, William T. "The Problem of Supply in the Trans-Mississippi Confederacy." *Journal of Southern History* 27, no. 2 (May 1961): 149–68.

Winther, Oscar Osburn, ed. *With Sherman to the Sea: The Civil War Letters, Diaries and Reminiscences of Theodore F. Upson*. Bloomington: Indiana Univ. Press, 1958.

"The Wreck of the *James Watson*: A Civil War Disaster." *Journal of the Illinois State Historical Society* 37, no. 3 (September 1944): 213–28.

Wright, T. J. *History of the Eighth Regiment Kentucky Vol. Inf.* St. Joseph, Mo.: St. Joseph Steam Printing Company, 1880.

INDEX

Peninsula campaign, 161, 178

Pennsylvania Railroad, 80, 82

Perkins, Simon, 21–22

Petersburg campaign, 146, 161, 254

Petersburg, Virginia, 141

Pettus, John J., 227

Petty, Elijah, P., 65

Philadelphia, Wilmington, and Baltimore Railroad, 82

Piedmont Railroad, 102, 290n95

Pittsburgh, Fort Wayne, and Chicago Railroad, 82

Platte Valley, 43

Pocahontas, 56

Poe, Orlando M., 186, 252

Poison Springs, battle of 256–257

Polk, Leonidas, 212, 220, 231

Pope, John, 148, 235–237

Port Hudson, siege of, 128, 218

Porter, David D., 58, 225–226, 228–229

Post Boy, 227

Prairie Rose, 55

Pratt, Edwin, xvii, 266

Premier, 118

Prima Donna, 218

Pringle, 59

Prussia, xvi–xvii, 11, 13–16, 270–274

Quartermaster Department, 7–8, 10, 17–33, 63, 112, 154–155, 273–274

Quartermaster Officers, 17–33, 280n3, 281n12, 281n31, 288n39

Rail-based system, xii–xiii, 13–16, 64, 265–267; accidents on, 71, 85, 106; as military transportation, 78–108; before the Civil War, 67–78; civilian passengers and freight on, 80–82, 93; compared to river-based system, 71, 201, 262–263;onfederate use of, 97–108, 289n83; cost of, 67, 70; fuel for, 77–78; government seizure of, 32, 86–87, 108, 289n83; military railroads as part of, 12, 274; passenger cars in, 288n39; size, composition, speed, and operation of, 71–78; soldier vandalism of, 82–85,

102; targeted by enemy, 235–254, 257–259; wrecking of, 249–253;

Rand, William Logan, 266

Ransom, Thomas E. G., 232

Rattler, 60, 225

Read, Charles W., 234

Red River campaign, 51

Redfield, H. V., 150

Reekie, John, 141

Reid, Harvey, 153, 176

Reindeer, 134

Republic, 65

Reynolds, Daniel H., 104, 208–109, 212–213

Rhode Island Units: Battery F, 1st Light Artillery, 124–125; 2nd Cavalry, 124, 127

Richard the Lionheart, 3

Richmond and Danville Railroad, 102

Richmond, Fredericksburg, and Potomac Railroad, 188

Risch, Erna, 265

River-based system, xii, 9, 128; aesthetics of, 40, 62–63; accidents, 59–61, 285n81; arming and armoring of, 226; as military transportation, 41–66, 199, 282n21; barges, 39, 53; before the Civil War, 35–41; charter method, 42–47; compared to coastal shipping, 129–131, 133; competition with rail-based system, 40–41, 64; Confederate use of, 64–66, 286n91; contract method, 42–47, 50; cost of transporting troops, 207, 261, 284n46; crew of steamers, 38, 54–55; fuel, 53–54; government compensation for damage, 49; government ownership of steamers, 46–47, 66; government profit in operating, 50; health on steamers, 58–59; ice, 60; pilots, 54–55, 59; sabotage, 226–229; sandbars and snags, 59–60; targeted by enemy, 215–234; troop transport on, 55–65, 199

Roads, 174–183; corduroy, 162, 181–183; dirt, 178; macadamized, 176–178; mountain, 179–180; plank, 175–176

Roemer, Jacob, 190

Rogers, George C., 241

Rome, ancient, xv, 1–2, 140

Rood, Hosea, 250